THE SACRED BOOKS OF THE EAST

Translated by
VARIOUS ORIENTAL SCHOLARS

and Edited by
F. MAX MÜLLER

Vol. 27

SACRED BOOKS OF THE EAST

(50 VOLUMES)

Series Editor : *F. Max-Müller*

ISBN: 978-81-208-0101-1 (Set)

These volumes of the Sacred Books of the East series include translations of all the most important works of the seven non-Christian religions that have exercised a profound influence on the civilisations of the continent of Asia. The Vedic Brahmanic system claims 21 volumes, Buddhism 10, and Jainism 2; 8 volumes comprise Sacred Books of the Parsis; 2 volumes represent Islam; and 6 the two main indigenous systems of China. Translated by twenty leading authorities in their respective fields, the volumes have been edited by the late F. Max Müller. The inception, publication and the compilation of these books cover almost 34 years.

I. BUDDHISM

Vol. 49: Buddhist Mahayana Texts (2 Parts)
Vol. 11: Buddhist Suttas
Vol. 10: The Dhammapada and Sutta Nipata
Vols. 35 & 36: The Questions of King Milinda (2 Parts)
Vol. 21: The Saddharma Pundarika or the Lotus of the True Law
Vols. 13, 17 & 20: Vinaya Texts (3 Parts)

II. CHINESE

Vol. 19: The Fo-Sho-Hing-Tsan-King
Vols. 3, 16, 27, 28, 39 & 40: The Sacred Books of China (6 Parts)

III. A GENERAL INDEX

Vol. 50: A General Index to the Names and Subject-matter of the Sacred Books of the East

IV. ISLAM

Vols. 6 & 9: The Qur'an (2 Parts)

V. JAINISM

Vols. 22 & 45: The Jaina Sutras (2 Parts)

VI. PARSIS

Vols. 5, 18, 24, 37 & 47: Pahlavi Texts (5 Parts)
Vols. 4, 23 & 31: The Zend-Avesta (3 Parts)

VII. VEDIC-BRAHMANIC SYSTEM

Vol. 8: The Bhagavadgita with the Sanatsujatiya and the Anugita
Vols. 29 & 30: The Grihya-Sutras: Rules of Vedic Domestic Ceremonies (2 Parts)
Vol. 42: Hymns of the Atharva Veda together with Extracts from the Ritual Books and the Commentaries
Vol. 7: The Institutes of Vishnu
Vol. 25: The Laws of Manu
Vol. 33: The Minor Law Books
Vols. 2 & 14: The Sacred Laws of the Aryas as Taught in the Schools of Apastamba, Gautama, Vasishtha and Baudhayana (2 Parts)
Vols. 12, 26, 41, 43 & 44: The Satapatha Brahmana According to the Text of the Madhyandina School (5 Parts)
Vols. 1 & 15: The Upanishads (2 Parts)
Vols. 34 & 38: The Vedanta Sutras (2 Parts)
Vol. 48: The Vedanta-Sutras (with the commentary by Ramanuja)
Vols. 32 & 46: Vedic Hymns (2 Parts)

THE SACRED BOOKS OF CHINA

The texts of Confucianism

Translated by

JAMES LEGGE

Part IV

The LĪ KĪ, I-X

MOTILAL BANARSIDASS PUBLISHERS
PRIVATE LIMITED • DELHI

Reprint: Delhi, 1964, 1967, 1970, 1976, 1986, 1992, 2001, 2008
First published by the Oxford University Press, 1885

ISBN: 978-81-208-0128-8

MOTILAL BANARSIDASS
41 U.A. Bungalow Road, Jawahar Nagar, Delhi 110 007
8 Mahalaxmi Chamber, 22 Bhulabhai Desai Road, Mumbai 400 026
203 Royapettah High Road, Mylapore, Chennai 600 004
236, 9th Main III Block, Jayanagar, Bangalore 560 011
Sanas Plaza, 1302 Baji Rao Road, Pune 411 002
8 Camac Street, Kolkata 700 017
Ashok Rajpath, Patna 800 004
Chowk, Varanasi 221 001

UNESCO COLLECTION OF REPRESENTATIVE WORKS— Indian Series
This book has been accepted in the Indian Translation Series of the UNESCO Collection of Representative Works, jointly sponsored by the United Nations Educational Scientific and Cultural Organization (UNESCO) and the Government of India

PRINTED IN INDIA

BY JAINENDRA PRAKASH JAIN AT SHRI JAINENDRA PRESS,
A-45 NARAINA, PHASE-I, NEW DELHI 110 028
AND PUBLISHED BY NARENDRA PRAKASH JAIN FOR
MOTILAL BANARSIDASS PUBLISHERS PRIVATE LIMITED,
BUNGALOW ROAD, DELHI 110 007

RASHTRAPATI BHAVAN,
NEW ḌELHI 4
June 10, 1962

I am very glad to know that the Sacred Books of the East, published years ago by the Clarendon Press, Oxford, which have been out of print for a number of years, will now be available to all students of religion and philosophy. The enterprise of the publishers is commendable and I hope the books will be widely read.

S. RADHAKRISHNAN

PREFATORY NOTE TO THE NEW EDITION

Since 1948 the United Nations Educational, Scientific and Cultural Organization (UNESCO), upon the recommendation of the General Assembly of the United Nations, has been concerned with facilitating the translation of the works most representative of the culture of certain of its Member States, and, in particular, those of Asia.

One of the major difficulties confronting this programme is the lack of translators having both the qualifications and the time to undertake translations of the many outstanding books meriting publication. To help overcome this difficulty in part, UNESCO's advisers in this field (a panel of experts convened every other year by the International Council for Philosophy and Humanistic Studies), have recommended that many worthwhile translations published during the 19th century, and now impossible to find except in a limited number of libraries, should be brought back into print in low-priced editions, for the use of students and of the general public. The experts also pointed out that in certain cases, even though there might be in existence more recent and more accurate translations endowed with a more modern apparatus of scholarship, a number of pioneer works of the greatest value and interest to students of Eastern religions also merited republication.

This point of view was warmly endorsed by the Indian National Academy of Letters (Sahitya Akademi), and the Indian National Commission for UNESCO.

It is in the spirit of these recommendations that this work from the famous series "Sacred Books of the East" is now once again being made available to the general public as part of the UNESCO Collection of Representative Works.

PUBLISHER'S NOTE

First, the man distinguished between eternal and perishable. Later, he discovered within himself the germ of the Eternal. This discovery was an epoch in the history of the human mind and the *East was the first to discover it.*

To watch in the Sacred Books of the East the dawn of this religious consciousness of man, must always remain one of the most inspiring and hallowing sights in the whole history of the world. In order to have a solid foundation for a comparative study of the Religions of the East, we must have before all things, complete and thoroughly faithful translation of their Sacred Books in which some of the ancient sayings were preserved because they were so true and so striking that they could not be forgotten. They contained eternal truths, expressed for the first time in human language.

With profoundest reverence for Dr. S. Radhakrishnan, President of India, who inspired us for the task; our deep sense of gratitude for Dr. C. D. Deshmukh & Dr. D. S. Kothari, for encouraging assistance; esteemed appreciation of UNESCO for the warm endorsement of the cause; and finally with indebtedness to Dr. H. Rau, Director, Max Müller Bhawan, New Delhi, in procuring us the texts of the Series for reprint, we humbly conclude.

CONTENTS

BOOK

I. *Kh*ü Lî or Summary of the Rules of Propriety.

Section I.

PREFACE.

I MAY be permitted to express my satisfaction that, with the two volumes of the Lî *K*î now published, I have done, so far as translation is concerned, all and more than all which I undertook to do on the Chinese Classics more than twenty-five years ago. When the first volume was published in 1861, my friend, the late Stanislas Julien, wrote to me, asking if I had duly considered the voluminousness of the Lî *K*î, and expressing his doubts whether I should be able to complete my undertaking. Having begun the task, however, I have pursued it to the end, working on with some unavoidable interruptions, and amidst not a few other engagements.

The present is the first translation that has been published in any European language of the whole of the Lî *K*î. In 1853 the late J. M. Callery published at the Imprimerie Royale, Turin, what he called 'Lî Kî, ou Mémorial des Rites, traduit pour la première fois du Chinois, et accompagné de Notes, de Commentaires, et du Texte Original.' But in fact the text which P. Callery adopted was only an expurgated edition, published by Fan Ʒze-tăng, a scholar of the Yüan dynasty, as commented on and annotated by *K*âu *K*ih, whose well-known work appeared in 1711, the 50th year of the Khang-hsî reign or period[1]. Callery has himself called attention to this in his introduction, and it is to be regretted that he did not indicate it in the title-page of his book. Fan's text omits entirely the 5th, 12th, 13th, 19th, 28th, 31st, 32nd, 33rd, 34th, 35th, 37th, and 39th Books in my translation, while of most of the others,

---

[1] The 禮記體註大全合參, for which Callery gives—'Combinaison des Commentaires Ta Tsüên (le Grand Complet) et Chu (l'explication), d'après le sens original du Mémorial des rites.' *K*âu *K*ih (周熾) has the alias of *K*âu Tan-lin (旦林).

'a good third' has been expurgated. I do not think that Callery's version contains above one half of the Lî *K*î, as it is found in the great editions of the Thang and present dynasties. The latter of these was commanded in an imperial rescript in 1748, the 13th year of the *Kh*ien-lung period. The committee charged with its execution consisted of 85 dignitaries and scholars, who used the previous labours of 244 authors, besides adding, on many of the most difficult passages, their own remarks and decisions, which are generally very valuable.

My own version is based on a study of these two imperial collections, and on an extensive compilation, made specially for my use by my Chinese friend and former helper, the graduate Wang Thâo, gathered mostly from more recent writers of the last 250 years. The *Kh*ien-lung editors make frequent reference to the work of *Kh*ăn Hâo, which appeared in 1322 under the modest title of, 'A Collection of Remarks on the Lî *K*î[1].' This acquired so great a celebrity under the Ming dynasty, that, as Callery tells us, an edict was issued in 1403 appointing it the standard for the interpretation of the Classic at the public examinations; and this pre-eminence was accorded to it on to the *Kh*ien-lung period. The whole of the Lî *K*î is given and expounded by *Kh*ăn, excepting the 28th and 39th Books, which had long been current as portions of 'The Four Books.' I may say that I have read over and over, and with much benefit, every sentence in his comments. Forming my own judgment on every passage, now agreeing with him and now differing, and frequently finding reason to attach a higher value to the views of the *Kh*ien-lung editors, I must say that 'he deserves well' of the Lî *K*î. His volumes are characterised by a painstaking study of the original text, and an honest attempt to exhibit the logical connexion of thought in its several parts.

[1] 禮記集說. The author has the aliases for Hâo of Kho Tâ (可大), Yün *K*wang (雲莊), and Tung Hui (東滙); the last, I suppose, from his having lived near the lake so called.

P. Callery's translation of his expurgated text is for the most part well executed, and his notes, of which I have often made use, are admirable. I have also enjoyed the benefit of the more recent work, 'Cursus Litteraturae Sinicae,' by P. Angelo Zottoli, in whom the scholarship of the earlier Jesuit missionaries has revived. In his third volume, published at Shang-hâi in 1880, there are good translations of the 1st, 5th, 10th, 20th, 21st, and 22nd Books; while the 28th and 39th are in his second volume. In the Latin which he employs, according to the traditions of his church and what is still a practice of some scholars, he is able to be more brief in his renderings than Callery and myself, but perhaps not so satisfactory to readers generally. I also referred occasionally to Signor Carlo Puini's 'Li-Ki: Instituzioni, Usi e Costumanze della Cina antica; Traduzione, Commento e Note (Fascicolo Primo; Firenze, 1883).'

The present translation is, as I said above, the first published in any European language of the whole of the Lî *K*î; but another had existed in manuscript for several years,—the work of Mr. Alexander Wylie, now unhappily, by loss of eye-sight and otherwise failing health, laid aside from his important Chinese labours. I was fortunate enough to obtain possession of this when I had got to the 35th Book in my own version, and, in carrying the sheets through the press, I have constantly made reference to it. It was written at an early period of Mr. Wylie's Chinese studies, and is not such as a Sinologist of his attainments and research would have produced later on. Still I have been glad to have it by me, though I may venture to say that, in construing the paragraphs and translating the characters, I have not been indebted in a single instance to him or P. Callery. The first six Books, and portions of several others, had been written out, more than once, before I finally left China in 1873; but I began again at the beginning, early in 1883, in preparing the present version. I can hardly hope that, in translating so extensive and peculiar a work, descriptive of customs and things at so remote a period of time, and without the assistance of any Chinese graduate with whom I could have talked over complicated and perplexing paragraphs, I may not have fallen into some mistakes; but I trust they will be found to be very few. My simple and only aim has been, first, to understand the text for myself, and then to render it in English, fairly and as well as I could in the time attain to, for my readers.

J. L.

OXFORD,
July 10, 1885.

THE LÎ *K*Î

OR

COLLECTION OF TREATISES ON THE RULES OF PROPRIETY OR CEREMONIAL USAGES.

THE LÎ *K*Î

OR

COLLECTION OF TREATISES ON THE RULES OF PROPRIETY OR CEREMONIAL USAGES.

INTRODUCTION.

CHAPTER I.

THREE DIFFERENT LÎ KING, OR RITUAL BOOKS, ACKNOWLEDGED IN CHINA. THE RECOVERY OF THE FIRST TWO, AND FORMATION OF THE THIRD, UNDER THE HAN DYNASTY.

How Confucius spoke of the Lî.

1. Confucius said, 'It is by the Odes that the mind is aroused; by the Rules of Propriety that the character is established; from Music that the finish is received[1].' On another occasion he said, 'Without the Rules of Propriety, respectfulness becomes laborious bustle; carefulness, timidity; boldness, insubordination; and straightforwardness, rudeness[1].'

These are two specimens of the manner in which Confucius expressed himself about the Lî, the Rules of Propriety or Ceremonial Usages, recognised in his time. It is a natural inference from his language that there were Collections of such Rules which could be read and studied; but he does not expressly say so.

How Mencius spoke of them.

The language of Mencius was more definite. In at least two passages of his works we find the usual form of quotation Lî Yüeh, 'The Lî says[2],' which, according to the analogy of Shih Yüeh, 'The Shih King, or Book of Poetry, says,' might be rendered,

---

[1] Confucian Analects, Book VIII, 8 and 2.

[2] Works of Mencius, II, Part ii, 2. 5; III, Part ii, 3. 3.

'The Lî King says.' In another passage, he says to a Mr. *K*ing *Kh*un, 'Have you not read the Lî[1]?' It does not appear that Mencius was always referring to one and the same collection of Lî; but it is clear that in his time there were one or more such collections current and well known among his countrymen.

Now there are three Lî King, or three Rituals.

There are now three Chinese classics into which the name Lî enters:—the Î Lî, the *K*âu Lî, and the Lî *K*î, frequently styled, both by the Chinese themselves and by sinologists, 'The Three Rituals[2].' The first two are books of the *K*âu dynasty (B.C. 1122–225). The third, of which a complete translation is given in the present work, may contain passages of an earlier date than either of the others; but as a collection in its present form, it does not go higher than the Han dynasty, and was not completed till our second century. It has, however, taken a higher position than those others, and is ranked with the Shû, the Shih, the Yî, and the *Kh*un *Kh*iû, forming one of 'The Five King,' which are acknowledged as the books of greatest authority in China. Other considerations besides antiquity have given, we shall see, its eminence to the Lî *K*î.

State of the Lî books at the rise of the Han dynasty.

2. The monuments of the ancient literature, with the exception, perhaps, of the Yî King, were in a condition of disorder and incompleteness at the rise of the Han dynasty (B.C. 206). This was the case especially with the Î Lî and *K*âu Lî. They had suffered, with the other books, from the fires and proscription of the short-lived dynasty of *Kh*in, the founder of which was bent especially on their destruction[3]; and during the closing centuries of *K*âu, in all the period of 'The Warring Kingdoms,' they had been variously mutilated by the contending princes[4].

[1] Works of Mencius, III, ii, 2. 2.

[2] See Wylie's Notes on Chinese Literature, p. 4, and Mayers' Chinese Reader's Manual, p. 300.

[3] Sze-mâ *Kh*ien's Biographies, Book 61 (儒林傳), p. 5b. Other testimonies to the fact could be adduced.

[4] Mencius V, ii, 2. 2. See also the note of Liû Hsin, appended to his catalogue of Lî works, in the Imperial library of Han.

Work of the emperors of Han in recovering the ancient books.

The sovereigns of Han undertook the task of gathering up and arranging the fragments of the ancient books, and executed it well. In B.C. 213 Shih Hwang Tî of *Kh*in had promulgated his edict forbidding any one to hide and keep in his possession the old writings. This was repealed in B.C. 191 by the emperor Hui, so that it had been in existence only twenty-two years, during most of which, we may presume, it had been inoperative. Arrangements were also made to receive and preserve old tablets which might be presented[1], and to take down in writing what scholars might be able to repeat. In B.C. 164, the emperor Wăn ordered 'the Great Scholars' of his court to compile 'the Royal Ordinances,' the fifth of the Books in our Lî *K*î[2].

Recovery of the Î Lî.

i. Internal evidence shows that when this treatise was made, the Î Lî, or portions of it at least, had been recovered; and with this agrees the testimony of Sze-mâ *Kh*ien, who was born perhaps in that very year[3], and lived to between B.C. 90 and 80. In the 61st Book of his Biographies, referred to in a note above, *Kh*ien says, 'Many of the scholars repeated (parts of) the Lî; but no other of them so much as Kâo Thang of Lû; and now we have only the Shih Lî, which he was able to recite.' In harmony with this statement of the great historian, is the first entry in Liû Hsin's Catalogue of Lî books in the Imperial library of Han:—'56 *k*üan or sections of Lî in the old text, and 17 phien in the (current) text (of the time);' forming, as is universally believed, the present Î Lî, for which the Shih Lî of *Kh*ien is merely another name.

That Kâo Thang should have been able to dictate so much of the work will not be thought wonderful by those who

[1] Such was the 'Stone-Conduit Gallery,' which Mayers (Manual, p. 185) describes as a building erected by Hsiâo Ho at *Kh*ang-an for the reception of the records of the extinct *Kh*in dynasty, about B.C. 200, adding that 'in B.C. 51, the emperor Hsüan appointed a commission of scholars to assemble in this building, and complete the revision of the classical writings.' But it had also been intended from the first as a repository for those writings as they were recovered.

[2] See the General Mirror of History under that year.

[3] Mayers puts his birth 'about B.C. 163,' and his death 'about 85.'

are familiar with the power of memory displayed by many Chinese scholars even at the present day. The sections in the old text were found in the reign of the emperor Wû (B.C. 140–87), and came into the possession of his brother, known as king Hsien of Ho-*k*ien. We do not know how much this mass of tablets added to the Î Lî, as we now have it, but they confirmed the genuineness of the portion obtained from Kâo.

King Hsien of Ho-*k*ien, and his recovery of the *K*âu Lî.

ii. The recovery of the *K*âu Lî came not long after, and through the agency of the same king Hsien. No one did so much as he in the restoration of the ancient literature. By name Teh, and one of the fourteen sons of the emperor *K*ing (B.C. 156–141), he was appointed by his father, in B.C. 155, king of Ho-*k*ien, which is still the name of one of the departments of *K*ih-lî, and there he continued till his death, in 129, the patron of all literary men, and unceasingly pursuing his quest for old books dating from before the *Kh*in dynasty. Multitudes came to him from all quarters, bringing to him the precious tablets which had been preserved in their families or found by them elsewhere. The originals he kept in his own library, and had a copy taken, which he gave to the donor with a valuable gift. We are indebted to him in this way for the preservation of the Tâo Teh King, the works of Mencius, and other precious treasures; but I have only to notice here his services in connexion with the Lî books[1].

Some one[2] brought to him the tablets of the *K*âu Lî, then called *K*âu Kwan, 'The Official Book of *K*âu,' and purporting to contain a complete account of the organised government of the dynasty of *K*âu in six sections. The sixth section, however, which should have supplied a list of the officers in the department of the minister of Works,

[1] See the account of king Hsien in the twenty-third chapter of the Biographies in the History of the first Han dynasty. Hsien was the king's posthumous title (獻), denoting 'The Profound and Intelligent.'

[2] The Catalogue of the Sui Dynasty's (A.D. 589–618) Imperial library says this was a scholar of the surname Lî (李). I have been unable to trace the authority for the statement farther back.

with their functions, was wanting, and the king offered to pay 1000 pieces of gold to any one who should supply the missing tablets, but in vain[1]. He presented the tablets which he had obtained at the court of his half-brother, the emperor Wû; but the treasure remained uncared for in one of the imperial repositories till the next century; when it came into the charge of Liû Hsin. Hsin replaced the missing portion from another old work, called Khâo Kung *K*î, which Wylie renders by 'The Artificers' Record.' This has ever since continued to appear as the sixth section of the whole work, for the charge of which Hsin obtained the appointment of a special board of scholars, such as had from the first been entrusted with the care of the Î Lî. The *K*âu Lî is a constitutional and not a ritual work. The last entry in Hsin's Catalogue of Lî Books is:—'The *K*âu Kwan in six sections; and a treatise on the *K*âu Kwan in four sections.' That is the proper name for it. It was not called the *K*âu Lî till the Thang dynasty[2].

Formation of the Lî *K*î.

iii. We come to the formation of the text of the Lî *K*î, in which we are more particularly interested. We cannot speak of its recovery, for though parts of it had been in existence during the *K*âu dynasty, many of its Books cannot claim a higher antiquity than the period of the Han. All that is known about the authorship of them all will be found in the notices which form the last chapter of this Introduction.

After the entry in Liû Hsin's Catalogue about the re-

[1] This is related in the Catalogue of the Sui dynasty. It could not be in *Kh*ien's sixty-first chapter of Biographies, because the *K*âu Kwan was not known, or, at least, not made public, in *Kh*ien's time. The Sui writers, no doubt, took it from some biography of the Han, which has escaped me.

[2] A complete translation of the *K*âu Lî appeared at Paris in 1851, the work of Edward Biot, who had died himself before its publication, before his fiftieth year. According to a note in Callery's 'Mémorial des Rites' (p. 191), the labour of its preparation hastened Biot's death. There are some errors in the version, but they are few. I have had occasion to refer to hundreds of passages in it, and always with an increasing admiration of the author's general resources and knowledge of Chinese. His early death was the greatest loss which the cause of sinology has sustained. His labours, chiefly on Chinese subjects, had been incessant from 1835. The perusal of them has often brought to my memory the words of Newton, 'If Mr. Cotes had lived, we should have known something.' Is there no sinologist who will now undertake a complete translation of the Î Lî?

covered text of the Î Lî, there follows—'131 phien of *K*î,' that is, so many different records or treatises on the subject of Lî. These had also been collected by king Hsien, and *K*û Hsî's note about them is that they were 'Treatises composed by the disciples of the seventy disciples,' meaning by 'the seventy disciples' those of Confucius' followers who had been most in his society and profited most from his instructions. These 131 phien contained, no doubt, the germ of our Lî *K*î; but there they remained for about a century in the imperial repositories, undigested and uncared for, and constantly having other treatises of a similar nature added to them.

At last, in B.C. 51, the emperor Hsüan (B.C. 73-47) convoked a large assembly of Great Scholars to meet in the Stone-Conduit Gallery, and discuss the text of the recovered classics[1]. A prominent member of this assembly, the president of it I suppose, was Liû Hsiang, himself a celebrated writer and a scion of the imperial house, who appears to have had the principal charge of all the repositories. Among the other members, and in special connexion with the Lî works, we find the name of Tâi Shăng, who will again come before us[2].

Council of B.C. 51.

We do not know what the deliberations of the Great Scholars resulted in, but twenty-five years later the emperor *Kh*ăng caused another search to be made throughout the empire for books that might hitherto have escaped notice; and, when it was completed, he ordered Hsiang to examine all the contents of the repositories, and collate the various copies of the classics. From this came the preparation of a catalogue; and Hsiang dying at the age of seventy-two, in B.C. 9, before it was completed, the work was delegated to his third and youngest son Hsin. His catalogue we happily possess. It mentions, in addition to the Î Lî and

B.C. 26.

[1] See the Details in the General Mirror of History, under B.C. 51.

[2] See the 58th Book of Biographies (儒林) in the History of the first Han, and the Catalogue of the Sui Library.

*K*âu Lî, 199 phien of Lî treatises. The résumé appended to the Lî books in the Catalogue of the Sui Dynasty, omitting works mentioned by Hsin, and inserting two others, says that Hsiang had in his hands altogether 214 phien. What was to be done with this mass of tablets, or the written copies made from them?

Hâu Ȝhang and the two Tâis.

The most distinguished of the Lî scholars in the time of the emperors Hsüan and *Kh*ăng was a Hâu Ȝhang, the author of the compilation called in Hsin's Catalogue *Kh*ü Tâi *K*î; and two of his disciples, Tâi Teh and Tâi Shăng, cousins[1], the name of the latter of whom has already been mentioned as a member of the council of B.C. 51, were also celebrated for their ability. Teh, the older of the two, and commonly called Tâ Tâi, or 'the Greater Tâi,' while Hsiang was yet alive, digested the mass of phien, and in doing so reduced their number to 85. The younger, called Hsiâo Tâi, or 'the Lesser Tâi,' doing the same for his cousin's work, reduced it to 46 treatises. This second condensation of the Lî documents met with general acceptance, and was styled the Lî *K*î. Shăng himself wrote a work in twelve chapters, called 'A Discussion of the Doubts of Scholars about the Lî *K*î,' which, though now lost, was existing in the time of Sui. Through *Kh*iâo *Z*ăn and others, scholars of renown in their day, the redaction passed on to the well-known

Mâ Yung and *K*ang Hsüan.

Mâ Yung (A.D. 79–166), who added to Shăng's books the Yüeh Ling, the Ming

[1] Sinologists, without exception I believe, have called Shăng a 'nephew' of Teh, overlooking the way in which the relationship between them is expressed in Chinese. Shăng is always Teh's 從兄之子, and not simply 兄之子. Foreign students have overlooked the force of the phrase 從兄 and, more fully, 從父兄. Teh and Shăng's father had the same grandfather, and were themselves the sons of brothers. They were therefore what we call first cousins, and Teh and Shăng were second cousins. The point is unimportant, but it is well to be correct even in small matters. Not unimportant, however, is the error of Callery (Introduction, p. 6), who says, 'Le neveu, homme dépravé, beaucoup plus adonné aux plaisirs, qu'à l'étude, retrancha encore davantage et fixa le nombre des chapitres à 46.' No such stigma rests on the character of Tâi Shăng, and I am sure translators have reason to be grateful to him for condensing, as he did, the result of his cousin's labours.

Thang Wei, and the Yo *K*î, making their number in all forty-nine, though, according to the arrangement adopted in the present translation, they still amount only to forty-six. From Mâ, again, it passed to his pupil *K*ăng Hsüan (A.D. 127–200), in whom he was obliged to acknowledge a greater scholar than himself.

Thus the Lî *K*î was formed. It is not necessary to pursue its history farther. *K*ăng was the scholar of his age, and may be compared, in scholarship, with the later *K*û Hsî. And he has been fortunate in the preservation of his works. He applied himself to all the three Rituals, and his labours on them all, the *K*âu Lî, the Î Lî, and the Lî *K*î, remain. His commentaries on them are to be found in the great work of 'The Thirteen King' of the Thang dynasty. There they appear, followed by the glosses, illustrations, and paraphrases of Khung Ying-tâ.

In A.D. 175, while *K*ăng was yet alive, 3hâi Yung, a scholar and officer of many gifts, superintended the work of engraving on stone the text of all the Confucian classics. Only fragments of that great manusculpt remain to the present day, but others of the same nature were subsequently made. We may feel assured that we have the text of the Lî *K*î and other old Chinese books, as it was 1800 years ago, more correctly than any existing manuscripts give us that of any works of the West, Semitic, or Greek, or Latin, of anything like equal antiquity.

3hâi Yung and his manusculpt.

3. A few sentences on the Lî of the Greater Tâi will fitly close this chapter. He handed down his voluminous compilation to a Hsü Liang of Lang Yeh in the present Shan-tung[1], and in his family it was transmitted; but if any commentaries on it were published, there is no trace of them in history. As the shorter work of his cousin obtained a wide circulation, his fell into neglect, and, as *K*û Î-3un says, was simply put upon the shelf. Still there appears in the Sui Catalogue these two entries:—'The Lî *K*î of Tâ Tâi, in 13 Sections,' and 'The Hsiâ

Lî of the Greater Tâi.

[1] 徐良, 字斿卿, 受禮於戴德.

Hsiâo Kăng, in 1 Section,' with a note by the editor that it was compiled by Tâ Tâi. This little tractate may, or may not, have been also included in one of the 13 Sections. There are entries also about Tâ Tâi's work in the catalogues of the Thang and Sung dynasties, which have given rise to many discussions. Some of the Sung scholars even regarded it as a 14th King. In the large collection of 'Books of Han and Wei,' a portion of the Lî of Tâ Tâi is still current, 39 Books in 10 Sections, including the fragment of the Hsiâ dynasty, of which a version, along with the text, was published in 1882 by Professor Douglas of King's College, under the title of 'The Calendar of the Hsiâ Dynasty.' I have gone over all the portion in the Han and Wei Collection, and must pronounce it very inferior to the compilation of the Hsiâo or Lesser Tâi. This inferiority, and not the bulk, merely, was the reason why from the first it has been comparatively little attended to.

CHAPTER II.

SIGNIFICANCE OF THE CHINESE CHARACTER CALLED LÎ. MEANING OF THE TITLE LÎ *KÎ*. VALUE OF THE WORK.

1. The Chinese character Lî admits of a great variety of terms in translating a work where it abounds into any of our western languages. In order fully to apprehend its significance, we must try to get hold of the fundamental ideas which it was intended to convey. And these are two. First, when we consult the Shwo Wăn, the oldest Chinese dictionary, we find Lî defined as 'a step or act; that whereby we serve spiritual beings and obtain happiness.' The character was to the author, Hsü Shăn, an ideagram of religious import; and we can see that he rightly interpreted the intention of its maker or makers. It consists of two elements, separately called *kh*ih and lî[1]. That on the left is the symbol,

Lî is a symbol of religious import.

[1] 示+豊=禮.

determining the category of meaning to which the compound belongs. It was the earliest figure employed to indicate spiritual beings, and enters into characters denoting spirits, sacrifices, and prayer[1]. That on the right, called lî, is phonetic, but even it is the symbol for 'a vessel used in performing rites;' and if, as the Khang-hsî dictionary seems to say, it was anciently used alone for the present compound, still the spiritual significance would attach to it, and the addition of the *kh*ih to complete the character, whensoever it was made, shows that the makers considered the rites in which the vessel was used to possess in the first place a religious import.

Next, the character is used, in moral and philosophical disquisitions, to designate one of the primary constituents of human nature. Those, as set forth by Mencius, are

Lî is a symbol for the feeling of propriety.

four; 'not fused into us from without,' not produced, that is, by any force of circumstances, but 'belonging naturally to us, as our four limbs do.' They are benevolence (*z*ăn), righteousness (î), propriety (lî), and understanding (*k*îh). Our possession of the first is proved by the feeling of distress at the sight of suffering; of the second, by our feelings of shame and dislike; of the third, by our feelings of modesty and courtesy; of the fourth, by our consciousness of approving and disapproving[2].

Thus the character lî, in the concrete application of it, denotes the manifestations, and in its imperative use, the rules, of propriety. This twofold symbolism of it—the religious and the moral—must be kept in mind in the study of our classic. A life ordered in harmony with it would realise the highest Chinese ideal, and surely a very high ideal, of human character.

But never and nowhere has it been possible for men to maintain this high standard of living. In China and elsewhere the lî have become, in the usages of society in its various relationships, matters of course, forms without the

---

[1] E.g. 神 (shăn), 祭 (*k*î), 祈 (*kh*î).

[2] Mencius, II, i, 6; VI, i, 6, 7.

spirit, and hence we cannot always translate the character by the same term. It would be easy to add to the number of words, more or less synonymous, in French or English or any other Aryan language, which Callery has heaped together in the following passage:—'Autant que possible, j'ai traduit Lî par le mot Rite, dont le sens est susceptible à une grande étendue; mais il faut convenir que, suivant les circonstances où il est employé, il peut signifier—Cérémonial, Cérémonies, Pratiques cérémoniales, L'étiquette, Politesse, Urbanité, Courtoisie, Honnêteté, Bonnes manières, Égards, Bonne éducation, Bienséance, Les formes, Les convenances, Savoir-vivre, Décorum, Décence, Dignité personnelle, Moralité de conduite, Ordre Social, Devoirs de Société, Lois Sociales, Devoirs, Droit, Morale, Lois hiérarchiques, Offrande, Usages, Coutumes[1].' I have made little use in my translation of the word Rite or Rites, which Callery says he had endeavoured to adhere to as much as possible, but I do not think I have allowed myself so much liberty in other terms in my English as he has done in his French. For the symbol in the title I have said 'Rules of Propriety or Ceremonial Usages.'

Translation of the title.

2. The meaning of the title—Lî *K*î—need not take us so long. There is no occasion to say more on the significance of Lî; the other character, *K*î, should have a plural force given to it. What unity belongs to the Books composing it arises from their being all, more or less, occupied with the subject of Lî. Each one, or at least each group, is complete in itself. Each is a *K*î; taken together, they are so many *K*îs. Only into the separate titles of seven of them, the 13th, 16th, 17th, 18th, 19th, 27th, and 29th, does the name of *K*î enter. That character is the symbol for 'the recording of things one by one,' and is often exchanged for another *K*î[2], in which the classifying element is sze, the symbol for 'a packet of cocoons,' the compound denoting the unwinding

---

[1] Introduction, p. 16.

[2] The classifier of *K*î in the title is 言 (yen), the symbol of words; that of this *K*î (紀) is 糸 (sze).

and arrangement of the threads[1]. Wylie's 'Book of Rites' and Callery's 'Mémorial des Rites' always failed to give me a definite idea of the nature of our classic. Sze-mâ *Kh*ien's work is called Sze *K*î[2], or 'Historical Records,' and Lî *K*î might in the same way be rendered 'Ceremonial Records,' but I have preferred to give for the title—'A Collection of Treatises on the Rules of Propriety or Ceremonial Usages.'

The value of the Lî *K*î.

3. The value of the work has been discussed fully by P. Callery in the sixth paragraph of the Introduction to his translation of an abbreviated edition of it, and with much of what he has said I am happy to feel myself in accord. I agree with him, for instance, that the book is 'the most exact and complete monography which the Chinese nation has been able to give of itself to the rest of the human race.' But this sentence occurs in a description of the Chinese spirit, which is little better than a caricature. 'Le cérémonial,' he says, 'résume l'esprit Chinois. . . . Ses affections, si elle en a, sont satisfaites par le cérémonial; ses devoirs, elle les remplit au moyen du cérémonial; la vertu et le vice, elle les reconnaît au cérémonial; en un mot, pour elle le cérémonial c'est l'homme, l'homme moral, l'homme politique, l'homme religieux, dans ses multiples rapports avec la famille, la société, l'état, la morale et la religion.'

To all this representation the first sentence of our classic is a sufficient reply:—'Always and in everything let there be reverence.' In hundreds of other passages the same thing is insisted on,—that ceremony without an inspiring reverence is nothing. I do not deny that there is much attention to forms in China with a forgetfulness of the spirit that should animate them. But where is the nation against whose people the same thing may not be charged? The treaties of western nations with China contain an article stipulating for the toleration of Chinese Christians on the ground that 'The Christian religion, as professed by

[1] Structure of Chinese Characters, p. 132.

[2] 史記.

Protestants or Roman Catholics, inculcates the practice of virtue, and teaches man to do as he would be done by[1].' Scores of Chinese, officers, scholars, and others, have, in conversations with myself, asked if such were indeed the nature of Christianity, appealing at the same time to certain things which they alleged that made them doubt it. All that can be said in the matter is this, that as the creeds of men elsewhere are often better than their practice, so it is in China. Whether it be more so there or here is a point on which different conclusions will be come to, according to the knowledge and prejudices of the speculators.

More may be learned about the religion of the ancient Chinese from this classic than from all the others together. Where the writers got their information about the highest worship and sacrifices of the most ancient times, and about the schools of Shun, we do not know. They expressed the views, doubtless, that were current during the Han dynasty, derived partly from tradition, and partly from old books which were not gathered up, or, possibly, from both those sources. But let not readers expect to find in the Lî *K*î anything like a theology. The want of dogmatic teaching of religion in the Confucian system may not be all a disadvantage and defect; but there is a certain amount of melancholy truth in the following observations of Callery:—'Le Lî *K*î, celui de tous les King où les questions religieuses auraient dû être traitées tout naturellement, à propos des sacrifices au Ciel, aux Dieux tutélaires, et aux ancêtres, glisse légèrement sur tout ce qui est de pure spéculation, et ne mentionne ces graves matières qu'avec une extrême indifférence. Selon moi ceci prouve deux choses: la première, que dans les temps anciens les plus grand génies de la Chine n'ont possédé sur le créateur, sur la nature et les destinées de l'âme, que des notions obscures, incertaines et souvent contradictoires; la seconde, que les Chinois possèdent à un très faible degré le sentiment religieux, et qu'ils n'éprouvent pas, comme les races de

[1] From the eighth article in the Treaty with Great Britain, 1858.

l'occident, le besoin impérieux de sonder les mystères du monde invisible.'

The number of the *K*î that are devoted to the subject of the mourning rites shows how great was the regard of the people for the departed members of their families. The solidarity of the family, and even the solidarity of the race, is a sentiment which has always been very strong among them. The doctrine of filial piety has also the prominence in several Books which we might expect.

As to the philosophical and moral ideas which abound in the work, they are, as Callery says, 'in general, sound and profound.' The way in which they are presented is not unfrequently eccentric, and hedged about with absurd speculations on the course of material nature, but a prolonged study of the most difficult passages will generally bring to light what Chinese scholars call a tâo-lî, a ground of reason or analogy, which interests and satisfies the mind.

The Lî *K*î as one of the Five King.

4. The position that came gradually to be accorded to the Lî *K*î as one of 'The Five King,' par excellence, was a tribute to its intrinsic merit. It did not, like the *K*âu Lî, treat of matters peculiar to one dynasty, but of matters important in all time; nor like the Î Lî, of usages belonging to one or more of the official classes, but of those that concerned all men. The category of 'Five King' was formed early, but the 'Three Rituals' were comprehended in it as of equal value, and formed one subdivision of it. So it was early in the Thang dynasty when the collection of 'The Thirteen King' was issued; but ere the close of that dynasty our classic had made good its eminence over the other two Rituals. In the 29th chapter of the Monographs of Thang, page 17, it is said, 'To the charge of each of the Five King two Great Scholars were appointed. The Yî of *K*âu, the Shang Shû, the Shih of Mâo, the *Kh*un *Kh*iû, and the Lî *K*î are the Five King.'

CHAPTER III.

Brief Notices of the different Books which make up the Collection.

Book I. *Kh*ü Lî.

This first Book in the collection is also the longest, and has been divided because of its length into two Books. In this translation, however, it appears only as one Book in two Sections, which again are subdivided, after the *Kh*ien-lung editors, into five Parts and three Parts respectively.

The name *Kh*ü Lî is taken from the first two characters in the first paragraph, and the first sentence, 'The *Kh*ü Lî says,' extends over all that follows to the end of the Book. P. Callery, indeed, puts only the first paragraph within inverted commas, as if it alone were from the *Kh*ü Lî, and the rest of the Book were by a different hand. He translates the title by 'Rites Divers,' and to his first sentence, 'Le Recueil des rites divers dit,' appends the following note:—'This work, that for a very long time has been lost, was, so far as appears, one of those collections of proverbs and maxims with which philosophy has commenced among nearly all peoples. Although the author does not say so, it is probable that this chapter and the next contain an analysis of that ancient collection, for the great unconnectedness which we find in it agrees well with the variety indicated by the title *Kh*ü Lî.' My own inference from the text, however, is what I have stated above, that the Book is a transcript of the *Kh*ü Lî, and not merely a condensation of its contents, or a redaction of them by a different author.

It is not easy to translate the title satisfactorily. According to *K*ăng Hsüan (or *K*ăng Khang-*kh*ăng), the earliest of all the great commentators on the Lî *K*î, 'The Book is named *Kh*ü Lî, because it contains matters relating to all the five ceremonial categories. What is said in it about sacrifices belongs to the "auspicious ceremonies;"

about the rites of mourning, and the loss or abandonment of one's state, to the "inauspicious;" about the payment of tributory dues and appearances at the royal court, to "the rites of hospitality;" about weapons, chariots, and banners, "to those of war;" and about serving elders, reverencing the aged, giving offerings or presents, and the marriage of daughters, to the "festive ceremonies."' On this view the title would mean 'Rules belonging to the different classes of ceremonies,' or, more concisely, the 'Rites Divers' of Callery; and Mr. Wylie has called the Book 'The Universal Ritual.'

But this rendering of the title does not suit the proper force of the character *Kh*ü, which is the symbol of 'being bent or crooked,' and is used, with substantival meaning, for what is small and appears irregularly. Mention is made in Book XXVIII, ii, 23, of 'him who cultivates the shoots of goodness in his nature,' those 'shoots' being expressed by this character *Kh*ü; and in a note on the passage there I have quoted the words of the commentator Pâi Lü:—'Put a stone on a bamboo shoot, or where the shoot would show itself, and it will travel round the stone, and come out crookedly at its side.' Thus *Kh*ü is employed for what is exhibited partially or in a small degree. Even *K*ăng Hsüan on that passage explains it by 'very small matters;' and the two ablest in my opinion of all the Chinese critics and commentators, *K*û Hsî and Wû *Kh*ăng (of the Yüan dynasty, A.D. 1249-1333), take our title to mean 'The minuter forms and smaller points of ceremony.' P. Zottoli is not to be blamed for following them, and styling the Book—'Minutiores Ritus.' Still even this does not satisfy my own mind. Great rites are mentioned in the treatise as well as small ones. Principles of ceremony are enunciated as well as details. The contents are marked indeed by the 'unconnectedness' which Callery mentions; but a translator cannot help that. The Book may not be as to method all that we could wish, but we must make the best we can of it as it stands; and I have ventured to call it 'A Summary of the Rules of Ceremony.' It occupies very properly the place at the beginning of the collection, and is a good introduction to the treatises that follow.

Among the Lî books in Liû Hsin's Catalogue of the Imperial Library of Han, is a Treatise in nine chapters (phien), compiled by Hâu Ʒhang, and called *Kh*ü Thâi *K*î, or 'Record made in the *Kh*ü Tower.' The *Kh*ü Tower was the name of an educational building, where scholars met in the time of the emperor Hsüan to discuss questions about ceremonies and other matters connected with the ancient literature, and Hâu Ʒhang (mentioned in the preceding chapter) kept a record of their proceedings. I should like to think that our *Kh*ü Lî is a portion of that *Kh*ü Thâi *K*î, and am sorry not to be able to adduce Chinese authorities who take the same view. It would relieve us of the difficulty of accounting for the use of *Kh*ü in the title.

Book II. Than Kung.

The name Than Kung given to this Book is taken from the first paragraph in it, where the gentleman so denominated appears attending the mourning rites for an officer of the state of Lû. Nowhere else in the Treatise, however, is there any mention of him, or reference to him. There can be no reason but this, for calling it after him, that his surname and name occur at the commencement of it. He was a native, it is understood, of Lû; but nothing more is known of him.

The Than Kung, like the *Kh*ü Lî, is divided into two Books, which appear in this translation as two Sections of one Book. Each Section is subdivided into three Parts. The whole is chiefly occupied with the observances of the mourning rites. It is valuable because of the information which it gives about them, and the views prevailing at the time on the subject of death. It contains also many historical incidents about Confucius and others, which we are glad to possess. Some of the commentators, and especially the *Kh*ien-lung editors, reject many of them as legendary and fabulous. The whole Book is reduced to very small compass in the expurgated editions of the Lî *K*î. We are glad, however, to have the incidents such as they are. Who would not be sorry to want the account of Confucius' death, which is given in I, ii, 20? We seem, moreover, to understand him better from accounts which the Book contains of his intercourse with his disciples. and of their mourning for him.

Ȝze-yû [1], an eminent member of his school, appears in the first paragraph much to his credit, and similarly afterwards on several occasions; and this has made the *Kh*ien-lung editors throw out the suggestion that the Book was compiled by his disciples. It may have been so.

Book III. Wang *K*ih.

According to Lû *K*ih (died A.D. 192)[2], the Wang *K*ih, or 'Royal Regulations,' was made by the Great Scholars of the time of the emperor Wăn (B.C. 179–157), on the requisition of that sovereign[3]. It professes to give the regulations of the early kings on the classes of the feudal nobles and officers and their emoluments, on their sacrifices, and their care for the aged. The emperor ordered it to be compiled after the death of *K*iâ Î, a Great scholar and highly esteemed by the sovereign, which event must have taken place about B.C. 170, when *K*iâ was only thirty-three. The Book is said to have contained, when it first appeared, an account of the royal progresses and of the altars and ceremonies of investiture, of which we do not now find any trace. Parts of it are taken from Mencius, from the Shû, and from the Commentaries of Kung-yang and Ȝo on the *Kh*un *Kh*iû; other parts again are not easily reconciled with those authorities.

---

[1] 子游.

[2] See the 54th Book of the Biographies in the History of the Second Han Dynasty.

[3] In B.C. 164. See the Mirror of History on that year.

The *Kh*ien-lung editors deliver their judgment on it to the following effect: When it was made, the Î Lî must have appeared, but not the *K*âu Lî. Hence the Banquet and Missions appear among the 'Six Subjects of Teaching,' and no mention is made of the minister of Religion, as one of the six great ministers, nor is anything said of the minister of War's management of the army. On a general view of it, many subjects are evidently based on Mencius, and whole paragraphs are borrowed from him. Nothing is said of the peculiar position of the son of Heaven, because in the Han dynasty, succeeding immediately to that of *Kh*in, the emperor was to be distinguished from, and not named along with, the feudal princes. In what is said about the reports of the Income and fixing the Expenditure, only the Grand ministers of Instruction, War, and Works are mentioned, because these were the three ducal ministers of the Han dynasty, and the ancient arrangements were represented so as to suit what had come into existence. That nothing is said about altars and investitures arose from Wăn's having disregarded in that matter the advice of Hsin-yüan Phing[1]. It only shows how much the information of the compilers exceeded that of Shû-sun Thung[2] and Sze-mâ Hsiang-*z*û[3]. The Book was received into the collection of the Lî *K*î, because it was made at no great distance from antiquity. It is foolish in later scholars to weigh and measure every paragraph of it by its agreement or disagreement with Mencius and the *K*âu Lî.

This account of the Wang *K*ih must commend itself to unprejudiced readers. To myself, the most interesting thing in the Book is the information to be gathered from it about the existence of schools in the earliest times. We see at the very commencement of history in China a

---

[1] 新垣平. A Tâoistic charlatan, honoured and followed for a few years by the emperor Wăn; put to death in B.C. 163.

[2] 叔孫通. A scholar of *Kh*in; was a counsellor afterwards of the first and second emperors of Han.

[3] 司馬相如. An officer and author. Died B.C. 126.

rudimentary education, out of which has come by gradual development the system of examinations of the present day.

BOOK IV. YÜEH LING.

The Yüeh Ling, or 'Proceedings of Government in the different Months,' appears in the *Kh*ien-lung edition of the Lî *K*î in six Sections; but it has seemed to me more in harmony with the nature of the Book and more useful for the student to arrange it in four Sections, and each Section in three Parts, a Section thus comprehending a season of the year, and every month having a part to itself. There is also a short supplementary Section in the middle of the year, at the end of the sixth month, rendered necessary by the Tâoist lines on which the different portions are put together.

Ȝhâi Yung (A.D. 133–192)[1] and Wang Sû[2], somewhat later (in our third century), held that the Book was the work of the duke of *K*âu, and must be assigned to the eleventh or twelfth century B.C. But this view of its antiquity may be said to be universally given up. Even *K*ăng Hsüan saw in the second century that it was a compilation from the *Kh*un *Kh*iû of Lü Pû-wei[3], still foolishly said by many Chinese writers to have been the real father of the founder of the *Kh*in dynasty, and who died in B.C. 237. Lû Teh-ming[4], writing in our seventh century, said, 'The Yüeh Ling was originally part of Lü's *Kh*un *Kh*iû, from which some one subsequently compiled this Memoir.' The *Kh*ien-lung editors unhesitatingly affirm this origin of the Yüeh Ling; as indeed no one, who has compared it with the work ascribed to Lü, can have any doubts on the matter. Of that work, Mayers says that 'it is a collection of quasi-historical notices, and, although nominally Lü's production, really compiled under his direction by an assemblage of scholars.'

---

[1] 蔡雍. [2] 王肅. [3] 呂不韋; 呂氏春秋. [4] 陸德命.

Mayers adds, that on the completion of the work, Lu Pû-wei suspended 1000 pieces of gold at the gate of his palace, which he offered as a reward to any one who could suggest an improvement of it by adding or expunging a single character[1].

Such was the origin of the Yüeh Ling. We do not know who compiled it from the *Kh*un *Kh*iû of Lü, but it was first received into the Lî *K*î by Mâ Yung. It can be explained only by noting the *Kh*in peculiarities in the names of titles and other things. It is in itself full of interest, throwing light on the ancient ways and religious views, and showing how the latter more especially came to be corrupted by the intrusion among them of Tâoistic elements.

The Book has sometimes been called 'A Calendar of the Months of *K*âu.' Callery translates the name Yüeh Ling by 'Attributs des Mois.' My own translation of it is after *K*ăng Hsüan, who says, 'The Book is called Yüeh Ling, because it records the proceedings of Government in the twelve months of the year.'

Book V. Ȝăng-ȝze Wăn.

This Book is named from the first three characters in it, meaning 'The Questions of Ȝăng-ȝze.' Most of the different paragraphs or chapters in the two Sections of it commence in the same way. It is not found at all in the expurgated editions of the classic.

Ȝăng-ȝze, or Mr. Ȝăng[2], about fifty years younger than Confucius, was one of the chief disciples of his school, perhaps the ablest among them. He was distinguished for his filial piety, and straightforward, honest simplicity.

[1] Mayers' Chinese Reader's Manual, p. 146. The 1000 pieces of gold suspended at Lü's gate are probably only a variation of what has been related in the preceding chapter of what was done by king Hsien of Ho-*k*ien towards the recovery of the missing Book of the *K*âu Kwan.

[2] 曾子; his name was (Shăn, 參), and that which he received in his maturity, Ȝze-yü (子輿).

There is an interesting account of his death in Book II, i, Part i, 18. In the department of Liû Hsin's Catalogue, which contains 'Works of the Literati,' there are entered '18 Treatises (phien) of Ȝăng-ȝze,' but without any further specification of them. Ten of those treatises, or fragments of them, are found in the Lî of the Greater Tâi, but this Book is not among them, nor have I seen it anywhere ascribed to him as the writer of it. It must have been compiled, however, from memoranda left by him or some of his intimate disciples. The names of only two other disciples of the Master occur in it—those of Ȝze-yû and Ȝze-hsiâ[1]. The reference to the disciples of the former in Section ii, 19, must be a note by the final compiler. The mention of Lâo-ȝze or Lâo Tan, and his views also, in Section ii, 22, 24, 28, strikes us as remarkable.

If it were necessary to devise a name for the Book, I should propose—'Questions of Casuistry on the subject of Ceremonial Rites.' Ȝăng-ȝze propounds difficulties that have struck him on various points of ceremony, especially in connexion with the rites of mourning; and Confucius replies to them ingeniously and with much fertility. Some of the questions and answers, however, are but so much trifling. Khung Ying-tâ says that only Ȝăng-ȝze could have proposed the questions, and only Confucius have furnished the answers. He applies to the Book the description of the Yî in the third of the Appendixes to that classic, i, 40, as 'Speaking of the most complex phenomena under the sky, and having nothing in it to awaken dislike, and of the subtlest movements under the sky, and having nothing in it to produce confusion.'

BOOK VI. WĂN WANG SHIH-ȜZE.

No hint is given, nothing has been suggested, as to who was the compiler of this Book, which the *Kh*ien-lung editors publish in two Sections. Its name is taken from the first

[1] 子游 and 子夏.

clause of the first paragraph, which treats of king Wăn, the founder of the *K*âu dynasty, as he demeaned himself in his youth, when he was Shih-ȝze, or son and heir of his father. This is followed by a similar account of his son, who became king Wû; and in paragraph 3 the writer goes on to the duke of *K*âu's training of king *Kh*ăng, the young son of Wû. In the last paragraph of the second Section, the subject of king Wăn as prince is resumed.

But the real subject-matter of the Book lies between those portions, and treats of three things.

First; Section i, paragraph 5 to the end, treats of the education and training of the eldest sons of the king and feudal princes, and of the young men of brightest promise throughout the kingdom, chosen to study with these. We learn much from it as to the educational institutions and methods of ancient times.

Second; in Section ii, paragraphs 1 to 15, we have the duties of the Shû-ȝze, the head of an official Section, belonging to the department of the premier, whose special business was with the direction of the young noblemen of the royal and feudal courts in all matters belonging to their instruction.

Third; from paragraph 17 to 23 of Section ii, we have an account of the various ceremonies or observances in the king's feasting and cherishing of the aged, and of his care that a similar course should be pursued by all the princes in their states.

BOOK VII. LÎ YUN.

Lî Yun means, literally, 'The Conveyance of Rites.' P. Callery translates the name, not unsuccessfully, by 'Phases du Cérémonial;' but I prefer my own longer rendering of it, because it gives the reader a better idea of the contents of the Book. *K*ăng Hsüan said it was called the Conveyance of Rites, because it records how the five Tîs and three Kings made their several changes in them, and how the Yin and the Yang, or the twofold movement and operation of nature, produced them by their revolutions. The whole is difficult and deep; and no other portion of the collection has tasked the ablest commentators more. The *Kh*ien-lung editors say that we have in the Book a grand expression of the importance of ceremonial usages, and that, if we are on our guard against a small Tâoistic element in it, it is pure and without a flaw. That depraving element, they think, was introduced by the smaller Tâi, who ignorantly thought he could make the Treatise appear to have a higher character by surreptitiously mixing it up with the fancies of Lâo and *K*wang. But the Tâoistic admixture is larger than they are willing to allow.

Some have attributed the Book to 3ze-yû, who appears, in the first of its Sections, three times by his surname and name of Yen Yen, as the questioner of Confucius, and thereby giving occasion to the exposition of the sage's views; others attribute it to his disciples. The second Section commences with an utterance of Confucius without the prompting of any interlocutor; and perhaps the compiler meant that all the rest of the Treatise should be received as giving not only the Master's ideas, but also his words. Whoever made the Book as we now have it, it is one of the most valuable in the whole work. Hwang *K*ăn (in the end of the Sung dynasty) says of it, that notwithstanding the appearance, here and there, of Tâoistic elements, it contains many admirable passages, and he instances what is said about creation or the processes of nature, in iii, 2; about government, in ii, 18; about man, in iii, 1, 7; and about ceremonial usages, in iv, 6.

But the Tâoistic element runs through the whole Book, as it does through Book IV. There is an attempt to sew the fancies about numbers, colours, elements, and other things on to the common-sense and morality of Confucianism. But nevertheless, the Treatise bears important testimony to the sense of religion as the first and chief element of ceremonies, and to its existence in the very earliest times.

Book VIII. Lî *Kh*î.

Book VII, it was said, has been attributed to Ʒze-yû. I have not seen this ascribed to any one; but it is certainly a sequel to the other, and may be considered as having proceeded from the same author. The more the two are studied together, the more likely will this appear.

Callery has not attempted to translate the title, and says that the two characters composing it give the sense of 'Utensils of Rites,' and have no plausible relation with the scope of the Book in which there is no question in any way of the material employed either in sacrifices or in other ceremonies; and he contends, therefore, that they should not be translated, but simply be considered as sounds[1].

But the rendering which I have given is in accordance with an acknowledged usage of the second character, *Kh*î. We read in the Confucian Analects, V, 3:—'Ʒze-kung asked, "What do you say of me?" The Master answered. "You are a vessel." "What vessel?" "A sacrificial vessel of jade."' The object of the Book is to show how ceremonial usages or rites go to form 'the vessel of honour,' 'the superior man,' who is equal to the most difficult and important services. *K*ăng Hsüan saw this clearly, and said, 'The Book was named Lî *Kh*î, because it records how ceremonies cause men to become perfect vessels.' 'The former Book shows the evolution of Rites; this shows the use of them:'—such was the dictum in A.D. 1113 of Fang *K*üeh, a commentator often quoted by *Kh*ăn Hâo and by the *Kh*ien-lung editors.

Throughout the Book it is mostly religious rites that are spoken of; especially as culminating in the worship of God. And nothing is more fully brought out than that all rites are valueless without truth and reverence.

---

[1] 禮器.

Book IX. *K*iâo Theh Săng.

The name of the Book is made up of the three characters with which it commences, just as the Hebrew name for the Book of Genesis in our Sacred Scriptures is Beraishith (בְּרֵאשִׁית). From the meaning, however, of *K*iâo Theh Săng the reader is led to suppose that he will find the Treatise occupied principally with an account of the great Border Sacrifice. But it is not so.

The main subject of the Book is sacrifice generally; and how that which is most valuable in it is the reverence and sincerity of the worshipper, finding its exhibition in the simplicity of his observances. In the preceding Book different conditions have been mentioned which are of special value in sacrifice and other ceremonies. Among them is the paucity of things (Section i, paragraph 8); and this consideration is most forcibly illustrated by 'the Single Victim' employed in the Border Sacrifice, the greatest of all ceremonies. At the same time various abuses of the ancient sincerity and simplicity are exposed and deplored.

The ceremonies of capping and marriage are dealt with in the third Section; and we are thankful for the information about them which it supplies. In the end the writer returns to the subject of sacrifices; and differences in the different dynasties, from the time of Shun downwards, in the celebration of them are pointed out.

The *Kh*ien-lung editors say that this Book was originally one with the last, and 'was separated from it by some later hand.' I had come to the same conclusion before I noticed their judgment. Books VII, VIII, and IX must have formed, I think, at first one Treatise.

Book X. Nêi Ʒeh.

The title of this book, meaning 'The Pattern of the Family,' rendered by Callery, 'Réglements Intérieurs,' approximates to a description of its contents more than most of the titles in the Lî *K*î. It is not taken, moreover, from any part of the text near the commencement or elsewhere. It is difficult to understand why so little of it is retained in the expurgated editions, hardly more than a page of P. Callery's work being sufficient for it.

*K*ăng Hsüan says:—'The Book takes its name of Nêi Ȝeh, because it records the rules for sons and daughters in serving their parents, and for sons and their wives in serving her parents-in-law in the family-home. Among the other Treatises of the Lî *K*î, it may be considered as giving the Rules for Children. And because the observances of the harem are worthy of imitation, it is called Nêi Ȝeh, "the Pattern of the Interior."' *K*û Hsî says, that 'it is a Book which was taught to the people in the ancient schools, an ancient Classic or Sacred Text.'

Because the name of Ȝăng-ȝze and a sentence from him occur, the *Kh*ien-lung editors are inclined to ascribe the authorship to his disciples; but the premiss is too narrow to support such a conclusion.

The position of the wife, as described in Section i, will appear to western readers very deplorable. Much in this part of the Treatise partakes of the exaggeration that is characteristic of Chinese views of the virtue of filial piety.

The account in Section ii of the attention paid to the aged, and the nourishing of them, is interesting, but goes, as the thing itself did, too much into details. What is it to us at the present time how they made the fry, the bake, the delicacy, and the other dishes to tempt the palate and maintain the strength? The observances in the relation of husband and wife, on the birth of a child, and the education and duties of the young of both sexes, which the Section goes on to detail, however, are not wanting in attraction.

BOOK XI. YÜ ȜÂO.

The name of the Book, Yü Ȝâo, is taken from the first clause of the first paragraph. The two characters denote the pendants of the royal cap worn on great occasions, and on which beads of jade were strung. There were twelve of those pendants hanging down, before and behind, from the ends of the square or rectangular top of the cap, as in the cardinal cap which is the crest of Christ Church, Oxford. But we read nothing more of this cap or its pendants after the first paragraph; and the contents of all the three Sections of the Book are so various, that it is impossible to give an account of them in small compass.

*K*ăng Hsüan said that the Book was named Yü 3âo, because it recorded the dresses and caps worn by the son of Heaven; but it is not confined to the king, but introduces rulers also and officers generally. It treats also of other matters besides dress, which it would be difficult to speak of in so many categories. Much, moreover, of the second Section seems to consist of disjecta membra, and the paragraphs are differently arranged by different editors. Here and there the careful reader will meet with sentiments and sentences that will remain in his memory, as in reading Book I; but he will only carry away a vague impression of the Book as a whole.

Book XII. Ming Thang Wei.

Readers will turn to this Book, as I did many years ago, expecting to find in it a full description of the Ming Thang, generally called by sinologists, 'The Brilliant Hall,' and 'The Hall of Light;' but they will find that the subject-matter is very different. I have here translated the name by 'the Hall of Distinction,' according to the meaning of it given in paragraph 5, taking 'distinction' in the sense of separation or discrimination.

The Treatise commences with, but does not fairly describe, the great scene in the life of the duke of *K*âu, when as regent of the kingdom, he received all the feudal lords and the chiefs of the barbarous tribes at the capital, on occasion of a grand audience or durbar. The duke was the ancestor of the lords or marquises of the state of

Lû,—part of the present province of Shan-tung. He was himself, indeed, invested with that fief by his nephew, king *Kh*ăng, though, remaining for reasons of state at the royal court, he never took possession of it in person, but sent his son Po-*kh*in to do so in his room. Because of his great services in the establishment and consolidation of the new dynasty, however, various privileges were conferred on the rulers of Lû above the lords of other states. These are much exaggerated in the Book; and after the sixth paragraph, we hear no more of the Hall of Distinction. All that follows is occupied with the peculiar privileges said to have been claimed, and antiques reported to have been possessed, by the marquises of Lû. What is said has no historical value, and the whole Book is excluded from the expurgated editions.

The *Kh*ien-lung editors say that its author must have been an ignorant and vainglorious scholar of Lû in the end of the *K*âu dynasty. Some have imagined that it was handed on, with additions of his own, by Mâ Yung to *K*ăng Hsüan; but the latter says nothing about the other in his brief prefatory note.

The Hall of Distinction was a royal structure. Part of it was used as a temple, at the sacrifices in which peculiar honour was done to king Wăn (The Shih, IV, i, 7). It was also used for purposes of audience, as on the occasion referred to in this Book; and governmental regulations were promulgated from it (Mencius, I, ii, 5). To this third use of it would belong the various references to it in Book IV of this collection.

The principal Hall was in the capital; but there were smaller ones with the same name at the four points where the kings halted in their tours of inspection to receive the feudal lords of the different quarters of the kingdom. It was one of these which Mencius had in his mind in the passage referred to above.

In the 67th Book of the Lî of the Greater Tâi there is a description of the building and its various parts; and among the 'Books of *K*âu' said to have been found in A. D. 279 in the grave of king Hsiang of Wei, the 55th chapter has the title of Ming Thang, but it is little more than a rifacimento of the first four paragraphs of this Book of the Lî *K*î.

In Morrison's Chinese Dictionary, vol. i, p. 512, there is a ground-plan of the Hall according to a common representation of it by Chinese authorities.

Book XIII. Sang Fû Hsiâo *K*î.

This 'Record of Smaller Points in connexion with the Dress of Mourning,' is the first of the many treatises in our collection, devoted expressly to the subject of the mourning rites, and especially of the dress worn by the mourners, according to the degree of their relationship. The expurgated editions do not give any part of it; and it is difficult—I may say impossible—to trace any general plan on which the compiler, who is unknown, put the different portions of it together. Occasionally two or three paragraphs follow one another on the same subject, and I have kept them together after the example of Khung Ying-tâ; but the different notices are put down as if at random, just as they occurred to the writer.

*K*û Hsî says that Ʒze-hsiâ made a supplementary treatise to the 11th Book of the Î Lî, and that we have here an explanation of many points in that Book. It is so; and yet we may not be justified in concluding that this is a remnant of the production of Ʒze-hsiâ.

Book XIV. Tâ *K*wan.

This Book, 'the Great Treatise,' has been compared to the Hsî Ʒhze, the longest and most important of the Appendixes to the Yî King, which is also styled Tâ *K*wan.

It is short, however, as compared with that other; nor is it easy to understand, the subjects with which it deals being so different in the conceptions of Chinese and western minds. 'It treats,' said *Kh*ăn Hsiang-tâo (early in the Sung dynasty), 'of the greatest sacrifice,—that offered by the sovereign to all his ancestors; of the greatest instance of filial piety,—that of carrying back to his forefathers the title gained by the sacrificer; of the greatest principle in the regulation of the family,—that expressed by the arrangement of the names of its members according to their relations to one another; and of the course of humanity as the greatest illustration of propriety and righteousness. On account of this it is called The Great Treatise.'

From this summary of its contents the importance of the Book will be seen. We know nothing either of its author or of the date of its compilation.

Book XV. Shâo Î.

The Shâo Î, or 'Smaller Rules of Conduct,' is akin to much of the first Book in our collection, 'the Summary of the Rules of Ceremony.' Shâo means 'few,' and often 'few in years,' or 'young;' and hence some have thought that the subject of the Book is 'Rules for the Young.' So Callery, who gives for the title, 'Règles de Conduite des Jeunes Gens.'

But the contents cannot be so restricted; and since the time of *K*ăng Hsüan, shâo has been taken by most Chinese commentators as equivalent to hsiâo[1], which occurs in the title of Book XIII. The difference between the two Chinese characters is not so great as that between these alphabetic exhibitions of their names. Lû Teh-ming says, 'Shâo is here equivalent to hsiâo;' and *K*ăng says, that the Book is named Shâo Î 'because it records the small rules of demeanour at interviews and in bringing in the provisions for a feast.' But the observances described are very various, and enable us to form a life-like picture of manners in those early days.

According to *K*û Hsî, the Book was intended to be a branch of the smaller learning, or lessons for youth; but

[1] 少 and 小.

was extended to a variety of subjects in daily life and the intercourses of society. When and by whom it was compiled is not known.

Book XVI. Hsio *K*î.

The Hsio *K*î, or 'Record of Studies,' is a treatise of very considerable interest and importance. *Kh*ăng-ȝze, whom *K*û Hsî was accustomed to call his 'Master,' considered it to be, after Books XXVIII and XXXIX, the *K*ung Yung and Tâ Hsio, the most correct and orthodox Book in the Lî *K*î.

The *Kh*ien-lung editors say that in paragraphs 4 and 5 we have the institutions of the ancient kings for purposes of education; in 6 to 19, the laws for teachers; and in what follows, those for learners. The summary is on the whole correct, but the compiler (who is unknown) did not always keep his subjects distinct. In the three commencing paragraphs the importance of education to the moral well-being of the people is strikingly exhibited. The whole displays an amount of observation and a maturity of reflection on the subject, which cannot but be deemed remarkable. The information about ancient schools and higher institutions may be found in the earlier Books, but we are glad to have this repetition of it.

Book XVII. Yo *K*î.

The Yo *K*î, or 'Record of Music,' will be found to have more interest for general readers than most of the other Books of the Lî. *Kh*ăng-ȝze speaks of it in terms similar to those quoted from him in the preceding notice about the Hsio *K*î. That, so far as correctness and orthodoxy are concerned, is next to the *K*ung Yung and Tâ Hsio; this is near to them. Its introduction into our collection is ascribed to Mâ Yung.

The old documents on music that had been recovered during the earlier Han dynasty, appear in Liû Hsin's Catalogue after those of the Lî, amounting in all to

165 phien, distributed in six collections. The first of these was the Yo *K*î, in 23 phien; the second, the *K*î of Wang Yü[1], in 24 phien. Khung Ying-tâ, deriving his information from a note in Hsin's Catalogue and other sources, sums up what he has to say about this Book in the following way:—On the rise of the Han dynasty, the treatises of former times on music, as well as the practice of the art, were in a state of special dilapidation. In the time of the emperor Wû, his brother Teh, with the help of many scholars, copied out all that remained on the subject of music, and made a Yo *K*î, or 'Record of Music,' in 24 phien or books, which Wang Yü presented to the court in the time of the emperor *Kh*ăng (B.C. 32-7); but it was afterwards hardly heard of. When Liû Hsiang (died B.C. 9) examined the books in the Imperial library, he found a 'Record of Music' in 23 phien, different from that which Wang Yü had presented. Our present Yo *K*î contains eleven of those phien, arranged with the names of their subjects. The other twelve are lost, though their names remain.

Most of the present text is found in Sze-mâ *Kh*ien's Monograph on Music; and as he was so long before Liû Hsiang (*Kh*ien died between B.C. 90 and 80), the *Kh*ien-lung editors suppose that it is one of the portions of *Kh*ien's work, supplied by *Kh*û Shâo-sun[2], who was a contemporary of Hsiang.

*K*û Hsî had a great admiration of many passages in the Yo *K*î, and finds in them the germs of the views on the constitution of humanity, and on the action and interaction of principle and passion, reason and force, in the economy of what we call Providence, on which he delighted to dwell in his philosophical speculations. We expect from the title, as Hwang Kan-hsing (Ming dynasty) says, that music will be the chief subject of the Treatise, but everywhere we find ceremonial usages spoken of equally and in their relation to it; for, according to the view of the author, the framework of society is built on the truth

[1] 王禹. [2] 褚少孫; see Wylie's Notes, p. 14.

underlying ceremonies, and music is the necessary expression of satisfaction in the resulting beauty and harmony.

Book XVIII. 3â *Kî*.

Book XVII is given nearly complete in the expurgated edition translated by Callery, while the 18th or 'Miscellaneous Records,' happily rendered by him by the one French word 'Mélanges,' is reduced to about a third of its length in the Chinese text. Notwithstanding its name of 'Miscellanies,' the greater part is occupied with the observances of the Mourning Rites. Interesting questions concerning them are discussed, and information is given on customs which we do not find in such detail elsewhere, —such, for instance, as those relating to the gifts of grave-clothes and other things for the burial of the dead. Towards the end other customs, besides those of the mourning rites, are introduced. It would be a mistake, however, to suppose that this is done to justify the name of Miscellaneous Records given to the whole. It is a peculiarity of many of the other Books that the writer, or writers, seem to get weary of confining themselves to one subject or even to a few subjects, and introduce entries of quite a different nature for no reason that we can discover but their arbitrary pleasure.

The correctness and integrity of many paragraphs have been justly called in question. The authority of the Book does not rank high. It must be classed in this respect with the Than Kung.

Book XIX. Sang Tâ *Kî*.

Book XIII deals with smaller points in connexion with the dress of mourning; Book XVIII, with miscellaneous points in mourning; and this Book with the greater points, especially with the two dressings of the dead, the coffining, and the burial. Beginning with the preparations for death in the case of a ruler, a Great officer, or an ordinary officer, it goes methodically over all the observances at and after death, until the burial has taken place. It takes us into the palace, the mansion, and the smaller official residence, and shows us what was done at the different steps that intervened between death and the committing of the coffin to the grave. Some of the observances differ in minor points from details in those other Books, and in the Than Kung or Book II; but taking them all together, we get from them a wonderfully minute account of all the rites of mourning in ancient China. Wû *Kh*ăng says, 'This Book relates the greater rules observed in each event which it mentions.' It was not intended to supplement the information elsewhere given about smaller details; and hence it is named 'The Greater Record of Mourning Rites.'

BOOK XX. *K*Î FÂ.

*K*î Fâ, so named from the first two characters in the Book, and meaning 'Laws or Rules of Sacrifices,' is the first of three treatises, all on the subject of sacrifices, that come together at this part of the collection of the Lî. They were not, perhaps, the production of the same hand; but the writer of this one evidently had before him the 17th article in the first Part of the Narratives connected with the state of Lû, which form the second Section of 'the Narratives of the States[1].' That article contains an exposition of the subject of sacrifices by a *K*en *Kh*in, in deprecation of a sacrifice ordered by Ȝang Wăn-*k*ang, who had been for about fifty years one of the ministers of Lû. Ȝang died in B.C. 617.

Difficulties attach to some of the historical statements in the Book, which cannot be cleared up from our want of sufficient documents. The whole consists of two Parts,—paragraphs 1–8, and paragraph 9. All the former is excluded from the expurgated editions; but in it, as well as in the other, the sacrifices are mainly those to departed worthies. There is no idea of deprecation in them; much less of atonement. They are expressions of gratitude, and commemorative of men whose laws and achievements were

[1] 國語.

beneficial to their own times, and helped on the progress of civilisation, so that they would be beneficial also to all ages.

In the conclusion, the sacrifices to the sun, moon, and other parts of nature appear; and it is said that they were instituted because the action of those bodies contributed to promote the comfort and agency of men. So far those sacrifices were a species of nature-worship; but the question arises whether they were not really offered to the spirits under whose guardianship those objects operated.

BOOK XXI. *Kî Î.*

The *Kî* Î, or 'The Meaning of Sacrifices,' 'Sens des Sacrifices' in Callery, embraces a wider extent of subjects than the last Book. It treats first of the sacrifices to Heaven, and to the sun and moon in connexion with it, as well as of those in the ancestral temple, though the latter are the principal subject. The writer, whoever he was, goes fully into the preparations of the sacrificer, and the spirit of reverence in which the services should be conducted.

No idea of deprecation or expiation is expressed as belonging to the sacrifices. It is said, indeed, in Section i, 18, that the sacrifice in the suburb of the capital was the great expression of gratitude to Heaven.

In Section ii other subjects besides sacrifice are treated of. It commences with a remarkable conversation between Confucius and his disciple Ȝâi Wo, on the constitution of man, as comprehending both the Kwei and Shăn, the former name denoting the animal soul, which, with the bones and flesh, 'moulders below and becomes the dust of the fields;' while the latter denotes the intelligent soul or spirit, which issues forth at death, and is displayed on high in a condition of glorious brightness.

The ploughing of the special fields by the king and rulers of states, and the regulations for the nourishment of silkworms and the preparation of silk by their wives, are set forth, both operations being to provide the sacrificial grain and robes.

After this we have the views of Ȝăng-ȝze and one of his disciples on filial piety, which subject again passes into the submission of the younger brother to the elder, and the respect to be paid generally by juniors to their elders.

BOOK XXII. *K*Î THUNG.

The 'Summary Account of Sacrifices' is the last and longest, and, it may be added, the most interesting, of the treatises, specially on that subject. We find nothing in it, any more than in the others, of the idea of propitiation; but it gives many details of the purposes which the institution of sacrifices served in the Chinese state. The old commentators took the character Thung[1] in the sense of 'Root' or 'Origin[2],' and hence some English sinologists have named the book 'The Origin of Sacrifices,' and P. Zottoli gives for the title 'Sacrificii Principium.' Callery calls it, better, 'Généralités sur les Sacrifices.' The very able commentator *Kh*ăn Hsiang-tâo compares the Treatise to 'the large rope which controls the meshes of a net,' saying, that it commences with sacrifice as coming from the feeling of the heart, and ends with the display of its influence in the conduct of government.

The concluding paragraph shows that it was written while the state of Lû still had an existence; and if the whole Book proceeded from the same hand, it must have been composed some time after the death of Confucius and before the extinction of Lû, which was consummated by *Kh*û in B.C. 248. I think we may refer it to the fourth century B.C.

The doctrine of Filial Piety occupies a prominent place in it. Paragraph 13 and the ten that follow, on the connexion between sacrifice and the ten relationships of men, are specially instructive. The author writes forcibly and often subtilely; and can hardly do himself justice in the

---

[1] 統. [2] 本.

expression of his ideas. What he says on the subject of Inscriptions towards the conclusion is interesting. He was a true Lû man, and his views on the sacrifices of his state are contrary to the standard of Chinese orthodoxy about them.

BOOK XXIII. *K*ING *K*IEH.

*K*ing *K*ieh has been translated 'Explanations of the Classics,' and Callery gives for the title 'Sens Général des Livres Canoniques.' A slight attention to the few paragraphs which compose the Book, however, will satisfy the reader that these translations of the name are incorrect. No explanation is attempted of passages in the different *K*ing. The true meaning of *K*ing *K*ieh was given by Hwang Khan in A.D. 538. '*K*ieh,' he says, 'is to be taken in the sense of "separation" or "division;" and the Treatise describes the difference between the subjects dealt with in the different *K*ing.'

The Book, though ingenious, is not entitled to much attention. The first two paragraphs, assigned to Confucius, could not have come from him. They assume that there were six *K*ing; but that enumeration of the ancient writings originated with the scholars of the Han dynasty. And among the six is the *Kh*un *Kh*iû, the work of Confucius himself, which he compiled only a year or two before his death. It was for posterity, and not for him, to raise it to the rank of a *K*ing, and place it on the same level with the Shû, the Shih, and the Yî. It may be doubted, moreover, if there were ever a Yo *K*ing, or 'Classic of Music.' Treatises on music, no doubt, existed under the *K*âu dynasty, but it does not appear that there was any collection of them made till the attempts that have been referred to in the introductory notice to Book XVII.

Who the ingenious, but uncritical, compiler of the *K*ing *K*ieh was is unknown.

Book XXIV. Âi Kung Wăn.

'Questions of Duke Âi' is a translation of the three characters with which the Book commences, and which mean there 'Duke Âi asked;' and the title is so far descriptive of the contents of the Book,—two conversations on ceremonies and the practice of government between the marquis Ȝiang of Lû, posthumously called duke Âi, and Confucius. The sage died in the sixteenth year of Ȝiang's marquisate. As an old minister of the state, after he had retired from public life, he had a right of entrance to the court, which, we know, he sometimes exercised. He may have conversed with the marquis on the subjects discussed in this Treatise; but whether he held the particular conversations here related can only be determined by the consideration of their style and matter. I am myself disposed to question their genuineness.

There are other recensions of the Treatise. It forms the third of the Books in the current editions of 'the Lî of the Greater Tâi,' purporting to be the forty-first of those which were in his larger collection; and is the same as in our Lî *K*î, with hardly a variation. The second conversation, again, appears as the fourth article in the collection called the 'Narratives of the School[1],' but with considerable and important variations, under the title of Tâ Hwăn, 'The Grand Marriage.' The first conversation is found also in the same collection, as part of the sixth article, called Wăn Lî, or 'Questions about Ceremonies.' There are also variations in it; but the questioner in both articles is duke Âi.

The most remarkable passages of the Book are some paragraphs of the second conversation towards its conclusion. P. Callery translates Thien Tâo, 'the Way of Heaven,' in paragraph 16, by 'La Vérité Céleste,' and

---

[1] 家語.

says in a note that Confucius speaks of this Tâo in a way not unlike Lâo-ȝze in the Tâo Teh *K*ing, adding that 'these two fathers of Chinese philosophy had on this mysterious Being ideas nearly similar.' But a close examination of the passage, which is itself remarkable, shows that this resemblance between it and passages of the Tâoist classic does not exist. See my concluding note on the Book. If there were a Tâoist semblance in the phraseology, it would make us refer the composition of the Treatise to the time of *Kh*in or the early days of Han, when Tâoism had taken a place in the national literature which it had not had under the dynasty of *K*âu.

BOOK XXV. *K*UNG-NÎ YEN *K*Ü.

The title of this Book is taken from the four characters with which it commences. Confucius has returned from his attendance at the court of Lû, and is at home in his own house. Three of his disciples are sitting by him, and his conversation with them flows on till it has reached the subject of ceremonial usages. In reply to their questions, he discourses on it at length, diverging also to the subjects of music and the practice of government in connexion with ceremonies, in a familiar and practical manner.

He appears in the title by his designation, or name as married, *K*ung-nî, which we find also two or three times in Book XXVIII, which is received as the composition of his grandson Khung *K*î, or Ȝze-sze. This Treatise, however, is much shorter than that, and inferior to it. The commentator Wang of Shih-liang[1], often quoted by *Kh*ăn Hâo, says, that though this Treatise has a beginning and end, the style and ideas are so disjected and loose, that many of the utterances attributed to Confucius cannot be accepted as really his.

[1] 石梁王氏.

BOOK XXVI. KHUNG-ȜZE HSIEN *K*Ü.

The title of this Book is akin to that of the last, the characters of that leading us to think of Confucius as having returned from court to 'his ease,' and those of this suggesting nothing of his immediate antecedents, but simply saying that he was 'at home and at leisure.' Instead of being called, as there, by his designation, he appears here as Khung-ȝze, 'the philosopher Khung,' or 'Mr. Khung.'

The Book also relates a conversation, but only one disciple is present, and to him the Master discourses on the description of a sovereign as 'the parent of the people,' and on the virtue of the founders of the three dynasties of Hsiâ, Shang, and *K*âu, illustrating his views by quotations from the Book of Poetry. His language is sometimes strange and startling, while the ideas underlying it are subtle and ingenious. And the poetical quotations are inapplicable to the subjects in connexion with which they are introduced. If the commentator Wang could not adopt the speeches attributed to Confucius in the last Book as really his, much less can we receive those in this as such.

From their internal analogies in form and sentiment, I suppose that the two Books were made by the same writer; but I have met with no guess even as to who he was.

BOOK XXVII. FANG *K*Î.

'The Dykes,' which is the meaning of the title of this Book, is suggestive of its subject-matter. We have in it the rules or usages of ceremony presented to us under the figure of dykes, dams, or barriers; defensive structures made to secure what is inside them from escaping or dispersion, and to defend it against inundation or other injurious assault and invasion from without. The character, called fang, is used for the most part with verbal force, 'acting as a dyke or barrier;' and it would often be difficult to say whether the writer was thinking of the particular institution or usage spoken of as fulfilling the purpose of defence against peril from within, or violence from without.

The illustrations are numerous, and they are all given as if they came from the lips of Confucius himself; but we cannot suppose that they were really from him. They are not in his style, and the reasonings are occasionally unworthy of him. Many paragraphs carry on their front a protest against our receiving them as really his. Nevertheless, the Book, though sometimes tedious, is on the whole interesting, and we like the idea of looking on the usages as 'dykes.' We do not know to whom we are indebted for it. One of the famous brothers *Kh*ăng of the Sung dynasty has said:—'We do not know who wrote the Treatise. Since we find such expressions in it as "The Lun Yü says," it is plainly not to be ascribed to Confucius. Passages in the Han scholars, *K*iâ Î and Tung *K*ung-shû, are to the same effect as what we find here; and perhaps this memoir was their production.'

BOOK XXVIII. *K*UNG YUNG.

The *K*ung Yung would be pronounced, I think, by Chinese scholars to be the most valuable of all the Treatises in the Lî *K*î; and from an early time it asserted a position peculiar to itself. Its place in the general collection of Ritual Treatises was acknowledged by Mâ Yung and his disciple *K*ăng Hsüan; but in Liû Hsin's Catalogue of the Lî Books, we find an entry of 'Observations on the *K*ung Yung, in two phien;' so early was the work thought to be deserving of special treatment by itself. In the records of the Sui dynasty (A. D. 589–617), in the Catalogue of its Imperial library, there are the names of three other special works upon it, one of them by the emperor Wû (A. D. 502–549) of the Liang dynasty.

Later on, under the Sung dynasty, the *K*ung Yung, the Tâ Hsio, or 'Great Learning,' which is also a portion of the Lî *K*î, the Confucian Analects, or the Lun Yü, and the works of Mencius, were classed together as 'The Four Books,' which have since that time formed so important a division of Chinese literature; and 'the *K*ung Yung, in chapters and sentences, with a digest of commentaries on it,' was published by *K*û Hsî early in A. D. 1189. About 125 years afterwards, the fourth emperor of the Yüan dynasty enacted that *K*û's edition and views should be the text-book of the classic at the literary examinations. From that time merely the name of the *K*ung Yung was retained in editions of the Lî *K*î, until the appearance of the Imperial edition of the whole collection in the *Kh*ien-lung period of the present dynasty. There the text is given in two Sections according to the old division of it, with the ancient commentaries from the edition of 'The Thirteen *K*ing' of the Thang dynasty, followed at the end of each paragraph by the Commentary of *K*û.

The authorship of the *K*ung Yung is ascribed to Khung *K*î, better known as Ȝze-sze, the grandson of Confucius. There is no statement to this effect, indeed, in the work itself; but the tradition need not be called in question. It certainly existed in the Khung family. The Book must have been written in the fifth century B. C., some time, I suppose, between 450 and 400. Since A. D. 1267, the author has had a place in the temples of Confucius as one of 'The Four Assessors,' with the title of 'The Philosopher Ȝze-sze, transmitter of the Sage.' I have seen his tomb-mound in the Confucian cemetery, outside the city of *Kh*ü-fû in Shantung, in front of those of his father and grandfather. There is a statue of him on it, bearing the inscription, 'Duke (or Prince) of the State of Î.'

It is not easy to translate the name of the Treatise, *K*ung Yung. It has been represented by 'Juste Milieu;' 'Medium Constans vel Sempiternum;' 'L'Invariable Milieu;' 'The Constant Medium;' 'The Golden Medium;' 'The True Medium;' and otherwise. I called it, in 1861, 'The Doctrine of the Mean,' which I have now changed for 'The State of Equilibrium and Harmony,' the reasons for which will be found in the notes on the first chapter of the present version.

I do not here enter on an exhibition of the scope and value of the Book. It gives the best account that we have of the Confucian philosophy and morals, and will amply repay careful study, and hold its place not only in China, but in the wider sphere beyond it. The writer had an exaggerated conception of the sage; but he deserves well of his own country and of the world.

Book XXIX. Piâo *K*î.

The character called Piâo is the symbol for the outer garments, and is used to indicate whatever is external in opposition to what is internal; the outside of things, what serves to mark them out and call attention to them. Hence comes its use in the sense which it bears in the title of this Book, for what serves as an example or model. Callery renders that title by 'Mémoire sur l'Exemple;' Wylie, by 'The Exemplar Record.'

Piâo is also used for the gnomon of a dial; and the *Kh*ien-lung editors fix on this application of the character in explaining the name of the Book. 'Piâo,' they say, 'is the gnomon of a dial, by which the movement of the sun is measured; it rises up in the centre, and all round is regulated by it. The Fang *K*î shows men what they ought to be on their guard against; the Piâo *K*î, what they should take as their pattern.' Then they add—'Of patterns there is none so honourable as benevolence (or humanity proper), and to aid that there is righteousness, while, to complete it, there is sincerity or good faith, and reverence is that by which the quest for humanity is pursued.' This second sentence may be considered a summary of the contents of the Book, which they conclude by saying, they have divided into eight chapters after the example of the scholar Hwang; meaning, I suppose, Hwang Khan, who has been already mentioned as having published his work on our classic in A. D. 538.

That division into eight chapters lies on the face of the Treatise. We have eight paragraphs commencing with the characters which I have rendered by 'These were the words of the Master;' and these are followed by a number of others, more or fewer as the case may be, in which the words of the Master ('The Master said') are adduced to substantiate what has been stated in that introductory passage. The arrangement is uniform, excepting in one instance to which I have called attention in a note, and suitably divides the whole into eight chapters.

But no one supposes that 'the words of the Master' are really those of Confucius, or were used by him in the connexion which is here given to them. They were invented by the author of the Treatise, or applied by him, to suit his own purpose; and scholars object to many of them as contrary to the sentiments of the sage, and betraying a tendency to the views of Tâoism. This appears, most strikingly perhaps, in the fifth chapter. On the statement, for instance, in paragraph 32, that the methods of Yin and *K*âu were not equal to the correction of the errors produced by those of Shun and Hsîa, the *Kh*ien-lung editors say:—'How could these words have come from the mouth of the Master? The disciples of Lâo-ȝze despised forms and prized the unadorned simplicity, commended what was ancient, and condemned all that was of their own time. In the beginning of the Han dynasty, the principles of Hwang and Lâo were widely circulated; students lost themselves in the stream of what they heard, could not decide upon its erroneousness, and ascribed it to the Master. Such cases were numerous, and even in several paragraphs of the Lî Yun (Book VII) we seem to have some of them. What we find there was the utterance, probably, of some disciple of Lâo-ȝze.'

No one, so far as I have noticed, has ventured to assign the authorship of this Book on example. I would identify him, myself, with the Kung-sun Nî-ȝze, to whom the next is ascribed.

BOOK XXX. ȜZE Î.

It is a disappointment to the reader, when he finds after reading the title of this Book, that it has nothing to do with the Black Robes of which he expects it to be an account.

That phrase occurs in the second paragraph, in a note to which its origin is explained; but the other name Hsiang Po, which is found in the same paragraph, might with equal appropriateness, or rather inappropriateness, have been adopted for the Treatise.

It is really of the same nature as the preceding, and contains twenty-four paragraphs, all attributed to 'the Master,' and each of which may be considered to afford a pattern for rulers and their people. It ought to form one Book with XXIX under the title of 'Pattern Lessons.' I have pointed out in the notes some instances of the agreement in their style and phraseology, and the intelligent reader who consults the translation with reference to the Chinese text will discover more. Lû Teh-ming (early in the Thang dynasty) tells us, on the authority of Liû Hsien, that the Ʒze Î was made by a Kung-sun Nî-ʒze. Liû Hsien was a distinguished scholar of the early Sung dynasty, and died about A. D. 500; but on what evidence he assigned the authorship of the Book to Kung-sun Nî-ʒze does not, in the present state of our knowledge, appear. The name of that individual is found twice in Liû Hsin's Catalogue, as belonging to the learned school, and among 'the Miscellaneous writers,' with a note that he was 'a disciple of the seventy disciples of the Master.' The first entry about him precedes that about Mencius, so that he must be referred to the closing period of the *K*âu dynasty, the third century B. C. He may, therefore, have been the author of 'The Black Robes,' and of the preceding Book as well, giving his own views, but attributing them, after the fashion of the time, to Confucius; but, as the commentator Făng Î (? Ming dynasty) observes:—'Many passages in the Book are made to resemble the sayings of a sage; but the style is not good and the meaning is inferior.'

BOOK XXXI. PĂN SANG.

This Book refers to a special case in connexion with the mourning rites, that of an individual who has been prevented, from taking part with the other relatives in the usual observances at the proper time. It might be that he was absent from the state, charged by his ruler with public business, or he might be in the same state but at a distance, and so occupied that he had been unable to take part in the mourning services.

But they were too sacred to be entirely neglected, and we have here the rules applicable to such a case, in a variety of circumstances and different degrees of consanguinity. Some other matter, more or less analogous, is introduced towards the end.

We have seen how the first of the 'Three Rituals' recovered in the Han dynasty was seventeen Books that now form the Î Lî. *K*ăng Hsüan supposed that the Păn Sang had been another Book of that collection, and was afterwards obtained from the tablets found in the village of Yen-*k*ung in Lû. It has been decided, however, that the style determines it to be from another hand than the Î Lî.

Here it is, and we have only to make the best of it that we can, without knowing who wrote it or when it came to light. The *Kh*ien-lung editors say:—'Anciently, in cases of mourning for a year or shorter period even, officers left their charges and hurried to the rites. In consequence of the inconvenience arising from this, it was enacted that officers should leave their charge only on the death of a parent. It was found difficult, however, to enforce this. The rule is that a charge cannot be left, without leave asked and obtained.'

BOOK XXXII. WĂN SANG.

The Wăn Sang, or 'Questions about Mourning Rites,' is a short Treatise, which derives its name from inquiries about the dressing of the corpse, the putting off the cap and replacing it by the cincture, and the use of the staff in mourning. Along with those inquiries there are accounts of some of the rites, condensed and imperfect. The Book should be read in connexion with the other Books of a similar character, especially XIII.

Much cannot be said in favour of the style, or of the

satisfactoriness of the replies to the questions that are propounded. The principal idea indeed in the mind of the author, whoever he was, was that the rites were the outcome of the natural feelings of men, and that mourning was a manifestation of filial piety. The most remarkable passage is that with which the Treatise concludes, that the use of the staff was not to be sought in any revelation from heaven or earth, but was simply from the good son's filial affection. The way in which the sentiment is expressed has often brought to my mind the question of the Apostle Paul about faith, in Romans x. 6–8.

BOOK XXXIII. FÛ WĂN.

Like the last two Books and the two that follow, the Fû Wăn is omitted in the expurgated editions. It is still shorter than the Wăn Sang, and treats also of the mourning rites, and specially of the dress in it, and changes in it, which naturally gave rise to questioning.

The writer, or compiler, often quotes from what he calls the *K*wan, a name which has sometimes been translated by 'Tradition.' But the Chinese term, standing alone, may mean what is transmitted by writings, as well as what is handed down by oral communication. It is used several times in Mencius in the sense of 'Record' and 'Records.' I have called it here 'The Directory of Mourning.' Wû *Kh*ăng says rightly that the Book is of the same character as XIII; that the mourning rites were so many, and some of them so peculiar, that collisions between different rites must have been of frequent occurrence. The Fû Wăn takes up several such cases and tells us how they were met satisfactorily, or, as we may think, unsatisfactorily.

BOOK XXXIV. *K*IEN *K*WAN.

The *K*ien *K*wan is a Treatise on subsidiary points in the mourning rites. It is not easy to render the name happily in English. I have met with it as 'The Intermediate Record.' *K* wan is the character spoken of in the preceding notice; *K* ien is the symbol for the space between two things, suggesting the idea of distinction or difference. *K*ăng Hsüan says that 'the name has reference to the distinctions suitably made in mourning, according as it was lighter or more important.'

However we translate or explain the name, we find the Book occupied with the manifestations of grief in the bearing of the mourners; in the modulation of their voices; in their eating and drinking; in their places; in the texture of their dress; and in the various changes which were made in it till it was finally put off. Some points in it are difficult to understand at this distance of time, and while we are still imperfectly acquainted with the mourning usages of the people at the present day.

Book XXXV. San Nien Wăn.

The 'Questions about the Mourning for three years' is occupied principally with the mourning for parents for that period, but it touches on all the other periods of mourning as well, explaining why one period differs in its duration from the others.

Mourning, it is said, is the outcome of the relative feeling proper to man; the materials of the dress, the duration of the rites, and other forms are from the ancient sages and legislators, to regulate and direct the expression of the feeling.

What is said in paragraph 4 about the mourning of birds and beasts is interesting, but fantastical. Though the mourning for a parent is said to last for three years, the western reader is not to suppose that it continues to the end of that time, but simply that it extends into the third year. Virtually it terminates with the twenty-fifth month, and positively with the twenty-seventh. It is the eastern mode in speaking of time to say that it lasts for three years. Similarly, I have often been told that a child, evidently not more than six months, was two years old, when a little cross-questioning has brought out the fact that it had been born towards the end of the previous year, that it had lived in two years, and was, therefore, spoken of as two years old.

Book XXXVI. Shăn Î.

The Shăn Î is what we should expect from the name, a description of the dress so-called. It was the garment of undress, worn by all classes of the people, from the highest to the lowest, when they were at home and at ease. What distinguished it from other dresses was that in those the jacket or upper garment was in one piece, and the skirt or lower garment in another, whereas in this they were joined together, so that it could be put on and off with ease.

In the *Kh*ien-lung edition of the Lî *K*î, chapter 29, second collection of Plates, there are pictures of the Shăn Î, taken from *K*û Hsî's 'Rules for the Family,' but they do not correspond with the description here. More accurate plates are to be found in a monograph on the subject by Yung *K*iang, a senior licentiate of the present dynasty, which forms the 251st chapter in the 'Explanations of the Classics under the Imperial dynasty of *Kh*ing.' The proper meaning of Shăn Î is 'The Deep Dress;' but the garment was also called 'The Long Dress,' which suits our nomenclature better; and 'The Inner Dress,' when it was worn under another.

The reasons assigned for fashioning it after the description in paragraphs 3 and 4 are of course fanciful; but M. Callery is too severe on the unknown author, when he says:—'On est tenté de rire en voyant les rapprochements que l'auteur cherche à établir entre la forme de cet habit et les principes les plus abstraits de la morale. Je suis porté à croire que toutes ces allégories ont été imaginées après coup; car si elles avaient dirigé la coupe primitive du Shăn Î, il faudrait dire que les ateliers des anciens tailleurs de la Chine étaient des écoles de mysticisme.'

Book XXXVII. Thâu Hû.

The Thâu Hû, or 'Pitching into a Jar,' gives the description of a game, played anciently, and probably at the present day also, at festal entertainments. It was a kind of archery, with darts instead of arrows, and the hand instead of a bow; 'the smallest,' as *K*ăng says, 'of all the games of archery,' and yet lessons for the practice of virtue and for judging of character might be learned from it. It is interesting to us, however, simply as a game for amusement, and a sufficient idea of it may be gained from this Book.

Two might play at it, or any number. The host and guest in the text are the representatives of two sides or parties. It was a contest at pitching darts into the mouth of a pot or vase, placed at a short distance from the players, —too short a distance, it appears to us. There was nothing peculiar in the form of the vase of which we have an account in paragraph 10. We are surprised to read the description of it in the late Dr. Williams' Syllabic Dictionary, under the character for Hû:—'One ancient kind (of vase) was made with tubes on each side of the mouth, and a common game, called Thâu Hû, was to pitch reeds into the three orifices.' This would have been a different jar, and the game would have been different from that here described, and more difficult.

The style of the Treatise is like that of the Î Lî, in the account of the contests of archery in Books VIII–XI, to which we have to refer to make out the meaning of several of the phrases.

The Book should end with paragraph 10. The three paragraphs that follow seem to have been jotted down by the compiler from some memoranda that he found, that nothing might be lost which would throw light on the game.

Then follows a paragraph, which may be pronounced unintelligible. The whole Book is excluded from the expurgated editions.

BOOK XXXVIII. *Z*û HSING.

The *Z*û Hsing, or 'Conduct of the Scholar,' professes to be a discourse delivered to duke Âi of Lû on the character and style of life by which scholars, or men claiming to possess literary acquirements, ought to be, and were in a measure, distinguished. Even so far back, such a class of men there was in China. They had certain peculiarities of dress, some of which are alluded to in Odes of the Shih. The duke, however, had not been accustomed to think highly of them; and struck by something in the dress of Confucius, he asks him if he wore the garb of a scholar. The sage disclaims this; and being questioned further as to the conduct of the scholar, he proceeds to dilate on that at great length, and with a remarkable magnificence of thought and diction. He pourtrayed to his ruler a man sans peur et sans reproche, strong in principle, of cultivated intelligence, and animated by the most generous, patriotic, and benevolent spirit. We are told in the conclusion that the effect on duke Âi was good and great. It made him a better man, and also made him think more highly of the class of scholars than he had done. The effect of the Book on many of the literati must have been great in the ages that have intervened, and must still be so.

But did such a conversation really take place between the marquis of Lû and the sage? The general opinion of Chinese scholars is that it did not do so. Lü Tâ-lin (of the eleventh century, and a contemporary of the brothers *Kh*ăng), as quoted by the *Kh*ien-lung editors, while cordially approving the sentiments, thinks the style too grandiloquent to allow of our ascribing it to Confucius. Another commentator of the Sung period, one of the Lîs[1], holds that the language is that of some ambitious scholar of the period of the Warring States, who wished to stir up the members of his order to a style of action worthy of it. P. Callery appends to his translation the following note:—'In general, the maxims of this chapter are sufficiently profound to justify us in ascribing them to Confucius, in preference to so many other passages which the author of this work places to the credit of the great philosopher. We find nevertheless in it some ideas of which the really authentic works of Confucius do not offer any trace.'

---

[1] 李氏.

Book XXXIX. Tâ Hsio.

Like the *K*ung Yung (XXVIII), the Tâ Hsio has long been published separately from the other Books of the Lî *K*î, and is now the first of the well-known 'Four Books.' As it appears in this translation, we follow the arrangement of the text given by the *Kh*ien-lung editors from that in the Thirteen King published by Khung Ying-tâ, who himself simply followed *K*ăng Hsüan. Early in the Sung dynasty the brothers *Kh*ăng occupied themselves with the Treatise; and thinking that errors had crept into the order of the paragraphs, and that portions were missing, made various alterations and additions. *K*û Hsî entered into their labours, and, as he thought, improved on them. It is now current in the Four Books, as he published it in 1189, and the difference between his arrangement and the oldest one may be seen by comparing the translation in the first volume of my Chinese Classics and that in the present publication. Despite the difference of arrangement, the substance of the work is the same.

There can be no doubt that the Tâ Hsio is a genuine monument of the Confucian teaching, and gives us a sufficient idea of the methods and subjects in the great or higher schools of antiquity. The enthusiasm of M. Pauthier is not to be blamed when he says:—'It is evident that the aim of the Chinese philosopher is to exhibit the duties of political government as the perfecting of self and the practice of virtue by all men.'

Pauthier adopts fully the view of *K*û, that the first chapter is a genuine relic of Confucius himself, for which view there really is no evidence. And he thinks also that all that follows should be attributed to the disciple, Ȝăng-ȝze, which is contrary to the evidence which the Treatise itself supplies.

If it were necessary to assign an author for the work, I should adopt the opinion of *K*iâ Kwei (A.D. 30–101), and assign it to Khung *K*î, the grandson of Confucius, and author of the *K*ung Yung. 'When Khung *K*î,' said *K*iâ, 'was still alive, and in straits, in Sung, being afraid that the lessons of the former sage (or sages) would become obscure, and the principles of the ancient Tîs and Kings fall to the ground, he made the Tâ Hsio as the warp of them, and the *K*ung Yung as the woof.' This would seem to have been the opinion of scholars in that early time, and the only difficulty in admitting it is that *K*ăng Hsüan does not mention it. Notwithstanding his silence, the conviction that Khung *K*î wrote both treatises has become very strong in my mind. There is that agreement in the matter, method, and style of the two, which almost demands for them a common authorship.

BOOK XL. KWAN Î.

A fuller account of the ceremony of capping is obtained from portions of the ninth and other Books, where it comes in only incidentally, than from this Book in which we might expect from the title to find all the details of it brought together. But the object of the unknown writer was to glorify the rite as the great occasion when a youth stepped from his immaturity into all the privileges and responsibilities of a man, and to explain some of the usages by which it had been sought from the earliest times to mark its importance. This intention is indicated by the second character in the title called Î, which we have met with only once before in the name of a Book,—in *K*î Î, 'the Meaning of Sacrifices,' the title of XXI. It is employed in the titles of this and the five Books that follow, and always with the same force of 'meaning,' 'signification,' 'ideas underlying the ceremony.' Callery renders correctly Kwan Î by Signification de la Prise du Chapeau Viril.'

The Chinese cap of manhood always suggests the toga virilis of the Romans; but there was a difference between the institutions of the two peoples. The age for assuming the toga was fourteen; that for receiving the cap was twenty. The capped Chinese was still young, but he had grown to man's estate; the gowned Roman might have reached puberty, but he was little more than a boy.

Until the student fully understands the object of the Treatise, the paragraphs seem intricate and heavy, and the work of translation is difficult.

Book XLI. Hwăn Î.

After capping comes in natural order the ceremony of marriage; and we are glad to have, in the first portion of this Book, so full an account of the objects contemplated in marriage, the way in which the ceremony was gone about, and the subsequent proceedings by which the union was declared to be established.

The writer made much use of the chapters on marriage in the Î Lî. Nothing is said of the age at which it was the rule for a young man to marry; and this, we have seen, is put down, in other parts of this collection, as thirty. The same age is mentioned in the *K*âu Lî, XIII, 55, on the duties of the marriage-contractor. But marriage, we may assume from the case of Confucius himself, actually took place earlier in ancient times, as it does now. The 3ze[1], or name of maturity, which was given at the capping, is commonly said to be the name taken at marriage, as in Morrison's Dictionary, I, i, page 627.

The duties set forth in the Book, however, are not those of the young husband, but those of the wife, all comprised in the general virtue of 'obedience.' After the tenth paragraph, the author leaves the subject of marriage, and speaks of the different establishments of the king and queen and of their functions. So far what is said on these topics bears on marriage as it sets forth, mystically, that union as analogous to the relations of heaven and earth, the sun and moon, and the masculine and feminine energies of nature; and the response made by these to the conduct of the human parties in their wedded union.

[1] 字.

BOOK XLII. HSIANG YIN *K*IÛ Î.

Hsiang was anciently the name for the largest territorial division of the state. Under the dominion of *K*âu, from the hamlet of five families, through the lü, the ȝû, the tang, and the *k*âu, we rise to the hsiang, nominally containing 12,500 families, and presided over by a 'Great officer.' The royal domain contained six hsiang, and a feudal state three.

In more than one of these territorial divisions, there were festive meetings at regular intervals, all said to be for the purpose of 'drinking.' There was feasting at them too, but the viands bore a small proportion to the liquor, called by the name of *K*iû, which has generally been translated wine, though the grape had nothing to do with it, and whether it was distilled or merely fermented is a disputed point.

The festivity described in this Book was at the true Hsiang meeting, celebrated once in three years, under the superintendence of 'the Great officer' himself, when, in the principal school or college of the district, he assembled the gentlemen of accomplishments and virtue, and feasted them. His object was to select, especially from among the young men, those who were most likely to prove useful to the government in various departments of service. There was in the celebration the germ of the competitive examinations which have been for so long a characteristic feature of the Chinese nation.

The writer had before him the sixth and seventh Books of the Î Lî on the same subject, or their equivalents. He brings out five things accomplished by the ceremony, all of a moral and social nature; but in trying to explain the arrangements, he becomes allegorical or mystical, and sometimes absurd.

BOOK XLIII. SHÊ Î.

There were various games or competitions of archery; at the royal court, at the feudal courts, at the meetings in the country districts which form the subject of the last Book, and probably others of a less public and distinguished character. We have references in this Book to at least one of the archery trials at the royal court; to that at the feudal courts; and to one presided over by Confucius himself, of which it is difficult to assign the occasion. The object of the author is to show the attention paid to archery in ancient times, and how it was endeavoured to make it subservient to moral and educational purposes.

He had before him the accounts of the archery for officers in Books VIII, IX, and X of the Î Lî; but he allows himself more scope, in his observations on them, than the authors of the two preceding Books, and explains several practices in his own way,—unsatisfactorily, as I have pointed out in my notes.

Book XLIV. Yen Î.

The Yen Î, or 'Meaning of the Banquet,' is a fragment of only five paragraphs, which, moreover, are inartistically put together, the first having no connexion with the others. The Book should begin with paragraph 2, commencing:— 'The meaning of the Banquet at the feudal courts was this.' It was of this banquet that the compiler intended to give his readers an idea.

The greatest of all the ancient banquets was that which immediately followed the sacrifices in the ancestral temple, given to all the kindred of the same surname as the ruler, and to which there are several references in the Shih King. Thang San-ʒhâi (Ming dynasty) specifies four other occasions for the banquet besides this:— It might be given by a feudal prince, without any special occasion,—like that described in the second of the Praise Songs of Lû; or to a high dignitary or Great officer, who had been engaged in the royal service,—like that in the Minor Odes of the Kingdom, iii, 3; or when a high dignitary returned from a friendly mission,—like that also in the Minor Odes, i, 2; or when an officer came from one state to another on a friendly mission. Many other occasions, however, can be imagined on which public banquets were appropriate and might be given. The usages at them would, for the most part, be of the same nature.

The eleventh and twelfth chapters of the Î Lî are occupied with the ceremony of the banquet. The author of this Treatise quotes passages here and there from them, and appends his own explanation of their educational significance. Two lessons, he says, were especially illustrated in them:—the right relations to be maintained between superiors and inferiors, and the distinction between the noble and the mean.

Book XLV. Phing Î.

The subject of the Phing Î is the interchange of missions between the ancient feudal states. It was a rule of the kingdom that those states should by such interchange maintain a good understanding with one another, as a means of preventing both internal disturbances and aggression from without. P. Callery gives for the title:—'Signification (du Rite) des Visites.' I have met with it rendered in English by 'The Theory of Embassies;' but the Phing was not an embassy on any great state occasion, nor was it requisite that it should be sent at stated intervals. It could not be long neglected between two states without risk to the good fellowship between them, but events might at any time occur in any one state which would call forth such an expression of friendly sympathy from others.

A mission occasioned a very considerable expenditure to the receiving state, and the author, with amusing ingenuity, explains this as a device to teach the princes and their peoples to care little for such outlay in comparison with the maintenance of the custom and its ceremonies.

Those visits are treated with all the necessary details in the Î Lî, Books XV–XVIII; and though the extracts from them are not many, we get from the author a sufficiently intelligible account of the nature of the missions and the way in which they were carried through.

In paragraph 11, however, he turns to another subject, and writes at some length about archery, while the concluding paragraphs (12 and 13) give a conversation between Confucius and his disciple Ȝze-kung on the reasons why jade is thought so much of. The three paragraphs have no connexion with those that precede on the subject of the missions; and the question arises—Whence were they derived? The previous paragraphs, taken from or based on the Î Lî, are found in one of the surviving Treatises of the larger collection of the Greater Tâi, the thirty-sixth Book, called *Kh*âo-sze, in consequence of which the *Kh*ien-lung editors suggest that these concluding paragraphs were an addition made by his relative, Tâi Shăng. It may have been so, but we should not thereby be impressed with a high idea of the skill or judgment with which Shăng executed his work.

Book XLVI. Sang Fû Sze *K*ih.

This Book, with which the collection of the Lî *K*î concludes, is an attempt to explain the usages of the mourning rites, and especially of the dress, wherein they agree, and wherein they differ, by referring them to the four constituents of man's nature,—love, righteousness, the sentiment of propriety, and knowledge, in harmony with the operations of heaven and earth in the course of nature. We do not know who was the author of it, but the *Kh*ien-lung editors contend that it could not have been in the original compilation of the Smaller Tâi, and owes its place in the collection to *K*ăng Hsüan.

The greater part of it is found in the thirty-ninth, or last but one[1], of the Books still current as the Lî of the Greater Tâi; and another part in the 'Narratives of the School,' the third article in the sixth chapter of that collection[2], the compilation of which in its present form is attributed to Wang Sû in the first half of our third century. But this second fragment must have existed previously, else *K*ăng

[1] 本命.   [2] 本命解.

himself could not have seen it. The argument of those editors, therefore, that some scholar, later than the Smaller Tâi, must have incorporated it with what we find in the Greater Tâi, adding a beginning and ending of his own, so as to form a Book like one of those of Tâi Shăng, and that *K*ăng thought it worth his while to preserve it as the last portion of Shăng's collection,—this argument is inconclusive. The fragment may originally have formed part of Tâi Teh's thirty-ninth Book or of some other, and the whole of this Book have been arranged, as we now have it by Shăng himself, working, as he is reported to have done, on the compilation or digest of his cousin. However this be, the views in the Book are certainly ingenious and deserve to be read with care.

A few lines in Callery's work are sufficient to translate all of the Book which is admitted into the expurgated editions.

THE LÎ *KÎ*.

A COLLECTION OF TREATISES ON THE RULES OF PROPRIETY OR CEREMONIAL USAGES.

BOOK I. *KHÜ* LÎ.

SUMMARY OF THE RULES OF PROPRIETY.

SECTION I. PART I.

Ch. 1. 1. The Summary of the Rules of Propriety says:—Always and in everything let there be reverence; with the deportment grave as when

---

On the names of the whole work and of this book, see the Introduction, pp. 9–12 and 15–17.

Part I is occupied with general principles and statements about Propriety rather than with the detail of particular rules. It may be divided into seven chapters, containing in all thirty-one paragraphs.

Ch. 1. 1, tells how reverence and gravity, with careful speech, are essential in Propriety; and shows its importance to a community or nation. 2. 2, specifies habits or tendencies incompatible with Propriety. 3. 3–5, gives instances of Propriety in superior men, and directions for certain cases. 4. 6, 7, states the rules for sitting, standing, and a mission to another state. 5. 8–22, sets forth how indispensable Propriety is for the regulation of the individual and society, and that it marks in fact the distinction between men and brutes. 6. 23–26, indicates how the rules, unnecessary in the most ancient times, grew with the progress of society, and were its ornament and security. 7. 27–31, speaks of the different stages of life, as divided into decades from ten years to a hundred; and certain characteristics belonging to them.

one is thinking (deeply), and with speech composed and definite. This will make the people tranquil.

2. 2. Pride should not be allowed to grow; the desires should not be indulged; the will should not be gratified to the full; pleasure should not be carried to excess.

3. 3. Men of talents and virtue can be familiar with others and yet respect them; can stand in awe of others and yet love them. They love others and yet acknowledge the evil that is in them. They accumulate (wealth) and yet are able to part with it (to help the needy); they rest in what gives them satisfaction and yet can seek satisfaction elsewhere (when it is desirable to do so). 4. When you find wealth within your reach, do not (try to) get it by improper means; when you meet with calamity, do not (try to) escape from it by improper means. Do not seek for victory in small contentions; do not seek for more than your proper share. 5. Do not positively affirm what you have doubts about; and (when you have no doubts), do not let what you say appear (simply) as your own view[1].

4. 6. If a man be sitting, let him do so as a personator of the deceased[2]; if he be standing, let him do so (reverently), as in sacrificing. 7. In

[1] The text in the second part of this sentence is not easily translated and interpreted. I have followed in my version the view of *K*ăng, *K*û Hsî, and the *Kh*ien-lung editors. Callery gives for the whole sentence, 'Ne donnez pas comme certain ce qui est douteux, mais exposez-le clairement sans arrière-pensée.' Zottoli's view of the meaning is probably the same as mine: 'Dubius rerum noli praesumere, sed sincerus ne tibi arroges.'

[2] On the personator of the deceased, see vol. iii, pp. 300, 301. According to the ritual of *K*âu, the representatives of the dead always sat, and bore themselves with the utmost gravity.

(observing) the rules of propriety, what is right (for the time and in the circumstances) should be followed. In discharging a mission (to another state), its customs are to be observed.

5. 8. They are the rules of propriety, that furnish the means of determining (the observances towards) relatives, as near and remote; of settling points which may cause suspicion or doubt; of distinguishing where there should be agreement, and where difference; and of making clear what is right and what is wrong. 9. According to those rules, one should not (seek to) please others in an improper way, nor be lavish of his words. 10. According to them, one does not go beyond the definite measure, nor encroach on or despise others, nor is fond of (presuming) familiarities. 11. To cultivate one's person and fulfil one's words is called good conduct. When the conduct is (thus) ordered, and the words are accordant with the (right) course, we have the substance of the rules of propriety. 12. I have heard that it is in accordance with those rules that one should be chosen by others (as their model); I have not heard of his choosing them (to take him as such). I have heard in the same way of (scholars) coming to learn; I have not heard of (the master) going to teach. 13. The course (of duty), virtue, benevolence, and righteousness cannot be fully carried out without the rules of propriety; 14. nor are training and oral lessons for the rectification of manners complete; 15. nor can the clearing up of quarrels and discriminating in disputes be accomplished; 16. nor can (the duties between) ruler and minister, high and low, father and son, elder brother and younger, be determined; 17. nor can students for office and

(other) learners, in serving their masters, have an attachment for them; 18. nor can majesty and dignity be shown in assigning the different places at court, in the government of the armies, and in discharging the duties of office so as to secure the operation of the laws; 19. nor can there be the (proper) sincerity and gravity in presenting the offerings to spiritual Beings on occasions of supplication, thanksgiving, and the various sacrifices[1]. 20. Therefore the superior man is respectful and reverent, assiduous in his duties and not going beyond them, retiring and yielding;—thus illustrating (the principle of) propriety. 21. The parrot can speak, and yet is nothing more than a bird; the ape can speak, and yet is nothing more than a beast[2]. Here now is a man who observes no rules of propriety; is not his heart that of a beast? But if (men were as) beasts, and without (the principle of) propriety, father and son might have the same mate. 22. Therefore, when the sages arose, they framed the rules of propriety in order to teach men, and cause them, by

---

[1] Four religious acts are here mentioned, in connexion with which the offerings to spiritual Beings were presented. What I have called 'various sacrifices' is in Chinese *K*î sze. Wû *Kh*ăng says: '*K*î means sacrificial offerings to the spirit (or spirits) of Earth, and sze those to the spirits of Heaven. Offerings to the manes of men are also covered by them when they are used together.'

[2] We know that the parrot and some other birds can be taught to speak; but I do not know that any animal has been taught to enunciate words even as these birds do. Williams (Dict. p. 809) thinks that the shăng shăng mentioned here may be the rhinopithecus Roxellana of P. David, found in Sze-*kh*üan; but we have no account of it in Chinese works, so far as I know, that is not evidently fabulous.

their possession of them, to make a distinction between themselves and brutes.

6. 23. In the highest antiquity they prized (simply conferring) good; in the time next to this, giving and repaying was the thing attended to[1]. And what the rules of propriety value is that reciprocity. If I give a gift and nothing comes in return, that is contrary to propriety; if the thing comes to me, and I give nothing in return, that also is contrary to propriety. 24. If a man observe the rules of propriety, he is in a condition of security; if he do not, he is in one of danger. Hence there is the saying, 'The rules of propriety should by no means be left unlearned.' 25. Propriety is seen in humbling one's self and giving honour to others. Even porters and pedlers are sure to display this giving honour (in some cases); how much more should the rich and noble do so (in all)! 26. When the rich and noble know to love propriety, they do not become proud nor dissolute. When the poor and mean know to love propriety, their minds do not become cowardly.

7. 27. When one is ten years old, we call him a boy; he goes (out) to school. When he is twenty, we call him a youth; he is capped. When he is thirty, we say, 'He is at his maturity;' he has a wife[2]. When

---

[1] Compare with this paragraph the state of 'the highest antiquity' described in the Tâo Teh King, chapters 18, 19, et al.

[2] When it is said that at thirty a man has a wife, the meaning must be that he ought not to reach that age without being married. Early marriages were the rule in ancient China, as they are now. Confucius was married when barely twenty. In the same way we are to understand the being in office at forty. A man might take office at thirty; if he reached forty before he did so, there was something wrong in himself or others.

he is forty, we say, 'He is in his vigour;' he is employed in office. When he is fifty, we say, 'He is getting grey;' he can discharge all the duties of an officer. When he is sixty, we say, 'He is getting old;' he gives directions and instructions. When he is seventy, we say, 'He is old;' he delegates his duties to others. At eighty or ninety, we say of him, 'He is very old.' When he is seven, we say that he is an object of pitying love. Such a child and one who is very old, though they may be chargeable with crime, are not subjected to punishment. At a hundred, he is called a centenarian, and has to be fed. 28. A great officer, when he is seventy, should resign (his charge of) affairs. 29. If he be not allowed to resign, there must be given him a stool and staff. When travelling on service, he must have the attendance of his wife[1]; and when going to any other state, he will ride in an easy carriage[2]. 30. (In another state) he will style himself 'the old man;' in his own state, he will call himself by his name. 31. When from another they ask (about his state), he must tell them of its (old) institutions[3].

---

[1] Perhaps we should translate here in the plural—'his women,' which would include his wife.

[2] An 'easy carriage' was small. Its occupant sat in it, and did not stand.

[3] It is supposed here that the foreign envoys first question the ruler, who then calls in the help of the aged minister.

PART II.

1\. 1. In going to take counsel with an elder, one must carry a stool and a staff with him (for the elder's use). When the elder asks a question, to reply without acknowledging one's incompetency and (trying to) decline answering, is contrary to propriety[1].

2\. 2. For all sons it is the rule:—in winter, to warm (the bed for their parents), and to cool it in summer; in the evening, to adjust everything (for their repose), and to inquire (about their health) in the morning; and, when with their companions, not to quarrel.

3\. 3. Whenever a son, having received the three (first) gifts (of the ruler), declines (to use) the carriage and horses, the people of the hamlets and smaller districts, and of the larger districts and neighbourhoods, will proclaim him filial; his brothers and relatives, both by consanguinity and affinity, will proclaim him

---

Part II enters more into detail about the rules of Propriety. It has been divided into seven chapters, containing in all thirty-two paragraphs.

Ch. 1. 1, speaks of a junior consulting an elder. 2. 2, describes services due from all sons to their parents. 3. 3, shows a filial son when raised to higher rank than his father. 4. 4–16, contains rules for a son in various circumstances, especially with reference to his father. 5. 17–26, gives the rules for younger men in their intercourse with their teachers and elders generally, and in various cases. 6. 27, is the rule for an officer in entering the gate of his ruler or coming out by it. 7. 28–32, deals with a host and visitor, and ceremonious visiting and intercourse generally.

[1] The reply of Tsăng Shăn to Confucius, as related in vol. iii, pp. 465, 466, is commonly introduced in illustration of this second sentence.

loving; his friends who are fellow-officers will proclaim him virtuous; and his friends who are his associates will proclaim him true[1].

4. 4. When he sees an intimate friend of his father, not to presume to go forward to him without being told to do so; nor to retire without being told; nor to address him without being questioned:—this is the conduct of a filial son. 5. A son, when he is going abroad, must inform (his parents where he is going); when he returns, he must present himself before them. Where he travels must be in some fixed (region); what he engages in must be some (reputable) occupation. 6. In ordinary conversation (with his parents), he does not use the term 'old' (with reference to them)[2]. 7. He should serve one twice as old as himself as he serves his father, one ten years older than himself as an elder brother; with one five years older he should walk shoulder to shoulder, but (a little) behind him. 8. When five are sitting together, the eldest must have a different mat (by himself)[3]. 9. A son should not occupy the south-west corner of the apartment, nor sit in the

[1] The gifts of distinction, conferred by the sovereign on officers, ministers, and feudal princes, were nine in all; and the enumerations of them are not always the same. The three intended here are the appointment to office, or rank; the robes belonging to it; and the chariot and horses. We must suppose that the rank placed the son higher than the father in social position, and that he declines the third gift from humility,—not to parade himself as superior to his father and others in his circle.

[2] Some understand the rule to be that the son is not to speak of himself as old; but the meaning in the translation is the more approved.

[3] Four men were the proper complement for a mat; the eldest of the five therefore was honoured with another mat for himself.

middle of the mat (which he occupies alone), nor walk in the middle of the road, nor stand in the middle of the doorway[1]. 10. He should not take the part of regulating the (quantity of) rice and other viands at an entertainment. 11. He should not act as personator of the dead at sacrifice[2]. 12. He should be (as if he were) hearing (his parents) when there is no voice from them, and as seeing them when they are not actually there. 13. He should not ascend a height, nor approach the verge of a depth; he should not indulge in reckless reviling or derisive laughing. A filial son will not do things in the dark, nor attempt hazardous undertakings, fearing lest he disgrace his parents. 14. While his parents are alive, he will not promise a friend to die (with or for him)[3], nor will he have wealth that he calls his own. 15. A son, while his parents are alive, will not wear a cap or (other) article of dress, with a white border[4]. 16. An orphan son, taking his father's place, will not wear a cap or (other article of) dress with a variegated border[5].

5. 17. A boy should never he allowed to see an

---

[1] The father is supposed to be alive; the south-west part of an apartment was held to be the most honourable, and must be reserved for him. So of the other things.

[2] This was in the ancestral worship. A son, acting such a part, would have to receive the homage of his father.

[3] I have known instances of Chinese agreeing to die with or for a friend, who wished to avenge a great wrong. See the covenant of the three heroes of the 'romance of the Three Kingdoms,' near the beginning.

[4] White was and is the colour worn in mourning.

[5] The son here is the eldest son and heir; even after the regular period of mourning is over, he continues to wear it in so far. The other sons were not required to do so.

instance of deceit[1]. 18. A lad should not wear a jacket of fur nor the skirt[2]. He must stand straight and square, and not incline his head in hearing. 19. When an elder is holding him with the hand, he should hold the elder's hand with both his hands. When the elder has shifted his sword to his back and is speaking to him with the side of his face bent down, he should cover his mouth with his hand in answering[3]. 20. When he is following his teacher[4], he should not quit the road to speak with another person. When he meets his teacher on the road, he should hasten forward to him, and stand with his hands joined across his breast. If the teacher speak to him, he will answer; if he do not, he will retire with hasty steps. 21. When, following an elder, they ascend a level height, he must keep his face towards the quarter to which the elder is looking. 22. When one has ascended the wall of a city, he should not point, nor call out[5]. 23. When he intends to go to a lodging-house, let it not be with the feeling that he must get whatever he asks for. 24. When about to go up to the hall (of a house), he must raise his voice. When outside the door there are two (pairs

---

[1] This maxim deserves to be specially noted. It will remind the reader of Juvenal's lines :—

'Maxima debetur puero reverentia. Si quid
Turpe paras, nec tu pueri contempseris annos.'

[2] To make him handy, and leave him free to execute any service required of him.

[3] The second sentence here is difficult to construe, and the critics differ much in dealing with it. Zottoli's version is—'Si e dorso vel latere transverso ore (superior) eloquatur ei, tunc obducto ore respondebit.'

[4] 'Teacher' is here 'the one born before him,' denoting 'an old man who teaches youth.'

[5] And thus make himself an object of general observation.

of) shoes[1], if voices be heard, he enters; if voices be not heard, he will not enter. 25. When about to enter the door, he must keep his eyes cast down. As he enters, he should (keep his hands raised as high as if he were) bearing the bar of the door. In looking down or up, he should not turn (his head). If the door were open, he should leave it open; if it were shut, he should shut it again. If there be others (about) to enter after him, while he (turns to) shut the door, let him not do so hastily. 26. Let him not tread on the shoes (left outside the door), nor stride across the mat (in going to take his seat); but let him hold up his dress, and move hastily to his corner (of the mat). (When seated), he must be careful in answering or assenting.

6. 27. A great officer or (other) officer should go out or in at the ruler's doors[2], on the right of the middle post, without treading on the threshold.

7. 28. Whenever (a host has received and) is entering with a guest, at every door he should give place to him. When the guest arrives at the innermost door (or that leading to the feast-

---

[1] It was the custom in China, as it still is in Japan, to take off the shoes, and leave them outside the door on entering an apartment. This paragraph and the next tell us how a new-comer should not enter an apartment hastily, so as to take those already there by surprise.

[2] It is necessary to translate here in the plural. Anciently, as now, the palace, mansion, or public office was an aggregate of courts, with buildings in them, so that the visitor passed from one to another through a gateway, till he reached the inner court which conducted to the hall, behind which again were the family apartments. The royal palace had five courts and gates; that of a feudal lord had three. Each gate had its proper name. The whole assemblage of buildings was much deeper than it was wide.

room), the host will ask to be allowed to enter first and arrange the mats. Having done this, he will come out to receive the guest, who will refuse firmly (to enter first). The host having made a low bow to him, they will enter (together). 29. When they have entered the door, the host moves to the right, and the guest to the left, the former going to the steps on the east, and the latter to those on the west. If the guest be of the lower rank, he goes to the steps of the host (as if to follow him up them). The host firmly declines this, and he returns to the other steps on the west[1]. 30. They then offer to each other the precedence in going up, but the host commences first, followed (immediately) by the other. They bring their feet together on every step, thus ascending by successive paces. He who ascends by the steps on the east should move his right foot first, and the other at the western steps his left foot. 31. Outside the curtain or screen[2] (a visitor) should not walk with the formal hasty steps, nor above in the hall, nor when carrying the symbol of jade. Above, in the raised hall, the foot-prints should be alongside each other, but below it free and separate. In the apartment the elbows should not be held out like wings in bowing. 32. When two (equals) are sitting side by side, they do not have their elbows extended crosswise. One should not kneel in handing anything to a (superior) standing, nor stand in handing it to him sitting.

[1] The host here is evidently of high dignity, living in a mansion.

[2] The screen was in front of the raised hall, in the courtyard; until they passed it visitors might not be in view of their host, and could feel at ease in their carriage and movements.

PART III.

1. 1. In all cases of (a lad's) carrying away the dirt that has been swept up from the presence of an elder, it is the rule that he (place) the brush on the basket, keeping his sleeve before it as he retires. The dust is not allowed to reach the elder, because he carries the basket with its mouth turned towards himself. 2. He carries the (elder's) mat in his arms like the cross-beam of a shadoof. 3. If it be a mat

---

Part III continues to lay down the rules for various duties and classes of duties. It extends to sixty-seven paragraphs, which may be comprised in twenty-one chapters.

Ch. 1. 1–4, describes a youth's ways in sweeping for an elder and in carrying and placing his mats. 2. 5–7, relates to host and guest. 3. 8–19, is about a youth, especially a pupil, in attendance on his elders. 4. 20–26, is about his ways in serving a superior. 5. 27–29, is about the shoes in visiting. 6. 30–39, gives rules about not interfering with people's private affairs, and avoiding, between male and female, what would cause suspicion. 7. 40, is a message of congratulation to a friend on his marriage. 8. 41, is about consideration for the poor and the old. 9. 42–46, gives rules for the naming of sons and daughters. 10. 47–51, describes the arrangement of the dishes, and the behaviour of the host and guests, at an entertainment. 11. 52, we have a youth and his host eating together. 12. 53, shows how people, eating together, ought to behave. 13. 54–58, is about things to be avoided in eating. 14. 59, shows us host and guest at the close of the entertainment. In 15. 60, we have a youth and elder drinking together. 16. 61, is about a gift from an elder. 17. 62, shows how the kernel of a fruit given by an elder is to be dealt with in his presence. 18. 63, 64, relates to gifts at a feast from the ruler, and how they are to be used. 19. 65, is about a ruler asking an attendant to share in a feast. 20. 66, is about the use of chopsticks with soup. 21. 67, gives the rules for paring a melon for the ruler and others.

to sit on, he will ask in what direction (the elder) is going to turn his face; if it be to sleep on, in what direction he is going to turn his feet. 4. If a mat face the south or the north, the seat on the west is accounted that of honour; if it face the east or the west, the seat on the south.

2. 5. Except in the case of guests who are there (simply) to eat and drink, in spreading the mats a space of ten cubits should be left between them[1]. 6. When the host kneels to adjust the mats (of a visitor), the other should kneel and keep hold of them, declining (the honour)[2]. When the visitor (wishes to) remove one or more, the host should firmly decline to permit him to do so. When the visitor steps on his mats, (the host) takes his seat. 7. If the host have not put some question, the visitor should not begin the conversation.

3. 8. When (a pupil) is about to go to his mat, he should not look discomposed. With his two hands he should hold up his lower garment, so that the bottom of it may be a cubit from the ground. His clothes should not hang loosely about him, nor should there be any hurried movements of his feet. 9. If any writing or tablets of his master, or his lute or cithern be in the way, he should kneel down and remove them, taking care not to disarrange them. 10. When sitting and doing nothing, he should keep quite at the back (of his mat); when eating, quite at the front of it[3]. He should sit quietly and keep

[1] To allow space and freedom for gesticulation.

[2] Two or more mats might be placed over each other in honour of the visitor.

[3] The dishes were placed before the mats.

a watch on his countenance. If there be any subject on which the elder has not touched, let him not introduce it irregularly. 11. Let him keep his deportment correct[1], and listen respectfully. Let him not appropriate (to himself) the words (of others), nor (repeat them) as (the echo does the) thunder. If he must (adduce proofs), let them be from antiquity, with an appeal to the ancient kings. 12. When sitting by his side, and the teacher puts a question, (the learner) should not reply till (the other) has finished. 13. When requesting (instruction) on the subject of his studies, (the learner) should rise; when requesting further information, he should rise. 14. When his father calls, (a youth) should not (merely) answer 'yes,' nor when his teacher calls. He should, with (a respectful) 'yes,' immediately rise (and go to them). 15. When one is sitting in attendance on another whom he honours and reveres, he should not allow any part of his mat to keep them apart[2], nor will he rise when he sees others (come in) of the same rank as himself. 16. When the torches come, he should rise; and also when the viands come in, or a visitor of superior rank[3]. 17. The torches should not (be allowed to burn) till their ends can be seen. 18. Before an honoured visitor we should not shout (even) at

[1] Here, and in some other places, we find the second personal pronoun; as if the text were made up from different sources. I have translated, however, as if we had only the third person.

[2] He should sit on the front of his mat, to be as near the other as possible.

[3] The torches were borne by boys. They were often changed, that the visitors might not be aware how the time was passing.

a dog. 19. When declining any food, one should not spit.

4. 20. When one is sitting in attendance on another of superior character or rank, and that other yawns or stretches himself, or lays hold of his staff or shoes, or looks towards the sun to see if it be early or late, he should ask to be allowed to leave. 21. In the same position, if the superior man put a question on a new subject, he should rise up in giving his reply. 22. Similarly, if there come some one saying (to the superior man), 'I wish, when you have a little leisure, to report to you,' he should withdraw to the left or right and wait. 23. Do not listen with the head inclined on one side, nor answer with a loud sharp voice, nor look with a dissolute leer, nor keep the body in a slouching position[1]. 24. Do not saunter about with a haughty gait, nor stand with one foot raised. Do not sit with your knees wide apart, nor sleep on your face. 25. Have your hair gathered up, and do not use any false hair[2]. 26. Let not the cap be laid aside; nor the chest be bared, (even) when one is toiling hard; nor let the lower garment be held up (even) in hot weather.

5. 27. When (going to) sit in attendance on an elder, (a visitor) should not go up to the hall with his shoes on, nor should he presume to take them off in front of the steps. 28. (When any single visitor is leaving), he will go to his shoes, kneel down and take them up, and then move to one side. 29. (When the visitors retire in a body) with their

[1] The style and form of 23–26 differ from the preceding. Perhaps they should form a paragraph by themselves.

[2] Which women were accustomed to do.

faces towards the elder, (they stand) by the shoes, which they then, kneeling, remove (some distance), and, stooping down, put on[1].

6. 30. When two men are sitting or standing together, do not join them as a third. When two are standing together, another should not pass between them. 31. Male and female should not sit together (in the same apartment), nor have the same stand or rack for their clothes, nor use the same towel or comb, nor let their hands touch in giving and receiving. 32. A sister-in-law and brother-in-law do not interchange inquiries (about each other). None of the concubines in a house should be employed to wash the lower garment (of a son)[2]. 33. Outside affairs should not be talked of inside the threshold (of the women's apartments), nor inside (or women's) affairs outside it. 34. When a young lady is promised in marriage, she wears the strings (hanging down to her neck)[3]; and unless there be some great occasion, no (male) enters the door of her apartment[4]. 35. When a married aunt, or sister, or daughter returns home (on a visit), no brother (of the family) should sit with her on the same mat or eat with her from the same dish. (Even) the father and daughter should not occupy the same mat[5]. 36.

[1] The host would be seeing the visitors off, and therefore they would keep their faces towards him.

[2] Concubines might be employed to wash clothes; delicacy forbade their washing the lower garments of the sons.

[3] Those strings were symbolic of the union with and subjection to her husband to which she was now pledged.

[4] Great sickness or death, or other great calamity, would be such an occasion.

[5] This is pushing the rule to an extreme. The sentence is also (but wrongly) understood of father and son.

Male and female, without the intervention of the matchmaker, do not know each other's name. Unless the marriage presents have been received, there should be no communication nor affection between them. 37. Hence the day and month (of the marriage) should be announced to the ruler, and to the spirits (of ancestors) with purification and fasting; and (the bridegroom) should make a feast, and invite (his friends) in the district and neighbourhood, and his fellow-officers:—thus giving its due importance to the separate position (of male and female). 38. One must not marry a wife of the same surname with himself. Hence, in buying a concubine, if he do not know her surname, he must consult the tortoise-shell about it[1]. 39. With the son of a widow, unless he be of acknowledged distinction, one should not associate himself as a friend.

7. 40. When one congratulates (a friend) on his marrying, his messenger says, 'So and So has sent me. Having heard that you are having guests, he has sent me with this present.'

8. 41. Goods and wealth are not to be expected from the poor in their discharge of the rules of propriety; nor the display of sinews and strength from the old.

9. 42. In giving a name to a son, it should not be that of a state, nor of a day or a month, nor of any hidden ailment, nor of a hill or river[2]. 43.

[1] Not to find out what her surname is, but to determine whether it be the same as that of the gentleman or not.

[2] Such names were so common, that if it became necessary to avoid them, as it might be, through the death of the party or on other grounds, it would be difficult and inconvenient to do so.

Sons and daughters should have their (relative) ages distinguished[1]. 44. A son at twenty is capped, and receives his appellation[2]. 45. Before his father a son should be called by his name, and before his ruler a minister[3]. 46. When a daughter is promised in marriage, she assumes the hair-pin, and receives her appellation.

10\. 47. The rules for bringing in the dishes for an entertainment are the following:—The meat cooked on the bones is set on the left, and the sliced meat on the right; the rice is placed on the left of the parties on the mat, and the soup on their right; the minced and roasted meat are put outside (the chops and sliced meat), and the pickles and sauces inside; the onions and steamed onions succeed to these, and the drink and syrups are on the right. When slices of dried and spiced meat are put down, where they are folded is turned to the left, and the ends of them to the right. 48. If a guest be of lower rank (than his entertainer), he should take up the rice[4], rise and decline (the honour he is receiving). The host then rises and refuses to allow the guest (to retire). After this the guest will resume his seat. 49. When the host leads on the guests to present an offering (to the father of cookery), they will begin

---

[1] As primus, prima; secundus, secunda, &c.

[2] The appellation was thus the name given (at a family meeting) to a youth who had reached man's estate. Morrison (Dict. i. 627) calls it the name taken by men when they marry. Such a usage testifies to the early marriages in ancient China, as referred to in note 2, p. 65.

[3] There might be some meaning in the appellation which would seem to place its bearer on the level of his father or his ruler.

[4] The rice is called 'the principal article in a feast.' Hence the humbler guest takes it up, as symbolical of all the others.

with the dishes which were first brought in. Going on from the meat cooked on the bones they will offer of all (the other dishes)[1]. 50. After they have eaten three times, the host will lead on the guests to take of the sliced meat, from which they will go on to all the other dishes. 51. A guest should not rinse his mouth with spirits till the host has gone over all the dishes.

11. 52. When (a youth) is in attendance on an elder at a meal, if the host give anything to him with his own hand, he should bow to him and eat it. If he do not so give him anything, he should eat without bowing.

12. 53. When eating with others from the same dishes, one should not try to eat (hastily) to satiety. When eating with them from the same dish of rice, one should not have to wash his hands[2].

13. 54. Do not roll the rice into a ball; do not bolt down the various dishes; do not swill down (the soup). 55. Do not make a noise in eating; do not crunch the bones with the teeth; do not put back fish you have been eating; do not throw the bones to the dogs; do not snatch (at what you want). 56. Do not spread out the rice (to cool); do not use chopsticks in eating millet[3].

---

[1] This paragraph refers to a practice something like our 'saying grace.' According to Khung Ying-tâ, a little was taken from all the dishes, and placed on the ground about them as an offering to 'the father of cookery.'

[2] As all ate from the same dish of rice without chopsticks or spoons, it was necessary they should try to keep their hands clean. Some say the 'washing' was only a rubbing of the hands with sand.

[3] A spoon was the proper implement in eating millet.

57. Do not (try to) gulp down soup with vegetables in it, nor add condiments to it; do not keep picking the teeth, nor swill down the sauces. If a guest add condiments, the host will apologise for not having had the soup prepared better. If he swill down the sauces, the host will apologise for his poverty[1]. 58. Meat that is wet (and soft) may be divided with the teeth, but dried flesh cannot be so dealt with. Do not bolt roast meat in large pieces.

14. 59. When they have done eating, the guests will kneel in front (of the mat), and (begin to) remove the (dishes) of rice and sauces to give them to the attendants. The host will then rise and decline this service from the guests, who will resume their seats.

15. 60. If a youth is in attendance on, and drinking with, an elder, when the (cup of) spirits is brought to him, he rises, bows, and (goes to) receive it at the place where the spirit-vase is kept. The elder refuses (to allow him to do so), when he returns to the mat, and (is prepared) to drink. The elder (meantime) lifts (his cup); but until he has emptied it, the other does not presume to drink his.

16. 61. When an elder offers a gift, neither a youth, nor one of mean condition, presumes to decline it.

17. 62. When a fruit is given by the ruler and in his presence, if there be a kernel in it, (the receiver) should place it in his bosom[2].

[1] The sauce should be too strong to be swallowed largely and hurriedly.

[2] Lest he should seem to throw away anything given by the ruler.

18. 63. When one is attending the ruler at a meal, and the ruler gives him anything that is left, if it be in a vessel that can be easily scoured, he does not transfer it (to another of his own); but from any other vessel he should so transfer it[1].

19. 64. Portions of (such) food should not be used as offerings (to the departed). A father should not use them in offering even to a (deceased) son, nor a husband in offering to a (deceased) wife[2].

20. 65. When one is attending an elder and (called to) share with him (at a feast), though the viands may be double (what is necessary), he should not (seek) to decline them. If he take his seat (only) as the companion of another (for whom it has been prepared), he should not decline them.

21. 66. If the soup be made with vegetables, chopsticks should be used; but not if there be no vegetables.

22. 67. He who pares a melon for the son of Heaven should divide it into four parts and then into eight, and cover them with a napkin of fine linen. For the ruler of a state, he should divide it into four parts, and cover them with a coarse napkin. To a great officer he should (present the four parts) uncovered. An inferior officer should receive it (simply) with the stalk cut away. A common man will deal with it with his teeth.

---

[1] A vessel of potter's ware or metal can be scoured, and the part which his mouth has touched be cleansed before the ruler uses it again.

[2] The meaning of this paragraph is not clear.

PART IV.

1. 1. When his father or mother is ill, (a young man) who has been capped should not use his comb, nor walk with his elbows stuck out, nor speak on idle topics, nor take his lute or cithern in hand. He should not eat of (different) meats till his taste is changed, nor drink till his looks are changed[1]. He should not laugh so as to show his teeth, nor be angry till he breaks forth in reviling. When the illness is gone, he may resume his former habits. 2. He who is sad and anxious should sit with his mat

---

Part IV contains fifty-two paragraphs, which have been arranged in ten chapters, stating the rules to be observed in a variety of cases.

Ch. 1. 1, 2, treats of the ways of a young man who is sorrowful in consequence of the illness or death of a parent. 2. 3-26, treats of the rules in giving and receiving, and of messages connected therewith. The presentations mentioned are all from inferiors to superiors. 3. 27, 28, does not lay down rules, but gives characteristics of the superior man, and the methods by which he preserves his friendships unbroken. 4. 29, 30, refers to the arrangement of the tablets in the ancestral temple, and to the personators of the dead. 5. 31, tells how one fasting should keep himself from being excited. 6. 32-34, sets forth cautions against excess in the demonstrations of mourning. 7. 35, 36, speaks of sorrowing for the dead and condoling with the living. 8. 37, 38, gives counsels of prudence for one under the influence of sympathy and benevolent feeling. 9. 39-48, describes rules in connexion with mourning, burials, and some other occasions. 10. 49-52, describes gradations in ceremonies and in the penal statutes; and how a criminal who has been punished should never be permitted to be near the ruler.

[1] Does the rule about eating mean that the anxious son should restrict himself to a single dish of meat?

spread apart from others; he who is mourning (for a death) should sit on a single mat[1].

2. 3. When heavy rains have fallen, one should not present fish or tortoises (to a superior)[2]. 4. He who is presenting a bird should turn its head on one side; if it be a tame bird, this need not be done. 5. He who is presenting a carriage and horses should carry in his hand (to the hall) the whip, and strap for mounting by[3]. 6. He who is presenting a suit of mail should carry the helmet (to the hall). He who is presenting a staff should hold it by its end[4]. 7. He who is presenting a captive should hold him by the right sleeve[5]. 8. He who is presenting grain unhulled should carry with him the left side of the account (of the quantity); if the hull be off, he should carry with him a measure-drum[6]. 9. He who is presenting cooked food, should carry with him the sauce and pickles for it. 10. He who is presenting fields and tenements should carry with him the writings about them, and give them up (to the superior). 11. In every case of giving a bow to another, if it be bent, the (string of) sinew should be kept upwards; but if unbent, the horn.

---

[1] Grief is solitary. A mourner afflicts himself.

[2] Because the fish in such a case are so numerous as not to be valuable, or because the fish at the time of the rains are not clean. Other reasons for the rule have been assigned.

[3] The whip and strap, carried up to the hall, represented the carriage and horses, left in the courtyard.

[4] For convenience; and because the end, going into the mud, was not so honourable.

[5] So that he could not attempt any violence.

[6] The account was in duplicate, on the same tablet. The right was held to be the more honourable part. 'Drum' was the name of the measure.

(The giver) should with his right hand grasp the end of the bow, and keep his left under the middle of the back. The (parties, without regard to their rank as) high and low, (bow to each other) till the napkins (at their girdles) hang down (to the ground). If the host (wish to) bow (still lower), the other moves on one side to avoid the salutation. The host then takes the bow, standing on the left of the other. Putting his hand under that of the visitor, he lays hold of the middle of the back, having his face in the same direction as the other; and thus he receives (the bow). 12. He who is giving a sword should do so with the hilt on his left side[1]. 13. He who is giving a spear with one hook should do so with the metal end of the shaft in front, and the sharp edge behind. 14. He who is presenting one with two hooks, or one with a single hook and two sharp points, should do so with the blunt shaft in front. 15. He who is giving a stool or a staff should (first) wipe it. 16. He who is presenting a horse or a sheep should lead it with his right hand. 17. He who is presenting a dog should lead it with his left hand. 18. He who is carrying a bird (as his present of introduction) should do so with the head to the left[2]. 19. For the ornamental covering of a lamb or a goose, an embroidered cloth should be used. 20. He who receives a pearl or a piece of jade should do so with both his hands. 21. He who receives a bow or a sword should do so (having his hands covered) with his sleeves[3]. 22. He who has

[1] That the receiver may take it with his right hand.

[2] Compare paragraph 4. In this case the bird was carried across the body of the donor with its head on his left.

[3] A different case from that in paragraph 11. It is supposed that

drunk from a cup of jade should not (go on to) shake it out[1]. 23. Whenever friendly messages are about to be sent, with the present of a sword or bow, or of (fruit, flesh, and other things, wrapped in) matting of rushes, with grass mats, and in baskets, round and square, (the messenger) has these things (carried with him, when he goes) to receive his commission, and deports himself as when he will be discharging it[2]. 24. Whenever one is charged with a mission by his ruler, after he has received from him his orders, and (heard all) he has to say, he should not remain over the night in his house. 25. When a message from the ruler comes (to a minister), the latter should go out and bow (to the bearer), in acknowledgment of the honour of it. When the messenger is about to return, (the other) must bow to him (again), and escort him outside the gate. 26. If (a minister) send a message to his ruler, he must wear his court-robes when he communicates it to the bearer; and on his return, he must descend from the hall, to receive (the ruler's) commands.

3. 27. To acquire extensive information and remember retentively, while (at the same time) he is modest; to do earnestly what is good, and not become weary in so doing:—these are the characteristics of him whom we call the superior man. 28. A superior man does not accept everything by which another would express his joy in him, or his devotion to him[3]; and thus he preserves their friendly intercourse unbroken.

here the two things were presented together, and received as on a cushion.

[1] Because of the risk to a thing so valuable.

[2] A rehearsal of what he would have to do.

[3] E. g., it is said, festive entertainments and gifts.

4. 29. A rule of propriety says, 'A superior man may carry his grandson in his arms, but not his son.' This tells us that a grandson may be the personator of his deceased grandfather (at sacrifices), but a son cannot be so of his father[1]. 30. When a great officer or (other) officer sees one who is to personate the dead (on his way to the ancestral temple), he should dismount from his carriage to him. The ruler himself, when he recognises him, should do the same[2]. The personator (at the same time) must bow forward to the cross-bar. In mounting the carriage, he must use a stool.

5. 31. One who is fasting (in preparation for a sacrifice) should neither listen to music nor condole with mourners[3].

6. 32. According to the rules for the period of mourning (for a father), (a son) should not emaciate himself till the bones appear, nor let his seeing and hearing be affected (by his privations). He should not go up to, nor descend from, the hall by the steps on the east (which his father used), nor go in or out by the path right opposite to the (centre of the) gate. 33. According to the same rules, if he have a scab on his head, he should wash it; if he have a sore on his body, he should bathe it. If he be ill, he should drink spirits, and eat flesh, returning to his former

[1] The tablets of a father and son should not be in the same line of shrines in the ancestral temple; and the fact in the paragraph—hardly credible—seems to be mentioned as giving a reason for this.

[2] The personator had for the time the dignity of the deceased whom he represented.

[3] The fasting and vigil extended to seven days, and were intended to prepare for the personating duty. What would distract the mind from this must be eschewed.

(abstinence) when he is better. If he make himself unable to perform his mourning duties, that is like being unkind and unfilial. 34. If he be fifty, he should not allow himself to be reduced (by his abstinence) very much; and, if he be sixty, not at all. At seventy, he will only wear the unhemmed dress of sackcloth, and will drink and eat flesh, and occupy (the usual apartment) inside (his house).

7. 35. Intercourse with the living (will be continued) in the future; intercourse with the dead (friend) was a thing of the past[1]. 36. He who knows the living should send (a message of) condolence; and he who knew the dead (a message also of his) grief. He who knows the living, and did not know the dead, will send his condolence without (that expression of) his grief; he who knew the dead, and does not know the living, will send the (expression of) grief, but not go on to condole.

8. 37. He who is condoling with one who has mourning rites in hand, and is not able to assist him with a gift, should put no question about his expenditure. He who is enquiring after another that is ill, and is not able to send (anything to him), should

---

[1] This gives the reasons for the directions in the next paragraph. We condole with the living—to console them; for the dead, we have only to express our grief for our own loss. P. Zottoli's translation is:—'Vivis computatur subsequens dies; mortuo computatur praecedens dies;' and he says in a note:—'Vivorum luctus incipit quarta a morte die, et praecedente die seu tertia fit mortui in feretrum depositio; luctus igitur et depositio, die intercipiuntur; haec precedit ille subsequctur.' This is after many critics, from *K*ăng Khang-*kh*ăng downwards; but it does great violence to the text. I have followed the view of the *Kh*ien-lung editors.

not ask what he would like. He who sees (a traveller), and is not able to lodge him, should not ask where he is stopping. 38. He who would confer something on another should not say, 'Come and take it;' he who would give something (to a smaller man), should not ask him what he would like.

9. 39. When one goes to a burying-ground, he should not get up on any of the graves. When assisting at an interment, one should (join in) holding the rope attached to the coffin[1]. 40. In a house of mourning, one should not laugh. 41. In order to bow to another, one should leave his own place. 42. When one sees at a distance a coffin with the corpse in it, he should not sing. When he enters among the mourners, he should not keep his arms stuck out. When eating (with others), he should not sigh. 43. When there are mourning rites in his neighbourhood, one should not accompany his pestle with his voice. When there is a body shrouded and coffined in his village, one should not sing in the lanes. 44. When going to a burying-ground, one should not sing, nor on the same day when he has wailed (with mourners). 45. When accompanying a funeral, one should not take a by-path. When taking part in the act of interment, one should not (try to) avoid mud or pools. When presenting himself at any mourning rite, one should have a sad countenance. When holding the rope, one should not laugh. 46. When present on an occasion of joy, one should not sigh. 47. When wearing his coat of

[1] The rope here may also be that, or one of those, attached to the low car on which the coffin was drawn to the grave. Compare paragraph 45.

mail and helmet, one's countenance should say, 'Who dares meddle with me?' 48. Hence the superior man is careful to maintain the proper expression of his countenance before others.

10. 49. Where the ruler of a state lays hold of the cross-bar, and bends forward to it, a great officer will descend from his carriage. Where a great officer lays hold of the bar and bends forward, another officer will descend. 50. The rules of ceremony do not go down to the common people[1]. 51. The penal statutes do not go up to great officers[2]. 52. Men who have suffered punishment should not (be allowed to) be by the side of the ruler[3].

[1] Not that the common people are altogether freed from the rules. But their occupations are engrossing, and their means small. Much cannot be expected from them.

[2] It may be necessary to punish them, but they should be beyond requiring punishment. The application of it, moreover, will be modified by various considerations. But the regulation is not good.

[3] To preserve the ruler from the contamination of their example, and the risk of their revenge.

Part V.

1. 1. A fighting chariot has no cross-board to assist its occupants in bowing; in a war chariot the

Part V contains forty-eight paragraphs, which may be arranged in ten chapters.

Ch. 1. 1–10, relates to carriages, especially to war chariots, and the use of them with their banners and other things in an expedition. 2. 10, gives the rules in avenging the deaths of a father, brother, and friend. 3. 11, shows the responsibility of ministers and officers generally in maintaining the defence and the cultivation

banner is fully displayed; in a chariot of peace it is kept folded round the pole. 2. A recorder should carry with him in his carriage his implements for writing[1]; his subordinates the (recorded) words (of former covenants and other documents). 3. When there is water in front, the flag with the green bird[2] on it should be displayed. 4. When there is (a cloud of) dust in front, that with the screaming kites. 5. For chariots and horsemen, that with wild geese in flight[3]. 6. For a body of troops, that with a tiger's (skin). 7. For a beast of prey, that with a leopard's (skin). 8. On the march the (banner with the) Red Bird should be in front; that with the Dark Warrior behind; that with the Azure Dragon on the left; and that with the White Tiger on the right; that

---

of their country. 4. 12–14, relates to sacrifices,—the sacrificers, their robes, the victims, &c. 5. 15–21, gives rules about avoiding the mention of certain names. 6. 22–27, is on the subject of divination,—of divining, especially, about the days for contemplated undertakings. 7. 28–33, describes the yoking the horses to a ruler's chariot, his taking his seat, and other points. 8. 34, 35, is about the strap which the driver handed to parties who wished to mount the carriage. 9. 36, gives three prohibitive rules:—about a visitor's carriage; a woman riding in a carriage; and dogs and horses. 10. 37–48, relates various rules about driving out, for the ruler and people generally.

[1] The original character denotes what is now used for 'pencils;' but the ordinary pencil had not yet been invented.

[2] Some kind of water-bird.

[3] A flock of geese maintains a regular order in flying, and was used to symbolise lines of chariots and horsemen. Khung Ying-tâ observes that chariots were used in the field before cavalry, and that the mention of horsemen here looks like the close of the *K*âu dynasty. One of the earliest instances of riding on horseback is in the 3o *K*wan under the year B.C. 517.

with the Pointer of the Northern Bushel should be reared aloft (in the centre of the host):—all to excite and direct the fury (of the troops)[1]. 9. There are rules for advancing and retreating; there are the various arrangements on the left and the right, each with its (proper) officer to look after it.

2. 10. With the enemy who has slain his father, one should not live under the same heaven. With the enemy who has slain his brother, one should never have his sword to seek (to deal vengeance). With the enemy who has slain his intimate friend, one should not live in the same state (without seeking to slay him).

3. 11. Many ramparts in the country round and near (a capital) are a disgrace to its high ministers and great officers[2]. Where the wide and open country is greatly neglected and uncultivated, it is a disgrace to the officers (in charge of it).

4. 12. When taking part in a sacrifice, one should not show indifference. 13. When sacrificial robes are worn out, they should be burnt: sacrificial vessels in the same condition should be buried, as should the tortoise-shell and divining stalks, and a victim that has died. 14. All who take part with the ruler in a sacrifice must themselves remove the stands (of their offerings).

---

[1] 'The Red Bird' was the name of the seven constellations of the southern quarter of the Zodiac; 'the Dark Warrior' embraced those of the northern; 'the Azure Dragon,' those of the eastern; and 'the Tiger,' those of the western. These flags would show the direction of the march, and seem to suggest that all heaven was watching the progress of the expedition.

[2] As showing that they had not been able to keep invaders at a distance.

5. 15. When the ceremony of wailing is over[1], a son should no longer speak of his deceased father by his name. The rules do not require the avoiding of names merely similar in sound to those not to be spoken. When (a parent had) a double name, the avoiding of either term (used singly) is not required. 16. While his parents (are alive), and a son is able to serve them, he should not utter the names of his grandparents; when he can no longer serve his parents (through their death), he need not avoid the names of his grandparents. 17. Names that would not be spoken (in his own family) need not be avoided (by a great officer) before his ruler; in the great officer's, however, the names proper to be suppressed by the ruler should not be spoken. 18. In (reading) the books of poetry and history, there need be no avoiding of names, nor in writing compositions. 19. In the ancestral temple there is no such avoiding. 20. Even in his presence, a minister need not avoid the names improper to be spoken by the ruler's wife. The names to be avoided by a wife need not be unspoken outside the door of the harem. The names of parties for whom mourning is worn (only) nine months or five months are not avoided[2]. 21. When one is crossing the boundaries (of a state), he should ask what are its prohibitory laws; when he has fairly entered it, he should ask about its customs; before entering the door (of a house), he should ask about the names to be avoided in it.

---

[1] After the burial. Till then they would not allow themselves to think of the departed as dead.

[2] As, in the first place, for uncles; and in the second, for cousins and grand-uncles.

6. 22. External undertakings should be commenced on the odd days, and internal on the even[1]. 23. In all cases of divining about a day, whether by the tortoise-shell or the stalks, if it be beyond the decade, it is said, 'on such and such a distant day,' and if within the decade, 'on such and such a near day.' For matters of mourning a distant day is preferred; for festive matters a near day[2]. 24. It is said, 'For the day we depend on thee, O great Tortoise-shell, which dost give the regular indications; we depend on you, O great Divining Stalks, which give the regular indications.' 25. Divination by the shell or the stalks should not go beyond three times. 26. The shell and the stalks should not be both used on the same subject[3]. 27. Divination by the shell is called pû; by the stalks, shih. The two were the methods by which the ancient sage kings made the people believe in seasons and days, revere spiritual beings, stand in awe of their laws and orders; the methods (also) by which they made them determine their perplexities and settle their misgivings. Hence it is said, 'If you doubted, and have consulted the stalks, you need not (any longer) think that you will do wrong. If the day (be clearly indicated), boldly do on it (what you desire to do).'

7. 28. When the ruler's carriage is about to have the horses put to it, the driver should stand before

[1] The odd days are called 'strong,' as belonging to the category of yang; the even days 'weak,' as of the category of yin.

[2] 'A distant day' gave a longer period for cherishing the memory of the departed; 'a near day' was desired for festive celebrations, because at them the feeling of 'respect' was supposed to predominate.

[3] To reverse by the one the indication of the other.

them, whip in hand. 29. When they are yoked, he will inspect the linch pin, and report that the carriage is ready. 30. (Coming out again), he should shake the dust from his clothes, and mount on the right side, taking hold of the second strap[1]. He should (then) kneel in the carriage[2]. 31. Holding his whip, and taking the reins separately, he will drive the horses on five paces, and then stop. 32. When the ruler comes out and approaches the carriage, the driver should take all the reins in one hand, and (with the other) hand the strap to him. The attendants should then retire out of the way. 33. They should follow quickly as the carriage drives on. When it reaches the great gate, the ruler will lay his hand on that of the driver (that he may drive gently), and, looking round, will order the warrior for the seat on the right to come into the carriage[3]. In passing through the gates (of a city) or village, and crossing the water-channels, the pace must be reduced to a walk.

8. 34. In all cases it is the rule for the driver to hand the strap (to the person about to mount the carriage). If the driver be of lower rank (than himself) that other receives it. If this be not the case, he should not do so[4]. 35. If the driver be of the lower rank, the other should (still) lay his own

[1] In a carriage the ruler occupied the seat on the left side; the driver avoided this by mounting on the right side. Each carriage was furnished with two straps to assist in mounting; but the use of one was confined to the chief occupant.

[2] But only till the ruler had taken his seat.

[3] This spearman occupied the seat on the right; and took his place as they were about to pass out of the palace precincts.

[4] That is, I suppose, he wishes the driver to let go the strap that he may take hold of it himself.

hand on his (as if to stop him). If this be not the case (and the driver will insist on handing it), the other should take hold of the strap below (the driver's hand).

9. 36. A guest's carriage does not enter the great gate; a woman does not stand up in her carriage; dogs and horses are not taken up to the hall[1].

10. 37. Hence[2], the ruler bows forward to his cross-board to (an old man of) yellow hair; he dismounts (and walks on foot) past the places of his high nobles (in the audience court)[3]. He does not gallop the horses of his carriage in the capital; and should bow forward on entering a village. 38. When called by the ruler's order, though through a man of low rank, a great officer, or (other) officer, must meet him in person. 39. A man in armour does not bow, he makes an obeisance indeed, but it is a restrained obeisance. 40. When the carriage of a deceased ruler is following at his interment, the place on the left should be vacant. When (any of his ministers on other occasions) are riding in (any of) the ruler's carriages, they do not presume to leave the seat on the left vacant, but he who occupies it should bend forward to the cross-board[4]. 41. A charioteer

[1] The carriage halted outside in testimony of the guest's respect. A man stood up in the carriage; a woman, as weaker, did not do so. For horses, see the rules in Part IV, 5. Dogs were too insignificant to be taken up.

[2] We do not see the connexion indicated by the 'hence.'

[3] Leaving the palace, he walks past those places to his carriage. Returning, he dismounts before he comes to them.

[4] The first sentence of this paragraph has in the original only four characters; as P. Zottoli happily renders them in Latin, 'Fausti currus vacante sinistra;' but they form a complete

driving a woman should keep his left hand advanced (with the reins in it), and his right hand behind him[1]. 42. When driving the ruler of a state, (the charioteer) should have his right hand advanced, with the left kept behind and the head bent down. 43. The ruler of a state should not ride in a one-wheeled carriage[2]. In his carriage one should not cough loudly, nor point with his hand in an irregular way. 44. Standing (in his carriage) one should look (forward only) to the distance of five revolutions of the wheels. Bending forward, he should (do so only till he) sees the tails of the horses. He should not turn his head round beyond the (line of the) naves. 45. In the (streets of the) capital one should touch the horses gently with the brush-end of the switch. He should not urge them to their speed. The dust should not fly beyond the ruts. 46. The ruler of a state should bend towards the cross-board when he meets a sacrificial victim, and dismount (in passing) the ancestral temple. A great officer or (other) officer should descend (when he comes to) the ruler's gate, and bend forward to the ruler's horses[3]. 47.

sentence. The left seat was that of the ruler in life, and was now left vacant for his spirit. Khung Ying-tâ calls the carriage in question, 'the Soul Carriage' (hwăn *k*ü). A ruler had five different styles of carriage, all of which might be used on occasions of state; as in the second sentence.

[1] The woman was on the driver's left, and they were thus turned from each other as much as possible.

[2] Common so long ago as now, but considered as beneath a ruler's dignity. So, Wang Tâo. See also the Khang-hsî dictionary under 奇 (*k*î).

[3] The text says that the ruler should dismount before a victim, and bow before the temple. The verbal characters have been misplaced, as is proved by a passage of the commentary on the

(A minister) riding in one of the ruler's carriages must wear his court robes. He should have the whip in the carriage with him, (but not use it). He should not presume to have the strap handed to him. In his place on the left, he should bow forward to the cross-board. 48. (An officer) walking the ruler's horses should do so in the middle of the road. If he trample on their forage, he should be punished, and also if he look at their teeth, (and go on to calculate their age).

Official Book of *K*âu, where one part is quoted. The *Kh*ien-lung editors approve of the alteration made in the version above.

SECTION II. PART I.

1. 1. When a thing is carried with both hands, it should be held on a level with the heart; when with one hand, on a level with the girdle. 2. An article belonging to the son of Heaven should be held higher than the heart; one belonging to a ruler of a state, on a level with it; one belonging to a Great officer, lower than it; and one belonging to an (inferior)

This Part I contains thirty-three paragraphs, which have been arranged in sixteen chapters.

Ch. 1. 1–5, describes the manner of carrying things belonging to superiors, and standing before them. 2. 6, relates to the not calling certain parties by their names. 3. 7, 8, to designations of themselves to be avoided or used by certain other parties. 4. 9, prescribes modesty in answering questions. 5. 10, 11, gives rules about the practice of ceremonies in another state. 6. 12, is a rule for an orphan son. 7. 13, 14, is for a son in mourning for his father, and other points. 8. 15–17, describes certain offences to be punished, and things to be avoided in the palace; and in private. 9. 18, shows us a superior man in building, preparing for sacrifice, and cognate matters; 10. 19–21, a great or other officer, leaving his own state to go to another, and in that other; 11. 22, 23, officers in interviews with one another and with rulers. 12. 24–26, gives the rules for the spring hunting; for bad years; and for the personal ornaments of a ruler, and the music of officers. 13. 27, is about the reply of an officer to a question of his ruler; 14. 28, about a great officer leaving his state on his own business. 15. 29, tells how parties entreat a ruler, and others, not to abandon the state. 16. 30–33, gives rules relating to the king: his appellations, designations of himself, &c.

officer should be carried lower still. 3. When one is holding an article belonging to his lord, though it may be light, he should seem unable to sustain it. In the case of a piece of silk, or a rank-symbol of jade, square or round, he should keep his left hand over it. He should not lift his feet in walking, but trail his heels like the wheels of a carriage. 4. (A minister) should stand (with his back) curved in the manner of a sounding-stone[1], and his girdle-pendants hanging down. Where his lord has his pendants hanging at his side, his should be hanging down in front; where his lord has them hanging in front, his should descend to the ground. 5. When one is holding any symbol of jade (to present it), if it be on a mat, he leaves it so exposed; if there be no mat, he covers it with (the sleeve of) his outer robe[2].

2. 6. The ruler of a state should not call by their names his highest ministers, nor the two noble ladies of her surname, who accompanied his wife to the harem[3]. A Great officer should not call in that way an officer who had been employed by his father, nor

[1] The sounding-stone which the writer had in mind could not have been so curved as it is ordinarily represented to be in pictures, or the minister must have carried himself as Scott in his 'Fortunes of Nigel,' ch. 10, describes Andrew the Scrivener.

[2] P. Zottoli translates this paragraph by:—'Deferens gemmas, si eae habent sustentaculum, tunc apertam indues diploidem; si non habent sustentaculum, tunc clausam.' The text is not easily construed; and the commentaries, very diffuse, are yet not clear.

[3] When a feudal prince married, two other states, of the same surname as the bride, sent each a daughter of their ruling house to accompany her to the new harem. These are 'the noble ladies' intended here.

the niece and younger sister of his wife (members of his harem)[1]. (Another) officer should not call by name the steward of his family, nor his principal concubine[2].

3. 7. The son of a Great officer (of the king, himself equal to) a ruler, should not presume to speak of himself as 'I, the little son[3].' The son of a Great officer or (other) officer (of a state) should not presume to speak of himself as 'I, the inheriting son, so-and-so[4].' They should not so presume to speak of themselves as their heir-sons do. 8. When his ruler wishes an officer to take a place at an archery (meeting), and he is unable to do so, he should decline on the ground of being ill, and say, 'I, so-and-so, am suffering from carrying firewood[5].'

4. 9. When one, in attendance on a superior man, replies to a question without looking round to see (if any other be going to answer), this is contrary to rule[6].

5. 10. A superior man[7], in his practice of cere-

---

[1] The bride (what we may call the three brides in the preceding note) was accompanied by a niece and a younger sister to the harem.

[2] This would be the younger sister of the wife, called in the text 'the oldest concubine.'

[3] So the young king styled himself during mourning.

[4] The proper style for the orphan son of such officer was, 'I, the sorrowing son.'

[5] Mencius on one occasion (I. ii. 2. 1) thus excused himself for not going to court. The son of a peasant or poor person might speak so; others, of higher position, adopted the style in mock humility.

[6] The action of 3ze-lû in Analects 9, 5. 4, is referred to as an instance in point of this violation of rule.

[7] The 'superior man' here must be an officer, probably the

monies (in another state), should not seek to change his (old) customs. His ceremonies in sacrifice, his dress during the period of mourning, and his positions in the wailing and weeping, will all be according to the fashions of his former (state). He will carefully study its rules, and carry them exactly into practice. 11. (But) if he (or his descendants) have been away from the state for three generations, and if his dignity and emoluments be (still) reckoned to him (or his representative) at the court, and his outgoings and incomings are announced to the state, and if his brothers or cousins and other members of his house be still there, he should (continue to) send back word about himself to the representative of his ancestor. (Even) after the three generations, if his dignity and emoluments be not reckoned to him in the court, and his outgoings and incomings are (no longer) announced in the state, it is only on the day of his elevation (to official rank) that he should follow the ways of his new state.

6. 12. A superior man, when left an orphan, will not change his name. Nor will he in such a case, if he suddenly become noble, frame an honorary title for his father[1].

7. 13. When occupied with the duties of mourning, and before the interment of (a parent), (a son) should study the ceremonies of mourning; and after

---

head of a clan or family. Does not the spirit of this chapter still appear in the unwillingness of emigrants from China to forget their country's ways, and learn those of other countries?

[1] The honorary title properly belonged to men of position, and was intended as a condensed expression of their character and deeds. A son in the position described would be in danger of styling his father from his own new standpoint.

the interment, those of sacrifice. When the mourning is over, let him resume his usual ways, and study the pieces of music. 14. When occupied with the duties of mourning, one should not speak of music. When sacrificing, one should not speak of what is inauspicious. In the ruler's court, parties should not speak of wives and daughters.

8. 15. For one to have to dust his (collection of) written tablets, or adjust them before the ruler, is a punishable offence; and so also is it to have the divining stalks turned upside down or the tortoise-shell turned on one side, before him[1]. 16. One should not enter the ruler's gate, (carrying with him) a tortoise-shell or divining stalks, a stool or a staff, mats or (sun-)shades, or having his upper and lower garments both of white or in a single robe of fine or coarse hempen cloth[2]. Nor should he do so in rush sandals, or with the skirts of his lower garment tucked in at his waist, or in the cap worn in the shorter periods of mourning. Nor, unless announcement of it has been made (and permission given), can one take in the square tablets with the written (lists of articles for a funeral), or the frayed sackcloth, or the coffin and its furniture[3]. 17. Public affairs should not be privately discussed.

9. 18. When a superior man, (high in rank), is about to engage in building, the ancestral temple should

[1] These things indicated a want of due preparation and care.

[2] All these things were, for various reasons, considered inauspicious.

[3] A death had in this case occurred in the palace, and the things mentioned were all necessary to prepare for the interment; but still they could not be taken in without permission asked and granted.

have his first attention, the stables and arsenal the next, and the residences the last. In all preparations of things by (the head of) a clan, the vessels of sacrifice should have the first place; the victims supplied from his revenue, the next; and the vessels for use at meals, the last. Those who have no revenue from lands do not provide vessels for sacrifice. Those who have such revenue first prepare their sacrificial dresses. A superior man, though poor, will not sell his vessels of sacrifice; though suffering from cold, he will not wear his sacrificial robes; in building a house, he will not cut down the trees on his grave-mounds.

10. 19. A Great or other officer, leaving his state[1], should not take his vessels of sacrifice with him across the boundary. The former will leave his vessels for the time with another Great officer, and the latter his with another officer. 20. A Great or other officer, leaving his state[2], on crossing the boundary, should prepare a place for an altar, and wail there, looking in the direction of the state. He should wear his upper garment and lower, and his cap, all of white; remove his (ornamental) collar, wear shoes of untanned leather, have a covering of white (dog's-fur) for his cross-board, and leave his horses' manes undressed. He should not trim his nails or beard, nor make an offering at his (spare) meals. He should not say to any one that he is not chargeable with guilt, nor have any of his women approach him. After three months he will return to his usual dress. 21. When a Great or other officer has an interview with the ruler of the state (to whom he has been sent),

[1] And expecting to return. [2] This is in case of exile.

if the ruler be condoling with him on the toils of his journey, he should withdraw on one side to avoid (the honour), and then bow twice with his head to the ground. If the ruler meet him (outside the gate) and bow to him, he should withdraw on one side to avoid (the honour), and not presume to return the bow.

11. 22. When Great or other officers are having interviews with one another, though they may not be equal in rank, if the host reverence (the greater worth of) the guest, he should first bow to him; and if the guest reverence the (greater worth of the) host, he should first bow. 23. In all cases but visits of condolence on occasion of a death, and seeing the ruler of one's state, the parties should be sure to return the bow, each of the other. When a Great officer has an interview with the ruler of (another) state, the ruler should bow in acknowledgment of the honour (of the message he brings); when an officer has an interview with a Great officer (of that state), the latter should bow to him in the same way. When two meet for the first time in their own state, (on the return of one from some mission), the other, as host, should bow in acknowledgment (of the service). A ruler does not bow to a (simple) officer; but if it be one of a different state, he should bow to his bow. A Great officer should return the bow of any one of his officers, however mean may be his rank. Males and females do (? not) bow to one another[1].

[1] The text says that they do bow to one another; but it is evident that *K*ăng Khang-*Kh*ăng understood it as saying the very opposite. Lû Teh-ming had seen a copy which had the character for 'not.'

12. 24. The ruler of a state, in the spring hunting, will not surround a marshy thicket, nor will Great officers try to surprise a whole herd, nor will (other) officers take young animals or eggs. 25. In bad years, when the grain of the season is not coming to maturity, the ruler at his meals will not make the (usual) offering of the lungs[1], nor will his horses be fed on grain. His special road will not be kept clean and swept[2], nor even at sacrifices will his musical instruments be suspended on their stands. Great officers will not eat the large grained millet; and (other) officers will not have music (even) at their drinkings. 26. Without some (sad) cause, a ruler will not let the gems (pendent from his girdle) leave his person, nor a Great officer remove his music-stand, nor an (inferior) officer his lutes.

13. 27. When an officer presents anything to the ruler of his state, and another day the ruler asks him, 'Where did you get that?' he will bow twice with his head to the ground, and afterwards reply[3].

14. 28. When a Great officer wishes to go beyond the boundaries (of the state) on private business, he must ask leave, and on his return must present some offering. An (inferior) officer in similar cir-

[1] The offering here intended was to 'the father of cookery;' see the first note on p. 80. Such offering, under the *K*âu dynasty, was of the lungs of the animal which formed the principal dish. It was not now offered, because it was not now on the ground, even the ruler not indulging himself in such a time of scarcity.

[2] The road was left uncared for that vegetables might be grown on it, available to the poor at such a time.

[3] The offering must have been rare and valuable. The officer had turned aside at the time of presenting it to avoid any compliment from his ruler.

cumstances, must (also) ask leave, and when he comes back, must announce his return. If the ruler condole with them on their toils, they should bow. If he ask about their journey, they should bow, and afterwards reply.

15. 29. When the ruler of a state (is proposing to) leave it, they should (try to) stop him, saying, 'Why are you leaving the altars of the spirits of the land and grain?' (In the similar case of) a Great officer, they should say, 'Why are you leaving your ancestral temple?' In that of an (inferior) officer, they should say, 'Why are you leaving the graves (of your ancestors)?' A ruler should die for his altars; a Great officer, with the host (he commands); an inferior officer, for his charge.

16. 30. As ruling over all, under the sky, (the king) is called 'The son of Heaven[1].' As receiving at court the feudal princes, assigning (to all) their different offices, giving out (the laws and ordinances of) the government, and employing the services of the able, he styles himself, 'I, the one man[2].' 31. When he ascends by the eastern steps, and presides at a sacrifice, if it be personal to himself and his family[3], his style is, 'I, so-and-so, the filial king;' if it be external to himself[4], 'I, so-and-so, the inheriting king.' When he visits the feudal princes[5], and sends to make announcement (of his

[1] Meaning, 'Heaven-sonned; constituted by Heaven its son, its firstborn.'

[2] An expression of humility as used by himself, 'I, who am but a man;' as used of him, 'He who is the one man.'

[3] In the ancestral temple.

[4] At the great sacrifices to Heaven and Earth.

[5] On his tours of inspection.

presence) to the spirits (of their hills and streams), it is said, 'Here is he, so-and-so, who is king by (the grace of) Heaven.' 32. His death is announced in the words, 'The king by (the grace of) Heaven has fallen[1].' In calling back (his spirit), they say, 'Return, O son of Heaven[2].' When announcement is made (to all the states) of the mourning for him, it is said, 'The king by (the grace of) Heaven has gone far on high[3].' When his place is given to him in the ancestral temple, and his spirit-tablet is set up, he is styled on it, 'the god[4].' 33. The son of Heaven, while he has not left off his mourning, calls himself, 'I, the little child.' While alive, he is so styled; and if he die (during that time), he continues to be so designated.

---

[1] A great landslip from a mountain is called păng, which I have rendered 'has fallen.' Like such a disaster was the death of the king.

[2] This ancient practice of calling the dead back is still preserved in China; and by the people generally. There are many references to it in subsequent Books.

[3] The body and animal soul went downward, and were in the grave; the intelligent soul (called 'the soul and spirit,' 'the essential breath') went far on high. Such is the philosophical account of death; more natural is the simple style of the text.

[4] The spirit-tablet was a rectangular piece of wood, in the case of a king, a cubit and two inches long, supposed to be a resting-place for the spirit at the religious services in the temple. *K*ăng says that the deceased king was now treated as 'a heavenly spirit,'—he was now deified. P. Zottoli translates the character here—Tî—by imperator; but there was in those times no 'emperor' in China.

PART II.

1. 1. The son of Heaven has his queen, his helpmates, his women of family, and his ladies of honour. (These) constituted his wife and concubines[1].

2. 2. The son of Heaven appoints the officers of Heaven's institution[2], the precedence among them belonging to the six grandees:—the Grand-governor; the Grand-minister of the ancestral temple; the Grand-historiographer; the Grand-minister of prayers; the Grand-minister of justice; and the Grand-diviner. These are the guardians and superintendents of the six departments of the statutes. 3. The five (administrative) officers of the son of Heaven are:—the minister of instruction; the minister of war; the

---

Part II consists of twenty-one paragraphs, which are distributed in eight chapters.

Ch. 1. 1, describes the members of the royal harem. 2. 2–6, relates to the various ministers and officers appointed by the king, with their departments and duties. 3. 7–10, gives the names and titles, applied to, and used by, the chiefs of regions, provinces, and of the barbarous tribes. 4. 11–16, is about audiences, meetings, and covenants, and the designations of the princes and others in various circumstances. 5. 17, is about the demeanour of the king and others. 6. 18, 19, is about the inmates of the harems, and how they designated themselves. 7. 20, is about the practice of sons or daughters, and various officers, in designating themselves. 8. 21, is about certain things that should not be said of the king, of princes, and of superior men.

[1] See the very different translation of this paragraph by P. Zottoli in his Cursus, iii. p. 653. It is confessed out of place here, should belong to paragraph 18, and is otherwise incomplete.

[2] So described, as 'Powers that be ordained' by the will of Heaven, equally with the king, though under him these grandees are not all in the *K*âu Kwan.

minister of works; the minister of offices; and the minister of crime. These preside over the multitude in (each of) their five charges. 4. The six treasuries of the son of Heaven are under the charge of the superintendent of the land; the superintendent of the woods; the superintendent of the waters; the superintendent of the grass; the superintendent of articles of employment; and the superintendent of wares. These preside over the six departments of their charges. 5. The six manufactures of the son of Heaven are under the care of (the superintendents of) the workers in earth; the workers in metal; the workers in stone; the workers in wood; the workers in (the skins of) animals; and the workers in twigs. These preside over the six departments of stores. 6. When the five officers give in their contributions, they are said to 'present their offerings[1].'

3. 7. Chief among the five officers are the presidents[2], to whom belong the oversight of quarters (of the kingdom). In any message from them transmitted to the son of Heaven, they are styled 'ministers of the son of Heaven.' If they are of the same surname as he, he styles them 'paternal uncles;' if of a different surname, 'maternal uncles.' To the feudal princes, they designate themselves, 'the ancients of the son of Heaven.' Outside (their own states), they are styled 'duke;' in their states, 'ruler.' 8. The head prince in each

[1] Who are the five officers here? Those of paragraph 3? or the feudal dukes, marquises, earls, counts, and barons? Both views have their advocates. The next paragraph favours the second view.

[2] Such presidents were the dukes of *K*âu and Shâo, at the commencement of the *K*âu dynasty.

of the nine provinces, on entering the state of the son of Heaven, is styled 'pastor.' If he be of the same surname as himself, the son of Heaven calls him 'my paternal uncle;' if he be of a different surname, 'my maternal uncle.' Outside (his own state) he is called 'marquis;' in it, 'ruler.' 9. The (chiefs) among (the wild tribes of) the Î on the east, the Tî on the north, the *Z*ung on the west, and the Man on the south, however great (their territories), are called 'counts.' In his own territories each one calls himself, 'the unworthy one;' outside them, 'the king's ancient.' 10. Any of the princelets of their various tracts[1], on entering the state of the son of Heaven, is styled, 'Such and such a person.' Outside it he is called 'count,' and calls himself 'the solitary.'

4. 11. When the son of Heaven stands with his back to the screen with axe-head figures on it, and the princes present themselves before him with their faces to the north, this is called *k*in (the autumnal audience). When he stands at the (usual) point (of reception) between the door and the screen, and the dukes have their faces towards the east, and the feudal princes theirs towards the west, this is called *Kh*âo (the spring audience)[2]. 12. When feudal princes see one another at a place and time not agreed on beforehand, the interview is called 'a meeting.' When they do so in some open place agreed on beforehand, it is called 'an assembly.'

---

[1] It is held, and I think correctly, that these princelets were the chiefs of the wild tribes.

[2] There were other audiences called by different names at the other two seasons.

When one prince sends a great officer to ask about another, it is called 'a message of friendly inquiry.' When there is a binding to mutual faith, it is called 'a solemn declaration.' When they use a victim, it is called 'a covenant.' 13. When a feudal prince is about to be introduced to the son of Heaven, he is announced as 'your subject so-and-so, prince of such-and-such a state.' He speaks of himself to the people as 'the man of little virtue.' 14. If he be in mourning (for his father), he is styled 'the rightful eldest son, an orphan;' if he be taking part at a sacrifice in his ancestral temple, 'the filial son, the prince of such-and-such a state, the prince so-and-so.' If it be another sacrifice elsewhere, the style is, 'so-and-so, prince of such-and-such a state, the distant descendant.' 15. His death is described by the character hung (disappeared). In calling back (his spirit), they say, 'Return, sir so-and-so.' When he has been interred and (his son) is presented to the son of Heaven, the interview, (though special), is said to be 'of the same kind as the usual interviews.' The honorary title given to him is (also) said to be 'after the usual fashion.' 16. When one prince sends a message to another, the messenger speaks of himself as 'the ancient of my poor ruler.'

5. 17. The demeanour of the son of Heaven should be characterised by majesty; of the princes, by gravity; of the Great officers, by a regulated composure; of (inferior) officers, by an easy alertness; and of the common people, by simplicity and humility.

6. 18. The partner of the son of Heaven is called

'the queen;' of a feudal prince, 'the helpmate;' of a Great officer, 'the attendant;' of an (inferior) officer, 'the serving woman;' and of a common man, 'the mate[1].' 19. A duke and (one of) the feudal princes had their helpmate, and their honourable women, (which) were their mates and concubines. The helpmate called herself, before the son of Heaven, 'the aged servant;' and before the prince (of another state), 'the small and unworthy ruler.' To her own ruler she called herself 'the small maid.' From the honourable women downwards, (each member of the harem) called herself 'your handmaid.'

7. 20. To their parents, sons and daughters called themselves by their names. A Great officer of any of the states, entering the state of the son of Heaven, was called 'the officer of such-and-such (a state),' and styled himself 'your subsidiary minister.' Outside (his own state), he was called 'sir;' and in that state, 'the ancient of our poor ruler.' A messenger (to any state) called himself 'so-and-so.'

8. 21. The son of Heaven should not be spoken of as 'going out (of his state)[2].' A feudal prince should not be called by his name, while alive. (When either of these things is done), it is because the superior man[3] will not show regard for wickedness. A prince who loses his territory is named, and also one who extinguishes (another state ruled by) lords of the same surname as himself.

---

[1] Here should come in paragraph 1.

[2] All the states are his. Wherever he may flee, he is still in what is his own land.

[3] This 'superior man' would be an upright and impartial historiographer, superior to the conventions of his order.

Part III.

1. 1. According to the rules of propriety for a minister, he should not remonstrate with his ruler openly. If he have thrice remonstrated and is still not listened to, he should leave (his service). In the service of his parents by a son, if he have thrice remonstrated and is still not listened to, he should follow (his remonstrance) with loud crying and tears. 2. When a ruler is ill, and has to drink medicine, the minister first tastes it. The same is the rule for a son and an ailing parent. The physic of a doctor, in whose family medicine has not been practised for three generations at least, should not be taken.

2. 3. In comparing (different) men, we can only do so when their (circumstances and conditions) are of the same class.

Part III contains twenty paragraphs, which may be comprised in eleven chapters.

Ch. 1. 1, 2, contains the rules for a minister and a son in remonstrating with a ruler or parent; and also in seeing about their medicine when ill. 2. 3, gives the rule in making comparisons. 3. 4, 5, gives the rules to be observed in asking about the age and wealth of different parties from the king downwards. 4. 6–10, is about sacrifices: those of different parties, the sacrificial names of different victims, &c. 5. 11, 12, gives the terms in which the deaths of different men, and of animals, are described. 6. 13, 14, gives the names of near relatives, when they are sacrificed to, and when they are alive. 7. 15, tells how different parties should look at others. 8. 16, 17, is about executing a ruler's orders, and things to be avoided in the conduct of business. 9. 18, is about great entertainments. 10. 19, is about presents of introduction. 11. 20, contains the language used in sending daughters to different harems.

3. 4. When one asks about the years of the son of Heaven, the reply should be—'I have heard that he has begun to wear a robe so many feet long[1].' To a similar question about the ruler of a state, the reply should be—'He is able to attend to the services in the ancestral temple, and at the altars of the spirits of the land and grain,' if he be grown up; and, if he be still young, 'He is not yet able to attend to the services in the ancestral temple, and at the altars of the spirits of the land and grain.' To a question about the son of a Great officer, the reply, if he be grown up, should be—'He is able to drive;' and, if he be still young, 'He is not yet able to drive.' To a question about the son of an (ordinary) officer, the reply, if he be grown up, should be—'He can manage the conveying of a salutation or a message;' and, if he be still young, 'He cannot yet manage such a thing.' To a question about the son of a common man, the reply, if he be grown up, should be—'He is able to carry (a bundle of) firewood;' and, if he be still young, 'He is not yet able to carry (such a bundle).' 5. When one asks about the wealth of the ruler of a state, the reply should be given by telling the extent of his territory, and the productions of its hills and lakes. To a similar question about a Great officer, it should be said, 'He has the lands allotted to him, and is supported by the labour (of his people). He needs not to borrow the vessels or dresses for his sacrificial occasions.' To the

[1] This would seem to imply that the king was still young.

same question about an (ordinary) officer, the reply should be by giving the number of his carriages; and to one about a common man, by telling the number of the animals that he keeps.

4. 6. The son of Heaven sacrifices (or presents oblations) to Heaven and Earth[1]; to the (spirits presiding over the) four quarters; to (the spirits of) the hills and rivers; and offers the five sacrifices of the house,—all in the course of the year. The feudal princes present oblations, each to (the spirit presiding over) his own quarter; to (the spirits of) its hills and rivers; and offer the five sacrifices of the house,—all in the course of the year. Great officers present the oblations of the five sacrifices of the house,—all in the course of the year. (Other) officers present oblations to their ancestors[2]. 7. There should be no presuming to resume any sacrifice which has been abolished (by proper authority)[3], nor to abolish any which has been so established. A sacrifice which it is not proper to offer, and which yet is offered, is called a licentious sacrifice. A licentious sacrifice brings no blessing. 8. The son of Heaven uses an ox of one colour, pure and unmixed; a feudal prince, a fatted ox; a Great officer, an ox selected for the occasion; an (ordinary) officer, a sheep or a pig. 9. The son of an inferior

---

[1] There were various sacrifices to Heaven and also to Earth. The great ones were—that to Heaven at the winter solstice, and that to Earth at the summer solstice. But all the sacrifices to Heaven and Earth were confined to the king.

[2] The king offered all the sacrifices in this paragraph. The other parties only those here assigned to them, and the sacrifices allowed to others of inferior rank. The five sacrifices of the house will come before the reader in Book IV and elsewhere.

[3] The 'proper authority' would be the statutes of each dynasty.

member of the harem cannot offer the sacrifice (to his grandfather or father); if (for some reason) he have to do so, he must report it to the honoured son, (the head of the family). 10. According to the rules for all sacrifices in the ancestral temple, the ox is called 'the creature with the large foot;' the pig, 'the hard bristles;' a sucking-pig, 'the fatling;' a sheep, 'the soft hair;' a cock, 'the loud voice;' a dog, 'the soup offering;' a pheasant, 'the wide toes;' a hare, 'the clear seer;' the stalks of dried flesh, 'the exactly cut oblations;' dried fish, 'the well-considered oblation;' fresh fish, 'the straight oblation.' Water is called 'the pure cleanser;' spirits, 'the clear cup;' millet, 'the fragrant mass;' the large-grained millet, 'the fragrant (grain);' the sacrificial millet, 'the bright grain;' paddy, 'the admirable vegetable;' scallions, 'the rich roots;' salt, 'the saline, briny substance;' jade, 'the admirable jade;' and silks, 'the exact silks.'

5. 11. The death of the son of Heaven is expressed by păng (has fallen); of a feudal prince, by hung (has crashed); of a Great officer, by ȝû (has ended); of an (ordinary) officer, by pû lû (is now unsalaried); and of a common man, by sze (has deceased). (The corpse) on the couch is called shih (the laid-out); when it is put into the coffin, that is called *k*iû (being in the long home). 12. (The death of) a winged fowl is expressed by hsiang (has fallen down); that of a quadruped, by ȝhze (is disorganised). Death from an enemy in fight is called ping (is slain by the sword).

6. 13. In sacrificing to them, a grandfather is

called 'the sovereign grandfather;' a grandmother, 'the sovereign grandmother;' a father, 'the sovereign father;' a mother, 'the sovereign mother;' a husband, 'the sovereign pattern.' 14. While (they are) alive, the names of father (fû), mother (mû), and wife (*kh*î) are used; when they are dead, those of 'the completed one (khâo),' 'the corresponding one (pî),' and 'the honoured one (pin).' Death in old age is called 'a finished course (ȝû);' an early death, 'being unsalaried (pû lû).'

7. 15. The son of Heaven does not look at a person above his collar or below his girdle; the ruler of a state looks at him a little lower (than the collar); a Great officer, on a line with his heart; and an ordinary officer, not from beyond a distance of five paces. In all cases looks directed above to the face denote pride, and below the girdle grief; directed askance, they denote villainy.

8. 16. When the ruler orders (any special business) from a Great officer or (other) officer, he should assiduously discharge it; in their offices speaking (only) of the official business; in the treasury, of treasury business; in the arsenals, of arsenal business; and in the court, of court business. 17. At court there should be no speaking about dogs and horses. When the audience is over, and one looks about him, if he be not attracted by some strange thing, he must have strange thoughts in his mind. When one keeps looking about him after the business of the court is over, a superior man will pronounce him uncultivated. At court the conversation should be according to the rules of propriety;

every question should be so proposed, and every answer so returned.

9. 18. For great entertainments[1] there should be no consulting the tortoise-shell, and no great display of wealth.

10. 19. By way of presents of introduction, the son of Heaven uses spirits of black millet; feudal princes, their symbols of jade; a high minister, a lamb; a Great officer, a goose; an (ordinary) officer, a pheasant; a common man, a duck. Lads should bring their article, and withdraw. In the open country, in the army, they do not use such presents;—a tassel from a horse's breast, an archer's armlet, or an arrow may serve the purpose. For such presents women use the fruits of the hovenia dulcis, or of the hazel tree, strings of dried meat, jujube dates, and chestnuts.

11. 20. In presenting a daughter for (the harem of) the son of Heaven it is said, 'This is to complete the providers of sons for you;' for that of the ruler of a state, 'This is to complete the providers of your spirits and sauces;' for that of a Great officer, 'This is to complete the number of those who sprinkle and sweep for you.'

---

[1] Instead of 'for great entertainments,' P. Zottoli has 'summo sacrificio;' but the *Kh*ien-lung editors decide in favour of the meaning which I have followed.

BOOK II. THE THAN KUNG.

SECTION I. PART I.

1. At the mourning rites for Kung-î *K*ung-ȝze, Than Kung (was there), wearing the mourning cincture for the head. *K*ung-ȝze had passed over his grandson, and appointed one of his (younger) sons as his successor (and head of the family). Than Kung said (to himself), 'How is this? I never heard of such a thing;' and he hurried to Ȝze-fû Po-ȝze at the right of the door, and said, 'How is it that *K*ung-ȝze passed over his grandson, and made a (younger) son his successor?' Po-ȝze replied, '*K*ung-ȝze perhaps has done in this, like others, according to the way of antiquity. Anciently, king Wăn passed over his eldest son Yî-khâo, and appointed king Wû; and the count of Wei passed over his grandson Tun, and made Yen, his (own) younger brother, his successor. *K*ung-ȝze perhaps did also in this according to the way of antiquity.' Ȝze-yû asked Confucius (about the matter), and he said, 'Nay, (the rule is to) appoint the grandson[1].'

On the name and divisions of this Book, see the Introduction, pp. 17, 18.

[1] Important as showing the rule of succession to position and property. We must suppose that the younger son, who had been made the head of the family, was by a different mother, and one whose position was inferior to that of the son, the proper heir who was dead. Of course the succession should have descended

2. In serving his father, (a son) should conceal (his faults), and not openly or strongly remonstrate with him about them; should in every possible way wait on and nourish him, without being tied to definite rules; should serve him laboriously till his death, and then complete the mourning for him for three years. In serving his ruler, (a minister) should remonstrate with him openly and strongly (about his faults), and make no concealment (of them); should in every possible way wait on and nourish him, but according to definite rules; should serve him laboriously till his death, and should then wear mourning for him according to rule for three years. In serving his master, (a learner) should have nothing to do with openly reproving him or with concealing (his faults); should in every possible way wait upon and serve him, without being tied to definite rules; should serve him laboriously till his death, and mourn for him in heart for three years[1].

3. *K*î Wû-ʒze had built a house, at the bottom of the western steps of which was the grave of the Tû family. (The head of that) asked leave to bury (some member of his house) in it, and leave was granted to him to do so. (Accordingly) he entered the house (with the coffin), but did not dare to wail (in the usual fashion). Wû-ʒze said to him, 'To bury in the same grave was not the way of antiquity. It was begun by the duke of *K*âu, and has not been

in the line of the rightful heir. Po-ʒze evaded the point of Than Kung's question; but Confucius did not hesitate to speak out the truth. On other matters which the paragraph might suggest we need not enter.

[1] On differences in the services rendered to a parent, a ruler, and a master or instructor.

changed since. I have granted you the great thing, and why should I not grant the less?' (With this) he ordered him to wail[1].

4. When 3ze-shang's mother died, and he did not perform any mourning rites for her, the disciples of (his father) 3ze-sze asked him, saying, 'Did your predecessor, the superior man, observe mourning for his divorced mother?' 'Yes,' was the reply. (And the disciples went on), 'Why do you not make Pâi also observe the mourning rites (for his mother)?' 3ze-sze said, 'My progenitor a superior man, never failed in pursuing the right path. When a generous course was possible, he took it and behaved generously; and when it was proper to restrain his generosity, he restrained it. But how can I attain to that? While she was my wife, she was Pâi's mother; but when she ceased to be my wife, she was no longer his mother.' It was in this way that the Khung family came not to observe mourning for a divorced mother; the practice began from 3ze-sze[2].

5. Confucius said, 'When (the mourner) bows to (the visitor), and then lays his forehead to the ground,

---

[1] This Wû-3ze was a great-grandson of *K*î Yû, the third son (by an inferior wife) of duke *K*wang of Lû (B.C. 693–662), and the ancestor of the *K*î-sun, one of the three famous families of Lû. It would appear that he had appropriated to himself the burying-ground of the Tû family.

[2] 3ze-shang, by name, Pâi, was the son of 3ze-sze, and great-grandson of Confucius. What is related here is important as bearing on the question whether Confucius divorced his wife or not. If I am correct in translating the original text by 'your predecessor, the superior man,' in the singular and not in the plural, and supposing that it refers to Confucius, the paragraph has been erroneously supposed to favour the view that he did divorce his wife.

this shows the predominance of courtesy. When he lays his forehead to the ground, and then bows (to his visitor), this shows the extreme degree of his sorrow. In the three years' mourning, I follow the extreme (demonstration)[1].'

6. When Confucius had succeeded in burying (his mother) in the same grave (with his father) at Fang, he said, 'I have heard that the ancients made graves (only), and raised no mound over them. But I am a man, who will be (travelling) east, west, south, and north. I cannot do without something by which I can remember (the place).' On this, he (resolved to) raise a mound (over the grave) four feet high. He then first returned, leaving the disciples behind. A great rain came on; and when they rejoined him, he asked them what had made them so late. 'The earth slipped,' they said, 'from the grave at Fang.' They told him this thrice without his giving them any answer. He then wept freely, and said, 'I have heard that the ancients did not need to repair their graves.'

7. Confucius was wailing for 3ze-lû in his court-yard. When any came to condole with him, he bowed to them. When the wailing was over, he made the messenger come in, and asked him all about (3ze-lû's death). 'They have made him into pickle,' said the

[1] In the former case the mourner first thought of his visitor; in the latter, of his dead and his own loss. The bow was made with the hands clasped, and held very low, the head being bowed down to them. They were then opened, and placed forward on the ground, on each side of the body, while the head was stretched forward between them, and the forehead made to touch the ground. In the second case the process was reversed.

messenger; and forthwith Confucius ordered the pickle (in the house) to be thrown away[1].

8. Ȝăng-ȝze said, 'When the grass is old[2] on the grave of a friend, we no (longer) wail for him.'

9. Ȝze-sze said, 'On the third day of mourning, when the body is put into the coffin, (a son) should exercise sincerity and good faith in regard to everything that is placed with it, so that there shall be no occasion for repentance[3]. In the third month when the body is interred, he should do the same in regard to everything that is placed with the coffin in the grave, and for the same reason. Three years are considered as the extreme limit of mourning; but though (his parents) are out of sight, a son does not forget them. Hence a superior man will have a lifelong grief, but not one morning's trouble (from without); and thus on the anniversary of a parent's death, he does not listen to music.'

10. Confucius, being quite young when he was left fatherless, did not know (his father's) grave (Afterwards) he had (his mother's) body coffined in the street of Wû-fû. Those who saw it all thought that it was to be interred there, so carefully was (everything done), but it was (only) the coffining. By inquiring of the mother of Man-fû of Ȝâu, he succeeded

[1] Ȝze-lû had died in peculiar circumstances in the state of Wei, through his hasty boldness, in B.C. 480. It was according to rule that the Master should wail for him. The order about the pickled meat was natural in the circumstances.

[2] The characters in the text imply that a year had passed since the friend's death.

[3] The graveclothes and coverlet. The things placed in the grave with the coffin were many, and will by-and-by come before the reader at length.

in burying it in the same grave (with his father) at Fang[1].

11. When there are mourning rites in the neighbourhood, one should not accompany his pestle with his voice[2]. When there is a body shrouded and coffined in his village, one should not sing in the lanes[2]. For a mourning cap the ends of the ties should not hang down.

12. (In the time of Shun) of Yü they used earthenware coffins[3]; under the sovereigns of Hsiâ, they surrounded these with an enclosure of bricks. The people of Yin used wooden coffins, the outer and inner. They of *K*âu added the surrounding curtains and the feathery ornaments. The people of *K*âu buried those who died between 16 and 19 in the coffins of Yin; those who died between 12 and 15 or between 8 and 11 in the brick enclosures of Hsiâ; and those who died (still younger), for whom no mourning is worn, in the earthenware enclosures of the time of the lord of Yü.

13. Under the sovereigns of Hsiâ they preferred what was black. On great occasions (of mourning), for preparing the body and putting it into the coffin, they used the dusk; for the business of war, they used black horses in their chariots; and the victims which they used were black. Under the Yin dynasty they preferred what was white. On occa-

[1] This paragraph is generally discredited. The *Kh*ien-lung editors say it is not to be relied on.

[2] These two rules are in Book I, i. Pt. iv, 43, page 89.

[3] In a still earlier time, according to the third Appendix of the Yî (vol. xvi, p. 385), they merely covered the body on the ground with faggots.

sions of mourning, for coffining the body, they used the midday; for the business of war they used white horses; and their victims were white. Under the *K*âu dynasty they preferred what was red. On occasions of mourning, they coffined the body at sunrise; for the business of war they used red horses, with black manes and tails; and their victims were red.

14. When the mother of duke Mû of Lû[1] died, he sent to ask Ʒăng-ʒze[2] what (ceremonies) he should observe. Ʒăng-ʒze said, 'I have heard from my father that the sorrow declared in the weeping and wailing, the feelings expressed in the robe of sackcloth with even or with frayed edges, and the food of rice made thick or in congee, extend from the son of Heaven to all. But the tent-like covering (for the coffin) is of (linen) cloth in Wei, and of silk in Lû.'

15. Duke Hsien of Ʒin, intending to put to death his heir-son Shăn-shăng, another son, *Kh*ung-*r*, said to the latter, 'Why should you not tell what is in your mind to the duke?' The heir-son said, 'I cannot do so. The ruler is happy with the lady *K*î of Lî. I should (only) wound his heart.' 'Then,' continued the other, 'Why not go away?' The heir-son replied, 'I cannot do so. The ruler says that I wish to murder him. Is there any state where the (sacredness) of a father is not recognised? Where should I go to obviate this charge?' (At the same time) he sent a man to take leave (for him) of Hû

[1] Duke Mû was marquis of Lû from B.C. 409 to 376.

[2] This was not the disciple of Confucius, but his son, also named Shăn like him; but the characters for the names are different.

Tû, with the message, 'I was wrong in not thinking (more) of your words, my old friend, and that neglect is occasioning my death. Though I do not presume to grudge dying, yet our ruler is old, and his (favourite) son is (quite) young. Many difficulties are threatening the state, and you, old Sir, do not come forth (from your retirement), and consult for (the good of) our ruler. If you will come forth and do this, I will die (with the feeling that I) have received a (great) favour from you.' He (then) bowed twice, laying his head to the ground, after which he died (by his own hand). On this account he became (known in history as) 'the Reverential Heir-son[1].'

16. There was a man of Lû, who, after performing in the morning the ceremony which introduced the 25th month of his mourning, began to sing in the evening. Ʒze-lû laughed at him, (but) the Master said, 'Yû, will you never have done with your finding fault with people? The mourning for three years is indeed long.' When Ʒze-lû went out, the Master said, 'Would he still have had to wait long? In another month (he might have sung, and) it would have been well.'

17. Duke *K*wang of Lû fought a battle with the men of Sung at Shăng-*kh*iû. Hsien Păn-fû was driving, and Pû Kwo was spearman on the right. The horses got frightened, and the carriage was broken, so that the duke fell down[2]. They handed the strap

[1] The marquis of Ʒin, who is known to us as duke Hsien, ruled from B.C. 676 to 651. Infatuated by his love for a barbarian captive from among the Lî, he behaved recklessly and unnaturally to his children already grown up. One very tragical event is the subject of this paragraph.

[2] The text would seem to say here that the army of the duke

of a relief chariot (that drove up) to him, when he said, 'I did not consult the tortoise-shell (about the movement).' Hsien Pân-fû said, 'On no other occasion did such a disaster occur; that it has occurred to-day is owing to my want of courage.' Forthwith he died (in the fight). When the groom was bathing the horses, a random arrow was found (in one of them), sticking in the flesh under the flank; and (on learning this), the duke said, 'It was not his fault;' and he conferred on him an honorary name. The practice of giving such names to (ordinary) officers began from this.

18. Ȝăng-ȝze was lying in his chamber very ill. Yo-*k*ăng Ȝze-*kh*un was sitting by the side of the couch; Ȝăng Yüan and Ȝăng Shăn were sitting at (their father's) feet; and there was a lad sitting in a corner holding a torch, who said, 'How beautifully coloured and bright! Is it not the mat of a Great officer?' Ȝze-*kh*un (tried to) stop him, but Ȝăng-ȝze had heard him, and in a tone of alarm called him, when he repeated what he had said. 'Yes,' said Ȝăng-ȝze, 'it was the gift of *K*î-sun, and I have not been able to change it. Get up, Yüan, and change the mat.' Ȝăng Yüan said, 'Your illness is extreme. It cannot now be changed. If you happily survive till the morning, I will ask your leave and reverently change it.' Ȝăng-ȝze said, 'Your love of me is not equal to his. A superior man loves another on grounds of virtue; a little man's love of another is seen in his indulgence of him. What do I seek for?

was defeated; but the victory was with the duke. See the Ȝo *K*wan, under B.C. 684, and there was a different reading, to which Lû Teh-ming refers on the passage, that leaves us free to translate as I have done.

I want for nothing but to die in the correct way.' They then raised him up, and changed the mat. When he was replaced on the new one, before he could compose himself, he expired.

19. When (a father) has just died, (the son) should appear quite overcome, and as if he were at his wits' end; when the corpse has been put into the coffin, he should cast quick and sorrowful glances around, as if he were seeking for something and could not find it; when the interment has taken place, he should look alarmed and restless, as if he were looking for some one who does not arrive; at the end of the first year's mourning, he should look sad and disappointed; and at the end of the second year's, he should have a vague and unreliant look.

20. The practice in *K*û-lü of calling the (spirits of the dead[1]) back with arrows took its rise from the battle of Shăng-hsing[2]. That in Lû of the women making their visits of condolence (simply) with a band of sackcloth round their hair took its rise from the defeat at Hû-thâi[3].

21. At the mourning for her mother-in-law, the Master instructed (his niece), the wife of Nan-kung Thâo[4], about the way in which she should tie up her hair with sackcloth, saying, 'Do not make it very high, nor very broad. Have the hair-pin of hazel-wood, and the hair-knots (hanging down) eight inches.'

22. Măng Hsien-ʒze, after the service which ended

---

[1] See p. 108, par. 32; p. 112, par. 15; and often, farther on.

[2] In B.C. 638. See the ʒo *K*wan of that year.

[3] See in the ʒo *K*wan, under B.C. 569.

[4] This must have been the Nan Yung of the Analects, V, 1, 2.

the mourning rites, had his instruments of music hung on their stands, but did not use them; and when he might have approached the inmates of his harem, he did not enter it. The Master said, 'Hsien-ʒze is a degree above other men[1].'

23. Confucius, after the service at the close of the one year's mourning, in five days more (began to) handle his lute, but brought no perfect sounds from it; in ten days he played on the organ and sang to it[2].

24. Yû-ʒze, it appears, after the service of the same period of mourning, wore shoes of (white) silk, and had ribbons of (white) silk for his cap-strings[3].

---

[1] The sacrificial service on the final putting off of the mourning dress, and to which reference is here made, was called than (禫). It will come several times before us hereafter. It is celebrated at the end of the 'three years' mourning' for a parent; that is, at the end of twenty-seven months from the death: see the Introduction, p. 49. Wang Sû of the Wei dynasty contended that the mourning was put off at the end of twenty-five months, and the editors of the Khang-hsî dictionary rather approve of his decision: see their note under the character than. I do not think the controversy as to the exact time when the mourning ceased can be entirely cleared up. Confucius praised Hsien-ʒze, because he could not forget his grief, when the outward sign of it was put off.

[2] The sacrificial service here is called by a different name from than; it is hsiang (祥); and in mourning for parents there was 'the small hsiang,' at the end of the first year, and 'the great hsiang,' at the end of the second. The character here probably denotes the mourning for one year, which is not continued beyond that time. Music was not used during any of the period of mourning; and it is doing violence to the text to take hsiang here as equivalent to than.

[3] In condemnation of Yû-ʒze (see Analects, I, 2), as quick to forget his grief.

25. There are three deaths on which no condolence should be offered:—from cowardice; from being crushed (through heedlessness); and from drowning[1].

26. When Ȝze-lû might have ended his mourning for his eldest sister, he still did not do so. Confucius said to him, 'Why do you not leave off your mourning?' He replied, 'I have but few brothers, and I cannot bear to do so.' Confucius said, 'When the ancient kings framed their rules, (they might have said that) they could not bear (to cease mourning) even for (ordinary) men on the roads.' When Ȝze-lû heard this, he forthwith left off his mourning.

27. Thâi-kung was invested with his state, (and had his capital) in Ying-*kh*iû; but for five generations (his descendants, the marquises of *Kh*î) were all taken back and buried in *K*âu. A superior man has said, 'For music, we use that of him from whom we sprang; in ceremonies, we do not forget him to whom we trace our root.' The ancients had a saying, that a fox, when dying, adjusts its head in the direction of the mound (where it was whelped); manifesting thereby (how it shares in the feeling of) humanity.

28. When the mother of Po-yü died, he kept on wailing for her after the year. Confucius heard him, and said, 'Who is it that is thus wailing?' The disciples said, 'It is Lî.' The Master said, 'Ah! (such a demonstration) is excessive.' When Po-yü heard it, he forthwith gave up wailing[2].

---

[1] The third death here must be supplemented, as I have done the second.

[2] Compare paragraph 4, and the note on it. Lî, designated Po-yü, was the son of Confucius, and it has been supposed that his mother had been divorced, so that his protracted wailing for her gave

29. Shun was buried in the wilderness of 3*h*ang-wû, and it would thus appear that the three ladies of his harem were not buried in the same grave with him[1]. *K*i Wû-ȝze said, 'Burying (husband and wife) in the same grave appears to have originated with the duke of *K*âu.'

Part II.

1. At the mourning rites for 3ăng-ȝze, his body was washed in the cook-room[2].

2. During the mourning for nine months[3] one should suspend his (musical) studies. Some one has said, 'It is permissible during that time to croon over the words (of the pieces).'

3. When 3ze-*k*ang was ill, he called (his son), Shăn-hsiang, and addressed him, saying, 'We speak of the end of a superior man, and of the death of

occasion to the rebuke of his father. But while his father was alive, a son did not wail for his mother beyond the year. The passage does not prove that Confucius had divorced his wife, but the contrary; though he might have shown more sympathy with his son's sorrow.

[1] From the first part of the Shû King we know that Shun married the two daughters of Yâo. The mention of 'three' wives here has greatly perplexed the commentators. Where 3hang-wû was is also much disputed.

[2] The proper place for the operation was the principal chamber. There is only conjecture to account for the different place in the case of 3ăng-ȝze.

[3] In relationships of the third degree: as by a man for a married aunt or sister, a brother's wife, a first cousin, &c.; by a wife, for her husband's grand-parents, uncles, &c.; by a married woman, for her uncle and uncle's wife, a spinster aunt, brothers, sisters, &c. See Appendix at the end of this Book.

a small man. I am to-day, perhaps, drawing near to my end (as a superior man).'

4. Ȝăng-ȝze said, 'May not what remains in the cupboard suffice to set down (as the offerings) by (the corpse of) one who has just died?'

5. Ȝăng-ȝze said, 'Not to have places (for wailing) in cases of the five months' mourning[1] is a rule which sprang from the ways in small lanes.' When Ȝze-sze wailed for his sister-in-law, he made such places, and his wife took the lead in the stamping. When Shăn-hsiang wailed for Yen-sze, he also did the same.

6. Anciently, (all) caps were (made) with the seams going up and down them; now the (mourning cap) is made with the seams going round. Hence to have the mourning cap different from that worn on felicitous occasions is not the way of antiquity[2].

7. Ȝăng-ȝze said to Ȝze-sze, '*Khî*, when I was engaged in the mourning for my parents, no water or other liquid entered my mouth for seven days.' Ȝze-sze said, 'With regard to the rules of ceremony framed by the ancient kings, those who would go beyond them should stoop down to them, and those who do not reach them should stand on tip-toe to do so. Hence, when a superior man is engaged in mourning for his parents, no water or other liquid

[1] In relationships of the fourth degree: as by a man for his grand-uncle and his wife, a spinster grand-aunt, a second cousin, &c.; by a wife for her husband's aunt, brother or sister, &c.; by a married woman, for her spinster aunt, married sister, &c. See Appendix.

[2] This paragraph does not seem to contain any lessons of censure or approval, but simply to relate a fact.

enters his mouth for three days, and with the aid of his staff he is still able to rise.'

8. Ȝăng-ȝze said, 'If, in cases coming under the five months' mourning, none be worn when the death is not heard of till after the lapse of that time, then when brethren are far apart there would be no wearing of mourning for them at all; and would this be right?'

9. On the mourning rites for Po-kâo, before the messenger from Confucius could arrive, *Z*an-ȝze had taken it on him, as his substitute, to present a parcel of silks and a team of four horses. Confucius said, 'Strange! He has only made me fail in showing my sincerity in the case of Po-kâo [1].'

10. Po-kâo died in Wei, and news of the event was sent to Confucius. He said, 'Where shall I wail for him? For brethren, I wail in the ancestral temple; for a friend of my father, outside the gate of the temple; for a teacher, in my chamber; for a friend, outside the door of the chamber; for an acquaintance, in the open country, (some distance off). (To wail) in the open country would in this case be too slight (an expression of grief), and to do so in the bed-chamber would be too great a one. But it was by Ȝhze that he was introduced to me. I will wail for him in Ȝhze's.' Accordingly he ordered Ȝze-kung to act as presiding mourner on the occa-

[1] We know almost nothing of the Po-kâo (the eldest son, Kâo) here. From the next paragraph it does not appear that his intimacy with Confucius had been great. *Z*an-ȝze had taken too much on himself. Perhaps the gift was too great, and sympathy cannot well be expressed by proxy. The parcel of silks contained five pieces.

sion, saying to him, 'Bow to those who come because you have a wailing in your house, but do not bow to those who come (simply) because they knew Po-kâo.'

11. Ȝăng-ȝze said, 'When one during his mourning rites falls ill, and has to eat meat and drink spirits, there must be added the strengthening flavours from vegetables and trees;' meaning thereby ginger and cinnamon.

12. When Ȝze-hsiâ was mourning for his son, he lost his eyesight. Ȝăng-ȝze went to condole with him, and said, 'I have heard that when a friend loses his eyesight, we should wail for him.' Thereupon he wailed, and Ȝze-hsiâ also wailed, and said, 'O Heaven, and I have no guilt!' Ȝăng-ȝze was angry, and said, 'Shang, how can you say that you have no guilt?'

'I and you served the Master between the *K*û and the Sze[1]; and (after his death) you retired, and grew old in the neighbourhood of the Western Ho, where you made the people compare you with the Master. This was one offence.

'When you mourned for your parents, you did so in such a way that the people heard nothing of it. This was a second offence.

'When you mourned for your son, you did it in such a way that you have lost your eyesight. This is a third offence. And how do you say that you have no guilt?'

---

[1] These were two streams of Lû, near which was the home of Confucius. I thought of this passage when I crossed at least one of them on my way to *Kh*ü-fû, 'the city of Confucius,' about twelve years ago.

3ze-hsiâ threw down his staff, and bowed, saying, 'I was wrong, I was wrong. It is a long time since I left the herd, and lived apart here.'

13. When a man stops during the daytime in his inner (chamber), it is allowable to come and ask about his illness. When he stops outside during the night, it is allowable to come and condole with him. Hence a superior man, except for some great cause[1], does not pass the night outside (his chamber); and unless he is carrying out a fast or is ill, he does not day and night stop inside.

14. When Kâo 3ze-kâo was engaged with the mourning for his parents, his tears flowed (silently) like blood for three years, and he never (laughed) so as to show his teeth. Superior men considered that he did a difficult thing.

15. It is better not to wear mourning at all than not to have it of the proper materials and fashion. When wearing the sackcloth with the edges even (for a mother), one should not sit unevenly or to one side, nor should he do any toilsome labour, (even) in the nine months' mourning[2].

16. When Confucius went to Wei, he found the mourning rites going on for a man with whom he had formerly lodged. Entering the house, he wailed for him bitterly; and when he came out, he told 3ze-kung to take out the outside horses of his carriage, and present them as his gift. 3ze-kung said, 'At the mourning for any of your disciples, you have

---

[1] 'A great cause:'—such as danger from enemies, or death and the consequent mourning, which, especially in the case of a father's death, required the son thus to 'afflict himself.'

[2] The whole of this paragraph seems overstrained and trivial.

never taken out those horses (for such a purpose); is it not excessive to do so for a man with whom you (merely) lodged?' The Master said, 'I entered a little ago, and wailed for him; and I found (the mourner) so dissolved in grief that my tears flowed (with his). I should hate it, if those tears were not (properly) followed. Do it, my child[1].'

17. When Confucius was in Wei, there was (a son) following his (father's) coffin to the grave. After Confucius had looked at him, he said, 'How admirably did he manage this mourning rite! He is fit to be a pattern. Remember it, my little children.' Ȝze-kung said, 'What did you, Master, see in him so admirable?' 'He went,' was the reply, 'as if he were full of eager affection. He came back (looking) as if he were in doubt.' 'Would it not have been better, if he had come back hastily, to present the offering of repose?' The Master said, 'Remember it, my children. I have not been able to attain to it.'

18. At the mourning rites for Yen Yüan, some of the flesh of the sacrifice at the end of (? two) years was sent to Confucius, who went out and received it. On re-entering he played on his lute, and afterwards ate it[2].

19. Confucius was standing (once) with his dis-

---

[1] We are willing to believe this paragraph, because it shows how the depths of Confucius' sympathy could be stirred in him. He was not in general easily moved.

[2] This paragraph has occasioned a good deal of discussion. The text does not make it clear whether the sacrifice was that at the end of one, or that at the end of two years. Why did Confucius play on his lute? and was he right in doing so?

ciples, having his hands joined across his breast, and the right hand uppermost. They also all placed their right hands uppermost. He said to them, 'You do so from your wish to imitate me, but I place my hands so, because I am mourning for an elder sister.' On this they all placed their left hands uppermost (according to the usual fashion).

20. Confucius rose early (one day), and with his hands behind him, and trailing his staff, moved slowly about near the door, singing—

'The great mountain must crumble;
The strong beam must break;
The wise man must wither away like a plant.'

Having thus sung, he entered and sat down opposite the door. ʒze-kung had heard him, and said, 'If the great mountain crumble, to what shall I look up? If the strong beam break, (on what shall I lean)[1]? If the wise man wither like a plant, whom shall I imitate? The Master, I am afraid, is going to be ill.' He then hastened into the house. The Master said, 'ʒhze, what makes you so late? Under the sovereigns of Hsiâ, the body was dressed and coffined at the top of the steps on the east, so that it was where the deceased used to go up (as master of the house). The people of Yin performed the same ceremony between the two pillars, so that the steps for the host were on one side of the corpse, and those for

[1] The original of this supplement has dropt out of the text. It is found in the 'Narratives of the School;' and in a Corean edition of the Lî *Kî*.

the guest on the other. The people of *K*âu perform it at the top of the western steps, treating the deceased as if he were a guest. I am a man (descended from the house) of Yin[1], and last night I dreamt that I was sitting with the offerings to the dead by my side between the two pillars. Intelligent kings do not arise; and what one under heaven is able to take me as his Master? I apprehend I am about to die.' With this he took to his bed, was ill for seven days, and died.

21. At the mourning rites for Confucius, the disciples were in perplexity as to what dress they should wear. 3ze-kung said, 'Formerly, when the Master was mourning for Yen Yüan, he acted in other respects as if he were mourning for a son, but wore no mourning dress. He did the same in the case of 3ze-lû. Let us mourn for the Master, as if we were mourning for a father, but wear no mourning dress[2].'

22. At the mourning for Confucius, Kung-hsî *Kh*ih made the ornaments of commemoration. As the adornments of the coffin, there were the wall-like curtains, the fan-like screens, and the cords at its sides, after the manner of *K*âu. There were the flags with their toothed edges, after the manner of Yin; and there were the flag-staffs bound with white silk, and

---

[1] It is well known that the Khung family was a branch of the ducal house of Sung, the lords of which were the representatives of the royal house of Shang. The Khungs were obliged to flee from Sung, and take refuge in Lû in the time of the great-grandfather of Confucius.

[2] It is doubtful whether this advice was entirely followed as regards the matter of the dress.

long streamers pendent from them, after the manner of Hsiâ[1].

23. At the mourning for Ȝze-*k*ang, Kung-ming Î made the ornaments of commemoration. There was a tent-like pall, made of plain silk of a carnation colour, with clusters of ants at the four corners, (as if he had been) an officer of Yin[2].

24. Ȝze-hsiâ asked Confucius, saying, 'How should (a son) conduct himself with reference to the man who has killed his father or mother?' The Master said, 'He should sleep on straw, with his shield for a pillow; he should not take office; he must be determined not to live with the slayer under the same heaven. If he meet with him in the market-place or the court, he should not have to go back for his weapon, but (instantly) fight with him.'

'Allow me to ask,' said (the other), 'how one should do with reference to the man who has slain his brother?' 'He may take office,' was the reply, 'but not in the same state with the slayer; if he be sent on a mission by his ruler's orders, though he may then meet with the man, he should not fight with him.'

'And how should one do,' continued Ȝze-hsiâ, 'in the case of a man who has slain one of his paternal cousins?' Confucius said, 'He should not take the lead (in the avenging). If he whom it chiefly concerns is able to do that, he should support him from behind, with his weapon in his hand.'

---

[1] See the full description of a coffin and hearse with all its ornaments in Book XIX.

[2] In honour of the Master, though Ȝze-*k*ang himself could not claim to be descended from the kings of Yin.

25. At the mourning rites for Confucius, his disciples all wore their head-bands of sackcloth, when they went out. For one of their own number, they wore them in the house (when condoling), but not when they went out.

26. Keeping (the ground about) their graves clear of grass was not a practice of antiquity[1].

27. Ȝze-lû said, 'I heard the Master say that in the rites of mourning, exceeding grief with deficient rites is better than little demonstration of grief with superabounding rites; and that in those of sacrifice, exceeding reverence with deficient rites is better than an excess of rites with but little reverence.'

28. Ȝăng-ȝze having gone on a visit of condolence to Fû-hsiâ, the chief mourner had already presented the sacrifice of departure, and removed the offerings. He caused the bier, however, to be pushed back to its former place, and made the women come down (again), after which (the visitor) went through his ceremony. The disciples who accompanied Ȝăng-ȝze asked him if this proceeding were according to rule, and he said, 'The sacrifice at starting is an unimportant matter. And why might he not bring (the bier) back, and let it rest (for a while)?'

The disciples further asked the same question of Ȝze-yû, who said, 'The rice and precious shell are put into the mouth of the corpse under the window (of the western chamber); the slighter dressing is

---

[1] Some would interpret this sentence as if it were—'changing the grave' (易 and not 易); but the *Kh*ien-lung editors say that this practice, originating in geomancy, arose in the time of Ȝin, and was unknown during the Han dynasty.

done inside the door, and the more complete one at (the top of) the eastern steps; the coffining takes place at the guests' place; the sacrifice at starting in the courtyard; and the interment at the grave. The proceedings go on in this way to what is more remote, and hence in the details of mourning there is a constant advance and no receding.' When 3ăng-ȝze heard of this reply, he said, 'This is a much better account than I gave of the going forth to offer the sacrifice of departure.'

29. 3ăng-ȝze went on a visit of condolence, wearing his fur robe over the silk one, while 3ze-yû went, wearing the silk one over his fur. 3ăng-ȝze, pointing to him, and calling the attention of others, said, 'That man has the reputation of being well versed in ceremonies, how is it that he comes to condole with his silk robe displayed over his fur one?' (By-and-by), when the chief mourner had finished the slighter dressing of the corpse, he bared his breast and tied up his hair with sackcloth, on which 3ze-yû hastened out, and (soon) came back, wearing his fur robe over the silk, and with a girdle of sackcloth. 3ăng-ȝze on this said, 'I was wrong, I was wrong. That man was right.'

30. When 3ze-hsiâ was introduced (to the Master) after he had put off the mourning (for his parents), a lute was given to him. He tried to tune it, but could hardly do so; he touched it, but brought no melody from it. He rose up and said, 'I have not yet forgotten my grief. The ancient kings framed the rules of ceremony, and I dare not go beyond them?' When a lute was given to 3ze-*k*ang in the same circumstances, he tried to tune it, and easily

did so; he touched it, and brought melody from it. He rose up and said, 'The ancient kings framed the rules of ceremony, and I do not dare not to come up to them.'

31. At the mourning rites for Hui-ȝze, who had been minister of Crime, Ȝze-yû (went to condole), wearing for him a robe of sackcloth, and a head-band made of the product of the male plant. Wăn-ȝze (the brother of Hui-ȝze), wishing to decline the honour, said, 'You condescended to be the associate of my younger brother, and now further condescend to wear this mourning; I venture to decline the honour.' Ȝze-yû said, 'It is in rule;' on which Wăn-ȝze returned and continued his wailing. Ȝze-yû then hastened and took his place among the officers (of the family); but Wăn-ȝze also declined this honour, and said, 'You condescended to be the associate of my younger brother, and now further condescend to wear for him this mourning, and to come and take part in the mourning rites; I venture to decline the honour.' Ȝze-yû said, 'I beg firmly to request you to allow me (to remain here).'

Wăn-ȝze then returned, and supporting the rightful son to take his position with his face to the south, said, 'You condescended to be the associate of my younger brother, and now you further condescend to wear this mourning for him, and to come and take part in the rites; dare Hû but return to his (proper) place?' Ȝze-yû on this hastened to take his position among the guests[1].

[1] The object of Ȝze-yû in all the movements detailed here is supposed to have been to correct some irregularity in the pro-

32. At the mourning rites for the general Wăn-ȝze, when the first year's mourning was at an end, there came a man from Yüeh[1] on a visit of condolence. The chief mourner, wearing the long robe (assumed on the completion of the first year's mourning), and the cap worn before that, wailed for him in the ancestral temple, with the tears running from his eyes and the rheum from his nose. Ȝze-yû saw it, and said, 'The son of the general Wăn is not far from being (a master of ceremonies). In his observances at this time, for which there is no special rule, his proceeding is correct.'

33. The giving of the name in childhood[2], of the designation at the capping, of the title of elder uncle or younger uncle at fifty, and of the honorary title after death, was the practice of the *K*âu dynasty.

The wearing of the sackcloth head-bands and girdles, to express the real (feeling of the heart); the digging a hole in the middle of the apartment (over which) to wash (the corpse); taking down the (tiles of the) furnace, and placing them at the feet (of it)[3]; and at the interment pulling down (part of the wall on the west of the door of) the ancestral temple, so as to pass by the upper side (of the altar to the spirit)

ceedings on the occasion. *K*ăng Hsüan thinks that Wăn-ȝze was supporting a grandson, instead of Hû, his deceased brother's rightful son, to be the principal mourner, and consequently to succeed Hui-ȝze as his representative and successor. Hui-ȝze and Wăn-ȝze (called Mei-mâu) were of the state of Wei.

[1] A distant state, south of Wû, on the seaboard.

[2] Three months after birth.

[3] To show the deceased had no more occasion for food, and to keep the feet straight, so that the shoes might be put on at the dressing of the corpse.

of the way, and issue by the great gate;—these were the practices of the Yin dynasty, and the learners (in the school of Confucius) followed them.

34. When the mother of Ȝze-liû died, (his younger brother) Ȝze-shih asked for the means (to provide what was necessary for the mourning rites). Ȝze-liû said, 'How shall we get them?' 'Let us sell (the concubines), the mothers of our half-brothers,' said the other. 'How can we sell the mothers of other men to bury our mother?' was the reply; 'that cannot be done.'

After the burial, Ȝze-shih wished to take what remained of the money and other things contributed towards their expenses, to provide sacrificial vessels; but Ȝze-liû said, 'Neither can that be done. I have heard that a superior man will not enrich his family by means of his mourning. Let us distribute it among the poor of our brethren.'

35. A superior man said, 'He who has given counsel to another about his army should die with it when it is defeated. He who has given counsel about the country or its capital should perish with it when it comes into peril.'

36. Kung-shû Wăn-ȝze ascended the mound of Hsiâ, with *K*ü Po-yü following him. Wăn-ȝze said, 'How pleasant is this mound! I should like to be buried here when I die.' *K*ü Po-yü said, 'You may find pleasure in such a thought, but allow me (to go home) before (you say any more about it)[1].'

37. There was a man of Pien who wept like a

[1] Was there anything more than a joke in this reply of Po-yü? The commentators make it out to be a reproof of Wăn-ȝze for wishing to appropriate for his grave the pleasant ground of another.

child on the death of his mother. Confucius said, 'This is grief indeed, but it would be difficult to continue it. Now the rules of ceremony require to be handed down, and to be perpetuated. Hence the wailing and leaping are subject to fixed regulations.'

38. When the mother of Shu-sun Wû-shû died, and the slighter dressing had been completed, the bearers went out at the door (of the apartment) with the corpse. When he had himself gone out at the door, he bared his arms, throwing down also his cap, and binding his hair with sackcloth. 3ze-yû said (in derision), 'He knows the rules[1]!'

39. (When a ruler was ill), the high chamberlain supported him on the right, and the assigner of positions at audiences did so on the left. When he died these two officers lifted (the corpse)[2].

40. There are the husband of a maternal cousin and the wife of a maternal uncle;—that these two should wear mourning for each other has not been said by any superior man. Some one says, 'If they have eaten together from the same fireplace, the three months' mourning[3] should be worn.'

41. It is desirable that affairs of mourning should be gone about with urgency, and festive affairs in a

[1] He should have made his preparations before, and not have had to throw down his cap on the ground.

[2] The text of this paragraph would make the assisting parties to be the chief diviner and the chief archer. The translation is according to an emendation of it from the *K*âu Lî.

[3] Worn in relationships of the fifth degree: as by a man for his great-grand-uncle and his wife, a spinster great-grand-aunt, the son of a mother's brother or sister, &c.; by a wife for her husband's great-great-grand-parents, &c. See Appendix.

leisurely way. Hence, though affairs of mourning require urgency, they should not go beyond the prescribed rules; and though festive affairs may be delayed, they should not be transacted negligently. Hurry therefore (in the former) becomes rudeness, and too much ease (in the latter) shows a small man. The superior man will conduct himself in them as they severally require.

42. A superior man is ashamed[1] to prepare (beforehand) all that he may require in discharging his mourning rites. What can be made in one or two days, he does not prepare (beforehand).

43. The mourning worn for the son of a brother should be the same as for one's own son: the object being to bring him still nearer to one's self. An elder brother's wife and his younger brother do not wear mourning for each other: the object being to maintain the distance between them. Slight mourning is worn for an aunt, and an elder or younger sister, (when they have been married); the reason being that there are those who received them from us, and will render to them the full measure of observance.

Part III.

1. When (the Master) was eating by the side of one who had mourning rites in hand, he never ate to the full.

2. Ȝăng-ȝze was standing with (another) visitor by the side of the door (of their house of entertainment), when a companion (of the other) came hurrying out.

[1] Lest he should seem not to be wishing individuals to live long.

'Where are you going?' said Ȝăng-ȝze; and the man replied, 'My father is dead, and I am going to wail for him in the lane.' 'Return to your apartment,' was the reply, 'and wail for him there.' (The man did so), and Ȝăng-ȝze made him a visit of condolence, standing with his face to the north.

3. Confucius said, 'In dealing with the dead, if we treat them as if they were entirely dead, that would show a want of affection, and should not be done; or, if we treat them as if they were entirely alive, that would show a want of wisdom, and should not be done. On this account the vessels of bamboo (used in connexion with the burial of the dead) are not fit for actual use; those of earthenware cannot be used to wash in; those of wood are incapable of being carved; the lutes are strung, but not evenly; the pandean pipes are complete, but not in tune; the bells and musical stones are there, but they have no stands. They are called vessels to the eye of fancy; that is, (the dead) are thus treated as if they were spiritual intelligences[1].'

---

[1] The *Kh*ien-lung editors say on this:—'To serve the dead as he served the living is the highest reach of a son's feeling. But there is a difference, it is to be presumed, between the ways of spirits and those of men. In the offerings put down immediately after death, there is an approach to treating the deceased as if he were still a (living) man. But at the burial the treatment of him approaches to that due to a (disembodied) spirit. Therefore the dealing with the dead may be spoken of generally as something between that due to a man and that due to a spirit,—a manifestation of the utmost respect without any familiar liberty.' We should like to have something still more definite. Evidently the subject was difficult to those editors, versed in all Chinese lore, and not distracted by views from foreign habits and ways of thinking. How much more difficult must it be for a foreigner to place

4. Yû-ʒze asked ʒăng-ʒze if he had ever questioned the Master about (an officer's) losing his place. 'I heard from him,' was the reply, 'that the officer in such a case should wish to become poor quickly, (just as) we should wish to decay away quickly when we have died.' Yû-ʒze said, 'These are not the words of a superior man.' 'I heard them from the Master,' returned ʒăng-ʒze. Yû-ʒze repeated that they were not the words of a superior man, and the other affirmed that both he and ʒze-yû had heard them. 'Yes, yes,' said Yû-ʒze, 'but the Master must have spoken them with a special reference.' ʒăng-ʒze reported Yû-ʒze's words to ʒze-yû, who said, 'How very like his words are to those of the Master! Formerly, when the Master was staying in Sung, he saw that Hwan, the minister of War, had been for three years having a stone coffin made for himself without its being finished, and said, "What extravagance! It would be better that when dead he should quickly decay away." It was with reference to Hwan, the minister of War, that he said, "We should wish to decay away quickly when we die." When Nan-kung *K*ing-shû returned (to the state), he made it a point to carry his treasures with him in his carriage when he went to court, on which the Master said, "Such an amount of property! It would have been better for him, when he lost his office, to make haste to become poor." It was with reference to Nan-kung *K*ing-shû that he said that

himself 'en rapport' with the thoughts and ways of men, so far removed from him in time and in mental training! The subject of these vessels, which yet were no vessels, will come up again.

"We should work to become poor quickly, when we have lost office."'

Ʒăng-ʒze reported these words of Ʒze-yû to Yû-ʒze, who said, 'Yes, I did say that these were not the words of the Master.' When the other asked him how he knew it, he said, 'The Master made an ordinance in *K*ung-tû that the inner coffin should be four inches thick, and the outer five. By this I knew that he did not wish that the dead should decay away quickly. And formerly, when he had lost the office of minister of Crime in Lû, and was about to go to *K*ing, he first sent Ʒze-hsiâ there, and afterwards *Z*an Yû. By this, I knew that he did not wish to become poor quickly[1].'

5. When *K*wang-ʒze of *Kh*ăn died, announcement of the event was sent to Lû. They did not want to wail for him there, but duke Mû[2] called Hsien-ʒze, and consulted him. He said, 'In old times, no messages from Great officers, not even such as were accompanied by a bundle of pieces of dried meat, went out beyond the boundaries of their states. Though it had been wished to wail for them, how could it have been done? Nowadays the Great officers share in the measures of government throughout the middle states. Though it may be wished not to wail for one, how can it be avoided? I have heard, moreover, that there are two grounds for the wailing; one from love, and one from fear.' The duke said, 'Very well; but how is the thing to be managed in this

[1] Confucius sent those two disciples, that he might get their report of *K*ing (or *Kh*û), and know whether he might himself go and take office there as he wished to do.

[2] B. C. 409–377.

case?' Hsien-ȝze said, 'I would ask you to wail for him in the temple of (a family of) a different surname;' and hereon the duke and he wailed for *K*wang-ȝze in (the temple of) the Hsien family.

6. *K*ung Hsien said to Ȝăng-ȝze, 'Under the sovereigns of the Hsiâ dynasty, they used (at burials) the vessels which were such only to the eye of fancy, intimating to the people that (the dead) had no knowledge. Under the Yin they used the (ordinary) sacrificial vessels, intimating to the people that (the dead) had knowledge. Under the *K*âu we use both, intimating to the people that the thing is doubtful.' Ȝăng-ȝze replied, 'It is not so! What are vessels (only) to the eye of fancy are for the shades (of the departed); the vessels of sacrifice are those of men; how should those ancients have treated their parents as if they were dead?'

7. An elder brother of Kung-shû Mû, by the same mother but a different father, having died, he asked Ȝze-yû (whether he should go into mourning for him), and was answered, 'Perhaps you should do so for the period of nine months.'

A brother, similarly related to Tî Î, having died, he consulted Ȝze-hsiâ in the same way, and was answered, 'I have not heard anything about it before, but the people of Lû wear the one year's mourning in such a case.' Tî Î did so, and the present practice of wearing that mourning arose from his question[1].

8. When Ȝze-sze's mother died in Wei, Liû *Z*o said to him, 'You, Sir, are the descendant of a sage.

[1] Confucius gives a decision against mourning at all in such a case, excepting it were exceptional,—in the 'Narratives of the School,' chapter 10, article 1.

From all quarters they look to you for an example in ceremonies; let me advise you to be careful in the matter.' ȝze-sze said, 'Of what have I to be careful? I have heard that when there are certain ceremonies to be observed, and he has not the necessary means for them, a superior man does not observe them, and that neither does he do so, when there are the ceremonies, and he has the means, but the time is not suitable; of what have I to be careful[1]?'

9. Hsien-ȝze So said, 'I have heard that the ancients made no diminution (in the degrees of mourning on any other ground); but mourned for every one above and below them according to his relationship. Thus Wăn, the earl of Thăng, wore the year's mourning for Măng-hû, who was his uncle, and the same for Măng Phî, whose uncle he was.'

10. Hâu Mû said, 'I heard Hsien-ȝze say about the rites of mourning, that (a son) should certainly think deeply and long about them all, and that (for instance) in buying the coffin he should see that, inside and outside, it be (equally) well completed. When I die, let it be so also with me[2].'

11. ȝăng-ȝze said, 'Until the corpse has its ornaments put on it, they curtain off the hall; and after the slighter dressing the curtain is removed.' *K*ung-liang-ȝze said, 'Husband and wife are at first all in

[1] ȝze-sze's mother, after his father's death, had married again into the Shû family of Wei. What mourning was ȝze-sze now to wear for her? Liû *Z*o seems to have apprehended that he would be carried away by his feelings and would do more than was according to rule in such a case. ȝze-sze's reply to him is not at all explicit.

[2] This record is supposed to be intended to ridicule Hâu Mû for troubling himself as he did.

confusion[1], and therefore the hall is curtained off. After the slighter dressing, the curtain is removed.'

12. With regard to the offerings to the dead at the time of the slighter dressing, Ʒze-yû said that they should be placed on the east (of the corpse). Ʒăng-ʒze said, 'They should be placed on the west, on the mat there at the time of the dressing.' The placing the offerings on the west at the time of the slighter dressing was an error of the later times of Lû.

13. Hsien-ʒze said, 'To have the mourning robe of coarse dolichos cloth, and the lower garment of fine linen with a wide texture, was not (the way of) antiquity.'

14. When Ʒze-phû died, the wailers called out his name Mieh[2]. Ʒze-kâo said, 'So rude and uncultivated are they!' On this they changed their style.

15. At the mourning rites for the mother of Tû *Kh*iâo no one was employed in the house to assist (the son in the ceremonies), which was accounted a careless omission.

16. The Master said, 'As soon as a death occurs, (the members of the family) should change their lamb-skin furs and dark-coloured caps, though they may do nothing more.' The Master did not pay a visit of condolence in these articles of dress.

17. Ʒze-yû asked about the articles to be provided for the mourning rites, and the Master said, 'They should be according to the means of the family.'

---

[1] Settling places for the wailers, &c. But this explanation is deemed unsatisfactory.

[2] The name was used only in calling the spirit back immediately after death; the wailing was a subsequent thing.

Ʒze-yû urged, 'How can a family that has means and one that has not have things done in the same way?' 'Where there are means,' was the reply, 'let there be no exceeding the prescribed rites. If there be a want of means, let the body be lightly covered from head to foot, and forthwith buried, the coffin being simply let down by means of ropes. Who in such a case will blame the procedure?'

18. Păn, superintendent of officers' registries, informed Ʒze-yû of his wish to dress his dead on the couch. 'You may,' said Ʒze-yû. When Hsien-ʒze heard of this, he said, 'How arrogant is the old gentleman! He takes it on himself to allow men in what is the proper rule[1].'

19. At the burial of his wife, duke Hsiang of Sung[2] placed (in the grave) a hundred jars of vinegar and pickles. Ʒăng-ʒze said, 'They are called "vessels only to the eye of fancy," and yet he filled them!'

20. After the mourning rites for Măng Hsien-ʒze, the chief minister of his family made his subordinates return their money-offerings to all the donors. The Master said that such a thing was allowable.

21. About the reading of the list of the material contributions (towards the service of a funeral), Ʒăng-

[1] On death, the body was lifted from the couch, and laid on the ground. When there was no response to the recalling of the spirit, it was returned to the couch and dressed. A practice seems to have arisen of slightly dressing it on the ground, which Păn did not wish to follow. Ʒze-yû ought to have told him that his proposal was according to rule; whereas he expressed his permission of it,—a piece of arrogance, which Hsien-ʒze condemned.

[2] Hsiang died in B. C. 637.

ʒze said, 'It is not an ancient practice; it is a second announcement (to the departed)[1]!'

22. When *Kh*ăng-ʒze Kâo was lying ill, *Kh*ing Î went in to see him, and asked his (parting) commands, saying, 'Your disease, Sir, is severe. If it should go on to be the great illness, what are we to do?' Ʒze-kâo said, 'I have heard that in life we should be of use to others, and in death should do them no harm. Although I may have been of no use to others during my life, shall I do them any harm by my death? When I am dead, choose a piece of barren ground, and bury me there.'

23. Ʒze-hsiâ asked the Master (how one should deport himself) during the mourning for the ruler's mother or wife, (and the reply was), 'In sitting and stopping with others, in his conversation, and when eating and drinking, he should appear to be at ease[2].'

24. When a stranger-visitor arrived, and had nowhere to lodge, the Master would say, 'While he is alive, let him lodge with me. Should he die, I will see to his coffining[3].'

25. Kwo-ʒze Kâo[4] said, 'Burying means hiding

---

[1] The contributions had been announced by the bier, as if to the departed, and a record of them made. To read the list, as is here supposed, as the procession was about to set forth, was a vain-glorious proceeding, which Ʒăng-ʒze thus derided.

[2] The supplements in this paragraph are from the 'Narratives of the School.' Some contend that the whole should be read as what Ʒze-hsiâ said, and that the Master gave him no reply, disapproving of his sentiments.

[3] This paragraph, like the preceding, appears in rather a different form in the 'Narratives of the School.'

[4] Kwo-ʒze Kâo was the same as the *Kh*ăng-ʒze Kâo of par. 22. Kwo was the surname, and *Kh*ăng the posthumous title. It is difficult to decide between Kwo-ʒze Kâo and Kwo Ʒze-kâo.

away; and that hiding (of the body) is from a wish that men should not see it. Hence there are the clothes sufficient for an elegant covering; the coffin all round about the clothes; the shell all round about the coffin; and the earth all round about the shell. And shall we farther raise a mound over the grave and plant it with trees?'

26. At the mourning for Confucius, there came a man from Yen to see (what was done), and lodged at 3ze-hsiâ's. 3ze-hsiâ said to him, 'If it had been for the sage's conducting a burial, (there would have been something worthy to see); but what is there to see in our burying of the sage? Formerly the Master made some remarks to me, saying, "I have seen some mounds made like a raised hall; others like a dyke on a river's bank; others like the roof of a large house; and others in the shape of an axe-head." We have followed the axe-shape, making what is called the horse-mane mound. In one day we thrice shifted the frame-boards, and completed the mound. I hope we have carried out the wish of the Master.'

27. Women (in mourning) do not (change) the girdle made of dolichos fibre.

28. When new offerings (of grain or fruits) are presented (beside the body in the coffin), they should be (abundant), like the offerings on the first day of the moon.

29. When the interment has taken place, everyone should make a change in his mourning dress.

30. The gutters of the tent-like frame over the coffin should be like the double gutters of a house.

31. When a ruler succeeds to his state, he makes

his coffin, and thereafter varnishes it once a year, keeping it deposited away.

32. Calling the departed back; plugging the teeth open; keeping the feet straight; filling the mouth; dressing the corpse; and curtaining the hall:—these things are set about together. The uncles and elder cousins give their charges to those who are to communicate the death (to friends).

33. The (soul of a deceased) ruler is called back in his smaller chambers, and the large chamber; in the smaller ancestral temples and in the great one: and at the gate leading to the court of the external audience, and in the suburbs all round.

34. Why do they leave the offerings of the mourning rites uncovered? May they do so with the flesh of sacrifice[1]?

35. When the coffining has taken place, in ten days after, provision should be made for the materials (for the shell), and for the vessels to the eye of fancy.

36. The morning offerings should be set forth (beside the body) at sunrise; the evening when the sun is about to set.

37. In mourning for a parent, there is no restriction to (set) times for wailing. If one be sent on a mission, he must announce his return (to the spirits of his departed).

38. After the twelfth month of mourning, the (inner) garment should be of white silk, with a yellow

[1] This short paragraph is difficult to construe. The *Kh*ien-lung editors seem to approve of another interpretation of it; but even that is not without its difficulties. The flesh of sacrifice, it is said, left uncovered, would become unfit for use or to be sold.

lining, and having the collar and the edges of the cuffs of a light purple. The waist-band should be of dolichos cloth; the shoes of hempen string, without the usual ornaments at the points; and the ear-plugs of horn. The lining of the deer's-fur (for winter) should be made broader and with longer cuffs, and a robe of thin silk may be worn over it[1].

39. When (a parent's) corpse has been coffined, if the son hear of mourning going on for a cousin at a distance, he must go (to condole), though the relationship would only require the three months' mourning. If the mourning be for a neighbour, who is not a relative, he does not go.

At (the mourning) for an acquaintance, he must pay visits of condolence to all his brethren, though they might not have lived with him.

40. The coffin of the son of Heaven is fourfold. The hides of a water-buffalo and a rhinoceros, overlapping each other, (form the first), three inches in thickness. Then there is a coffin of Î wood[2], and there are two of the Rottlera. The four are all complete enclosures. The bands for the (composite) coffin are (five); two straight, and three cross; with a double wedge under each band (where it is on the edge).

---

[1] The outer sackcloth remained unchanged; but inside it was now worn this robe of white silk, a good deal ornamented. Inside this and over the deer's-fur in winter might be worn another robe of thin silk, through which the fur was seen. Inside the fur was what we should call the shirt, always worn.

[2] Tracing the Î tree, through the dictionaries from synonym to synonym, we come at last to identify it with the 'white aspen;' whether correctly or not I do not know.

The shell is of cypress wood, in pieces six cubits long, from the trunk near the root.

41. When the son of Heaven is wailing for a feudal prince, he wears the bird's-(head) cap[1], a headband of sackcloth, and black robes. Some one says, 'He employs an officer to wail for him.' While so engaged, he has no music at his meals.

42. When the son of Heaven is put into his coffin it is surrounded with boards plastered over, and (rests on the hearse), on whose shafts are painted dragons, so as to form a (kind of) shell. Then over the coffin is placed a pall with the axe-heads figured on it. This being done, it forms a plastered house. Such is the rule for (the coffining of) the son of Heaven[2].

43. It is only at the mourning rites for the son of Heaven that the feudal princes are arranged for the wailing according to their different surnames.

44. Duke Âi of Lû eulogised Khung *Kh*iû in the words, 'Heaven has not left the old man, and there is no one to assist me in my place. Oh! Alas! Nî-fû[3]!'

45. When a state had lost a large tract of terri-

---

[1] This cap, it is said, was of leather, of the dark colour of a male sparrow's head. Hence its name.

[2] See Book XIX.

[3] Confucius' death took place on the 18th of the fourth month of duke Âi's 16th year, B.C. 479. The eulogy is given somewhat differently in the Ȝo *K*wan under that year: 'Compassionate Heaven vouchsafes me no comfort, and has not left me the aged man, to support me, the One man, on my seat. Dispirited I am, and full of distress. Woe is me! Alas! O Nî-fû. There is no one now to be a rule to me!' *Kh*iû was Confucius' name, and *K*ung-nî his designation! After this eulogy, Nî-fû was for a time his posthumous title.

tory with its cities, the highest and other ministers, and the Great and other officers, all wailed in the grand ancestral temple, in mourning caps, for three days; and the ruler (for the same time) had no full meal with music. Some one says, 'The ruler has his full meals and music, but wails at the altar to the spirit of the land.'

46. Confucius disliked those who wailed in the open fields[1].

47. (A son) who has not been in office should not presume to give away anything belonging to the family. If he should have to do so[2], he ought to have the order of his father or elder brother for the act.

48. When the (ordinary) officers[3] are all entered, then (the chief mourner and all the others) fall to their leaping, morning and evening.

49. After the service on the conclusion of the twenty-fourth month of mourning, the plain white cap is assumed. In that month the service on leaving off mourning is performed, and after another month (the mourners) may take to their music[4].

50. The ruler may confer on any officer the small curtain (as a pall for his father's coffin).

---

[1] It was the rule to mourn in the open country for an acquaintance. See p. 134. There must have been some irregularity in the practice adverted to.

[2] That is, supposing him to have been in office; though some suppose that the necessity might arise, even in the case of a son who had not been in office.

[3] Of course the higher officers must also be there. This refers to the mourning rites for a ruler.

[4] See the note on page 130. It is difficult, notwithstanding all the references to it, to say definitely in what month the than sacrifice was performed.

SECTION II. PART I.

1. (At the funeral of) a ruler's eldest son by his acknowledged wife, who has died under age, there are three (small) carriages (with the flesh of sacrifice to be put in the grave). At that of an eldest son by one of his concubines, dying under age, there is one such carriage; as at the funeral of the eldest rightful son of a Great officer in the same circumstances[1].

2. At the mourning rites for a feudal lord, his chief officers who had received their appointments directly from him, carried their staffs.

3. When a Great officer of a state was about to be buried, its ruler (went to) condole with (his son) in the hall where the coffin was. When it was

[1] This refers to a strange custom which was practised at the burial of men of rank, or of others who were treated as such, as in the cases here. 'The carriages employed in it,' says Ying-tâ, 'were very small. When the funeral car was about to set off from the temple, and all to be done at the grave was arranged, they took portions of the bodies which had supplied the offerings put down by the coffin, broke them in small pieces, wrapped them up, and placed them in these carriages, to be conveyed after the car. At the grave the little bundles were placed one by one, inside the outer shell at its four corners.' The number of these small carriages varied according to the rank of the deceased. We shall find the practice mentioned again and again. It is not easy for a foreigner fully to understand it, and I have found great haziness in the attempts of native scholars to explain it. 'The eldest sons' would have died between sixteen and nineteen.

being taken out, he ordered some one to draw the (bier-carriage) for him. This moved on for three paces and stopped; in all for three times; after which the ruler retired. The same proceeding was gone through, when the bier entered the ancestral temple, and also at the place of (special) grief[1].

4. Men of fifty, who had no carriage, did not make visits of condolence beyond the boundaries (of their states).

5. When *K*î Wû-ȝze was lying ill in his chamber, *K*iâo Kû entered and appeared before him without taking off the mourning with its even edges (which he happened to wear). 'This practice,' said he, 'has nearly fallen into disuse. But it is only at the gate of the ruler that an officer should take off such mourning as I have on.' Wû-ȝze replied, 'Is it not good that you should act thus[2]? A superior man illustrates the smallest points (of propriety).'

At the mourning rites for Wû-ȝze, Ȝăng Tien leant against his gate and sang[3].

6. If a Great officer pay a visit of condolence

---

[1] Where visitors had been lodged during the mourning rites, outside the great gate.

[2] Wû-ȝze was the posthumous title of *K*i-sun Suh, the principal minister of Lû in the time of duke Hsiang (B.C. 572–543). He was arrogant, and made other officers pay to him the same observances as to the ruler; but he was constrained to express his approval of the bold rectitude of *K*iâo.

[3] This is added by the writer, and implies a condemnation of Ȝăng Tien, who did not know how to temper his censure of the minister, as *K*iâo Kû had done. But there must be an error in the passage. Tien (the father of Ȝăng Shăn) could have been but a boy when Wû-ȝze died.

(to an ordinary officer), and he arrive when (the latter) is occupied with the business of the occasion, an apology is made (for not coming to the gate to receive him).

7. When one has paid a visit of condolence, he should not on the same day show manifestations of joy[1].

8. A wife should not go beyond the boundaries of the state on a visit of condolence.

9. On the day when he has made a visit of condolence, one should not drink spirits nor eat flesh.

10. When one pays a visit of condolence, and the arrangements for the funeral are going on, he should take hold of the ropes (attached to the car). Those who follow to the grave should take hold of those attached to the coffin.

11. During the mourning rites, if the ruler send a message of condolence, there must be some one to acknowledge it, by bowing to the messenger. A friend, or neighbour, or even a temporary resident in the house, may perform the duty. The message is announced in the words:—'Our unworthy ruler wishes to take part in your (sad) business.' The chief mourner responds:—'We acknowledge your presence with his message[2].'

12. When a ruler meets a bier on the way, he must send some one to present his condolences (to the chief mourner).

---

[1] Or it may be, 'should not have music;' toning one of the characters differently.

[2] It is supposed that the deceased had left no son to preside at the mourning rites.

13. At the mourning rites for a Great officer, a son by an inferior wife should not receive the condolences[1].

14. On the death of his wife's brother who was the successor of their father, (the husband) should wail for him in (the court of) the principal chamber[2]. He should appoint his (own) son to preside (on the occasion). With breast unbared and wearing the cincture instead of the cap, he wails and leaps. When he enters on the right side of the gate, he should make some one stand outside it, to inform comers of the occasion of the wailing; and those who were intimate (with the deceased) will enter and wail. If his own father be in the house, the wailing should take place (before) his wife's chamber. If (the deceased) were not the successor of his father, the wailing should take place before a different chamber.

15. If a man have the coffin of a parent in his hall, and hear of mourning going on for a cousin of the same surname at a distance, he wails for him in a side apartment. If there be no such apartment, he should wail in the court on the right of the gate. If the deceased's body be in the same state, he should go to the place, and wail for him there.

16. When Ȝze-*k*ang died, Ȝăng-ȝze was in mourning for his mother, and went in his mourning dress

[1] But if there be no son by the wife proper, the oldest son by an inferior wife may receive the condolences. See the *Kh*ien-lung editors in loc.

[2] For some reason or other he has not gone to the house of the deceased, to wail for him there.

to wail for him. Some one said, 'That dress of sackcloth with its even edges is not proper for a visit of condolence.' 3ăng-ȝze replied, 'Am I condoling (with the living)?'

17. At the mourning rites for Yû *Z*o, duke Tâo[1] came to condole. 3ze-yû received him, and introduced him by (the steps on) the left[2].

18. When the news was sent from *Kh*î of the mourning for the king's daughter who had been married to the marquis, duke *K*wang of Lû wore the nine months' mourning for her. Some have said, 'She was married from Lû[3]; therefore he wore the same mourning for her as for a sister of his own.' Others have said, 'She was his mother's mother, and therefore he wore it.'

19. At the mourning rites for duke Hsien of 3in, duke Mû of *Kh*in sent a messenger to present his condolences to Hsien's son *Kh*ung-*r* (who was then an exile), and to add this message:—'I have heard that a time like this is specially adapted to the

---

[1] B.C. 467–431. Yû *Z*o had been a disciple of Confucius, and here we find the greater follower of the sage, 3ze-yû, present and assisting at the mourning rites for him.

[2] That is, the prince went up to the hall by the steps on the east, set apart for the use of the master and father of the house. But the ruler was master everywhere in his state, as the king was in his kingdom. An error prevailed on this matter, and 3ze-yû took the opportunity to correct it.

[3] That is, she had gone from the royal court to Lû, and been married thence under the superintendence of the marquis of that state, who also was of the royal surname. This was a usual practice in the marriage of kings' daughters; and it was on this account the lord of the officiating state wore mourning for them. The relationship assigned in the next clause is wrong; and so would have been the mourning mentioned, if it had been correct.

losing of a state, or the gaining of a state. Though you, my son, are quiet here, in sorrow and in mourning, your exile should not be allowed to continue long, and the opportunity should not be lost. Think of it and take your measures, my young son.' *Kh*ung-*r* reported the words to his maternal uncle Fan, who said, 'My son, decline the proffer. An exile as you are, nothing precious remains to you; but a loving regard for your father is to be considered precious. How shall the death of a father be told? And if you take advantage of it to seek your own profit, who under heaven will be able to give a good account of your conduct? Decline the proffer, my son.'

On this the prince replied to his visitor:—'The ruler has kindly (sent you) to condole with his exiled servant. My person in banishment, and my father dead, so that I cannot take any share in the sad services of wailing and weeping for him;—this has awakened the sympathy of the ruler. But how shall the death of a father be described? Shall I presume (on occasion of it) to think of any other thing, and prove myself unworthy of your ruler's righteous regard?' With this he laid his head to the ground, but did not bow (to the visitor); wailed and then arose, and after he had risen did not enter into any private conversation with him.

Ȝze-hsien reported the execution of his commission to duke Mû, who said, 'Truly virtuous is this prince *Kh*ung-*r*. In laying his forehead on the ground and not bowing (to the messenger), he acknowledged that he was not his father's successor, and therefore he did not complete the giving of thanks. In wailing before he rose, he showed how he loved his father. In having no private conversation after he arose, he showed how he put from him the thought of gain[1].'

20. The keeping the curtain up before the coffin with the corpse in it was not a custom of antiquity. It originated with the wailing of *K*ing *K*iang for Mû-po[2].

21. The rites of mourning are the extreme expression of grief and sorrow. The graduated reduction of that expression in accordance with the natural changes (of time and feeling) was made by the superior men, mindful of those to whom we owe our being[3].

22. Calling (the soul) back is the way in which love receives its consummation, and has in it the mind which is expressed by prayer. The looking for it to return from the dark region is a way of seeking for it among the spiritual beings. The turning the face to the north springs from the idea of its being in the dark region.

23. Bowing to the (condoling) visitor, and laying the forehead on the ground are the most painful demonstrations of grief and sorrow. The laying the forehead in the ground is the greatest expression of the pain (from the bereavement).

---

[1] Fully to understand this paragraph, one must know more particulars of the history of *K*h*ung-r*, and his relations with his father and the duke of *K*h*in, than can be given here in a note. He became the ablest of the five chiefs of the *K*h*un *K*h*iû period.

[2] This was a prudish action of the young widow, but it changed an old custom and introduced a new one.

[3] This has respect to the modifications adopted in regulating the mourning rites for parents.

24. Filling the mouth with rice uncooked and fine shells arises from a feeling which cannot bear that it should be empty. The idea is not that of giving food; and therefore these fine things are used.

25. The inscription[1] forms a banner to the eye of fancy. Because (the person of) the deceased can no longer be distinguished, therefore (the son) by this flag maintains the remembrance of him. From his love for him he makes this record. His reverence for him finds in this its utmost expression.

26. The first tablet for the spirit (with this inscription on it) serves the same purpose as that (subsequently) placed in the temple, at the conclusion of the mourning rites. Under the Yin dynasty the former was still kept. Under the *K*âu, it was removed[1].

27. The offerings to the unburied dead are placed in plain unornamented vessels, because the hearts

[1] This inscription contained the surname, name, and rank of the deceased. It was at first written, I suppose, on a strip of silk, and fastened up under the eaves above the steps on the east. In the meantime a tablet of wood called *Kh*ung, the first character in the next paragraph, and for which I have given 'The first tablet for the spirit,' was prepared. The inscription was transferred to it, and it was set up on or by the coffin, now having the body in it, and by and by it was removed to the east of the coffin pit, where it remained till after the interment.

The observances in this paragraph and the next remain substantially the same at the present day. 'The bier,' writes Wang Thâo, 'is placed in the apartment, and the tablet with the inscription, as a resting-place for the spirit, is set up, while the offerings are set forth near it morning and evening. After the interment this tablet is burned, and the permanent tablet (神主) is made, before which the offerings are presented at the family sacrifices from generation to generation. Thus "the dead are served as the living have been."'

of the living are full of unaffected sorrow. It is only in the sacrifices (subsequent to the interment), that the principal mourner does his utmost (in the way of ornament). Does he know that the spirit will enjoy (his offerings)? He is guided only by his pure and reverent heart.

28. Beating the breast (by the women), and leaping (by the men) are extreme expressions of grief. But the number of such acts is limited. There are graduated rules for them.

29. Baring the shoulders and binding up the hair (with the band of sackcloth) are changes, (showing) the excited feeling which is a change in the grief. The removal of the (usual) ornaments and elegancies (of dress) has manifold expression, but this baring of the shoulders and the sackcloth band are the chief. But now the shoulders are quite bared, and anon they are covered (with a thin garment);—marking gradations in the grief.

30. At the interment they used the cap of plain white (silk), and the headband of dolichos fibre; thinking these more suitable for their intercourse with (the departed) now in their spirit-state. The feeling of reverence had now arisen. The people of *K*âu use the pien cap at interments; those of Yin used the hsü[1].

---

[1] The 'Three Rituals Explained' (三禮通釋), ch. 238, give the figures of these caps thus:—

The hsü 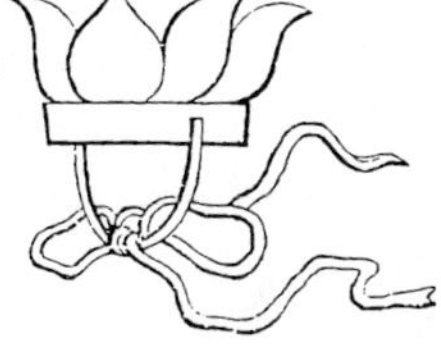 The pien 

31. The gruel of the chief mourner (the son), the presiding wife[1], and the steward of the family (of a Great officer) is taken by them at the order of the ruler lest they should get ill.

32. On returning (from the grave) to wail, (the son) should ascend the hall (of the ancestral temple);—returning to the place where (the deceased) performed his rites. The presiding wife should enter the chamber;—returning to the place where he received his nourishment.

33. Condolences should be presented (to the son) when he returns (from the grave) and is wailing, at which time his grief is at its height. He has returned, and (his father) is not to be seen; he feels that he has lost him. (His grief is) then most intense. Under the Yin, they presented condolences immediately at the grave; under the *K*âu, when the son had returned and was wailing. Confucius said, 'Yin was too blunt; I follow *K*âu.'

34. To bury on the north (of the city), and with the head (of the dead) turned to the north, was the common practice of the three dynasties:—because (the dead) go to the dark region.

35. When the coffin has been let down into the grave, the chief mourner presents the (ruler's) gifts (to the dead in the grave[2]), and the officer of prayer (returns beforehand) to give notice of the sacrifice of repose[3] to him who is to personate the departed.

---

[1] This would be the wife of the deceased, or the wife of his son.

[2] These were some rolls of purplish silks, sent by the ruler as his parting gifts, when the hearse-car reached the city gate on its way to the grave.

[3] Where was the spirit of the departed now? The bones and

36. When he has returned and wailed, the chief mourner with the (proper) officer inspects the victim. (In the meantime other) officers have set out a stool and mat with the necessary offerings on the left of the grave[1]. They return, and at midday the sacrifice of repose is offered[2].

37. The sacrifice is offered on the day of interment; they cannot bear that the departed should be left a single day (without a place to rest in).

38. On that day the offerings, (previously) set forth (by the coffin), are exchanged for the sacrifice of repose. The (continuous) wailing is ended, and they say, 'The business is finished.'

39. On that day the sacrifices of mourning were exchanged for one of joy. The next day the service of placing the spirit-tablet of the departed next to that of his grandfather was performed.

40. The change to an auspicious sacrifice took place on that day, and the placing the tablet in its place on the day succeeding:—(the son) was unable

---

flesh had returned to the dust, but the soul-spirit might be anywhere (魂氣無所不之[=至]). To afford it a resting-place, the permanent tablet was now put in the shrine, and this sacrifice of repose (虞[=安]祭) was offered, so that the son might be able to think that his father was never far from him. For a father of course the personator was a male; for a mother, a female; but there are doubts on this point.

[1] For the spirit of the ground.

[2] If the grave were too far distant to allow all this to be transacted before midday, then the sacrifice was performed in the chamber where the coffin had rested. So says Wang Thâo on the authority of *Z*ăn Yî-shăng (任翼聖).

to bear that (the spirit of the departed) should be a single day without a resting-place.

41. Under the Yin, the tablet was put in its place on the change of the mourning at the end of twelve months; under the *K*âu, when the (continuous) wailing was over. Confucius approved the practice of Yin.

42. When a ruler went to the mourning rites for a minister, he took with him a sorcerer with a peach-wand, an officer of prayer with his reed-(brush), and a lance-bearer,—disliking (the presence of death), and to make his appearance different from (what it was at any affair of) life[1]. In the mourning rites it is death that is dealt with, and the ancient kings felt it difficult to speak of this[2].

43. The ceremony in the mourning rites of (the coffined corpse) appearing in the court (of the ancestral temple) is in accordance with the filial heart of the deceased. He is (supposed to be) grieved at leaving his chamber, and therefore he is brought to the temple of his fathers, and then (the coffin) goes on its way.

Under the Yin, the body was thus presented and then coffined in the temple; under the *K*âu the interment followed immediately after its presentation (in the coffin).

44. Confucius said, 'He who made the vessels

---

[1] When visiting a minister when alive, the ruler was accompanied by the lance-bearer, but not by those other officers;—there was the difference between life and death.

[2] I suspect that the sorcerer and exorcist were ancient superstitions, not established by the former kings, but with which they did not care to interfere by saying anything about them.

which are so (only) in imagination, knew the principles underlying the mourning rites. They were complete (to all appearance), and yet could not be used. Alas! if for the dead they had used the vessels of the living, would there not have been a danger of this leading to the interment of the living with the dead?'

45. They were called 'vessels in imagination,' (the dead) being thus treated as spiritual intelligences. From of old there were the carriages of clay and the figures of straw,—in accordance with the idea in these vessels in imagination. Confucius said that the making of the straw figures was good, and that the making of the (wooden) automaton was not benevolent.—Was there not a danger of its leading to the use of (living) men?

PART II.

1. Duke Mû[1] asked Ȝze-sze whether it was the way of antiquity for a retired officer still to wear the mourning for his old ruler. 'Princes of old,' was the reply, 'advanced men and dismissed them equally according to the rules of propriety; and hence there was that rule about still wearing mourning for the old ruler. But nowadays princes advance men as if they were going to take them on their knees, and dismiss them as if they were going to push them into an abyss. Is it not good if (men so treated) do not head rebellion? How should there be the observance of that rule about still wearing mourning (for old rulers)?'

[1] Of Lû, B.C. 409–377.

2. At the mourning rites for duke Tâo[1], *K*î *K*âo-ʒze asked Măng *K*ing-ʒze what they should eat (to show their grief) for the ruler. *K*ing-ʒze replied, 'To eat gruel is the general rule for all the kingdom.' (The other said), 'It is known throughout the four quarters that we three ministers[2] have not been able to live in harmony with the ducal house. I could by an effort make myself emaciated; but would it not make men doubt whether I was doing so in sincerity? I will eat rice as usual.'

3. When Sze-thû *K*ing-ʒze of Wei died, Ʒze-hsiâ made a visit of condolence (to his house); and, though the chief mourner had not completed the slight dressing (of the corpse), he went in the head-band and robe of mourning. Ʒze-yû paid a similar visit; and, when the chief mourner had completed the slight dressing, he went out, put on the bands, returned and wailed. Ʒze-hsiâ said to him, 'Did you ever hear (that) that (was the proper method to observe)?' 'I heard the Master say,' was the reply, 'that until the chief mourner had changed his dress, one should not assume the mourning bands[3].'

4. Ʒăng-ʒze said, 'An-ʒze may be said to have known well the rules of propriety;—he was humble and reverent.' Yû *Z*o said, 'An-ʒze wore the same (robe of) fox-fur for thirty years. (At the burial of

[1] B.C. 467–431.

[2] The heads of the *K*ung-sun, Shû-sun, and *K*i-sun families; whose power Confucius had tried in vain to break.

[3] In this case Ʒze-yû was correct, according to rule, following the example of the chief mourner. Sze-thû was a name of office,—the ministry of Instruction; but it had become in this case the family name; from some ancestor of *K*ing-ʒze, who had been minister of Instruction.

his father), he had only one small carriage (with the offerings to be put into the grave[1]); and he returned immediately from the grave (without showing the usual attentions to his guests). The ruler of a state has seven bundles of the offerings, and seven such small carriages for them, and a Great officer five. How can it be said that An-ȝze knew propriety?' Ȝăng-ȝze replied, 'When a state is not well governed, the superior man is ashamed to observe all ceremonies to the full. Where there is extravagance in the administration of the state, he shows an example of economy. If the administration be economical, he shows an example of (the strict) observance of all rules.'

5. On the death of the mother of Kwo *K*âo-ȝze, he asked Ȝze-*k*ang, saying, 'At the interment, when (all) are at the grave, what should be the places of the men and of the women?' Ȝze-*k*ang said, 'At the mourning rites for Sze-thû *K*ing-ȝze, when the Master directed the ceremonies, the men stood with their faces to the west and the women stood with theirs to the east.' 'Ah!' said the other, 'that will not do;' adding, 'All will be here to see these mourning rites of mine. Do you take the sole charge of them. Let the guests be the guests, while I (alone) act as the host. Let the women take their places behind the men, and all have their faces towards the west[2].'

---

[1] See the note on paragraph 1, page 161. An-ȝze was the chief minister of *Kh*î.

[2] 'The master' here would seem to be Confucius; and yet he died before Sze-thû *K*ing-ȝze. There are other difficulties in parts of the paragraph.

6. At the mourning for Mû-po (her husband), *K*ing *K*iang wailed for him in the daytime, and at that for Wăn-po (her son), she wailed for him both in the daytime and the night. Confucius said, 'She knows the rules of propriety[1].'

At the mourning for Wăn-po, *K*ing *K*iang (once) put her hand on the couch (where his body lay), and without wailing said, 'Formerly, when I had this son, I thought that he would be a man of worth. (But) I never went with him to the court (to see his conduct there); and now that he is dead, of all his friends, the other ministers, there is no one that has shed tears for him, while the members of his harem all wail till they lose their voices. This son must have committed many lapses in his observance of the rules of propriety!'

7. When the mother of *K*î Khang-ȝze died, (her body was laid out with) her private clothes displayed. *K*ing *K*iang (Khang-ȝze's grand-uncle's wife) said, 'A wife does not dare to see her husband's parents without the ornament (of her upper robes); and there will be the guests from all quarters coming;—why are her under-clothes displayed here?' With this she ordered them to be removed.

8. Yû-ȝze and Ȝze-yû were standing together when they saw (a mourner) giving all a child's demonstrations of affection. Yû-ȝze said, 'I have never understood this leaping in mourning, and have long wished to do away with it. The sincere feeling (of sorrow) which appears here is right, (and

---

[1] It is said, 'She mourned for her husband according to propriety; for her son according to her feelings.'

should be sufficient).' Ȝze-yû replied, 'In the rules of propriety, there are some intended to lessen the (display of) feeling, and there are others which purposely introduce things (to excite it). To give direct vent to the feeling and act it out as by a short cut is the way of the rude *Z*ung and Tî. The method of the rules is not so. When a man rejoices, he looks pleased; when pleased, he thereon sings; when singing, he sways himself about; swaying himself about, he proceeds to dancing; from dancing, he gets into a state of wild excitement[1]; that excitement goes on to distress; distress expresses itself in sighing; sighing is followed by beating the breast; and beating the breast by leaping. The observances to regulate all this are what are called the rules of propriety.

'When a man dies, there arises a feeling of disgust (at the corpse). Its impotency goes on to make us revolt from it. On this account, there is the wrapping it in the shroud, and there are the curtains, plumes (and other ornaments of the coffin), to preserve men from that feeling of disgust. Immediately after death, the dried flesh and pickled meats are set out (by the side of the corpse). When the interment is about to take place, there are the things sent and offered (at the grave); and after the interment, there is the food presented (in the sacrifices of repose). The dead have never been seen to partake of these things. But from

[1] Evidently there is a lacuna in the text here; there should be some mention of stamping. Many of the critics have seen this, especially the *Kh*ien-lung editors; and various additions have been proposed by way of correction and supplement.

the highest ages to the present they have never been neglected;—all to cause men not to revolt (from their dead). Thus it is that what you blame in the rules of propriety is really nothing that is wrong in them.'

9. Wû made an incursion into *Kh*ăn, destroying the (places of) sacrifice, and putting to death those who were suffering from a pestilence (which prevailed). When the army retired, and had left the territory, Phî, the Grand-administrator of *Kh*ăn, was sent to the army (of Wû). Fû *Kh*âi (king of Wû) said to his internuncius Î, 'This fellow has much to say. Let us ask him a question.' (Then, turning to the visitor), he said, 'A campaign must have a name. What name do men give to this expedition?' The Grand-administrator said, 'Anciently, armies in their incursions and attacks did not hew down (trees about the) places of sacrifice; did not slay sufferers from pestilence; did not make captives of those whose hair was turning. But now, have not you in this campaign slain the sufferers from pestilence? Do they not call it the sick-killing expedition?' The king rejoined, 'If we give back your territory, and return our captives, what will you call it?' The reply was, 'O ruler and king, you came and punished the offences of our poor state. If the result of the campaign be that you now compassionate and forgive it, will the campaign be without its (proper) name[1]?'

---

[1] This incursion must be that mentioned in the Ȝo *K*wan under B.C. 494. Various corruptions and disruptions of the text of the paragraph have to be rectified, however; and the interpretation is otherwise difficult.

10. Yen Ting[1] deported himself skilfully during his mourning. Immediately after the death (of his father), he looked grave and restless, as if he were seeking for something, and could not find it. When the coffining had taken place, he looked expectant, as if he were following some one and could not get up with him. After the interment he looked sad, and as if, not getting his father to return (with him), he would wait for him[2].

11. Ȝze-*k*ang asked, saying, 'The Book of History says, that Kâo Ȝung for three years did not speak; and that when he did his words were received with joy[3]. Was it so?' *K*ung-nî replied, 'Why should it not have been so? Anciently, on the demise of the son of Heaven, the king, his heir, left everything to the chief minister for three years.'

12. When *K*ih Tâo-ȝze died[4], before he was buried, duke Phing was (one day) drinking along with the music-master Kwang and Lî Thiâo. The bells struck up; and when Tû Khwâi, who was coming in from outside, heard them, he said, 'Where is the music?' Being told that it was in the (principal) apartment, he entered it; and having ascended the steps one by one, he poured out a cup of spirits, and said, 'Kwang, drink this.' He then poured out another, and said, 'Thiâo, drink this.' He poured out a third cup; and kneeling in the hall, with his face to the north, he drank it himself, went down the steps, and hurried out.

[1] An officer of Lû.

[2] Compare above, paragraph 17, p. 137 et al.

[3] See vol. iii, p. 113. The Shû is not quoted exactly.

[4] This was in B.C. 533. *K*ih Tâo-ȝze was a great officer of Ȝin. See the story in the Ȝo *K*wan under that year.

Duke Phing called him in again, and said, 'Khwâi, just now I thought you had something in mind to enlighten me about, and therefore I did not speak to you. Why did you give the cup to Kwang?' 'On the days (*K*iâ-)ʒze and (*K*î-)mâo,' was the reply, 'there should be no music; and now *K*ih Tâo-ʒze is (in his coffin) in his hall, and this should be a great ʒze or mâo day. Kwang is the grand music-master, and did not remind you of this. It was on this account that I made him drink.'

'And why did you give a cup to Thiâo?' Tû Khwâi said, 'Thiâo is your lordship's favourite officer; and for this drinking and eating he forgot the fault you were committing. It was on this account I made him drink.'

'And why did you drink a cup yourself?' Khwâi replied, 'I am (only) the cook; and neglecting my (proper work of) supplying you with knives and spoons, I also presumed to take my part in showing my knowledge of what should be prohibited. It was on this account that I drank a cup myself.'

Duke Phing said, 'I also have been in fault. Pour out a cup and give it to me.' Tû Khwâi then rinsed the cup, and presented it. The duke said to the attendants, 'When I die, you must take care that this cup is not lost.' Down to the present day, (at feasts in Ʒin), when the cups have been presented all round, they then raise up this cup, and say, 'It is that which Tû presented.'

13. When Kung-shû Wăn-ʒze died, his son Shû begged the ruler (of the state) to fix his honorary title, saying, 'The sun and moon have brought the time;—we are about to bury him. I beg that you will fix the title, for which we shall change his name.'

The ruler said, 'Formerly when our state of Wei was suffering from a severe famine, your father had gruel made, and gave it to the famishing;—was not this a proof of how kind he was? Moreover, in a time of trouble[1], he protected me at the risk of his own life;—was not this a proof of how faithful he was? And while he administered the government of Wei, he so maintained the regulations for the different classes, and conducted its intercourse with the neighbouring states all round, that its altars sustained no disgrace;—was not this a proof of how accomplished he was? Therefore let us call him "The Faithful, Kind, and Accomplished."'

14. Shih Tâi-*k*ung died, leaving no son by his wife proper, and six sons by concubines. The tortoise-shell being consulted as to which of them should be the father's successor, it was said that by their bathing and wearing of their girdle-pendants the indication would be given. Five of them accordingly bathed and put on the girdle-pendants with their gems. Shih *Kh*î-ȝze, however, said, 'Whoever, being engaged with the mourning rites for a parent, bathed his head or his body, and put on his girdle-pendants?' and he declined to do either, and this was considered to be the indication. The people of Wei considered that the tortoise-shell had shown a (true) knowledge.

15. *Kh*ăn Ȝze-*k*ü having died in Wei, his wife and the principal officer of the family consulted together

---

[1] This was in B.C. 512. Twice in the Analects (XIV, 14, 19) Kung-shuh Wăn-ȝze, 'Kung-shu, the accomplished,' is mentioned. Whether he received the long honorary title given in the conclusion of this paragraph is considered doubtful.

about burying some living persons (to follow him). When they had decided to do so, (his brother), *Kh*ăn 3ze-khang arrived[1], and they informed him about their plan, saying, 'When the master was ill, (he was far away) and there was no provision for his nourishment in the lower world; let us bury some persons alive (to supply it).' 3ze-khang said, 'To bury living persons (for the sake of the dead) is contrary to what is proper. Nevertheless, in the event of his being ill, and requiring to be nourished, who are so fit for that purpose as his wife and steward? If the thing can be done without, I wish it to be so. If it cannot be done without, I wish you two to be the parties for it.' On this the proposal was not carried into effect.

16. 3ze-lû said, 'Alas for the poor! While (their parents) are alive, they have not the means to nourish them; and when they are dead, they have not the means to perform the mourning rites for them.' Confucius said, 'Bean soup, and water to drink, while the parents are made happy, may be pronounced filial piety. If (a son) can only wrap the body round from head to foot, and inter it immediately, without a shell, that being all which his means allow, he may be said to discharge (all) the rites of mourning.'

17. Duke Hsien of Wei having (been obliged to) flee from the state, when he returned[2], and had

---

[1] *Kh*ăn 3ze-khang was one of the disciples of Confucius, mentioned in the Analects I, 10; VII, 25. It is difficult to follow the reasoning of the wife and steward in justification of their proposals.

[2] Duke Hsien fled from Wei in B.C. 559, and returned to it in 547.

reached the suburbs (of the capital), he was about to grant certain towns and lands to those who had attended him in his exile before entering. Liû *K*wang said, 'If all had (remained at home) to guard the altars for you, who would have been able to follow you with halter and bridle? And if all had followed you, who would have guarded the altars? Your lordship has now returned to the state, and will it not be wrong for you to show a partial feeling?' The intended allotment did not take place.

18. There was the grand historiographer of Wei, called Liû *K*wang, lying ill. The duke said[1], 'If the illness prove fatal, though I may be engaged at the time in sacrificing, you must let me know.' (It happened accordingly, and, on hearing the news), the duke bowed twice, laying his head to the ground, and begged permission from the personator of the dead, saying, 'There was the minister Liû *K*wang,—not a minister of mine (merely), but a minister of the altars of the state. I have heard that he is dead, and beg leave to go (to his house).' On this, without putting off his robes, he went; and on the occasion presented them as his contribution (to the mourning rites). He also gave the deceased the towns of *Kh*iû-shih and Hsien-fan-shih by a writing of assignment which was put into the coffin, containing the words:—'For the myriads of his descendants, to hold from generation to generation without change.'

19. When *Kh*ăn Kan-hsî was lying ill, he assembled his brethren, and charged his son Ʒun-*k*î,

[1] The same duke Hsien of Wei. *Kh*ăn Hâo and others condemn his action in this case. Readers may not agree with them.

saying, 'When I am dead, you must make my coffin large, and make my two concubines lie in it with me, one on each side.' When he died, his son said, 'To bury the living with the dead is contrary to propriety; how much more must it be so to bury them in the same coffin!' Accordingly he did not put the two ladies to death.

20. *K*ung Sui died in *Kh*ui; and on the next day, which was *Z*ăn-wû, the sacrifice of the previous day was notwithstanding repeated (in the capital of Lû). When the pantomimes entered, however, they put away their flutes. *K*ung-nî said, 'It was contrary to rule. When a high minister dies, the sacrifice of the day before should not be repeated[1].'

21. When the mother of *K*î Khang-ȝze died, Kung-shû *Z*o was still young. After the dressing[2], Pan asked leave to let the coffin down into the grave by a mechanical contrivance. They were about to accede, when Kung-*k*ien *K*iâ said, 'No. According to the early practice in Lu, the ducal house used (for this purpose) the arrangement looking like large stone pillars, and the three families that like large wooden columns. Pan, you would, in the case of another man's mother, make trial of your ingenuity;—could you not in the case of your own mother do so? Would that distress you? Bah!' They did not allow him to carry out his plan[3].

---

[1] See this incident in the Chinese Classics, V, i, pp. 301, 302, where the account of it is discussed in a note.

[2] This must be the greater dressing.

[3] Pan and *Z*o were probably the same man; but we know that Pan lived at a later period. The incident in this paragraph therefore is doubted.

22. During the fight at Lang[1], Kung-shu *Z*ü-*z*ăn saw (many of) the men, carrying their clubs on their shoulders, entering behind the shelter of the small wall, and said, 'Although the services required of them are distressing, and the burdens laid on them heavy, (they ought to fight); but though our superiors do not form (good) plans, it is not right that soldiers should not be prepared to die. This is what I say.' On this along with Wang Î, a youth, (the son) of a neighbour, he went forward, and both of them met their death.

The people of Lû wished to bury the lad Wang Î not as one who had died prematurely, and asked *K*ung-nî about the point. He said, 'As he was able to bear his shield and spear in the defence of our altars, may you not do as you wish, and bury him as one who has not died prematurely?'

23. When 3ze-lû was going away from Lû, he said to Yen Yüan, 'What have you to send me away with?' 'I have heard,' was the reply, 'that, when one is leaving his state, he wails at the graves (of his fathers), and then takes his journey, while on his return to it, he does not wail, but goes to look at the graves, and (then) enters (the city).' He then said to 3ze-lû, 'And what have you to leave with me here?' 'I have heard,' was the reply, 'that, when you pass by a grave, you should bow forward to the cross-bar, and, when you pass a place of sacrifice, you should dismount.'

24. Shang Yang, director of Works (in *Kh*û), and

[1] The fight at Lang is mentioned in the *Kh*un *Kh*iû under B.C. 484. 3o's description of the battle gives the incident mentioned here, but somewhat differently.

*Kh*ăn *Kh*î-*k*î[1] were pursuing the army of Wû, and came up with it. The latter said to Shang Yang, 'It is the king's[2] business. It will be well for you to take your bow in hand.' He did so, and *Kh*î-*k*î told him to shoot, which he did, killing a man, and returning immediately the bow to its case. They came up with the enemy again, and being told as before to shoot, he killed other two men; whenever he killed a man, he covered his eyes. Then stopping the chariot, he said, 'I have no place at the audiences; nor do I take part in the feasts. The death of three men will be sufficient for me to report.' Confucius said, 'Amidst his killing of men, he was still observant of the rules of propriety[3].'

25. The princes were engaged in an invasion of *Kh*in, when duke Hwan of Ȝhâo died at their meeting[4]. The others asked leave to (see) the plugging of his teeth with the jade, and they were made to enshroud (his corpse)[5].

Duke Hsiang being in attendance at the court of *K*ing, king Khang died[6]. The people of *K*ing said to him, 'We must beg you to cover (the corpse

[1] *Kh*î-*k*î was a son of the king of *Kh*û, and afterwards became king Phing. *Kh*û, in B.C. 534, reduced *Kh*ăn to be a dependency of itself, and put it under *Kh*î-*k*î, who became known as *Kh*î-*k*î of *Kh*ăn.

[2] 'The king's business;' that is, the business of the count of *Kh*û, who had usurped the title of king.

[3] It is not easy to discover the point of Confucius' reply. Even Ȝze-lû questioned him about it (as related in the Narratives of the School), and got an answer which does not make it any clearer.

[4] In B.C. 578.

[5] Probably by the marquis of Ȝin—duke Wăn—as 'lord of Meetings and Covenants.'

[6] In B.C. 545.

with your gift of a robe).' The men of Lû (who were with him) said, 'The thing is contrary to propriety.' They of *Kh*û, however, obliged him to do what they asked; and he first employed a sorcerer with his reed-brush to brush (and purify) the bier. The people of *K*ing then regretted what they had done[1].

26. At the mourning rites for duke *Kh*ăng of Thăng[2], ʒze-shû *K*ing-shû was sent (from Lû) on a mission of condolence, and to present a letter (from duke Âi), ʒze-fû Hui-po being assistant-commissioner. When they arrived at the suburbs (of the capital of Thăng), because it was the anniversary of the death of Î-po, (Hui-po's uncle), *K*ing-shû hesitated to enter the city. Hui-po, however, said, 'We are on government business, and should not for the private affair of my uncle's (death) neglect the duke's affairs.' They forthwith entered.

Part III.

1. Duke Âi sent a message of condolence to Khwâi Shang, and the messenger met him (on the way to the grave). They withdrew to the way-side, where Khwâi drew the figure of his house, (with the coffin in it), and there received the condolences[3].

ʒăng-ʒze said, 'Khwâi Shang's knowledge of the

---

[1] *K*ing was another name for *Kh*û. Duke Hsiang went from Lû in B.C. 545; and it was in the spring of the next year, probably, that the incident occurred. The sorcerer and his reed-brush were used when a ruler went to the mourning for a minister (see Part i. 42), so that *Kh*û intending to humiliate Lû was itself humiliated.

[2] Duke *Kh*ăng of Thăng died in B.C. 539.

[3] This must have been a case for which the rule is given in Part i. 12.

rules of ceremony was not equal to that of the wife of *Kh*î Liang. When duke *K*wang fell on *K*ü by surprise at Thui, *Kh*î Liang met his death. His wife met his bier on the way, and wailed for him bitterly. Duke *K*wang sent a person to convey his condolences to her; but she said, 'If his lordship's officer had been guilty of any offence, then his body should have been exposed in the court or the market-place, and his wife and concubines apprehended. If he were not chargeable with any offence, there is the poor cottage of his father. This is not the place where the ruler should demean himself to send me a message[1].'

2. At the mourning rites for his young son Tun, duke Âi wished to employ the (elm-juice) sprinklers, and asked Yû *Z*o about the matter, who said that it might be done, for his three ministers even used them. Yen Liû said, 'For the son of Heaven dragons are painted on (the shafts of) the funeral carriage, and the boards surrounding the coffin, like the shell, have a covering over them. For the feudal princes there is a similar carriage (without the painted dragons), and the covering above. (In both cases) they prepare the elm-juice, and therefore employ sprinklers. The three ministers, not employing (such a carriage), and yet employing the sprinklers, thus appropriate a ceremony which is not suitable for them; and why should your lordship imitate them[2]?'

---

[1] See the 3o *K*wan under B.C. 550, the twenty-third year of duke Hsiang. The name of the place in the text (To, read Thui by *K*ăng Hsüan) seems to be a mistake. See the Khang-hsî dictionary on the character To (奪).

[2] There is a good deal of difficulty and difference of opinion in

3. After the death of the mother of (his son, who became) duke Tâo, duke Âi wore for her the one year's mourning with its unfrayed edges. Yû *Z*o asked him, if it was in rule for him to wear that mourning for a concubine. 'Can I help it?' replied the duke. 'The people of Lû will have it that she was my wife.'

4. When *K*î 3ze-kâo buried his wife, some injury was done to the standing corn, which Shăn-hsiang told him of, begging him to make the damage good. 3ze-kâo said, 'The Măng has not blamed me for this, and my friends have not cast me off. I am here the commandant of the city. To buy (in this manner a right of) way in order to bury (my dead) would be a precedent difficult to follow [1].'

5. When one receives no salary for the official duties which he performs [2], and what the ruler sends to him is called 'an offering,' while the messenger charged with it uses the style of 'our unworthy ruler;' if such an one leave the state, and afterwards the ruler dies, he does not wear mourning for him.

6. At the sacrifice of Repose a personator of the

---

the interpretation of this paragraph. According to the common view, the funeral carriage used by the king and princes was very heavy, and difficult to drag along. To ease its transit, a juice was prepared from the elm bark, and sprinkled on the ground to make it slippery. But this practice was because of the heaviness of the carriage; and was not required in the case of lighter conveyances.

[1] This *K*î 3ze-kâo was Kâo *Kh*âi, one of the disciples of Confucius. Shăn-hsiang was the son of 3ze-*k*ang; see paragraph 3, page 132.

[2] Such was 3ze-sze in Lû, and Mencius in *Kh*î. They were 'guests,' not ministers. Declining salary, they avoided the obligations incurred by receiving it.

dead is appointed, and a stool, with a mat and viands on it, is placed (for him). When the wailing is over, the name of the deceased is avoided. The service of him as living is over, and that for him in his ghostly state has begun. When the wailing is over, the cook, with a bell having a wooden clapper, issues an order throughout the palace, saying, 'Give up disusing the names of the former rulers, and henceforth disuse (only) the name of him who is newly deceased.' This was done from the door leading to the chambers to the outer gate.

7. When a name was composed of two characters they were not avoided when used singly. The name of the Master's mother was *K*ăng-ʒâi. When he used ʒâi, he did not at the same time use *K*ăng; nor ʒâi, when he used *K*ăng.

8. When any sad disaster occurred to an army, (the ruler) in plain white robes wailed for it outside the Khû gate[1]. A carriage conveying the news of such disaster carried no cover for buff-coats nor case for bows.

9. When the (shrine-)apartment of his father was burned, (the ruler) wailed for it three days. Hence it is said, 'The new temple took fire;' and also, 'There was a wailing for three days[2].'

10. In passing by the side of mount Thâi, Confucius came on a woman who was wailing bitterly by a grave. The Master bowed forward to the cross-bar, and hastened to her; and then sent

[1] The Khû (arsenal or treasury gate) was the second of the palace gates, and near the ancestral temple. Hence the position selected for the wailing.

[2] See the *Kh*un *Kh*iû, under B.C. 588.

Ȝze-lû to question her. 'Your wailing,' said he, 'is altogether like that of one who has suffered sorrow upon sorrow.' She replied, 'It is so. Formerly, my husband's father was killed here by a tiger. My husband was also killed (by another), and now my son has died in the same way.' The Master said, 'Why do you not leave the place?' The answer was, 'There is no oppressive government here.' The Master then said (to the disciples), 'Remember this, my little children. Oppressive government is more terrible than tigers.'

11. In Lû there was one *K*âu Făng[1], to whom duke Âi went, carrying an introductory present, and requesting an interview, which, however, the other refused. The duke said, 'I must give it up then.' And he sent a messenger with the following questions:—'(Shun), the lord of Yü, had not shown his good faith to the people, and yet they put confidence in him. The sovereign of Hsiâ had not shown his reverence for the people, and yet the people revered him:—what shall I exhibit that I may obtain such things from the people?' The reply was:—'Ruins and graves express no mournfulness to the people, and yet the people mourn (amidst them). The altars of the spirits of the land and grain and the ancestral temples express no reverence to the people, and yet the people revere them. The kings of Yin made their solemn proclamations, and yet the people began to rebel; those of *K*âu made their covenants, and the people began to distrust them. If there be not the heart

[1] This *K*âu Făng must have been a worthy who had withdrawn from public life.

observant of righteousness, self-consecration, good faith, sincerity, and guilelessness, though a ruler may try to knit the people firmly to him, will not all bonds between them be dissolved?'

12. While mourning (for a father), one should not be concerned about (the discomfort of) his own resting-place [1], nor, in emaciating himself, should he do so to the endangering of his life. He should not be the former;—he has to be concerned that (his father's spirit-tablet) is not (yet) in the temple. He should not do the latter, lest (his father) should thereby have no posterity.

13. *K*î-ȝze of Yen-ling [2] had gone to *Kh*î; and his eldest son having died, on the way back (to Wû), he buried him between Ying and Po. Confucius (afterwards) said, '*K*î-ȝze was the one man in Wû most versed in the rules of propriety, so I went and saw his manner of interment. The grave was not so deep as to reach the water-springs. The grave-clothes were such as (the deceased) had ordinarily worn. After the interment, he raised a mound over the grave of dimensions sufficient to cover it, and high enough for the hand to be easily placed on it. When the mound was completed, he bared his left arm;

[1] Referring, I think, to the discomfort of the mourning shed. But other interpretations of the paragraph are to be found in *Kh*ăn Hâo's work, and elsewhere.

[2] This *K*î-ȝze is better known as *K*î *K*â (季札), a brother of the ruler of Wû. Having declined the state of Wû, he lived in the principality of Yen-ling. He visited the northern states Lû, *Kh*î, Ȝin, and the others, in B.C. 515; and his sayings and doings in them are very famous. He was a good man and able, whom Confucius could appreciate. Ying and Po were two places in *Kh*î.

and, moving to the right, he went round it thrice, crying out, "That the bones and flesh should return again to the earth is what is appointed. But the soul in its energy can go everywhere; it can go everywhere." And with this he went on his way.' Confucius (also) said, 'Was not *K*î-ȝze of Yen-ling's observance of the rules of ceremony in accordance with (the idea of them)?'

14. At the mourning rites for the duke Khâo of *K*û-lü[1], the ruler of Hsü sent Yung *K*ü with a message of condolence, and with the articles to fill the mouth of the deceased. 'My unworthy ruler,' said he, 'hath sent me to kneel and put the jade for a marquis which he has presented into your (deceased) ruler's mouth. Please allow me to kneel and do so.' The officers of *K*ü replied, 'When any of the princes has deigned to send or come to our poor city, the observances have been kept according to their nature, whether simple and easy, or troublesome and more difficult; but such a blending of the easy and troublesome as in your case, we have not known.' Yung *K*ü replied, 'I have heard that in the service of his ruler one should not forget that ruler, nor be oblivious of his ancestral (rules). Formerly, our ruler, king *K*ü, in his warlike operations towards the west, in which he crossed the Ho, everywhere used this style of speech. I am a plain, blunt man, and do not presume to forget his example[2].'

[1] Khâo should probably be Ting. Duke Khâo lived after the period of the *Kh*un *Kh*iû, during which the power of Hsü had been entirely broken.

[2] Here was Yung *K*ü, merely a Great officer, wishing to do what only a prince could do, according to the rules of propriety.

15. When the mother of Ʒze-sze died in Wei, and news of the event was brought to him, he wailed in the ancestral temple. His disciples came to him and said, 'Your mother is dead, after marrying into another family[1]; why do you wail for her in the temple of the Khung family?' He replied, 'I am wrong, I am wrong.' And thereon he wailed in one of the smaller apartments of his house.

16. When the son of Heaven died, three days afterwards, the officers of prayer[2] were the first to assume mourning. In five days the heads of official departments did so; in seven days both males and females throughout the royal domain; and in three months all in the kingdom.

The foresters examined the trees about the various altars, and cut down those which they thought suitable for the coffins and shell. If these did not come up to what was required, the sacrifices were abolished, and the men had their throats cut[3].

17. During a great dearth in *Kh*î, *Kh*ien Âo had food prepared on the roads, to wait the approach of hungry people and give to them. (One day), there came a famished man, looking as if he could

---

He defends himself on the ground that the lords of Hsü claimed the title of King. The language of the officers of *K*û shows that they were embarrassed by his mission.

[1] Literally, 'The mother of the Shû family is dead,' but the interpretation of the text is disputed. The *Kh*ien-lung editors and many others question the genuineness of the whole paragraph.

[2] The officers of prayer were divided into five classes; the first and third of which are intended here. See the Official Book of *K*âu, ch. 25.

[3] Great efforts are made to explain away this last sentence.

hardly see, his face covered with his sleeve, and dragging his feet together. *Kh*ien Âo, carrying with his left hand some rice, and holding some drink with the other, said to him, 'Poor man! come and eat.' The man, opening his eyes with a stare, and looking at him, said, 'It was because I would not eat "Poor man come here's" food, that I am come to this state.' *Kh*ien Âo immediately apologised for his words, but the man after all would not take the food and died.

When Ȝăng-ȝze heard the circumstances, he said, 'Was it not a small matter? When the other expressed his pity as he did, the man might have gone away. When he apologised, the man might have taken the food.'

18. In the time of duke Ting of *K*û-lü[1], there occurred the case of a man killing his father. The officers reported it; when the duke, with an appearance of dismay, left his mat and said, 'This is the crime of unworthy me!' He added, 'I have learned how to decide on such a charge. When a minister kills his ruler, all who are in office with him should kill him without mercy. When a son kills his father, all who are in the house with him should kill him without mercy. The man should be killed; his house should be destroyed; the whole place should be laid under water and reduced to a swamp. And his ruler should let a month elapse before he raises a cup to his lips.'

[1] This duke Ting became ruler of *K*û in B.C. 613. Some interpret the paragraph as if it said that all the officers, as well as the whole family of a regicide or parricide, should be killed with him. But that cannot be, and need not be, the meaning.

19. (The ruler of) 3in having congratulated Wăn-ʒze on the completion of his residence, the Great officers of the state went to the house-warming[1]. *K*ang Lâo said, 'How elegant it is, and lofty! How elegant and splendid! Here will you have your songs! Here will you have your wailings! Here will you assemble the representatives of the great families of the state!' Wăn-ʒze replied, 'If I can have my songs here, and my wailings, and assemble here the representatives of the great families of the state, (it will be enough). I will then (only) seek to preserve my waist and neck to follow the former Great officers of my family to the Nine Plains.' He then bowed twice, laying his head also on the ground.

A superior man will say (of the two), that the one was skilful in the expression of his praise and the other in his prayer.

20. The dog kept by *K*ung-nî having died, he employed 3ze-kung to bury it, saying, 'I have heard that a worn-out curtain should not be thrown away, but may be used to bury a horse in; and that a worn-out umbrella should not be thrown away, but may be used to bury a dog in. I am poor and have no umbrella. In putting the dog into the grave, you can use my mat; and do not

[1] It is doubtful how this first sentence should be translated. Most naturally we should render Hsien-wăn-ʒze of 3in having completed his house, but binomial honorary titles were not yet known; and the view seems to be correct that this Wăn-ʒze was *K*âo Wû, a well-known minister of 3in. The 'Nine Plains' below must have been the name of a burying-place used by the officers of 3in. There seems to be an error in the name in the text, which is given correctly in paragraph 25.

let its head get buried in the earth. When one of the horses of the ruler's carriage dies, it is buried in a curtain (in good condition)[1].'

21. When the mother of *K*î-sun died, duke Âi paid a visit of condolence to him. (Soon after) Ʒăng-ʒze and Ʒze-kung arrived for the same purpose; but the porter declined to admit them, because the ruler was present. On this they went into the stable, and adjusted their dress more fully. (Shortly) they entered the house, Ʒze-kung going first[2]. The porter said to him, 'I have already announced your arrival;' and when Ʒăng-ʒze followed, he moved on one side for him. They passed on to the inner place for the droppings from the roof, the Great officers all moving out of their way, and the duke descending a step and bowing to them. A superior man has said about the case, 'So it is when the toilet is complete! Immediately its influence extends far[3].'

22. A man-at-arms at the Yang gate (of the capital of Sung) having died, Ʒze-han, the superintendent of Works, went to (his house), and wailed for him bitterly. The men of Ʒin who were in Sung as spies returned, and reported the thing to

[1] The concluding sentence is found also in the 'Narratives of the School,' and may have been added to the rest by the compiler of this Than Kung. We are not prepared for the instance which Confucius gives of his poverty; but perhaps we like him better for keeping a dog, and seeing after its burial.

[2] Because he was older than Ʒăng-ʒze.

[3] This concluding sentence is much objected to; seeming, as it does, to attribute to their toilet what was due to the respectful demeanour of the two worthies, and their established reputation. But the text must stand as it is.

the marquis of Ʒin, saying, 'A man-at-arms at the Yang gate having died, Ʒze-han wailed for him bitterly, and the people were pleased; (Sung), we apprehend, cannot be attacked (with success).'

When Confucius heard of the circumstances, he said, 'Skilfully did those men do their duty as spies in Sung. It is said in the Book of Poetry,—

"If there was any mourning among the people,
I did my utmost to help them."

Though there had been other enemies besides Ʒin, what state under the sky could have withstood one (in the condition of Sung)[1]?'

23. At the mourning rites for duke *K*wang of Lû, when the interment was over, (the new ruler) did not enter the outer gate with his girdle of dolichos cloth. The ordinary and Great officers, when they had finished their wailing, also did not enter in their sackcloth[2].

24. There was an old acquaintance of Confucius, called Yüan *Z*ang. When his mother died, the Master assisted him in preparing the shell for the coffin. Yüan (then) got up on the wood, and said, 'It is long since I sang to anything;' and (with this he struck the wood), singing:—

'It is marked like a wild cat's head;
It is (smooth) as a young lady's hand which you hold.'

The Master, however, made as if he did not hear, and passed by him.

---

[1] The whole narrative here is doubted. See the Shih, I. iii. Ode 10. 4. The reading of the poem, but not the meaning, is different from the text. The application is far-fetched

[2] The time was one of great disorder; there may have been reasons for the violations of propriety, which we do not know.

The disciples who were with him said, 'Can you not have done with him?' 'I have heard,' was the reply, 'that relations should not forget their relationship, nor old acquaintances their friendship[1].'

25. *K*âo Wăn-ȝze and Shû-yü were looking about them at the Nine Plains[2], when Wăn-ȝze said, 'If these dead could arise, with whom would I associate myself?' Shû-yü asked, 'Would it be with Yang Khû-fû[3]?' 'He managed by his course,' was the reply, 'to concentrate in himself all the power of Ȝin, and yet he did not die a natural death. His wisdom does not deserve to be commended.'

'Would it be with uncle Fan[4]?' Wăn-ȝze said, 'When he saw gain in prospect, he did not think of his ruler; his virtue does not deserve to be commended[4]. I think I would follow Wû-ȝze of Sui[5]. While seeking the advantage of his ruler, he did not forget himself; and while consulting for his own advantage, he was not forgetful of his friends.'

The people of Ȝin thought that Wăn-ȝze knew men. He carried himself in a retiring way, as if he could not bear even his clothes. His speech

---

[1] We have another instance of Confucius's relations with Yüan *Z*ang in the Analects, XIV, 46. He was evidently 'queer,' with a sort of craze. It gives one a new idea of Confucius to find his interest in, and kindly feeling for, such a man.

[2] See paragraph 19 and note.

[3] Master of duke Hsiang B.C. 627–621, and an important minister afterwards.

[4] See in paragraph 19, Part i. But scant measure is dealt here to 'uncle Fan.'

[5] Wû-ȝze of Sui had an eventful life, and played an important part in the affairs of Ȝin and *Kh*in in his time. See a fine testimony to him in the Ȝo *K*wan, under B.C. 546.

was low and stuttering, as if he could not get his words out. The officers whom he advanced to responsible charges in the depositories of Ʒin were more than seventy. During his life, he had no contentions with any of them about gain, and when dying he required nothing from them for his sons.

26. Shû-*k*ung Phî instructed (his son) Ʒze-liû (in the rules of ceremony); and when he died, Ʒze-liû's wife, who was a plain, blunt woman, wore for him the one year's mourning and the headband with its two ends tied together. (Phî's brother), Shû-*k*ung *Kh*ien spoke to Ʒze-liû about it, and requested that she should wear the three months' mourning and the simple headband; saying, 'Formerly, when I was mourning for my aunts and sisters, I wore this mourning, and no one forbade it.' When he withdrew, however, (Ʒze-liû) made his wife wear the three months' mourning and the simple headband[1].

27. There was a man of *Kh*ăng, who did not go into mourning on the death of his elder brother. Hearing, however, that Ʒze-kâo was about to become governor of the city, he forthwith did so. The people of *Kh*ăng said, 'The silkworm spins

---

[1] Shû-*k*ung Phî was the first of a branch of the Shû-sun clan, descended from the ruling house of Lû. The object of the paragraph seems to be to show, that Ʒze-liû's wife, though a plain simple woman, was taught what to do, by her native feeling and sense, in a matter of ceremony, more correctly than the two gentlemen, mere men of the world, her husband and his uncle. The paragraph, however, is not skilfully constructed, nor quite clear. *K*ăng Hsüan thought that Ʒze-liû was Phî's son, which, the *Kh*ien-lung editors say, some think a mistake. They do not give definitely their own opinion.

its cocoons, but the crab supplies the box for them; the bee has its cap, but the cicada supplies the strings for it. His elder brother died, but it was 3ze-kâo who made the mourning for him[1].'

28. When Yo *K*ăng, 3ze-*kh*un's mother, died, he was five days without eating. He then said, 'I am sorry for it. Since in the case of my mother's death, I could not eat according to my feelings, on what occasion shall I be able to do so?'

29. In a year of drought duke Mû[2] called to him Hsien-ȝze, and asked him about it. 'Heaven,' said he, 'has not sent down rain for a long time. I wish to expose a deformed person in the sun (to move its pity), what do you say to my doing so?' 'Heaven, indeed,' was the reply, 'does not send down rain; but would it not be an improper act of cruelty, on that account to expose the diseased son of some one in the sun?'

'Well then,' (said the duke), 'I wish to expose in the sun a witch; what do you say to that?' Hsien-ȝze said, 'Heaven, indeed, does not send down rain; but would it not be wide of the mark to hope anything from (the suffering of) a foolish woman, and by means of that to seek for rain[3]?'

---

[1] The 3ze-kâo here was the same as Kâo *Kh*âi; see the note on paragraph 4. The incident here shows the influence of his well-known character. He is the crab whose shell forms a box for the cocoons, and the cicada whose antennae form the strings for the cap.

[2] 'Duke Mû and Hsien-ȝze;' see Section I. Part iii. 5.

[3] In the 3o *K*wan, under B. C. 639, duke Hsî of Lû makes a proposal about exposing a deformed person and a witch like that which is recorded here. Nothing is said, however, about changing the site of the market. Reference is made, however, to that

'What do you say then to my moving the market-place elsewhere?' The answer was, 'When the son of Heaven dies, the market is held in the lanes for seven days; and it is held in them for three days, when the ruler of a state dies. It will perhaps be a proper measure to move it there on account of the present distress.'

30. Confucius said, 'The people of Wei, in burying husband and wife together (in the same grave and shell), leave a space between the coffins. The people of Lû, in doing the same, place them together;—which is the better way.

APPENDIX TO BOOK II.

THE reader will have been struck by the many references in the Than Kung to the degrees and dress of mourning; and no other subject occupies so prominent a place in many of the books of the Lî *K*î that follow. It is thought well, therefore, to introduce here, by way of appendix to it, the following passage from a very valuable paper on 'Marriage, Affinity, and Inheritance in China,' contributed, on February 8th, 1853, to the China Branch of the Royal Asiatic Society, by Mr. W. H. Medhurst, jun., now Sir Walter H. Medhurst. The information and subjoined illustrative tables were taken by him mainly from the Ritual and Penal Code of China, a preliminary chapter of which is devoted to the subject of 'The Dress of Mourning:'—

'The ideas of the Chinese as to nearness of kin, whether by

---

practice in a work of Tung *K*ung-shu (second century, B. C.), of which Wang Thâo ventures to give a geomantic explanation. The narrative in the text is probably taken from the Ȝo *K*wan, the compiler having forgotten the time and parties in the earlier account.

blood or marriage, differ widely from our own. They divide relationships into two classes, Nêi *kh*in (內親) and Wâi yin (外因), terms analogous to our "consanguinity" and "affinity," but conveying, nevertheless, other associations than those which we attach to these words. The former (Nêi *kh*in) comprehends all kindred derived from common stock with the individual, but only by descent through the male line; the latter (Wâi yin) includes what the Chinese designate mû tang (母黨), *kh*î tang (妻黨), and nü tang (女黨), three terms best translated, perhaps, by "mother's kin," "wife's kin," and "daughter's kin," and understood by them to mean a mother's relatives, relatives of females received into one's kindred by marriage, and members of families into which one's kinswomen marry. Thus, for example, a first cousin twice removed, lineally descended from the same great-great-grandfather through the male line, is a nêi-*kh*in relative; but a mother's parents, wife's sister, and a sister's husband or child, are all equally wâi-yin kindred. The principle on which the distinction is drawn appears to be, that a woman alienates herself from her own kin on marriage, and becomes a part of the stock on which she is grafted; and it will be necessary to keep this principle distinctly in mind in perusing any further remarks that may be made, as otherwise it will be found impossible to reconcile the many apparent contradictions in the theory and practice of the Chinese Code.

'The indication of the prohibited degrees (in marriage) depends then upon a peculiar genealogical disposition of the several members of a family with respect to the mourning worn for deceased relatives; and this I shall now proceed to explain. The Ritual prescribes five different kinds of mourning, called wû fû (五服), to be worn for all relatives within a definite proximity of degree, graduating the character of the habit in proportion to the nearness of kin. These habits are designated by certain names, which by a species of metonymy come to be applied to the relationships themselves, and are used somewhat as we apply the terms "1st degree," "2nd degree," and so on; and plans, similar to our genealogical tables, are laid down, showing the specific habit suitable for each kinsman. The principal one of these tables, that for a married or unmarried man, comprises cousins twice removed, that is, derived by lineal descent from a common great-great-grandfather, that ancestor himself, and all relatives included within the two lines of descent from him to them; below the individual, it comprehends his own descendants (in the male line) as far as great-great-grandchildren, his brother's as far as great-grandchildren, his cousin's as far as grandchildren, and the children of his cousin once removed. In this table nêi-*kh*in relationships will alone be found; mourning is worn for very few of the wâi-yin, and these, though actually, that is, in our eyes, ties of consanguinity, and deserving far more consideration than many for which a deeper habit is prescribed, are classed among the very lowest degrees of mourning.

'Six tables are given in the Ritual to which the five habits are common; they prescribe the mourning to be worn by

1st, A man for his kinsmen and kinswomen;
2nd, A wife for her husband's kinsfolk;
3rd, A married female for her own kinsfolk;
4th, A man for his mother's kinsfolk;
5th, A man for his wife's kinsfolk;
6th, A concubine for her master's kinsfolk.

'A seventh table is given, exhibiting the mourning to be worn for step-fathers and fathers by adoption, and for step- and foster-mothers, &c.; but I have not thought it necessary to encumber my paper by wandering into so remote a portion of the field.

'To render these details more easily comprehensible, I shall class the relationships in each table under their appropriate degrees of mourning, and leave the reader to examine the tables at his leisure. It need only be borne in mind, that, excepting where otherwise specified, the relationship indicated is male, and only by descent through the male line, as, for example, that by "cousin" a father's brother's son alone is meant, and not a father's sister's son or daughter.

'The five kinds of mourning, the names of which serve, as has been said, to indicate the degrees of relationship to which they belong, are :—

1st, *K*an-ʒui (斬衰), nominally worn for three years, really for twenty-seven months ;

2nd, Ʒze-ʒui (齊衰), worn for one year, for five months, or for three months ;

3rd, Tâ-kung (大功), worn for nine months ;

4th, Hsiâo-kung (小功), worn for five months ;

5th, Sze-mâ (緦麻), worn for three months.

'The character of each habit, and the relatives for whom it is worn, are prescribed as follows :—

'1st, *K*an-ʒui indicates relationships of the first degree. The prescribed habit for it is composed of the coarsest hempen fabric, and left unhemmed at the borders. It is worn :—

'By a man, for his parents ; by a wife, for her husband, and husband's parents ; and by a concubine, for her master.

'2nd, Ʒze-ʒui indicates relationships of the second degree. The prescribed habit for it is composed of coarse hempen fabric, with hemmed borders. It is worn for one year :—

'By a man, for his grandparents ; uncle ; uncle's wife ; spinster aunt ; brother ; spinster sister ; wife ; son (of wife or concubine) ; daughter-in-law (wife of first-born) ; nephew ; spinster niece ; grandson (first-born son of first-born) ; by a wife, for her husband's nephew, and husband's spinster niece ; by a married woman, for her parents, and grandparents ; and by a concubine, for her master's wife ; her master's parents ; her master's sons (by wife or other concubine), and for sons. It is worn for five months :—

'By a man, for his great-grandparents; and by a married woman, for her great-grandparents. It is worn for three months:—

'By a man, for his great-great-grandparents; and by a married woman, for her great-great-grandparents.

'3rd, Tâ-kung indicates relationships of the third degree. The prescribed habit for it is composed of coarse cotton fabric[1]. It is worn:—

'By a man, for his married aunt; married sister; brother's wife; first cousin; spinster first cousin; daughter-in-law (wife of a younger son, or of a son of a concubine); nephew's wife; married niece; and grandson (son of a younger son, or of a concubine's son); by a wife, for her husband's grandparents; husband's uncle; husband's daughter-in-law (wife of a younger son, or of a concubine's son); husband's nephew's wife; husband's married niece; and grandson; by a married woman, for her uncle; uncle's wife; spinster aunt; brother; sister; nephew; spinster niece; and by a concubine, for her grandson.

'4th, Hsiâo-kung indicates relationships of the fourth degree. The habit prescribed for it is composed of rather coarse cotton fabric. It is worn:—

'By a man, for his grand-uncle; grand-uncle's wife; spinster grand-aunt; father's first cousin; father's first cousin's wife; father's spinster first cousin; married female first cousin; first cousin once removed; spinster female first cousin once removed; second cousin; spinster female second cousin; grand-daughter-in-law (wife of first-born of first-born son); grand-nephew; spinster grand-niece; mother's parents; mother's brother; mother's

[1] In the very brief account of this preliminary chapter in the Penal Code, given by Sir George Staunton, in his translation of the Code (page lxxv), he gives for the material 'coarse' linen cloth. The Chinese character is simply 'cloth.' I suppose the material originally was linen; but since the use of cotton, both of native and foreign manufacture, has increased in China, it is often substituted for linen. I have seen some mourners wearing linen, and others wearing cotton.

sister[1]; by a wife, for her husband's aunt; husband's brother; husband's brother's wife; husband's sister; husband's second cousin; spinster female second cousin of husband; husband's grand-nephew; and spinster grand-niece of husband; by a married woman, for her spinster aunt; married sister; first cousin; and married niece; and by a concubine, for her master's grand-parents.

'5th, Sze-mâ indicates relationships of the fifth degree. The prescribed dress for it is composed of rather fine cotton cloth. It is worn :—

'By a man, for his great-grand-uncle; great-grand-uncle's wife; spinster great-grand-aunt; married grand-aunt; grandfather's first cousin; grandfather's first cousin's wife; spinster first cousin of grandfather; married female first cousin of father; father's first cousin once removed; wife of father's first cousin once removed; father's spinster first cousin once removed; first cousin's wife; married female first cousin once removed; first cousin twice removed; spinster first cousin twice removed; married female second cousin; second cousin once removed; spinster second cousin once removed; grand-daughter-in-law (wife of son of a younger son, or of son of a concubine); grand-nephew's wife; married grand-niece; third cousin; spinster third cousin; great-grandson; great-grand-nephew; spinster great-grand-niece; great-great-grandson; aunt's son; mother's brother's son; mother's sister's son; wife's parents; son-in-law; daughter's child: by a wife, for her husband's great-great-grand-parents; husband's great-grand-parents; husband's grand-uncle; husband's spinster grand-aunt; father-in-law's first cousin; father-in-law's first cousin's wife; spinster first cousin of father-in-law; female first cousin of husband; husband's second cousin's wife; married female second cousin of husband; husband's second cousin once removed; husband's

[1] These names and others farther on, printed with spaced letters, all belong to the Wâi-yin relationships.

spinster second cousin once removed; grand-daughter-in-law (wife of own or a concubine's grandson); husband's grand-nephew's wife; husband's married grand-niece; husband's third cousin; spinster third cousin of husband; great-grandson; great-grand-daughter-in-law; husband's great-grand-nephew; spinster great-grand-niece of husband; and great-great-grandson: and by a married woman, for her grand-uncle; spinster grand-aunt; father's first cousin; spinster first cousin of father; spinster first cousin; second cousin; spinster second cousin.'

BOOK III. THE ROYAL REGULATIONS[1].

SECTION I.

1. According to the regulations of emolument and rank framed by the kings, there were the duke; the marquis; the earl; the count; and the baron[2]:—in all, five gradations (of rank). There were (also), in the feudal states, Great officers[3] of the highest grade,—the ministers; and Great officers of the lowest grade; officers of the highest, the middle, and the lowest grades:—in all, five gradations (of office).

2. The territory of the son of Heaven amounted to 1000 lî square; that of a duke or marquis to 500 lî square; that of an earl to 70 lî square; and that of a count or baron to 50 lî square[4]. (Lords) who could not number 50 lî square, were not

---

[1] See the Introduction, chapter iii, pages 18–20.

[2] Most sinologists have adopted these names for the Chinese terms. Callery says, 'Les ducs, les marquis, les comtes, les vicomtes, et les barons.' See the note on Mencius, V, i, 2, 3, for the meaning given to the different terms.

[3] 'Great officers' are in Chinese Tâ Fû, 'Great Sustainers.' The character fû (夫) is different from that for 'officer,' which follows. The latter is called shih (士), often translated 'scholar,' and is 'the designation of one having a special charge.' Callery generally retains the Chinese name Tâ Fû, which I have not liked to do.

[4] A lî is made up of 360 paces. At present 27·8 lî = 10 English miles, and one geographical lî = 1458·53 English feet. The territories were not squares, but when properly measured, 'taking the length with the breadth,' were equal to so many lî square. The Chinese term rendered 'territory' is here (田), meaning 'fields;' but it is not to be supposed that that term merely denotes 'ground that could be cultivated,' as some of the commentators maintain.

admitted directly to (the audiences of) the son of Heaven. Their territories were called 'attached,' being joined to those of one of the other princes.

3. The territory assigned to each of the ducal ministers of the son of Heaven was equal to that of a duke or marquis; that of each of his high ministers was equal to that of an earl; that of his Great officers to the territory of a count or baron; and that of his officers of the chief grade to an attached territory.

4. According to the regulations, the fields of the husbandmen were in portions of a hundred acres[1] According to the different qualities of those acres, when they were of the highest quality, a farmer supported nine individuals; where they were of the next, eight; and so on, seven, six, and five. The pay of the common people, who were employed in government offices[2], was regulated in harmony with these distinctions among the husbandmen.

5. The officers of the lowest grade in the feudal states had an emolument equal to that of the husbandmen whose fields were of the highest quality; equal to what they would have made by tilling the fields. Those of the middle grade had double that of the lowest grade; and those of the highest grade double that of the middle. A Great officer of the lowest grade had double that of an officer of the highest. A high minister had four times that of

---

[1] The mâu is much less than an English acre, measuring only $733\frac{1}{3}$ square yards. An English acre is rather more than 6 mâu.

[2] But held their appointments only from the Head of their department, and were removable by him at pleasure, having no commission from the king, or from the ruler of the state in which they were.

a Great officer; and the ruler had ten times that of a high minister. In a state of the second class, the emolument of a minister was three times that of a Great officer; and that of the ruler ten times that of a minister. In small states, a high minister had twice as much as a Great officer; and the ruler ten times as much as a minister.

6. The highest minister, in a state of the second class, ranked with the one of the middle grade in a great state; the second, with the one of the lowest grade; and the lowest, with a Great officer of the highest grade. The highest minister in a small state ranked with the lowest of a great state; the second, with the highest Great officer of the other; and the lowest, with one of the lower grade.

7. Where there were officers of the middle grade and of the lowest, the number in each was three times that in the grade above it[1].

8. Of the nine provinces embracing all within the four seas[2], a province was 1000 lî square, and there were established in it 30 states of 100 lî (square) each; 60 of 70 lî; 120 of 50 lî:—in all, 210 states. The famous hills and great meres were not included in the investitures[3]. The rest of the

---

[1] Some of the critics think that this sentence is out of place, and really belongs to paragraph 5 of next section. As the text stands, and simple as it appears, it is not easy to construe.

[2] The expression 'the four seas' must have originated from an erroneous idea that the country was an insular square, with a sea or ocean on each side. The explanation of it in the *R* Ya as denoting the country surrounded by 'The 9 Î, the 8 Tî, the 7 *Z*ung, and the 6 Man,' was an attempt to reconcile the early error with the more accurate knowledge acquired in the course of time. But the name of 'seas' cannot be got over.

[3] That is, these hills and meres were still held to belong to all

ground formed attached territories and unoccupied lands of the eight provinces (apart from that which formed the royal domain), each contained (the above) 210 states[1].

9. Within the domain[2] of the son of Heaven there were 9 states of 100 lî square; 21 of 70 lî; and 63 of 50 lî:—in all, 93 states. The famous hills and great meres were not assigned[3]. The rest of the ground served to endow the officers, and to form unoccupied lands.

10. In all, in the nine provinces, there were 1773 states, not counting in (the lands of) the officers of the chief grade of the son of Heaven, nor the attached territories in the feudal states.

Section II.

1. (The contributions from) the first hundred lî (square) of the son of Heaven served to supply (the needs of) the (various) public offices; (those from the rest of) the thousand lî were for his own special use[4].

2. Beyond his thousand lî, chiefs of regions were appointed. Five states formed a union, which had

---

the people, and all had a right to the game on the hills and the fish of the waters. The princes could not deny to any the right of access to them; though I suppose they could levy a tax on what they caught.

[1] This statement must be in a great degree imaginary, supposing, as it does, that the provinces were all of the same size. They were not so; nor are the eighteen provinces of the present day so.

[2] The character in the text here is different from that usually employed to denote the royal domain.

[3] The term is different from the 'invested' of the previous paragraph. The tenures in the royal domain were not hereditary.

[4] Such seems to be the view of the *Kh*ien-lung editors. Callery translates the paragraph substantially as I have done.

a President. Ten formed a combination, which had a Leader. Thirty formed a confederation, which had a Director. Two hundred and ten formed a province, which had a Chief. In the eight provinces there were eight Chiefs, fifty-six Directors, one hundred and sixty-eight Leaders, and three hundred and thirty-six Presidents. The eight Chiefs, with those under them, were all under the two Ancients of the son of Heaven. They divided all under the sky between them, one having charge of the regions on the left and the other of those on the right, and were called the two (Great) Chiefs [1].

3. All within the thousand lî (of the royal domain) was called the Tien (or field Tenure). Outside that domain there were the 3hâi (or service territories) and the Liû (or territory for banished persons).

4. The son of Heaven had three dukes [2], nine high ministers [2], twenty-seven Great officers, and eighty-one officers of the chief grade.

5. In a great state there were three high ministers [3], all appointed by the son of Heaven; five Great

---

[1] Of these two great chiefs, we have an instance in the dukes of *K*âu and Shâo, at the rise of the *K*âu dynasty, the former having under his jurisdiction all the states west of the Shen river, and the other, all east of it. But in general, this constitution of the kingdom is imaginary.

[2] Compare the Shû V, xx. The three dukes (Kung) were the Grand Tutor, Grand Assistant, and Grand Guardian. The nine ministers were the Prime Minister, the Ministers of Instruction, Religion, War, Crime, and Works, with the Junior Tutor, Junior Assistant, and Junior Guardian added. The six ministers exist still, substantially, in the six Boards. The titles of the three Kung and their Juniors also still exist.

[3] These appear to have been the Ministers of Instruction, War, and Works. The first had also the duties of Premier, the second those of minister of Religion, and the third those of minister of Crime.

officers of the lower grade; and twenty-seven officers of the highest grade. In a state of the second class there were three high ministers, two appointed by the son of Heaven and one by the ruler; five Great officers of the lower grade; and twenty-seven officers of the highest grade. In a small state there were two high ministers, both appointed by the ruler; five Great officers of the lower grade; and twenty-seven officers of the highest grade.

6. The son of Heaven employed his Great officers as the Three Inspectors,—to inspect the states under the Chiefs of Regions[1]. For each state there were three Inspectors.

7. Within the domain of the son of Heaven the princes enjoyed their allowances; outside it they had their inheritances[2].

8. According to the regulations, any one of the three ducal ministers might wear one additional symbol of distinction,—that of the descending dragon[3].

---

[1] The *Kh*ien-lung editors think that this was a department first appointed by the Han dynasty, and that the compilers of this Book took for it the name of 'the Three Inspectors,' from king Wû's appointment of his three brothers to watch the proceedings of the son of the last sovereign of Yin, in order to give it an air of antiquity. Was it the origin of the existing Censorate?

[2] Outside the royal domain, the feudal states were all hereditary. This is a fact of all early Chinese history. In the domain itself the territories were appanages rather than states. Yet they were in some sense hereditary too. The descendants of all who had served the country well, were not to be left unprovided for. Compare Mencius I, ii, 5, 3.

[3] See the Shih, Part I, xv, Ode 6. 1, with the note in my edition of 'the Chinese Classics.' The old symbols of distinction gave rise to 'the Insignia of Civil and Military Officers' of the present dynasty, called *K*iu phin (九品). See Williams' Dictionary, p. 698. This paragraph is in the expurgated edition

But if such an addition were made (to his eight symbols), it must be by special grant. There were only nine symbols (in all). The ruler of a state of the second class wore only seven of them, and the ruler of a small state only five.

9. The high minister of a great state could not wear more than three of the symbols, and the ministers below him only two. The high ministers of a small state, and Great officers of the lowest class, wore only one.

10. The rule was that the abilities of all put into offices over the people should first be discussed. After they had been discussed with discrimination, the men were employed. When they had been (proved) in the conduct of affairs, their rank was assigned; and when their position was (thus) fixed, they received salary.

11. It was in the court that rank was conferred, the (already existing) officers being (thus) associated in the act[1]. It was in the market-place that punishment was inflicted; the multitude being (thus) associated in casting the criminals off. Hence, neither the ruler, nor (the head of) a clan, would keep a criminal who had been punished about him; a Great officer would not maintain him; nor would an officer, meet-

of the Lî *Kî*, used by Callery, and he gives for it, unfortunately, the following version:—'Il est de règle que les trois ministres (qui d'habitude n'appartiennent qu'au 8e ordre de dignitaires), en montant un degré portent l'habit des dragons en broderie. Si, après cela, il y a lieu de leur accorder de nouvelles récompenses, on leur donne des objets de valeur, car on ne va pas au delà du 9e ordre.'

[1] The presence of the officers generally would be a safeguard against error in the appointments, as they would know the individuals.

ing him on the road, speak to him. Such men were sent away to one of the four quarters, according to the sentence on each. They were not allowed to have anything to do with affairs of government, to show that there was no object in allowing them to live[1].

12. In their relation to the son of Heaven, the feudal princes were required to send every year a minor mission to the court, and every three years a greater mission; once in five years they had to appear there in person.

13. The son of Heaven, every five years, made a tour of Inspection through the fiefs[2].

14. In the second month of the year, he visited those on the East, going to the honoured mountain of Tâi. There he burnt a (great) pile of wood, and announced his arrival to Heaven; and with looks directed to them, sacrificed to the hills and rivers. He gave audience to the princes; inquired out those who were 100 years old, and went to see them: ordered the Grand music-master to bring him the poems (current in the different states)[3], that he might see the manners of the people; ordered the superintendents of markets to present (lists of prices), that he might see what the people liked and disliked, and whether they were set on extravagance and loved

[1] It has been said that these were rules of the Yin or Shang dynasty. The *Kh*ien-lung editors maintain that they were followed by all the three feudal dynasties.

[2] Compare vol. iii, pp. 39, 40.

[3] These would include ballads and songs. Perhaps 'Grand music-master' should be in the plural, meaning those officers of each state. Probably these would have given them to the king's Grand music-master.

what was bad; he ordered the superintendent of rites to examine the seasons and months, and fix the days, and to make uniform the standard tubes, the various ceremonies, the (instruments of) music, all measures, and (the fashions of) clothes. (Whatever was wrong in these) was rectified.

15. Where any of the spirits of the hills and rivers had been unattended to, it was held to be an act of irreverence, and the irreverent ruler was deprived of a part of his territory. Where there had been neglect of the proper order in the observances of the ancestral temple, it was held to show a want of filial piety, and the rank of the unfilial ruler was reduced. Where any ceremony had been altered, or any instrument of music changed, it was held to be an instance of disobedience, and the disobedient ruler was banished. Where the statutory measures and the (fashion of) clothes had been changed, it was held to be rebellion, and the rebellious ruler was taken off. The ruler who had done good service for the people, and shown them an example of virtue, received an addition to his territory and rank.

16. In the seventh month, (the son of Heaven) continued his tour, going to the south, to the mountain of that quarter[1], observing the same ceremonies as in the east. In the eighth month, he went on to the west, to the mountain of that quarter[2], observing the

[1] Mount Hăng; in the present district of Hăng-shan, dept. Hăng-*k*âu, Hu-nan.

[2] Mount Hwa; in the present district of Hwa-yin, dept. Thung *k*âu, Shen-hsî.

same ceremonies as in the south. In the eleventh month, he went on to the north, to the mountain of that quarter[1], observing the same ceremonies as in the west. (When all was done), he returned (to the capital), repaired (to the ancestral temple) and offered a bull in each of the fanes, from that of his (high) ancestor to that of his father[2].

17. When the son of Heaven was about to go forth, he sacrificed specially, but with the usual forms, to God, offered the Î sacrifice at the altar of the earth, and the Ȝhâo in the fane of his father[3]. When one of the feudal princes was about to go forth, he offered the Î sacrifice to the spirits of the land, and the Ȝhâo in the fane of his father.

18. When the son of Heaven received the feudal princes, and there was no special affair on hand, it was (simply) called an audience. They examined their ceremonies, rectified their punishments, and made uniform what they considered virtuous; thus giving honour to the son of Heaven[4].

19. When the son of Heaven gave (an instrument of) music to a duke or marquis, the presentation was

---

[1] Mount Hăng; in the present district of *Kh*ü-yang, dept. Ting-*k*âu, *K*ih-lî.

[2] I have followed here the view of Khung Ying-tâ. It seems to me that all the seven fanes of the son of Heaven were under one roof, or composed one great building, called 'the Ancestral Temple.' See p. 224.

[3] The meaning of the names of the different sacrifices here is little more than guessed at.

[4] The second sentence of this paragraph is variously understood.

preceded by a note from the signal box[1]; when giving one to an earl, count, or baron, the presentation was preceded by shaking the hand-drum. When the bow and arrows were conferred on a prince, he could proceed to execute the royal justice. When the hatchet and battle-axe were conferred, he could proceed to inflict death. When a large libation-cup was conferred, he could make the spirits from the black millet for himself. When this cup was not conferred, he had to depend for those spirits (as a gift) from the son of Heaven.

20. When the son of Heaven ordered a prince to institute instruction, he proceeded to build his schools; the children's[2], to the south of his palace, on the left of it; that for adults, in the suburbs. (The college of) the son of Heaven was called (the palace of) Bright Harmony, (and had a circlet of water). (That of) the princes was called the Palace with its semicircle of water.

[1] A representation of the signal box is here given (1). The note was made by turning the upright handle, which then struck on some arrangement inside. The hand-drum is also represented (2). It was merely a sort of rattle; only that the noise was

(1)

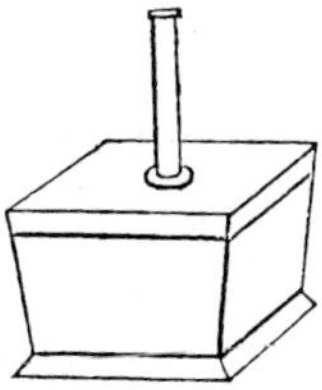

(2)

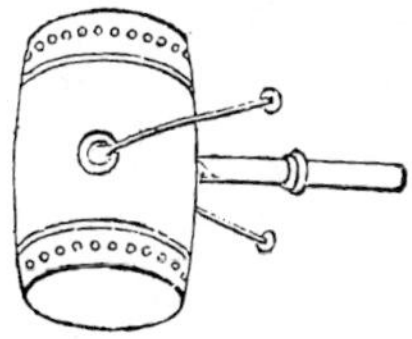

made by the two little balls striking against the ends of the drum. It is constantly seen and heard in the streets of Chinese cities at the present day, in the hands of pedlers and others.

[2] That is, the children of the princes; but an impulse was thus given to the education of children of lower degree.

21. When the son of Heaven was about to go forth on a punitive expedition, he sacrificed specially, but with the usual forms, to God; offered the Î sacrifice at the altar of the Earth, and the 3hâo in the fane of his father. He offered sacrifice also to the Father of War (on arriving) at the state which was the object of the expedition. He had received his charge from his ancestors, and the complete (plan) for the execution of it in the college. He went forth accordingly, and seized the criminals; and on his return he set forth in the college his offerings, and announced (to his ancestors) how he had questioned (his prisoners), and cut off the ears (of the slain)[1].

22. When the son of Heaven and the princes had no (special) business in hand, they had three huntings[2] in the year. The first object in them was to supply the sacrificial dishes with dried flesh; the second, to provide for guests and visitors; and the third, to supply the ruler's kitchen.

23. Not to hunt when there was no (special) business in the way was deemed an act of irreverence[3]. To hunt without observing the rules (for hunting) was deemed cruelty to the creatures of Heaven.

24. The son of Heaven did not entirely surround (the hunting ground)[4]; and a feudal prince did not

[1] Compare paragraph 17, and vol. iii, pp. 392, 393.

[2] The huntings were in spring, summer, and winter, for each of which there was its proper name. In autumn the labours of the field forbade hunting.

[3] Irreverence, in not making provision for sacrifices; disrespect, in not providing properly for guests.

[4] He left one opening for the game. This paragraph contains some of the rules for hunting.

take a (whole) herd by surprise. When the son of Heaven had done killing, his large flag was lowered; and when the princes had done, their smaller flag. When the Great officers had done, the auxiliary carriages were stopped[1]; and after this, the common people fell a hunting (for themselves).

25. When the otter sacrificed its fish[2], the foresters entered the meres and dams. When the wolf sacrificed its prey, the hunting commenced. When the dove changed into a hawk, they set their nets, large and small. When the plants and trees began to drop their leaves, they entered the hills and forests (with the axe). Until the insects had all withdrawn into their burrows, they did not fire the fields. They did not take fawns nor eggs. They did not kill pregnant animals, nor those which had not attained to their full growth. They did not throw down nests[3].

26. The chief minister determined the expenditure of the states, and it was the rule that he should do so at the close of the year. When the five kinds of grain had all been gathered in, he then determined the expenditure;—according to the size of each territory, as large or small, and the returns of the year, as abundant or poor. On the average of thirty years he determined the expenditure, regulating the outgoing by the income.

---

[1] These were light carriages used in driving and keeping the game together.

[2] See the next Book, where all these regulations are separately mentioned.

[3] The Chinese have a reputation for being callous in the infliction of punishment and witnessing suffering; and I think they are so. But these rules were designed evidently to foster kindness and sympathy.

27. A tenth of the (year's) expenditure was for sacrifices. During the three years of the mourning rites (for parents), the king did not sacrifice (in person), excepting to Heaven, Earth, and the Spirits of the land and grain; and when he went to transact any business, the ropes (for his chariot) were made of hemp (and not of silk)[1]. A tithe of three years' expenditure was allowed for the rites of mourning. When there was not sufficient for the rites of sacrifice and mourning, it was owing to lavish waste; when there was more than enough, the state was described as affluent. In sacrifices there should be no extravagance in good years, and no niggardliness in bad.

28. If in a state there was not accumulated (a surplus) sufficient for nine years, its condition was called one of insufficiency; if there was not enough for six years, one of urgency. If there was not a surplus sufficient for three years, the state could not continue. The husbandry of three years was held to give an overplus of food sufficient for one year; that of nine years, an overplus sufficient for three years. Going through thirty years (in this way), though there might be bad years, drought, and inundations, the people would have no lack or be reduced to (eating merely) vegetables, and then the son of Heaven would every day have full meals and music at them.

SECTION III.

1. The son of Heaven was encoffined on the seventh day (after his death), and interred in the seventh month. The prince of a state was en-

[1] Such is the meaning of the text here given by the *Kh*ien-lung editors. It is found also in the Khang-hsî dictionary, under the character 越, called in this usage hwo.

coffined on the fifth day, and interred in the fifth month. A Great officer, (other) officers, and the common people were encoffined on the third day, and interred in the third month. The mourning rites of three years (for parents) extended from the son of Heaven to all.

2. The common people let the coffin down into the grave by ropes, and did not suspend the interment because of rain. They raised no mound, nor planted trees over the grave. That no other business should interfere with the rites of mourning was a thing extending from the son of Heaven to the common people.

3. In the mourning rites they followed (the rank of) the dead; in sacrificing to them, that of the living. A son by a concubine did not (preside at) the sacrifices[1].

4. (The ancestral temple of) the son of Heaven embraced seven fanes (or smaller temples); three on the left and three on the right, and that of his great ancestor (fronting the south):—in all, seven. (The temple of) the prince of a state embraced five such fanes: those of two on the left, and two on the right, and that of his great ancestor:—in all, five. Great officers had three fanes:—one on the left, one on the right, and that of his great ancestor:—in all, three. Other officers had (only) one. The common people presented their offerings in their (principal) apartment[2].

---

[1] Even though he might attain to higher rank than the son of the wife proper, who represented their father.

[2] The technical terms (as they may be called) in the text make it impossible to translate this paragraph concisely, so as to make it intelligible to a foreign reader unacquainted with the significance of

5. The sacrifices in the ancestral temples of the son of Heaven and the feudal princes were that of

---

those terms. The following ground-plan of an ancestral temple of a king of *K*âu is given in the plates of the *Kh*ien-lung edition of the Lî *K*î:—after *K*û Hsî. I introduce it here with some condensations.

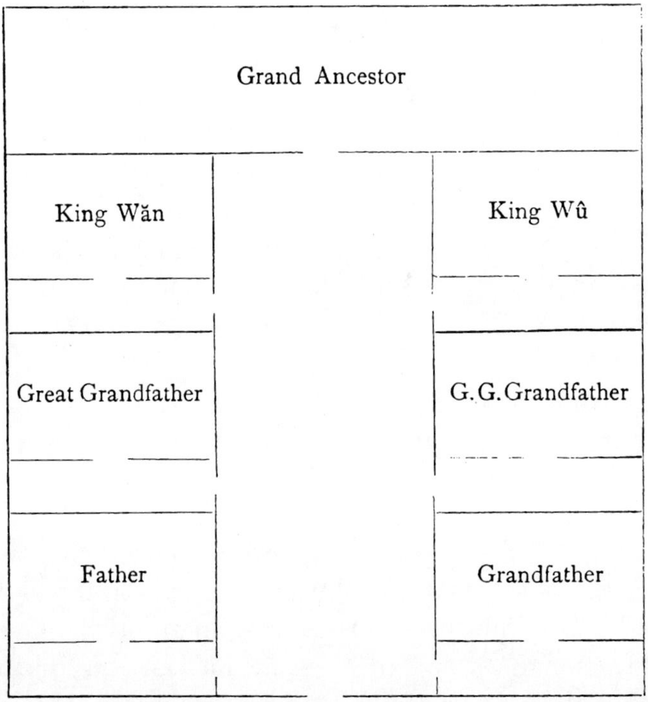

Entering at the gate on the south, we have, fronting us, at the northern end, the fane of the grand ancestor to whom, in the distant past, the family traced its line. South of his fane, on the right and left, were two fanes dedicated to kings Wăn and Wû, father and son, the joint founders of the dynasty. The four below them, two on each side, were dedicated to the four kings preceding the reigning king, the sacrificer. At the back of each fane was a comparatively dark apartment, called *kh*in (寢), where the spirit tablet was kept during the intervals between the

spring, called Yo; that of summer, called Tî; that of autumn, called *Kh*ang; and that of winter, called *Kh*ăng[1].

6. The son of Heaven sacrificed to Heaven and Earth; the princes of the states, to the (spirits of the) land and grain; Great officers offered the five sacrifices (of the house). The son of Heaven sacrificed to all the famous hills and great streams under the sky, the five mountains[2] receiving (sacrificial) honours like the honours paid (at court) to the three ducal ministers, and the four rivers[2] honours like those paid to the princes of states; the princes sacrificed to the famous hills and great streams which were in their own territories.

7. The son of Heaven and the feudal lords sacrificed to the ancient princes who had no successors to

sacrifices. When a sacrifice was offered, the tablet was brought out and placed in the centre of a screen, in the middle of the fane. As the line lengthened, while the tablets of the grand ancestor and joint ancestors always remained untouched, on a death and accession, the tablet of the next oldest occupant was removed and placed in a general apartment for the keeping of all such tablets, and that of the newly deceased king was placed in the father's fane, and the other three were shifted up, care being always taken that the tablet of a son should never follow that of his father on the same side. The number of the lower fanes was maintained, as a rule, at four. Those on the east were called *K*âo (昭), and on the west Mû (穆), the names in the text here. See the Chinese Classics, I, pp. 266, 267, and the note there.

[1] The names of some of these sacrifices and their order are sometimes given differently.

[2] For four of these mountains, see pages 217, 218, notes. The fifth was that of the centre, mount Sung, in the present district of Sung, department Ho-nan, Ho-nan. The four rivers were the *K*iang, the Hwâi, the Ho, and the *K*î.

preside over the sacrifices to them, and whose possessions now formed part of the royal domain or of their respective states.

8. The son of Heaven offered the spring sacrifice apart and by itself alone, but his sacrifices of all the other seasons were conducted on a greater scale in the fane of the high ancestor. The princes of the states who offered the spring sacrifice omitted that of the summer; those who offered that of the summer omitted that of the autumn; those who sacrificed in autumn did not do so in winter; and those who sacrificed in winter did not do so in spring[1].

In spring they offered the sacrifice of the season by itself apart; in summer, in the fane of the high ancestor[2]; in autumn and winter both the sacrifices were there associated together.

9. In sacrificing at the altars to the spirits of the land and grain, the son of Heaven used in each case a bull, a ram, and a boar; the princes, (only) a ram and a boar. Great and other officers, at the sacrifices in their ancestral temples, if they had lands, sacrificed an animal; and, if they had no lands, they only presented fruits. The common people, in the spring, presented scallions; in summer, wheat; in autumn, millet; and in winter, rice unhulled. The scallions were set forth with eggs; the wheat with

[1] The princes who omitted one sacrifice in the year would probably be absent in that season, attending at the royal court. They paid that attendance in turns from the several quarters.

[2] If in this summer service the seasonal and the sacrifice in the fane of the high sacrifice were associated together, the rule for the princes was the same as for the king. There was the ordinary associate sacrifice, and 'the great;' about which the discussions and different views have been endless.

fish; the millet with a sucking-pig; and the rice with a goose.

10. Of the bulls used in sacrificing to Heaven and Earth, the horns were (not larger than) a cocoon or a chestnut[1]. Those of the one used in the ancestral temple could be grasped with the hand; those of the ox used for (feasting) guests were a foot long.

Without sufficient cause, a prince did not kill an ox, nor a Great officer a sheep, nor another officer a dog or a pig, nor a common person eat delicate food.

The various provisions (at a feast) did not go beyond the sacrificial victims killed; the private clothes were not superior to the robes of sacrifice; the house and its apartments did not surpass the ancestral temple.

11. Anciently, the public fields were cultivated by the united labours of the farmers around them, from the produce of whose private fields nothing was levied. A rent was charged for the stances in the market-places, but wares were not taxed. Travellers were examined at the different passes, but no duties were levied from them. Into the forests and plains at the foot of mountains the people went without hindrance at the proper seasons. None of the produce was levied from the fields assigned to the younger sons of a family, nor from the holy fields. Only three days' labour was required (by the state) from the people in the course of a year. Fields and residences in the hamlets, (when once assigned), could

[1] The victims must all have been young animals; 'to show,' says Wang Thâo, 'that the sincerity of the worshipper is the chief thing in the view of Heaven.'

not be sold. Ground set apart for graves could not be sought (for any other purpose)[1].

12. The minister of Works with his (various) instruments measured the ground for the settlements of the people. About the hills and rivers, the oozy ground and the meres, he determined the periods of the four seasons. He measured the distances of one spot from another, and commenced his operations in employing the labour of the people. In all his employment of them, he imposed (only) the tasks of old men (on the able-bodied), and gave (to the old) the food-allowance of the able-bodied.

13. In all their settlements, the bodily capacities of the people are sure to be according to the sky and earthly influences, as cold or hot, dry or moist. Where the valleys are wide and the rivers large, the ground was differently laid out; and the people born in them had different customs. Their temperaments,

---

[1] Compare Mencius III, i, 3, 6–9, et al.; II, i, 5, 2–4; I, i, 3, 3, 4; III, i, 3, 15–17; with the notes. I give here also the note of P. Callery on the first sentence of this paragraph:—'Sous les trois premières dynasties, époque éloignée où il y avait peu de terrains cultivés dans l'empire, le gouvernement concédait les terres incultes par carrés équilatères ayant 900 mâu, ou arpents, de superficie. Ces carrés, qu'on nommait 3ing (井), d'après leur analogie de tracé avec le caractère 3ing, "a well," étaient divisés en neuf carrés égaux de 100 mâu chacun, au moyen de deux lignes médianes que deux autres lignes coupaient à angle droit à des distances égales. Il résultait de cette intersection de lignes une sorte de damier de trois cases de côté, ayant huit carrés sur la circonférence, et un carré au milieu. Les huit carrés du pourtour devenaient la propriété de huit colons; mais celui du centre était un champ de réserve dont la culture restait bien à la charge des huit voisins, mais dont les produits appartenaient à l'empereur.'

as hard or soft, light or grave, slow or rapid, were made uniform by different measures; their preferences as to flavours were differently harmonised; their implements were differently made; their clothes were differently fashioned, but always suitably. Their training was varied, without changing their customs; and the governmental arrangements were uniform, without changing the suitability (in each case).

14. The people of those five regions—the Middle states, and the *Z*ung, Î, (and other wild tribes round them)—had all their several natures, which they could not be made to alter. The tribes on the east were called Î. They had their hair unbound, and tattooed their bodies. Some of them ate their food without its being cooked. Those on the south were called Man. They tattooed their foreheads, and had their feet turned in towards each other. Some of them (also) ate their food without its being cooked. Those on the west were called *Z*ung. They had their hair unbound, and wore skins. Some of them did not eat grain-food. Those on the north were called Tî. They wore skins of animals and birds, and dwelt in caves. Some of them also did not eat grain-food.

The people of the Middle states, and of those Î, Man, *Z*ung, and Tî, all had their dwellings, where they lived at ease; their flavours which they preferred; the clothes suitable for them; their proper implements for use; and their vessels which they prepared in abundance. In those five regions, the languages of the people were not mutually intelligible, and their likings and desires were different. To make what was in their minds apprehended, and to communicate their likings and desires, (there were officers),—in the east, called transmitters; in the south, representationists; in the west, Tî-tîs[1]; and in the north, interpreters.

15. In settling the people, the ground was measured for the formation of towns, and then measured again in smaller portions for the allotments of the people. When the division of the ground, the cities, and the allotments were thus fixed in adaptation to one another, so that there was no ground unoccupied, and none of the people left to wander about idle, economical arrangements were made about food; and its proper business appointed for each season. Then the people had rest in their dwellings, did joyfully what they had to do, exhorted one another to labour, honoured their rulers, and loved their superiors. This having been secured, there ensued the institution of schools.

Section IV.

1. The minister of Instruction defined and set forth the six ceremonial observances[2]:—to direct and control the nature of the people; clearly illustrated the seven lessons (of morality)[3] to stimulate their virtue; inculcated uniformity in the eight objects of government[2], to guard against all excess; taught the

[1] I cannot translate Tî-tî. It was the name of a region (Williams says, 'near the Koko-nor'), the people of which had a reputation for singing.

[2] See the last paragraph of these Regulations, at the end of next Section.

[3] It has become the rule, apparently with all sinologists, to call the minister in the text here, Sze Thû, by the name of 'The minister

sameness of the course (of duty) and virtue, to assimilate manners; nourished the aged, to secure the completion of filial piety; showed pity to orphans and solitaries, to reach those who had been bereaved; exalted men of talents and worth, to give honour to virtue; and dealt summarily with the unworthy, to discountenance wickedness.

2. He commanded that, throughout the districts[1], there should be marked and pointed out to him those who were disobedient to his lessons. (This having been done), the aged men were all assembled in the school[2], and on a good day archery was practised and places were given according to merit. (At the same time) there was a feast, when places were given according to age. The Grand minister of Instruction[3] conducted thither the eminent scholars of the state and along with them superintended the business.

---

of Instruction.' Callery describes him as 'Le ministre qui a dans ses attributions l'instruction publique et les rites.' And this is correct according to the account of his functions here, in the *K*âu Lî, and in the Shû (V, xx, 8); but the characters (司 徒) simply denote 'superintendent of the multitudes.' This, then, was the conception anciently of what government had to do for the multitudes,—to teach them all moral and social duties, how to discharge their obligations to men living and dead, and to spiritual beings. The name is now applied to the president and vice-president of the board of Revenue.

[1] That is, the six districts embraced in the royal domain, each nominally containing 12,500 families.

[2] The great school of the district. The aged men would be good officers retired from duty, and others of known worth.

[3] Here we have 'the Grand minister of Instruction;' and it may be thought we should translate the name in the first paragraph in the plural. No doubt, where there is no specification of 'the grand,' it means the board or department of Education.

If those (who had been reported to him) did not (now) change, he gave orders that they who were noted as continuing disobedient in the districts on the left should be removed to those on the right, and those noted on the right to the districts on the left. Then another examination was held in the same way, and those who had not changed were removed to the nearest outlying territory. Still continuing unchanged, they were removed, after a similar trial, to the more distant territory. There they were again examined and tried, and if still found defective, they were cast out to a remote region, and for all their lives excluded from distinction.

3. Orders were given that, throughout the districts, the youths who were decided on as of promising ability should have their names passed up to the minister of Instruction, when they were called 'select scholars.' He then decided which of them gave still greater promise, and promoted them to the (great) college[1], where they were called 'eminent scholars[2].' Those who were brought to the notice of the minister were exempted from services in the districts; and those who were promoted to the (great) school, from all services under his own department, and (by and by) were called 'complete scholars[2].'

4. The (board for) the direction of Music gave all honour to its four subjects of instruction[3], and

---

[1] This would be the college at the capital.

[2] Have we not in these the prototypes of the 'Flowering Talents' (Hsiû Ʒhai 秀才) and 'Promoted Men' (*K*ü *Z*ăn 舉人) of to-day?

[3] In the text these are called 'the four Arts' and 'the four Teachings;' but the different phrases seem to have the same meaning.

arranged the lessons in them, following closely the poems, histories, ceremonies, and music of the former kings, in order to complete its scholars. The spring and autumn were devoted to teaching the ceremonies and music; the winter and summer to the poems and histories[1]. The eldest son of the king and his other sons, the eldest sons of all the feudal princes, the sons, by their wives proper, of the high ministers, Great officers, and officers of the highest grade, and the eminent and select scholars from (all) the states, all repaired (to their instruction), entering the schools according to their years.

5. When the time drew near for their quitting the college, the smaller and greater assistants[2], and the inferior director of the board, put down those who had not attended to their instructions, and reported them to the Grand director, who in turn reported them to the king. The king ordered the three ducal ministers, his nine (other) ministers, the Great officers, and the (other) officers, all to enter the school (and hold an examination). If this did not produce the necessary change; the king in person inspected the school; and if this also failed, for three days he took no full meal nor had music, after which the (culprits) were cast out to the remote regions. Sending them to those of the west was called 'a (temporary) expul-

[1] The *Kh*ien-lung editors say that 'in spring and autumn the temperature is equable and the bodily spirits good, well adapted for the practice of ceremonies and moving in time to the music, whereas the long days of summer and long nights of winter are better adapted for the tasks of learning the poems and histories.'

[2] The smaller assistants of the Grand director of Music were eighteen, and the greater four. See the *K*âu Lî, XVII, 21. Their functions are described in XXII, 45-53.

sion;' to the east, 'a temporary exile.' But all their lives they were excluded from distinction.

6. The Grand director of Music, having fully considered who were the most promising of the 'completed scholars,' reported them to the king, after which they were advanced to be under the minister of War, and called 'scholars ready for employment[1].'

7. The minister of War gave discriminating consideration (to the scholars thus submitted to him), with a view to determine the offices for which their abilities fitted them. He then reported his decisions concerning the best and ablest of them to the king, to have that judgment fixed[2]. When it was, they were put into offices. After they had discharged the duties of these, rank was given them; and, their positions being thus fixed, they received salary.

8. When a Great officer was dismissed as incompetent from his duties, he was not (again) employed in any office to the end of his life. At his death, he was buried as an (ordinary) officer.

---

[1] Exactly the name to the candidates of to-day who have succeeded at the triennial examinations at the capital; 'the Metropolitan Graduates,' as Mayers (page 72) calls them.

[2] It is strange to find the minister of War performing the services here mentioned, and only these. The *Kh*ien-lung editors say that the compilers of this Book had not seen the *K*âu Lî nor the Shû. It has been seen in the Introduction, pages 4, 5, how the *K*âu Lî came to light in the reign of Wû, perhaps fifty years after this Book was made, and even then did not take its place among the other restored monuments till the time of Liû Hsin. To make the duties here ascribed to the minister of War (literally, 'Master of Horse,' 司馬) appear less anomalous, *K*ăng and other commentators quote from the Shû (V, xx, 14) only a part of the account of his functions.

9. If any expedition of war were contemplated, orders were given to the Grand minister of Instruction to teach the scholars the management of the chariot and the wearing of the coat of mail.

10. In the case of all who professed any particular art, respect was had to their strength. If they were to go to a distant quarter, they had to display their arms and legs, and their skill in archery and charioteering was tested. All who professed particular arts for the service of their superiors, such as prayer-makers, writers, archers, carriage-drivers, doctors, diviners, and artizans,—all who professed particular arts for the service of their superiors, were not allowed to practise any other thing, or to change their offices; and when they left their districts, they did not take rank with officers. Those who did service in families (also), when they left their districts, did not take rank with officers.

11. The minister of Crime adapted the punishments (to the offences for which they were inflicted), and made the laws clear in order to deal with criminal charges and litigations. He required the three references as to its justice (before the infliction of a capital punishment)[1]. If a party had the intention, but there were not evidence of the deed, the charge was not listened to. Where a case appeared as doubtful, it was lightly dealt with; where it might be pardoned, it was (still) gravely considered.

12. In all determining on the application of any of the five punishments[2], it was required to decide

[1] See the *K*âu Lî, XXXVII, 45, 46.

[2] Branding; cutting off the nose; cutting off the feet; castration; death. See vol. iii, p. 40.

according to the judgment of Heaven. Inadvertent and redeemable offences were determined by (the circumstances of) each particular case[1].

13. When hearing a case requiring the application of any of the five punishments, (the judge) was required to have respect to the affection between father and son[2], or the righteousness between ruler and minister[3] (which might have been in the mind of the defendant), to balance his own judgment. He must consider the gravity or lightness (of the offence), and carefully try to fathom the capacity (of the offender) as shallow or deep, to determine the exact character (of his guilt). He must exert his intelligence to the utmost, and give the fullest play to his generous and loving feeling, to arrive at his final judgment. If the criminal charge appeared to him doubtful, he was to take the multitude into consultation with him; and if they also doubted, he was to pardon the defendant. At the same time he was to examine analogous cases, great and small, and then give his decision.

14. The evidence in a criminal case having thus been all taken and judgment given, the clerk reported it all to the director (of the district), who heard it and reported it to the Grand minister of Crime. He also heard it in the outer court[4], and then reported it to the king, who ordered the three ducal ministers,

[1] Vol. iii, pp. 260–263. The compilers in this part evidently had some parts of the Shû before them.

[2] Which might make either party conceal the guilt of the other.

[3] Which might in a similar way affect the evidence.

[4] The text says, 'Under the Zizyphus trees.' These were planted in the outer court of audience, and under them the different ministers of the court had their places.

with the minister and director, again to hear it. When they had (once more) reported it to the king, he considered it with the three mitigating conditions[1], and then only determined the punishment.

15. In all inflictions of punishments and fines, even light offenders (that were not doubtful) were not forgiven. Punishment may be compared to the body. The body is a complete thing; when once completed, there cannot be any subsequent change in it[2]. Hence the wise man will do his utmost (in deciding on all these inflictions).

16. Splitting words so as to break (the force of) the laws; confounding names so as to change what had been definitely settled; practising corrupt ways so as to throw government into confusion: all guilty of these things were put to death. Using licentious music; strange garments; wonderful contrivances and extraordinary implements, thus raising doubts among the multitudes: all who used or formed such things were put to death. Those who were persistent in hypocritical conduct and disputatious in hypocritical speeches; who studied what was wrong, and went on to do so more and more, and whoever increasingly followed what was wrong so as to bewilder the multitudes: these were put to death. Those

---

[1] Callery gives for this, 'qui pardonne trois fois.' The conditions were—ignorance, mistake, forgetfulness.

[2] There is here a play upon the homophonous names of different Chinese characters, often employed, as will be pointed out, in the Lî *K*î, and in which the scholars of Han set an example to future times. Callery frames a French example of the reasoning that results from it: 'Un saint est un ceint; or, la ceinture signifiant au figuré la continence, il s'ensuit que la vertu de continence est essentielle à la sainteté!'

who gave false reports about (appearances of) spirits, about seasons and days, about consultings of the tortoise-shell and stalks, so as to perplex the multitudes: these were put to death. These four classes were taken off, and no defence listened to.

17. All who had charge of the prohibitions for the regulation of the multitudes[1] did not forgive transgressions of them.

Those who had rank-tokens, the long or the round, and gilt libation-cups were not allowed to sell them in the market-places; nor were any allowed to sell robes or chariots, the gift of the king; or vessels of an ancestral temple; or victims for sacrifice; or instruments of war; or vessels which were not according to the prescribed measurements; or chariots of war which were not according to the same; or cloth or silk, fine or coarse, not according to the prescribed quality, or broader or narrower than the proper rule; or of the illegitimate colours, confusing those that were correct[2]; or cloth, embroidered or figured; or vessels made with pearls or jade; or clothes, or food, or drink, (in any way extravagant); or grain which was not in season, or fruit which was unripe; or wood which was not fit for the axe; or birds, beasts, fishes, or reptiles, which were not fit to be killed. At the frontier gates, those in charge of the prohibitions, examined travellers, forbidding such as wore strange clothes, and taking note of such as spoke a strange language.

18. The Grand recorder had the superintendence of

---

[1] These would be, especially, the superintendents of the markets.

[2] The five correct colours were—black, carnation, azure, white, and yellow.

ceremonies. He was in charge of the tablets of record, and brought before the king what (names) were to be avoided[1], and what days were unfavourable (for the doing of particular affairs)[1]. The son of Heaven received his admonitions with reverence[2].

19. (The office of) the accountants[3] prepared the complete accounts of the year to be submitted to the son of Heaven which were reverently received by the chief minister. The Grand director of Music, the Grand minister of Crime, and the (chief) superintendent of the markets, these three officers, followed with the completed accounts of their departments to be submitted to the son of Heaven. The Grand minister of Instruction, the Grand minister of War, and the Grand minister of Works, reverently received the completed accounts of their several departments from their various subordinates, and examined them, then presenting them to the son of Heaven. Those subordinates then reverently received them after being so examined and adjudicated on. This being done, the aged were feasted and the royal sympathy shown to the husbandmen. The business of the year was concluded, and the expenditure of the states was determined.

---

[1] See pages 93, 180, et al.

[2] Some of the functions here belonged to the assistant recorder, according to the *K*âu Lî, but the two were of the same department.

[3] This office was under the board of the chief minister, and consisted of sixty-two men of different grades under the *K*âu dynasty (the *K*âu Lî, I, 38; their duties are described in Book VI). It is not easy to understand all the text of the rest of the paragraph, about the final settlement of the accounts of the year.

Section V.

1. In nourishing the aged, (Shun), the lord of Yü, used the ceremonies of the drinking entertainment; the sovereigns of Hsiâ, those at entertainments (after) a reverent sacrifice or offering[1]; the men of Yin, those of a (substantial) feast; and the men of *K*âu cultivated and used all the three.

2. Those of fifty years received their nourishment in the (schools of the) districts; those of sixty, theirs in the (smaller school of the) state; and those of seventy, theirs in the college. This rule extended to the feudal states. An old man of eighty made his acknowledgment for the ruler's message, by kneeling once and bringing his head twice to the ground. The blind did the same. An old man of ninety employed another to receive (the message and gift for him).

3. For those of fifty the grain was (fine and) different (from that used by younger men). For those of sixty, flesh was kept in store. For those of seventy, there was a second service of savoury meat. For those of eighty, there was a constant supply of delicacies. For those of ninety, food and drink were never out of their chambers. Wherever they wandered (to another place), it was required that savoury meat and drink should follow them.

---

[1] The commentators make this to have been a Barmecide feast, merely to show respect for the age; and Callery, after them, gives for the text: 'La dynastie des Hsiâ faisait servir un repas qu'on ne mangeait point.' But Ying-tâ's authorities adduced to support this view do not appear to me to bear it out. See the commencing chapter of Book X, Section ii, where all this about nourishing the aged is repeated.

4. After sixty, (the coffin and other things for the mourning rites) were seen to be in readiness, (once) in the year; after seventy, once in the season; after eighty, once in the month; and after ninety, every day they were kept in good repair. But the bandages, sheet, and coverlets and cases (for the corpse) were prepared after death.

5. At fifty, one begins to decay; at sixty, he does not feel satisfied unless he eats flesh; at seventy, he does not feel warm unless he wears silk; at eighty, he does not feel warm unless there be some one (to sleep) with him; and at ninety, he does not feel warm even with that.

6. At fifty, one kept his staff always in his hand in his family; at sixty, in his district; at seventy, in the city; at eighty, (an officer) did so in the court. If the son of Heaven wished to put questions to (an officer) of ninety, he went to his house, and had rich food carried after him.

7. At seventy, (an officer) did not wait till the court was over (before he retired); at eighty, he reported every month (to the ruler's messenger) that he was still alive; at ninety, he (had delicate food sent) regularly to him every day.

8. At fifty, a (common) man was not employed in services requiring strength; at sixty, he was discharged from bearing arms along with others; at seventy, he was exempted from the business of receiving guests and visitors; and at eighty, he was free from the abstinences and other rites of mourning.

9. When one was fifty, he received the rank (of a

Great officer)[1]; at sixty, he did not go in person to the college; at seventy, he retired from the service of the government; and in mourning, he used only the dress of sackcloth (without adopting the privations of the mourning rites).

10. (Shun), the lord of Yü, nourished the aged (who had retired from the service) of the state in (the school called) the higher hsiang, and the aged of the common people (and officers who had not obtained rank) in (the school called) the lower hsiang. The sovereigns of Hsiâ nourished the former in (the school called) the hsü on the east, and the latter in (that called) the hsü on the west. The men of Yin nourished the former in the school of the right, and the latter in that of the left. The men of *K*âu entertained the former in (the school called) the eastern *k*iâo, and the latter in (what corresponded to) the hsiang of Yü. This was in the suburb of the capital on the west[2].

11. The lord of Yü wore the hwang cap in sacri-

---

[1] See Book X, Section ii 1. This was, say the *Kh*ien-lung editors, a lesson against forwardness in seeking office and rank, as retirement at seventy was a lesson against cleaving to these too long.

[2] It is wearisome to try and thread one's way through the discussions about the schools, called by all these different names. One thing is plain, that there were the lower schools which boys entered when they were eight, and the higher schools into which they passed from these. But in this paragraph these institutions are mentioned not in connexion with education, but as they were made available for the assembling and cherishing of the aged. They served various purposes. A school-room with us may do the same, occasionally; it was the rule in ancient China that the young should be taught and the old ministered to in the same buildings.

ficing (in the ancestral temple), and the white robes in nourishing the aged. The sovereigns of Hsiâ used the shâu cap in sacrificing, and the upper and lower dark garments of undress in nourishing the aged. During the Yin, they used the hsü cap in sacrificing, and the upper and lower garments, both of white thin silk, in nourishing the aged. During the *K*âu dynasty, they used the mien cap in sacrificing, and the dark-coloured upper and lower garments in nourishing the aged.

12. The kings of the three dynasties[1], in nourishing the old, always had the years of those connected with them brought to their notice. Where (an officer) was eighty, one of his sons was free from all duties of government service; where he was ninety, all the members of his family were set free from them. In cases of parties who were disabled or ill, and where the attendance of others was required to wait upon them, one man was discharged from those duties (for the purpose). Parties mourning for their parents had a discharge for three years. Those mourning for one year or nine months had a discharge for three months. Where an officer was about to move to another state, he was discharged from service for three months beforehand. When one came from another state, he was not required to take active service for a round year.

13. One who, while quite young, lost his father was called an orphan; an old man who had lost his sons was called a solitary. An old man who had lost his wife was called a pitiable (widower); an old woman who had lost her husband was called a poor

[1] Hsiâ, Shang or Yin, and *K*âu.

(widow). These four classes were the most forlorn of Heaven's people, and had none to whom to tell their wants; they all received regular allowances.

14. The dumb, the deaf, the lame, such as had lost a member, pigmies, and mechanics, were all fed according to what work they were able to do.

15. On the roads, men took the right side and women the left; carriages kept in the middle. A man kept behind another who had a father's years; he followed one who might be his elder brother more closely, but still keeping behind, as geese fly after one another in a row. Friends did not pass by one another, when going the same way. (In the case of an old and a young man, carrying burdens,) both were borne by the younger; and if the two were too heavy for one, he took the heavier. A man with grey hair was not allowed to carry anything, though he might do it with one hand.

16. An officer of superior rank, of the age of sixty or seventy, did not walk on foot. A common man, at that age, did not go without flesh to eat.

17. A Great officer, (having land of his own), was not permitted to borrow the vessels for sacrifice; nor to make vessels for his own private use before he had made those for sacrifice.

18. A space of one lî square contained fields amounting to 900 mâu[1]. Ten lî square were equal to 100 spaces of one lî square, and contained 90,000 mâu. A hundred lî square were equal to 100 spaces of ten lî square, and contained 9,000,000 mâu. A

[1] See note as to the size of the mâu on page 218.

thousand lî square were equal to 100 spaces of 100 lî square, and contained 900,000,000 mâu.

19. From mount Hăng[1] to the southernmost point of the Ho was hardly 1000 lî. From that point to the *K*iang was hardly 1000 lî. From the *K*iang to mount Hăng in the south was more than 1000 lî. From the Ho on the east to the eastern sea was more than 1000 lî. From the Ho on the east to the same river on the west was hardly 1000 lî; and from that to the Moving Sands[2] was more than 1000 lî. (The kingdom) did not pass the Moving Sands on the west, nor mount Hăng on the south. On the east it did not pass the eastern sea, nor on the north did it pass (the other) mount Hăng. All within the four seas, taking the length with the breadth, made up a space of 3000 lî square, and contained eighty trillions of mâu[3].

20. A space of 100 lî square contained ground to the amount of 9,000,000 mâu. Hills and mounds, forests and thickets, rivers and marshes, ditches and canals, city walls and suburbs, houses, roads, and

---

[1] See notes on pages 217, 218. I have said below '(the other) mount Hăng;' but the names, or characters for the names, of the two mountains are different in Chinese.

[2] What is now called the desert of Gobi.

[3] As it is in the text $= 80 \times 10000 \times 100000 \times 10000 \times 100000$ mâu. A translator, if I may speak of others from my own experience, is much perplexed in following and verifying the calculations in this and the other paragraphs before and after it. The *Kh*ien-lung editors and Wang Thâo use many pages in pointing out the errors of earlier commentators, and establishing the correct results according to their own views, and I have thought it well to content myself with simply giving a translation of the text.

lanes took up one third of it, leaving 6,000,000 mâu.

21. Anciently, according to the cubit of *K*âu, eight cubits formed a pace. Now, according to the same, six cubits and four inches make a pace. One hundred ancient mâu were equal to 146 of the present day and thirty paces. One hundred ancient lî were equal to 121 of the present day, sixty paces, four cubits, two inches and two-tenths.

22. A space of 1000 lî square contained 100 spaces of 100 lî square each. In this were constituted thirty states of 100 lî square, leaving what would have been enough for other seventy of the same size. There were also constituted sixty states of 70 lî square, twenty-nine of 100 lî square, and forty spaces of 10 lî square; leaving enough for forty states of 100 lî square, and sixty spaces of 10 lî square. There were also constituted a hundred and twenty states of 50 lî square, and thirty of 100 lî square, leaving enough for ten of the same size, and sixty spaces of 10 lî square.

The famous hills and great meres were not included in the fiefs; and what remained was assigned for attached territories and unoccupied lands. Those unappropriated lands were taken to reward any of the princes of acknowledged merit, and what was cut off from some others (because of their demerit) became unappropriated land.

23. The territory of the son of Heaven, amounting to 1000 lî square, contained 100 spaces of 100 lî square each. There were constituted nine appanages of 100 lî square, leaving ninety-one spaces of the same size. There were also constituted twenty-one

appanages of 70 lî square, ten of 100 lî, and twenty-nine spaces of 10 lî square; leaving enough for eighty of 100 lî square, and seventy-one of 10 lî. There were further constituted sixty-three appanages of 50 lî square, fifteen of 100 lî, and seventy-five spaces of 10 lî, while there still remained enough for sixty-four appanages of 100 lî square, and ninety-six spaces of 10 lî each.

24. The officers of the lowest grade in the feudal states received salary sufficient to feed nine individuals; those of the second grade, enough to feed eighteen; and those of the highest, enough for thirty-six. A Great officer could feed 72 individuals; a minister, 288; and the ruler, 2880.

In a state of the second class, a minister could feed 216; and the ruler, 2160.

A minister of a small state could feed 144 individuals; and the ruler, 1440.

In a state of the second class, the minister who was appointed by its ruler received the same emolument as the minister of a small state.

25. The Great officers of the son of Heaven acted as 'the three inspectors.' When they were inspecting a state, their salary was equal to one of its ministers, and their rank was that of a ruler of a state of the second class. Their salaries were derived from the territories under the chiefs of regions[1].

26. The chiefs of regions, on occasion of their appearing at the court of the son of Heaven, had cities assigned them for purification[2] within his domain like those of his officers of the chief grade.

[1] See page 212, paragraph 2, and note 1, page 213.

[2] The text says, 'Cities for bathing and washing the hair;'

27. The (appointed) heir-sons[1] of the feudal princes inherited their states. Great officers (in the royal domain) did not inherit their rank. They were employed as their ability and character were recognised, and received rank as their merit was proved. Till their rank was conferred (by the king), (the princes) were in the position of his officers of the chief grade, and so they ruled their states. The Great officers of the states did not inherit their rank and emoluments.

28. The six ceremonial observances were:—capping; marrying; mourning rites; sacrifices; feasts; and interviews. The seven lessons (of morality) were:—(the duties between) father and son; elder brother and younger; husband and wife; ruler and minister; old and young; friend and friend; host and guest. The eight objects of government were:—food and drink; clothes; business (or, the profession); maintenance of distinctions; measures of length; measures of capacity; and definitely assigned rules[2].

---

but preparing by mental exercises for appearing before the king is also intimated by the phrase.

[1] A son, generally the eldest son by the wife proper, had to be recognised by the king before he could be sure of succeeding to his father.

[2] See page 230, paragraph 1.

BOOK IV. THE YÜEH LING

OR

PROCEEDINGS OF GOVERNMENT IN THE DIFFERENT MONTHS.

SECTION I. PART I.

1. In the first month of spring the sun is in Shih, the star culminating at dusk being 3han, and that culminating at dawn Wei[1].

2. Its days are *k*iâ and yî[2].

---

[1] In this month the conjunction of the sun and moon took place in Shih or α Markab Pegasi. 3han is a constellation embracing Betelguese, Bellatrix, Rigel, γ, δ, ϵ, ζ, η, of Orion; and Wei is ϵ, μ, of Scorpio. Shih is called in the text Ying Shih, 'the Building Shih,' because this month was the proper time at which to commence building.

[2] *K*iâ and yî are the first two of the 'ten heavenly stems,' which are combined with the 'twelve earthly branches,' to form the sixty binomial terms of 'the cycle of sixty,' that was devised in a remote antiquity for the registration of successive days, and was subsequently used also in the registration of successive years. The origin of the cycle and of the names of its terms is thus far shrouded in mystery; and also the application of those terms to the various purposes of divination. The five pairs of the stems correspond, in the jargon of mysterious speculation, to the five elements of wood, fire, earth, metal, and water, and, as will be seen in this Book, to the seasons of spring, summer, the intermediate centre, autumn, and winter. Whether there be anything more in this short notice than a declaration of this fact, or any indication of the suitableness of 'the days' for certain 'undertakings' in them, as even the *Kh*ien-lung editors seem to think, I cannot say.

3. Its divine ruler is Thâi Hâo, and the (attending) spirit is Kâu-mang[1].

4. Its creatures are the scaly[2].

5. Its musical note is *K*io, and its pitch-tube is the Thâi Ȝhâu[3].

6. Its number is eight[4]; its taste is sour; its smell is rank.

---

[1] Thâi Hâo, 'the Grandly Bright,' is what is called 'the dynastic designation' of Fû-hsî and his line. By the time that the observances described in this Book had come into use, Fû-hsî and other early personages had been deified (帝), and were supposed to preside over the seasons of the year. To him as the earliest of them was assigned the presidency of the spring, and the element of wood, the phenomena of vegetation being then most striking. He was the 'divine ruler' of the spring, and sacrificed to in its months; and at the sacrifices there was associated with him, as assessor, an inferior personage called Kâu-mang (literally, 'curling fronds and spikelets'), said to have been a son of Shâo Hâo, another mythical sovereign, founder of the line of *K*in Thien (金天氏). But Shâo Hâo was separated from Thâi Hâo by more than 1000 years. The association at these sacrifices in the spring months of two personages so distant in time from each other as Fû-hsî and Kâu-mang, shows how slowly and irregularly the process of deification and these sacrifices had grown up.

[2] The character for which I have given 'creatures' is often translated by 'insects;' but fishes, having scales, must form a large portion of what are here intended. 'The seven (zodiacal) constellations of the east,' says Wû *Kh*ăng, 'make up the Azure Dragon, and hence all moving creatures that have scales belong to (the element of) wood.'

[3] *K*io is the name of the third of the five musical notes of the Chinese scale, corresponding to our B (?); and Thâi Ȝhâu is the name of one of the twelve tubes by which, from a very early date, music was regulated. The Thâi Ȝhâu, or 'Great Pipe,' was the second of the tubes that give the 'six upper musical accords.'

[4] The 'number' of wood is three, which added to five, the

7. Its sacrifice is that at the door[1], and of the parts of the victim the spleen has the foremost place[1].

8. The east winds resolve the cold. Creatures that have been torpid during the winter begin to move. The fishes rise up to the ice. Otters sacrifice fish. The wild geese make their appearance[2].

9. The son of Heaven occupies the apartment on the left of the *Kh*ing Yang (Fane); rides in the carriage with the phœnix (bells), drawn by the azure-dragon (horses), and carrying the green flag; wears the green

'number' of earth, gives eight, the 'number' of the months of spring; but this, to me at least, is only a jargon.

[1] This was one of the sacrifices of the house; see paragraph 6, page 116, and especially the seventh paragraph of Book XX. As the door is the place of exodus, it was the proper place for this sacrifice in the spring, when all the energies of nature begin to be displayed afresh. Among the five viscera,—the heart, the liver, the spleen, the lungs, and the kidneys,—the spleen corresponds to the element of earth, and therefore it was made prominent in this service, in the season when the earth seems to open its womb beneath the growing warmth of the year.

[2] These are all phenomena of the spring. The third of them is differently expressed in Hwai-nan Ȝze, the Tâoist grandson of the founder of the Han dynasty (see Book V of his works), and in the Hsiâ Hsiâo *K*ăng, showing that this text of the Lî *K*î was taken from Lü Pû-wei, if the whole Book were not written by him. They read 魚陟負氷, which Professor Douglas renders, 'Fish mount (to the surface of) the water, bearing on their backs pieces of ice.' But the meaning of the longer text is simply what I have given. Ying-tâ says, 'Fishes, during the intense cold of winter, lie close at the bottom of the water, attracted by the greater warmth of the earth; but, when the sun's influence is felt, they rise and swim near to the ice.' 負冰 = 'with their backs near to the ice.' What is said about the otter is simply a superstitious misinterpretation of its habit of eating only a small part of its prey, and leaving the rest on the bank. The geese come from the south on the way to their quarters during the warmer season in the north.

robes, and the (pieces of) green jade (on his cap and at his girdle pendant). He eats wheat and mutton. The vessels which he uses are slightly carved, (to resemble) the shooting forth (of plants)[1].

[1] The *Kh*ing Yang ('Green and Bright') was one of the principal divisions in the Hall of Distinction of Book XII. We must suppose that the sovereign went there (among other purposes) to give out the first day of the month, and did so in the apartment indicated, and in the style and robes and ornaments of the text, in the first month of spring. The ancient Shun, it is said, set the example of the carriage with bells, whose tinkling was supposed to resemble the notes of the lwan, a bird at which we can only guess, and which has been called the phœnix, and the argus pheasant. Horses above eight feet high were called dragon steeds. The predominating green colour suits the season and month; but what made wheat and mutton then peculiarly suitable for the royal mat, I do not know the fancies of Tâoism sufficiently to be able to understand.

In the plates to the *Kh*ien-lung edition of our classic, the following rude ground-plan of the structure is given to illustrate the various references to it in this Book:—

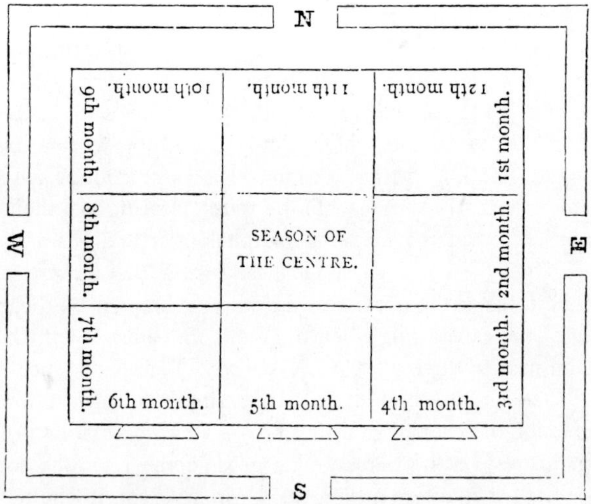

10. In this month there takes place the inauguration of spring. Three days before this ceremony, the Grand recorder informs the son of Heaven, saying, 'On such and such a day is the inauguration of the spring. The energies of the season are fully seen in wood.' On this the son of Heaven devotes himself to self-purification, and on the day he leads in person the three ducal ministers, his nine high ministers, the feudal princes (who are at court), and his Great officers, to meet the spring in the eastern suburb[1];

The building is made to consist of nine large apartments or halls; three fronting the different points of the compass, and one in the centre; making nine in all. That in the centre was called 'The Grand Apartment of the Grand Fane;' south from it was 'The Ming Thang Grand Fane;' on the east 'The *Kh*ing Yang Grand Fane;' on the west 'The Ȝung Yang Grand Fane;' and on the north 'The Hsüan Thang Grand Fane.'

In the second month of the seasons, the king went the round of the Grand Fanes. The four corner apartments were divided into two each, each one being named from the Grand Fane on the left or right of which it was. Commencing with the half on the left of the *Kh*ing Yang Fane, the king made the circuit of all the others and of the Fanes, returning to the other half on the right of the Hsüan Thang Fane in the twelfth month. The Grand Apartment in the centre was devoted to the imaginary season of the centre, between the sixth and seventh months, or the end of summer and beginning of autumn.

[1] We are not told what the ceremonies in the inauguration of the spring were. The phrase li *kh*un (立春) is the name of the first of the twenty-four terms into which the Chinese year is divided, dating now from the sun's being in the fifteenth degree of Aquarius. Kăng Hsüan thought that the meeting of the spring in the eastern suburb was by a sacrifice to the first of 'the five planetary gods,' corresponding to Jupiter, 'the Azure Tî, called Ling-wei-jang' (靈威仰). But where he found that name, and what is its significance, is a mystery; and the whole doctrine

and on their return, he rewards them all in the court[1].

11. He charges his assistants[2] to disseminate (lessons of) virtue, and harmonise the governmental orders, to give effect to the expressions of his satisfaction and bestow his favours; down to the millions of the people. Those expressions and gifts thereupon proceed, every one in proper (degree and direction).

12. He also orders the Grand recorder to guard the statutes and maintain the laws, and (especially) to observe the motions in the heavens of the sun and moon, and of the zodiacal stars in which the conjunctions of these bodies take place, so that there should be no error as to where they rest and what they pass over; that there should be no failure in the record of all these things, according to the regular practice of early times.

13. In this month the son of Heaven on the first (hsin)[3] day prays to God for a good year; and afterwards, the day of the first conjunction of the sun and moon having been chosen, with the handle and share of the plough in the carriage, placed between the man-at-arms who is its third occupant and the driver, he conducts his three ducal ministers, his nine high ministers, the feudal princes and his Great officers, all with their own hands to plough the field of

of five planetary Tîs is held to be heresy, and certainly does not come from the five King.

[1] This rewarding, it is understood, was that mentioned in paragraph 15, p. 217.

[2] These assistants are supposed to be the 'three ducal ministers.

[3] This took and takes place on the first hsin (辛) day, the first day commencing with that character, the eighth of the 'stems.'

God. The son of Heaven turns up three furrows, each of the ducal ministers five, and the other ministers and feudal princes nine[1]. When they return, he takes in his hand a cup in the great chamber, all the others being in attendance on him and the Great officers, and says, 'Drink this cup of comfort after your toil.'

14. In this month the vapours of heaven descend and those of the earth ascend. Heaven and earth are in harmonious co-operation. All plants bud and grow.

15. The king gives orders to set forward the business of husbandry. The inspectors of the fields are ordered to reside in the lands having an eastward exposure, and (see that) all repair the marches and divisions (of the ground), and mark out clearly the paths and ditches. They must skilfully survey the mounds and rising grounds, the slopes and defiles, the plains and marshes, determining what the different lands are suitable for, and where the different grains will grow best. They must thus instruct and lead on the people, themselves also engaging in the tasks. The business of the fields being thus ordered, the guiding line is first put in requisition, and the husbandry is carried on without error[2].

16. In this month orders are given to the chief director of Music to enter the college, and practise the dances (with his pupils)[3].

---

[1] The services described here are still performed, in substance, by the emperors of China and their representatives throughout the provinces. The field is generally called 'the imperial field,' through error. The grain produced by it was employed in the sacrifices or religious services of which God (Shang Tî) was the object, and hence arose the denomination.

[2] Compare vol. iii, pp. 320–322, 370–373.

[3] 'The chief director of Music' would be the same as the Tâ

17. The canons of sacrifice are examined and set forth, and orders are given to sacrifice to the hills and forests, the streams and meres, care being taken not to use any female victims[1].

18. Prohibitions are issued against cutting down trees.

19. Nests should not be thrown down; unformed insects should not be killed, nor creatures in the womb, nor very young creatures, nor birds just taking to the wing, nor fawns, nor should eggs be destroyed.

20. No congregating of multitudes should be allowed, and no setting about the rearing of fortifications and walls[2].

21. Skeletons should be covered up, and bones with the flesh attached to them buried.

22. In this month no warlike operations should be undertaken; the undertaking of such is sure to be followed by calamities from Heaven. The not undertaking warlike operations means that they should not commence on our side[3].

Sze Yo of the *K*âu Lî, Book XXII. There were dances of war (wan), and dances of peace (wân); but neither is in the text. But either term may include both classes of dancing. Callery translates by 'faire des évolutions.'

[1] Not to destroy the life unborn. At 'the great sacrifices,' those to Heaven and Earth, and in the ancestral temple, only male victims were used, females being deemed 'unclean.' The host of minor sacrifices is intended here.

[2] Such operations would interfere with the labours of husbandry.

[3] War is specially out of time in the genial season of spring; but a state, when attacked, must, and might, defend itself even then.

23. No change in the ways of heaven is allowed; nor any extinction of the principles of earth; nor any confounding of the bonds of men[1].

24. If in the first month of spring the governmental proceedings proper to summer were carried out, the rain would fall unseasonably, plants and trees would decay prematurely, and the states would be kept in continual fear. If the proceedings proper to autumn were carried out, there would be great pestilence among the people; boisterous winds would work their violence; rain would descend in torrents; orach, fescue, darnel, and southernwood would grow up together. If the proceedings proper to winter were carried out, pools of water would produce their destructive effects, snow and frost would prove very injurious, and the first sown seeds would not enter the ground[2].

PART II.

1. In the second month of spring, the sun is in Khwei, the star culminating at dusk being Hû, and that culminating at dawn *K*ien-hsing[3].

2. Its days are *k*iâ and yî. Its divine ruler is Thâi Hâo, the attending spirit is Kâu-mang. Its

[1] Compare what is said in the fifth Appendix to the Yî King, paragraph 4 (vol. xvi, pp. 423, 424). The next paragraph is the sequel of this.

[2] Such government would be comparable to the inversion of the seasons in the course of nature. Compare Proverbs xxvi. 1.

[3] The constellation Khwei contains β (Mirac), δ, ϵ, ζ, μ, ν, π of Andromeda, and some stars of Pisces. Hû or Hû *K*ih contains δ, ϵ, η, κ, of Canis Major; and δ, ω, of Argo; and *K*ien-hsing ν, ξ, π, ρ, σ, of Sagittarius' head.

creatures are the scaly. Its musical note is *K*io, and its pitch-tube is the *K*iâ *K*ung[1].

3. Its number is eight; its taste is sour; its smell is rank. Its sacrifice is that at the door, and of the parts of the victim the spleen has the foremost place.

4. The rain begins to fall[2]. The peach tree begins to blossom. The oriole sings. Hawks are transformed into doves[3].

5. The son of Heaven occupies the *Kh*ing Yang Grand Fane[4]; rides in the carriage with the phœnix bells, drawn by the azure dragon-(horses), and bearing the green flag. He is dressed in the green robes, and wears the azure gems. He eats wheat

---

[1] *K*iâ *K*ung, 'the double tube,' is the second tube of the six lower accords.

[2] Literally, 'There commence the rains.' 'The rains' is now the name of the second of the twenty-four terms (February 15 to March 4).

[3] This is the converse of the phenomenon in page 277, paragraph 3. Both are absurd, but the natural rendering in the translation is the view of Kăng, Ying-tâ, Kâo Yû (the glossarist of Hwâi-nan Ȝze), and the *Kh*ien-lung editors. Seeking for the actual phenomenon which gave rise to the superstitious fancy, Professor Douglas renders the corresponding sentence of the Hsiâ *K*ăng by 'hawks become crested hawks,' and thinks that the notice is based on the appearance of the hawks when 'the rearing instinct becomes excessive, and birds of prey become excited.' It may be so, but this meaning cannot be brought out of the text, and should not be presented as that of the writer of the Book.

[4] See the note on p. 252. The three apartments (two of them subdivided) on the east of the Hall of Distinction, all received the general designation of *Kh*ing Yang, 'the Green and Bright,' as characteristic of the season of Spring. It was now the second month of that season, and the king takes his place in the principal or central apartment, 'the Grand Fane.'

and mutton. The vessels which he uses are slightly carved, (to resemble) the bursting forth (of nature).

6. In this month, they keep both the young buds and those more advanced from being disturbed; they nourish both the young animals and those not fully grown; they especially watch over all orphans.

7. The fortunate day is chosen, and orders are given to the people to sacrifice at their altars to the spirits of the ground[1].

8. Orders are given to the (proper) officers to examine the prisons; to remove fetters and handcuffs; that there shall be no unregulated infliction of the bastinado; and that efforts shall be made to stop criminal actions and litigations.

9. In this month the swallow makes its appearance[2]. On the day of its arrival, the son of Heaven sacrifices to the first match-maker with a bull, a ram, and a boar. He goes to do so in person, with his queen and help-mates, attended by his nine ladies of honour. Peculiar courtesy is shown to those whom he has (lately) approached. Bow-cases have been brought, and a bow and arrows are given to each before (the altar of) the first match-maker.

10. In this month day and night are equal[3]. Thunder utters its voice, and the lightning begins

---

[1] The sacrifice here was not that to Earth, which it was competent to the king alone to offer; nor to the spirits of the territories of the different states. It was offered by the people generally to the spirits presiding over their fields.

[2] The swallow is 'the dark-coloured bird,' of the third sacrificial ode of the Shang dynasty; see vol. iii, p. 307.

[3] The vernal equinox.

to be seen. Insects in their burrows are all in motion, opening their doors and beginning to come forth.

11. Three days before the thunder[1], a bell with a wooden tongue is sounded, to give notice to all the people. 'The thunder,' it is said, 'is about to utter its voice. If any of you be not careful of your behaviour, you shall bring forth children incomplete; there are sure to be evils and calamities.'

12. At the equinox they make uniform the measures of length and capacity; the weight of 30 catties, the steelyard, and the weight of 120 catties. They correct the peck and bushel, the steelyard weights and the bushel-scraper[2].

13. In this month few of the husbandmen remain in their houses in the towns. They repair, however, their gates and doors, both of wood and wattles; and put their sleeping apartments and temples all in good repair. No great labours, which would interfere with the work of husbandry, should be undertaken[3].

14. In this month (the fishermen) should not let the streams and meres run dry, nor drain off all the water from the dams and ponds, (in order to catch all the fish), nor should (the hunters) fire the hills and forests.

---

[1] We are not told how they knew this third day.

[2] A catty (*k*in) at present = $1\frac{1}{3}$lb. avoirdupois. The *kh*ün, or 30 catties, = 40lbs. av.; and the shih, or 120 catties, = 160 lbs. av.; see Williams' Commercial Guide, pp. 278–231. The tâu (or peck, in use in the market) contains 10 catties of dry, cleaned rice, and measures 316 cubic ȝhun, or inches; and the hû, or bushel, = 5 tâu. The bushel-scraper is a piece of wood or roller used to level the top of the hû. But see Williams, pp. 281, 282.

[3] Compare vol. iii, pp. 368–373.

15. The son of Heaven at this time offers a lamb (to the ruler of cold), and opens the (reservoirs of) ice. Before (using it generally), they offer some in their principal apartment or in the ancestral temple[1].

16. On the first ting day[2] orders are given to the chief director of Music to exhibit the civil dances and unfold the offerings of vegetables[3] (to the inventor of music). The son of Heaven, at the head of the three ducal ministers, his nine high ministers, the feudal princes (at court), and his Great officers, goes in person to see the ceremony. On the second ting[2] day orders are given again to the same chief to enter the college, and practise music (with his pupils).

17. In this month at the (smaller) services of supplication[4] they do not use victims. They use offerings of jade, square and round, and instead (of victims) skins and pieces of silk.

18. If in this second month of spring the governmental proceedings proper to autumn were observed,

---

[1] Compare vol. iii, page 445. Where there was an ancestral temple, the ice would be presented there. The people who had no such temple might present it before the spirit-tablets of their deceased in their principal apartment, where these were set up.

[2] The fourth and fourteenth cycle days.

[3] The offerings were small and scanty in this month, fruits not yet being ready for such a use. Cress and tussel-pondweed are mentioned among the vegetables which were presented on this occasion.

[4] The received text here means not 'services of supplication,' but sacrifices. That which I have adopted is found in 3hâi Yung, and is approved by the *Kh*ien-lung editors. It is a necessary alteration, for in paragraphs 9 and 15 we have instances of victims used this month at sacrifices. The change in the text is not great in Chinese, the character 祈 for 祀.

there would be great floods in the states; cold airs would be constantly coming; and plundering attacks would be frequent. If those of winter were observed, the warm and genial airs would be insufficient; the wheat would not ripen; and raids and strifes would be rife among the people. If those of summer were observed, there would be great droughts among the people; the hot airs would come too early; and caterpillars and other insects would harm the grain[1].

PART III.

1. In the last month of spring, the sun is in Wei, the constellation culminating at dusk being *Kh*ih-hsing, and that culminating at dawn *Kh*ien-niû[2].

2. Its days are *k*iâ and yî. Its divine ruler is Thâi Hâo, and the attending spirit is Kâu-mang. Its creatures are the scaly. Its musical note is the *K*io, and its pitch-tube is the Kû Hsien[3]. Its number is eight. Its taste is sour. Its smell is rank.

3. Its sacrifice is that at the door, and of the parts of the victim the spleen has the foremost place.

---

[1] Before this and the corresponding paragraphs in the Parts of the Book that follow, we must always understand paragraph 23 of the last Part, of which these concluding paragraphs are supposed to be the natural sequence.

[2] Wei is the seventeenth of the twenty-eight Chinese constellations (longitude in 1800, 44° 8′ 17″) corresponding to Musca borealis. *Kh*ih-hsing is understood to be α (Alphard) of Hydra, and small stars near it. *Kh*ien-niû corresponds to certain stars (ε, μ, ν) in the neck of Aquila.

[3] Kû Hsien, 'the lady bathes,' is the third of the tubes that give the six upper musical accords.

4. The Elaeococca begins to flower[1]. Moles are transformed into quails[2]. Rainbows begin to appear. Duckweed begins to grow.

5. The son of Heaven occupies the apartment on the right of the *Kh*ing Yang (Fane); rides in the carriage with the phœnix bells, drawn by the azure dragon-(horses), and bearing the green flag. He is dressed in the green robes, and wears the azure gems. He eats wheat and mutton. The vessels which he uses are slightly carved, (to resemble) the bursting forth (of nature).

6. In this month the son of Heaven presents robes yellow as the young leaves of the mulberry tree to the ancient divine ruler (and his queen)[3].

7. Orders are given to the officer in charge of the boats to turn a boat bottom up. Five times he does so, and five times he turns it back again, after which he reports that it is ready for the son of Heaven, who

---

[1] This would probably be the Elaeococca vernicia, or Aleurites cordata.

[2] This statement, perhaps, arose from seeing quails running about among the mole-hills. The *Kh*ien-lung editors say that the quails fly at night, and in the day keep hidden among the grass; but they seem to admit the transformation. Professor Douglas explains the error from a want of recognition of the migration of quails.

[3] Callery translates this by:—'L'empereur offre de la belle jaune de céréales (aux empereurs anciens et modernes qui l'ont précédé),' following a different reading for the article offered. The general view is what I have followed. The offering is supposed to have been in connexion with a sacrifice preparatory to the silkworm season. The rearing of silkworms was due, it was supposed, to Hsî-ling, the wife of the Yellow Tî. He is the 'Ancient Tî' intended here, I suppose. The name is not to be taken as in the plural. See the Khang-hsî dictionary on the character *kh*ü (鞠).

then gets into it for the first time (this spring). He offers a snouted sturgeon (which he has caught) in the rear apartment of the ancestral temple, and also prays that the wheat may yield its produce[1].

8. In this month the influences of life and growth are fully developed; and the warm and genial airs diffuse themselves. The crooked shoots are all put forth, and the buds are unfolded. Things do not admit of being restrained.

9. The son of Heaven spreads his goodness abroad, and carries out his kindly promptings. He gives orders to the proper officers to distribute from his granaries and vaults, giving their contents to the poor and friendless, and to relieve the needy and destitute; and to open his treasuries and storehouses, and to send abroad through all the nation the silks and other articles for presents, thus stimulating the princes of states to encourage the resort to them of famous scholars and show courtesy to men of ability and virtue.

10. In this month, he charges the superintendents of works, saying, 'The rains of the season will be coming down, and the waters beneath will be swelling up. Go in order over the states and visit the towns, inspecting everywhere the low and level grounds. Put the dykes and dams in good repair, clear the ditches and larger channels, and open all paths, allowing no obstruction to exist.'

[1] The five times repeated inspection of the boat does seem rather ridiculous. We must regard the king's taking to the boat as an encouragement to the fishermen, as his ploughing was to the husbandmen. The long-snouted sturgeon has always been called 'the royal sturgeon.' How the praying for a good wheat harvest seems to be connected with this ceremony I do not know.

11. The nets used in hunting animals and birds, hand nets, archers' disguises, and injurious baits should not (in this month) issue from (any of) the nine gates[1].

12. In this month orders are given to the foresters throughout the country not to allow the cutting down of the mulberry trees and silk-worm oaks. About these the cooing doves clap their wings, and the crested birds light on them[2]. The trays and baskets with the stands (for the worms and cocoons) are got ready. The queen, after vigil and fasting, goes in person to the eastern fields to work on the mulberry trees. She orders the wives and younger women (of the palace) not to wear their ornamental dresses, and to suspend their woman's-work, thus stimulating them to attend to their business with the worms. When this has been completed, she apportions the cocoons, weighs out (afterwards) the silk, on which they go to work, to supply the robes for the solstitial and other great religious services, and for use in the ancestral temple. Not one is allowed to be idle.

13. In this month orders are given to the chiefs of works, to charge the workmen of their various departments to inspect the materials in the five storehouses:—those of iron and other metals; of skins

---

[1] 'On each side of the wall of the royal city,' says Lû Tien (early in the Sung dynasty), 'there were three gates.' Wû *Kh*ăng says, 'The three gates on the south were the chief gates. Generally, such things as are mentioned here might issue from the other gates, but not from these; but in this month they could not issue from any of the nine.' Other explanations of 'the nine gates' have been attempted. The 'baits' (or medicines) were used to attract and to stupefy.

[2] Perhaps the hoopoe.

and hides and sinews; of horn and ivory; of feathers, arrows and wood (for bows); and of grease, glue, cinnabar, and varnish. (They are to see) that all these things be good. The workmen then labour at their several tasks. (The chiefs) inspect their work, and daily give them their orders. They must not produce anything contrary to what the time requires; nor can they practise a licentious ingenuity, which would dissipate the minds of their superiors.

14. In the end of this month a fortunate day is chosen for a grand concert of music. The son of Heaven, at the head of the three ducal ministers, the nine high ministers, the feudal princes (at court), and his great officers, goes in person to witness it.

15. In this month they collect the large, heavy bulls, and fiery stallions, and send them forth to the females in the pasture grounds. They number and make a list of the animals fit for victims, with the foals and calves.

16. Orders are given for the ceremonies against pestilence throughout the city; at the nine gates (also) animals are torn in pieces in deprecation (of the danger):—to secure the full development of the (healthy) airs of the spring[1].

17. If, in this last month of spring, the governmental

[1] Compare Analects X, 10, 2. The ceremonies there referred to were the same as those here, carried out in the villages and, indeed, throughout the land. Diseases prevailing were attributed by superstition to the action of evil spirits, and ridiculous measures adopted to drive them away. Confucius and others, even the government itself, gave countenance to these, seeing, perhaps, that in connexion with them the natural causes of disease would be in a measure dispelled.

proceedings proper to winter were observed, cold airs would constantly be prevailing; all plants and trees would decay; and in the states there would be great terrors. If those proper to summer were observed, many of the people would suffer from pestilential diseases; the seasonable rains would not fall; and no produce would be derived from the mountains and heights. If those proper to autumn were observed, the sky would be full of moisture and gloom; excessive rains would fall early; and warlike movements would be everywhere arising.

SECTION II. PART I.

1. In the first month of summer, the sun is in Pî; the constellation culminating at dusk being Yî, and that culminating at dawn Wû-nü[1].

2. Its days are ping and ting[2].

3. Its divine ruler is Yen Tî, and the (attending) spirit is *K*û-yung[3].

4. Its creatures are the feathered.

5. Its musical note is *K*ih, and its pitch-tube is the *K*ung Lü[4].

6. Its number is seven[5]. Its taste is acrid. Its smell is that of things burning.

---

[1] Pî is the name for the Hyades, or, more exactly, of six stars in Hyades, with μ and ν of Taurus; it is the nineteenth of the Chinese constellations. Yî is crater. Wû-nü is not so well identified. Williams says that it is 'a star near the middle of Capricorn,' but others say in Hercules. The *R* Yâ makes it the same as Hsü-nü (須女). Probably it was a star in the constellation Nü of Aquarius.

[2] The third and fourth stem characters of the cycle.

[3] Yen Tî ('the blazing Tî') is the dynastic designation of Shăn Năng, generally placed next to Fû-hsî in Chinese chronology, and whose date cannot be assigned later than the thirty-first century B.C. *K*û-yung in one account is placed before Fû-hsî; in a second, as one of the ministers of Hwang Tî; and in a third, as a son of *Kh*wan-hsü (B.C. 2510–2433). He was 'the Director of Fire,' and had the presidency of summer.

[4] *K*ih is the fourth of the notes of the Chinese scale, and *K*ung Lü ('the middle Spine') the third of the tubes that give the six lower accords.

[5] The number of fire is 2, which + 5, that of earth, = 7.

7. Its sacrifice is that at the furnace[1]; and of the parts of the victim the lungs have the foremost place.

8. The green frogs croak. Earth-worms come forth. The royal melons grow[2]. The sow-thistle is in seed.

9. The son of Heaven occupies the apartment on the left of the Ming Thang (Grand Fane); rides in the vermilion carriage, drawn by the red horses with black tails, and bearing the red flag. He is dressed in the red robes, and wears the carnation jade. He eats beans and fowls. The vessels which he uses are tall, (to resemble) the large growth (of things).

10. In this month there takes place the inauguration of summer. Three days before this ceremony, the Grand recorder informs the son of Heaven, saying, 'On such-and-such a day is the inauguration of summer. The energies of the season are most fully seen in fire.' On this the son of Heaven devotes himself to self-purification; and on the day, at the head of the three ducal ministers, the nine high ministers, and his Great officers, he proceeds to meet the summer in the southern suburbs. On their return, rewards are distributed. He grants to the feudal princes (an increase of) territory. Congratulations and gifts proceed, and all are joyful and pleased.

11. Orders are also given to the chief master of

[1] It was natural that they should sacrifice here in the summer. 'The lungs' is the fourth of the five viscera, and 'metal' the fourth of the five elements; but 'fire subdues metal.' This is supposed to account for the prominence given to the lungs in this sacrifice.

[2] According to Williams this is the 'common cucumber.'

music to teach the practice of ceremonies and music together.

12. Orders are given to the Grand Peace-maintainer[1] to recommend men of eminence, allow the worthy and good to have free course and bring forward the tall and large. His conferring of rank and regulation of emolument must be in accordance with the position (of the individual).

13. In this month what is long should be encouraged to grow longer, and what is high to grow higher. There should be no injuring or overthrowing of anything; no commencing of works in earth; no sending forth of great multitudes (on expeditions); no cutting down of large trees.

14. In this month the son of Heaven begins to wear thin dolichos cloth.

15. Orders are given to the foresters throughout the country to go forth over the fields and plains, and, for the son of Heaven, to encourage the husbandmen, and stimulate them to work, and not let the season slip by unimproved.

Orders are (also) given to the minister of Instruction to travel in order through the districts to the borders, charging the husbandmen to work vigorously, and not to rest in the towns.

16. In this month they chase away wild animals to prevent them from doing harm to any of the

---

[1] The 'Grand Peace-maintaïner' (大尉) was a title under the *Kh*in dynasty, and instituted by it, of the Minister of War. The functions of the latter, as described in the last Book, page 234, are in harmony with what is said here. The occurrence of the name bears out the attributing of this Book to Lü Pû-wei.

(growing) grain; but they should not have a great hunting.

17. When the husbandmen present (the first-fruits of) their wheat, the son of Heaven tastes it along with some pork, first offering a portion in the apartment behind (the hall of the) ancestral temple.

18. In this month they collect and store up the various medicinal herbs. Delicate herbs (now) die; it is the harvest time (even) of the wheat. They decide cases for which the punishments are light; they make short work of small crimes, and liberate those who are in prison for slight offences[1].

19. When the work with the silk-worms is over, the queen presents her cocoons; and the tithe-tax of cocoons generally is collected, according to the number of mulberry trees; for noble and mean, for old and young there is one law. The object is with such cocoons to provide materials for the robes to be used at the sacrifices in the suburbs and in the ancestral temple.

20. In this month the son of Heaven (entertains his ministers and princes) with strong drink and with (much) observance of ceremony and with music[2].

---

[1] There does not appear to be any connexion between the first sentence of this paragraph and the remainder of it. The medicinal herbs are collected while all their vigour is in them. For the things in the second sentence the 'summer heats' make a premature harvest; and this seems to lead to the third topic,—the saving those charged with slight offences from the effects of that heat in confinement.

[2] The *Kh*ien-lung editors have a note here, which is worth quoting, to the effect that as the great solstitial sacrifices and the seasonal sacrifices of the ancestral temple do not appear in this Book, the drinking here was at court entertainments.

21. If, in this first month of summer, the proceedings proper to autumn were observed, pitiless rains would be frequent; the five esculent plants[1] would not grow large, and in all the borders people would have to enter the places of shelter. If those proper to winter were observed, all plants and trees would wither early, and afterwards there would be great floods, destroying city and suburban walls. If those proper to spring were observed, there would be the calamity of locusts, violent winds would come, and plants in flower would not go on to seed.

PART II.

1. In the second month of summer the sun is in the eastern 3ing, the constellation culminating at dusk being Khang, and that culminating at dawn Wei[2].

2. Its days are ping and ting. Its divine ruler is Yen Tî, and the (attending) spirit is *Kh*û-yung. Its creatures are the feathered. Its musical note is *K*ih, and its pitch-tube is Sui Pin[3].

3. Its number is seven. Its taste is acrid. Its smell is that of things burning. Its sacrifice is that at the furnace; and of the parts of the victim the lungs have the foremost place.

4. The (period of) slighter heat arrives; the praying mantis is produced; the shrike begins to give its notes; the mocking-bird ceases to sing[4].

---

[1] Hemp or flax, millet, rice, bearded grain, and pulse.

[2] 3ing comprehends $\gamma, \epsilon, \zeta, \lambda, \mu, \nu$, Gemini; Khang, $\iota, \kappa, \lambda, \mu, \rho$, Virgo; and Wei corresponds to α, Aquarius, and ϵ, θ, Pegasus.

[3] Sui Pin, 'the flourishing Guest,' is the fourth of the tubes that give the six upper musical accords.

[4] This is here 'the inverted Tongue.' The Khang-hsî dictionary

5. The son of Heaven occupies the Ming Thang Grand Fane; rides in the vermilion carriage, drawn by the red horses with black tails, and bearing the red flag. He is dressed in the red robes, and wears the carnation gems. He eats beans and fowls. The vessels which he uses are tall, (to resemble) the large growth (of things).

6. They encourage the (continued) growth of what is strong and beautiful[1].

7. In this month orders are given to the music-masters to put in repair the hand-drums, smaller drums, and large drums; to adjust the lutes, large and small, the double flutes, and the pan-pipes; to teach the holding of the shields, pole-axes, lances, and plumes; to tune the organs, large and small, with their pipes and tongues; and to put in order the bells, sonorous stones, the instrument to give the symbol for commencing, and the stopper[2].

8. Orders are given to the (proper) officers to pray for the people and offer sacrifice to the (spirits of the) hills, streams, and all springs. (After that) comes the great summer sacrifice for rain to God, when all

says it is the same as 'the hundred Tongues;' the Chinese mocking-bird.

[1] *K*û Hsî would remove this paragraph to the thirteenth of the last Part. It seems to me to be in its proper place.

[2] See vol. iii, p. 324. The stopper is represented thus:—

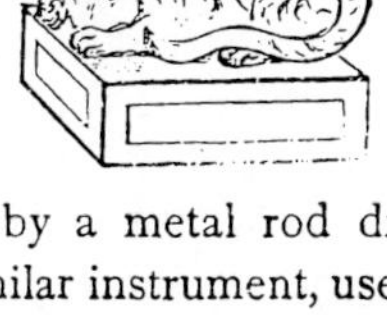

It was made to sound by a metal rod drawn along the spinous back. I have seen a similar instrument, used for the same purpose, brought from Madras.

the instruments of music are employed. Then orders are given throughout all the districts to sacrifice to the various princes, high ministers, and officers who benefited the people; praying that there may be a good harvest of grain[1].

9. The husbandmen present (the first-fruits of) their millet; and in this month the son of Heaven partakes of it along with pullets, and with cherries set forth beside them, first offering a portion in the apartment behind the ancestral temple.

10. The people are forbidden to cut down the indigo plant to use it in dyeing[2],

11. Or to burn wood for charcoal, or to bleach cloth in the sun.

12. The gates of cities and villages should not be shut[3], nor should vexatious inquiries be instituted at the barrier gates or in the markets.

---

[1] The first and last of the three sacrificial services in the paragraph were subsidiary to the second, the great praying for rain to God by the sovereign; the motive is not mentioned in the text, but only he could conduct a service to God. Callery renders:—'En même temps l'empereur invoque le ciel avec grand apparat (afin d'obtenir de la pluie), et cette cérémonie est accompagnée de grande musique.' All Chinese commentators admit that the performer was the sovereign. *K*ăng Khang-*kh*ăng says: 'For this sacrifice to God, they made an altar (or altars) by the side of the (grand altar in the) southern suburb, and sacrificed to the five essential (or elemental) gods with the former rulers as their assessors.' But the *Kh*ien-lung editors insist on the text's having 'God,' and not 'five gods,' and that the correct view is that the sacrifice was to the one God dwelling in the bright sky, or, as Williams renders the phrase, 'the Shang Tî of the glorious heaven.'

[2] The plant would not yet be fully fit for use.

[3] Every facility should be afforded for the circulation of air during the summer heats.

13. Leniency should be shown to prisoners charged (even) with great crimes, and their allowance of food be increased[1].

14. Impregnated mares are collected in herds by themselves, and the fiery stallions are tied up. The rules for the rearing of horses are given out.

15. In this month the longest day arrives. The influences in nature of darkness and decay and those of brightness and growth struggle together; the tendencies to death and life are divided[2]. Superior men give themselves to vigil and fasting. They keep retired in their houses, avoid all violent exercise, restrain their indulgence in music and beautiful sights, eschew the society of their wives, make their diet spare, use no piquant condiments, keep their desires under rule, and maintain their spirits free from excitement. The various magistrates keep things quiet and inflict no punishments[3];—to bring about that state of settled quiet in which the influence of darkness and decay shall obtain its full development.

16. Deer shed their horns. Cicadas begin to sing. The midsummer herb is produced. The tree hibiscus flowers[4].

17. In this month fires should not be lighted (out of doors) in the southern regions (of the country).

---

[1] The leniency would be seen in the lightening of their fetters for one thing,—in consequence of the exhaustion produced by the season.

[2] Decay begins to set in, while growth and vigour seek to maintain their hold.

[3] The *Kh*ien-lung editors approve a reading here, which means, instead of 'no punishments,' 'no rash or hurried action.'

[4] The 'tree hibiscus' is the 'hibiscus syriacus.' The 'half-summer herb' is medicinal. It is 'white, with round seeds, and of a hot and pungent taste.'

18. People may live in buildings high and bright. They may enjoy distant prospects. They may ascend hills and heights. They may occupy towers and lofty pavilions[1].

19. If, in the second month of summer, the governmental proceedings of winter were observed, hail and cold would injure the grain; the roads would not be passable; and violent assaults of war would come. If the proceedings proper to spring were observed, the grains would be late in ripening; all kinds of locusts would continually be appearing; and there would be famine in the states. If those proper to autumn were observed, herbs and plants would drop their leaves; fruits would ripen prematurely; and the people would be consumed by pestilence.

Part III.

1. In the third month of summer the sun is in Liû, the constellation culminating at dusk being Kwo, and that culminating at dawn Khwei[2].

2. Its days are ping and ting Its divine ruler is Yen Tî, and the (assisting) spirit is *Kh*û-yung. Its musical note is *K*ih, and its pitch-tube is Lin *K*ung[3].

---

[1] At the beginning of this paragraph there should be—'In this month.'

[2] Liû comprehends δ, ε, ζ, η, θ, ρ, σ, and ω Hydræ; Hwo is the same as Hsin, the fifth of the Chinese zodiacal constellations comprehending Antares, σ, τ, and two c. 2584, 2587, Scorpio; Khwei (as stated above, p. 257) comprehends β (Mirac), δ, ε, ζ, μ, ν, π of Andromeda, and some stars of Pisces.

[3] The fourth of the tubes that give the six lower musical accords.

3. Its number is seven. Its taste is acrid. Its smell is that of things burning. Its sacrifice is that at the furnace; and of the parts of the victim the lungs have the foremost place.

4. Gentle winds begin to blow. The cricket takes its place in the walls. (Young) hawks learn to practise (the ways of their parents)[1]. Decaying grass becomes fire-flies.

5. The son of Heaven occupies the apartment on the right of the Ming Thang (Fane); rides in the vermilion carriage, drawn by the red horses with black tails, and bearing the red flag. He is dressed in the red robes, and wears the carnation gems. He eats beans and fowls. The vessels which he uses are tall, (to resemble) the large growth (of things).

6. Orders are given to the master of the Fishermen to attack the alligator, to take the gavial, to present the tortoise, and to take the great turtle[2].

7. Orders are given to the superintendent of the Meres to collect and send in the rushes available for use.

8. In this month orders are given to the four

---

[1] Compare what is said about hawks in paragraph 4, page 258. 'Here,' says Wang Thao, 'we have the turtle-doves transformed back to hawks, showing that the former notice was metaphorical.' What is said about the fire-flies is, of course, a mistaken fancy.

[2] The first of these animals—the *k*iâo—is, probably, the alligator or crocodile; it was taken only after a struggle or fight. The second—the tho—had a skin used in making drums; and its flesh, as well as that of the fourth—the yûan—was used in making soup.

inspectors[1] to make a great collection over all the districts of the different kinds of fodder to nourish the sacrificial victims; and to require all the people to do their utmost towards this end;—to supply what is necessary for (the worship of) God (who dwells in) the great Heaven, and for the spirits of the famous hills, great streams, and four quarters, and for the sacrifices to the Intelligences of the ancestral temple, and at the altars to the spirits of the land and grain; that prayer may be made for blessing to the people.

9. In this month orders are given by the officers of women's (work), on the subject of dyeing[2]. (They are to see) that the white and black, the black and green, the green and carnation, the carnation and white be all according to the ancient rules, without error or change; and that their black, yellow, azure, and carnation be all genuine and good, without any presumptuous attempts at imposition. These furnish the materials for the robes used at the sacrifices in the suburbs and the ancestral temple; for flags and their ornaments; and for marking the different degrees of rank as high or low.

10. In this month the trees are luxuriant; and orders are given to the foresters to go among the hills and examine the trees, and see that the people do not cut any down or lop their branches[3].

---

[1] Of hills, forests, rivers, and meres.

[2] We find full details of the number and duties of the superintendents of women's work, with its tailoring, dyeing, and other things, in the *K*âu Lî, Books I and VII.

[3] The *Kh*ien-lung editors say that this was to let the process of growth have its full course; and, besides, that wood cut down in spring and summer will be found full of insects.

11. There should not be any work in earth[1] (now) undertaken; nor any assembling of the princes of the states; nor any military movements, causing general excitement. There should be no undertaking of (such) great affairs, which will disturb the nourishing growth that is proceeding, nor any issuing of orders to be hereafter carried into effect. All these things will interfere with the business of husbandry, (which is specially dear to) the Spirits[2]. The floods are now great and overflow the roads; husbandry (dear to) the Spirits has to take in hand its various tasks. The curse of Heaven will come on the undertaking of great affairs (at this time).

---

[1] Such as building walls and fortifications, or laying out the ground.

[2] The text is—'will interfere with the business of Shăn Năng (妨神農之事).' How is it that 'husbandry' has here the epithet of Shăn, or 'spiritual,' 'mysterious,' applied to it? The *Kh*ien-lung editors say:—'3hâi Yung (our second century) makes Shăn Năng to be Yen Tî (the divine ruler of the summer). *K*ăng made the name to be that of "the spirit of the ground." Kâo Yû (second century) took it as a name for the minister of Husbandry. To some extent each of these views might be admitted, but none of them is very certain. Looking carefully at the text it simply says that no great undertakings should be allowed to interfere with husbandry. That it does not plainly say husbandry, but calls it the Shăn husbandry, is from a sense of its importance, and therefore making it out to be Spirit-sanctioned. Heaven produced the people, and the grain to nourish them; is not sowing and reaping the business of Heaven? When a ruler knows this, he feels that he is under the inspection of Heaven in his reverent regard of the people, and the importance which he attaches to husbandry. He will not dare lightly to use the people's strength, so as to offend against Heaven.' I have tried to bring out their view in my version.

12. In this month the ground lies steaming and wet beneath the heats, for great rains are (also) continually coming. They burn the grass lying cut upon the ground[1] and bring the water over it. This is as effectual to kill the roots as hot water would be; and the grass thus serves to manure the fields of grain and hemp, and to fatten the ground which has been but just marked out for cultivation.

13. If, in the last month of summer, the governmental proceedings proper to spring were observed, the produce of grain would be scanty and fail; in the states there would be many colds and coughs; and the people would remove to other places. If the proceedings proper to autumn were observed, even the high grounds would be flooded; the grain that had been sown would not ripen; and there would be many miscarriages among women. If those proper to winter were observed, the winds and cold would come out of season; the hawks and falcons would prematurely attack their prey; and all along the four borders people would enter their places of shelter.

Supplementary Section.

1. Right in the middle (between Heaven and Earth, and the other elements) is earth.

2. Its days are wû and *k*î.

3. Its divine ruler is Hwang Tî; and the (attending) spirit is Hâu-thû.

[1] Compare what is said on the duties of those who cut the grass, as is here assumed to be done, in the *K*âu Lî, Book XXXVII, paragraphs 80, 81 (薙氏).

4. Its creature is that without any natural covering but the skin.

5. Its musical note is *K*ung, and its pitch-tube gives the *k*ung note from the tube Hwang *K*ung.

6. Its number is five. Its taste is sweet. Its smell is fragrant.

7. Its sacrifice is that of the middle court; and of the parts of the victim the heart has the foremost place.

8. The son of Heaven occupies the Grand apartment of the Grand fane; rides in the great carriage drawn by the yellow horses with black tails, and bearing the yellow flag; is clothed in the yellow robes, and wears the yellow gems. He eats panicled millet and beef. The vessels which he uses are round, (and made to resemble) the capacity (of the earth)[1].

---

[1] I have called this a supplementary section. It is dropt in, in all its brevity, without mention of any proceedings of government, between the end of summer and the beginning of autumn. It has all the appearance of an after-thought, suggested by the superstitious fancies of the compiler. Callery says on it:—

'This passage can only be comprehended by help of the intimate affinities which Chinese philosophers have attributed to the different beings of nature. According to them, the four seasons are related to the four cardinal points: spring to the east, summer to the south, autumn to the west, and winter to the north. Each of the cardinal points is related to an element: the east to wood, the south to fire, the west to metal, and the north to water. But as there is a fifth element, that of earth, and the four cardinal points have no reason for being distinguished as they are, but that there is a point in the middle between them, which is still the earth, it follows from this that the earth ought to have its place in the midst of the four seasons, that is, at the point of separation between summer and autumn. Here a difficulty presented itself. The bamboo flutes to which the Chinese months are referred being but twelve, where shall be found the musical affinities of the earth? But the Chinese philosopher did not find himself embarrassed. See how he reasoned. The sound of the first flute, that is, of the longest and largest, is the strongest and most grave, and, like a bass, harmonizes with all the other sounds more acute. So the earth, likewise, is the most important of all the elements; it extends towards all the cardinal points, and intervenes in the products of each season. Hence the earth ought to correspond to the sound of the first flute! These affinities extend to colours, tastes, and a crowd of other categories.'

The *Kh*ien-lung editors say:—

'Speaking from the standpoint of Heaven, then the earth is in the midst of Heaven; that is, (the element of) earth. Speaking from the standpoint of the Earth, then wood, fire, metal, and water are all supported on it. The manner in which the way of Earth is affected by that of Heaven cannot be described by reference to one point, or one month. Speaking from the standpoint of the heavenly stems, then wû and *k*î occupy the middle places, and are between the stems for fire and metal, to convey the system of mutual production. Speaking from the standpoint of the "earthly branches," the *kh*ăn, hsü, *kh*âu, and wi occupy the corners of the four points; wood, fire, metal, and water, all turn to earth. This is what the idea of reciprocal ending, and that of elemental flourishing, arise from. This may be exhibited in the several points, and reckoned by the periods of days. The talk about the elements takes many directions, but the underlying principle comes to be the same!'

I shall be glad if my readers can understand this.

Section III. Part I.

1. In the first month of autumn, the sun is in Yî; the constellation culminating at dusk being *K*ien-hsing, and that culminating at dawn Pî[1].

2. Its days are kăng and hsin.

3. Its divine ruler is Shâo Hâo, and the (attending) spirit is *Z*û-shâu[2].

4. Its creatures are the hairy.

5. Its musical note is Shang; its pitch-tube is Î Ȝeh[3].

6. Its number is nine. Its taste is bitter. Its smell is rank.

7. Its sacrifice is that at the gate; and of the parts of the victim the liver has the foremost place.

8. Cool winds come; the white dew descends[4]; the cicada of the cold chirps[5]. (Young) hawks at this

---

[1] Yî corresponds to Crater. *K*ien-hsing comprehends stars in Sagittarius (see page 257). Pî corresponds to the Hyades.

[2] Shâo Hâo follows Hwang Tî, whose eldest son he was, as the fourth in the list of the five Tî, or divine rulers (B.C. 2594). His capital was at *Kh*ü-fâu, the city of Confucius; and I have seen, at a little distance from it, perhaps the only pyramid in China, which is in memory of him, and said to be on or near his grave. His personal appellation is *K*in-thien (金天), or Thien-*k*in, the element to which he and his reign are assigned being *k*in, or metal. *Z*û-shâu was one of his sons.

[3] Î Ȝeh, 'the equalization of the Laws,' is the tube giving the fifth of the upper musical accords.

[4] White dew is a name for hoar-frost.

[5] This cicada (Williams thinks the cicada viridis) is called

time sacrifice birds, as the first step they take to killing (and eating) them[1].

9. The son of Heaven occupies the apartment on the left of the 3ung-*k*ang (Fane); rides in the war chariot, drawn by the white horses with black manes, and bearing the white flag. He is clothed in the white robes, and wears the white jade. He eats hemp-seeds and dog's flesh. The vessels which he uses are rectangular, and going on to be deep[2].

10. In this month there takes place the inauguration of autumn. Three days before the ceremony, the Grand recorder informs the son of Heaven, saying, 'On such-and-such a day is the inauguration of the autumn. The character of the season is fully seen in metal.' On this the son of Heaven devotes himself to self-adjustment; and on the day he leads in person the three ducal ministers, the nine high ministers, the princes of states (at court), and his Great officers, to meet the autumn in the western suburb, and on their return he rewards the general-in-chief, and the military officers in the court.

11. The son of Heaven also orders the leaders and commanders to choose men and sharpen weapons, to select and exercise those of distinguished merit, and

---

'the dumb.' Now it begins to chirp. Its colour is 'green and red.'

[1] Compare what is said about the otter, page 251.

[2] 3ung-*k*ang is made out to mean, 'all bright,' and the apartment was on the west; with mystical reference to the maturity and gathering of all things in the autumn, or season of the west. The vessels were rectangular, having sharp corners in harmony with the sharp weapons made of metal, to which element the season of autumn is referred; and they were deep, to resemble the deep bosom of the earth, to which things now begin to return.

to give their entire trust only to men whose services have been proved;—thereby to correct all unrighteousness. (He instructs them also) to make enquiries about and punish the oppressive and insolent;—thereby making it clear whom he loves and whom he hates, and giving effect to (the wishes of) the people, even the most distant from court.

12. In this month orders are given to the proper officers to revise the laws and ordinances, to put the prisons in good repair, to provide handcuffs and fetters, to repress and stop villainy, to maintain a watch against crime and wickedness, and to do their endeavour to capture criminals. Orders are (also) given to the managers (of prisons) to look at wounds, examine sores, inspect broken members, and judge particularly of dislocations. The determination of cases, both criminal and civil, must be correct and just. Heaven and earth now begin to be severe;—there should be no excess in copying that severity, or in the opposite indulgence[1].

13. In this month the husbandmen present their grain. The son of Heaven tastes it, while still new, first offering some in the apartment at the back of the ancestral temple.

14. Orders are given to all the officers to begin their collecting and storing the contributions (from

[1] For this last sentence Callery has:—'(Ce mois-ci) la nature commençant à devenir rigoureuse, on ne doit pas augmenter (ses rigeurs par l'application de châtiments trop sévères).' Wang Thâo takes an opposite view. I think I have got the thought that was in the compiler's mind. See the note of the *Kh*ien-lung editors with reference to the advocacy of it by commentators of 'the Brief Calendar of Hsiâ.'

the husbandmen); to finish the embankments and dykes; to look to the dams and fillings up in preparation for the floods, and also to refit all houses; to strengthen walls and enclosures; and to repair city and suburban walls.

15. In this month there should be no investing of princes, and no appointment of great ministers. There should be no dismemberment of any territory, no sending out on any great commission, and no issuing of great presents.

16. If, in this first month of autumn, the proceedings of government proper to winter were observed, then the dark and gloomy influence (of nature) would greatly prevail; the shelly insects would destroy the grain; and warlike operations would be called for. If the proceedings proper to spring were observed, there would be droughts in the states; the bright and growing influence would return; and the five kinds of grain would not yield their fruit. If the proceedings proper to summer were observed, there would be many calamities from fire in the states; the cold and the heat would be subject to no rule; and there would be many fevers among the people.

PART II.

1. In the second month of autumn the sun is in *K*io, the constellation culminating at dusk being *Kh*ien-niû, and that culminating at dawn Ȝze-hsî[1].

2. Its days are *k*ăng and hsin. Its divine ruler

[1] *K*io corresponds to α (Spica) and ζ of Virgo; *Kh*ien-niû (see on page 262) to certain stars in the neck of Aquila; and Ȝze-hsî is said to be λ Orion.

is Shâo Hâo, and the (attending) spirit is *Z*û-shâu. Its insects are the hairy. Its musical note is Shang, and its pitch-tube is Nan Lü[1].

3. Its number is nine. Its taste is bitter. Its smell is rank. Its sacrifice is that of the gate; and of the parts of the victim the liver has the foremost place.

4 Sudden and violent winds come. The wild geese arrive[2]. The swallows return (whence they came)[2]. Tribes of birds store up provisions (for the future)[3].

5. The son of Heaven occupies the 3ung-*k*ang Grand Fane; rides in the war chariot, drawn by the white horses with black manes, and bearing the white flag. He is clothed in the white robes, and wears the white gems. He eats hemp-seed and dog's flesh. The vessels which he uses are rectangular or cornered, and rather deep.

6. In this month they take especial care of the

[1] Nan Lü, 'the southern spine,' is the tube that gives the fifth of the lower musical accords.

[2] The wild geese are now returning to their winter quarters, from which they had come in the first month of spring; see page 251. So with the swallows, who had appeared in the second month of spring; see page 259.

[3] This sentence is hardly translatable or intelligible. Some would read as in paragraph 95 of 'the Brief Calendar of Hsiâ' (丹鳥羞白鳥), translated by Professor Douglas: 'The red birds (i.e. fire-flies) devour the white birds (i. e. mosquitoes),' which he ingeniously supports by a reference to the habits of the fire-fly from Chambers' Encyclopædia. But his translation of hsiû by 'devour' is inadmissible. Wang Thâo says that this view is 'chisseling.' 'Sparrows and other birds,' he says, 'now collect seeds of grapes and trees, and store them in their nests and holes against the time of rain and snow.'

decaying and old; give them stools and staves, and distribute supplies of congee for food.

7. Orders are given to the superintendent of robes to have ready the upper and lower dresses with their various ornaments. For the figures and embroidery on them there are fixed patterns. Their size, length, and dimensions must all be according to the old examples. For the caps and girdles (also) there are regular rules.

8. Orders are given to the proper officers to revise with strict accuracy (the laws about) the various punishments. Beheading and (the other) capital executions must be according to (the crimes) without excess or defect. Excess or defect out of such proportion will bring on itself the judgment (of Heaven).

9. In this month orders are given to the officers of slaughter and prayer to go round among the victims for sacrifice, seeing that they are entire and complete, examining their fodder and grain, inspecting their condition as fat or thin, and judging of their looks. They must arrange them according to their classes. In measuring their size, and looking at the length (of their horns), they must have them according to the (assigned) measures. When all these points are as they ought to be, God will accept the sacrifices[1].

10. The son of Heaven performs the ceremonies against pestilence, to secure development for the (healthy) airs of autumn.

11. He eats the hemp-seed (which is now pre-

[1] *K*ăng says here: 'And if God accept them, of course there is no other spirit that will not do so.'

sented) along with dog's flesh, first offering some in the apartment at the back of the ancestral temple.

12. In this month it is allowable to rear city and suburban walls, to establish cities and towns, to dig underground passages and grain-pits, and to repair granaries, round and square.

13. Orders are given to the proper officers to be urgent with the people, and (to finish) receiving their contributions and storing them. They should do their best to accumulate (large) stores of vegetables and other things.

14. They should (also) stimulate the wheat-sowing. (The husbandmen) should not be allowed to miss the proper time for the operation. Any who do so shall be punished without fail.

15. In this month day and night are equal. The thunder begins to restrain its voice. Insects stop up the entrances to their burrows. The influence to decay and death gradually increases. That of brightness and growth daily diminishes. The waters begin to dry up.

16. At the equinox, they make uniform the measures of length and capacity; equalise the steelyards and their weights; rectify the weights of 30 and 120 catties; and adjust the pecks and bushels.

17. In this month they regulate and reduce the charges at the frontier gates and in the markets, to encourage the resort of both regular and travelling traders, and the receipt of goods and money; for the convenience of the business of the people. When merchants and others collect from all quarters, and come from the most distant parts, then the resources (of the government) do not fail. There is no want

of means for its use; and all things proceed prosperously.

18. In commencing great undertakings, there should be no opposition to the great periods (for them) as defined (by the motion of the sun). They must be conformed to the times (as thereby marked out), and particular attention paid to the nature of each[1].

19. If in this second month of autumn the proceedings proper to spring were observed, the autumnal

---

[1] Callery translates this paragraph by: 'Toute personne ayant une chose importante à accomplir ne doit pas se mettre en opposition avec les grands principes (yin et yang); il doit se conformer au temps (propre à agir; mais il doit aussi) bien examiner la nature même de l'entreprise.' He appends to this the following note:—'Les deux principes yin et yang auxquels se rapportent tous les êtres, ayant tour-à-tour la prédominance dans certaines époques de l'année, le temps convenable pour une chose quelconque est celui auquel prédomine le principe dont cette chose dépend par son affinité naturelle. Ainsi, par exemple, les travaux de terrassement et de construction conviennent en automne, parce que le principe yin dont ils dépendent est en progrès pendant l'automne. Néanmoins, de ce que cette époque de l'année est favorable sous ce point de vue, il ne s'ensuit pas que toute entreprise de construction faite en automne soit avantageuse en elle-même; une foule de circonstances peuvent la rendre ruineuse, et c'est à l'entrepreneur de bien l'examiner, abstraction faite de la saison.'

The text rendered by Callery, 'les deux principes (yin et yang),' is simply tâ shû, 'the grand numbers,' the meaning of which I have endeavoured to bring out by the supplements in my version. The yin and yang are not mentioned in the text of the paragraph. They are simply a binomial phrase for the course of nature, with special reference to the weather and its conditions, as regulated by the action of the sun on the earth in the course of the seasons.

rains would not fall; plants and trees would blossom; and in the states there would be alarms. If those proper to summer were observed, there would be droughts in the states; insects would not retire to their burrows; and the five grains would begin to grow again. If those proper to winter were observed, calamities springing from (unseasonable) winds would be constantly arising; the thunder now silent would be heard before its time; and plants and trees would die prematurely.

PART III.

1. In the last month of autumn the sun is in Fang, the constellation culminating at dusk being Hsü[1], and that culminating at dawn Liû.

2. Its days are kăng and hsin. Its divine ruler is Shâo Hâo, and the (attending) spirit is Ʒû-shâu. Its creatures are the hairy. Its musical note is Shang, and its pitch-tube is Wû Yî[2].

3. Its number is nine. Its taste is bitter. Its smell is rank. Its sacrifice is that at the gate; and of the parts of the victim the liver has the foremost place.

4. The wild geese come, (and abide) like guests[3].

---

[1] Fang comprehends β, δ, π, ρ Scorpio. Hsü corresponds to β Aquarius; and Liû comprehends δ, ε, ζ, η, θ, ρ, σ, φ Hydra.

[2] Wû Yî, 'the unwearied,' is the tube giving the sixth upper musical accord.

[3] The addition of guests here is a difficulty. It is said on the previous month that 'the wild geese come;' are these here the same as those, or are they others,—the younger birds, as some suppose, which had waited after the former, and still found it necessary to remain on their passage to recruit their strength?

Small birds enter the great water and become mollusks[1]. Chrysanthemums show their yellow flowers. The *kh*âi sacrifice larger animals, and kill (and devour) the smaller[2].

5. The son of Heaven occupies the apartment on the right of the Ȝung-*k*ang (Fane); rides in the war chariot, drawn by the white horses with black manes, and bearing the white flags; is dressed in the white robes, and wears the white jade. He eats hemp-seeds and dog's flesh. The vessels which he uses are rectangular, cornered, and rather deep.

6. In this month the orders are renewed and

---

[1] Professor Douglas has made it more than probable that the 'small birds' here are sand-pipers. What is said about them, however, will not admit of his version, that they 'go into the sea or lakes for crustaceae.' His 'crustaceae' should be 'mollusks.' According to all rules of Chinese composition, what he renders 'for' must be taken verbally, = 'to become.' It is not merely the Chinese 'commentators,' who consider the sentence to mean, 'Sparrows go into the sea and become crustaceae (? mollusks);' it is what the text says. It is indeed an absurd statement, but a translator is not responsible for that. The *Kh*ien-lung editors observe that there is no mention here of the little birds being 'transformed,' as in the paragraph about the 'hawks' on page 258, and hence they argue that we cannot understand the notice here metaphorically. They accept the fact (?). The marine Ko, which is mentioned here, as figured in the plates of the Păn Ȝhâo Kang-mû, is the Calyptroida Trochita.

[2] Compare what is said about the otter, page 251. Professor Douglas argues that the *kh*âi is the polecat. But this identification cannot yet be received as certain. The *kh*âi is 'dog-footed,' 'hunts in troops,' and has 'a voice like that of the dog.' In Japanese plates it is not at all like 'the polecat.' An English naturalist, to whom I submitted a Japanese work illustrative of the Shih King, many years ago, has written over the *kh*âi, 'a wild dog or wolf.'

strictly enjoined, charging the various officers (to see) that noble and mean all exert themselves in the work of ingathering, in harmony with the storing of heaven and earth. They must not allow anything to remain out in the fields.

7. Orders are also given to the chief minister, after the fruits of husbandry have all been gathered in, to take in hand the registers of the produce of the different grains (from all the country), and to store up the produce that has been gathered from the acres of God in the granary of the spirits; doing this with the utmost reverence and correctness[1].

8. In this month the hoar-frost begins to fall; and all labours cease (for a season).

9. Orders are given to the proper officers, saying, 'The cold airs are all coming, and the people will not be able to endure them. Let all enter within their houses (for a time).'

10. On the first ting day orders are given to the chief Director of music to enter the college, and to practise (with his pupils) on the wind instruments.

11. In this month an announcement is made to the son of Heaven that the victims for the great sacrifice to God, and the autumnal sacrifice in the ancestral temple[2] are fit and ready.

---

[1] 'This,' says Hsü Sze-ȝăng (Ming dynasty), 'is the great rule of making provision for the sustenance of men and for serving spiritual beings,—two things demanding the utmost inward reverence and outward reverential vigour.' I suppose that the 'spirit-granary' contained the grain for all governmental sacrifices, as well as that gathered from 'the acres of God,' and to be used specially in sacrifices to Him.

[2] This paragraph gives great trouble to the *Kh*ien-lung editors; but we need not enter on their discussions.

12. The princes of the states are assembled, and orders given to the officers of the various districts (in the royal domain). They receive the first days of the months for the coming year[1], and the laws for the taxation of the people by the princes, both light and heavy, and the amount of the regular contribution to the government, which is determined by the distance of the territories and the nature of their several productions. The object of this is to provide what is necessary for the suburban sacrifices and those in the ancestral temple. No private considerations are allowed to have place in this.

13. In this month the son of Heaven, by means of hunting, teaches how to use the five weapons of war, and the rules for the management of horses.

14. Orders are given to the charioteers and the seven (classes of) grooms[2] to see to the yoking of the several teams, to set up in the carriages the flags and various banners[3], to assign the carriages according to the rank (of those who were to occupy them), and to arrange and set up the screens outside (the royal tent). The minister of Instruction, with his baton

[1] This last month of autumn, the ninth from the first month of spring, was the last month of the year with the dynasty of Ȝhin, when it was high time to give out the calendar for the months of the next year.

[2] The sovereign's horses were divided into six classes, and every class had its own grooms, with one among them who had the superintendence of the rest. See a narrative in the Ȝo *K*wan, under the eighteenth year of duke *Kh*ăng.

[3] Two of these insignia are mentioned in the text;—the Ȝing, which was only a pennant, and the *K*âo, a large banner with a tortoise and serpent intertwined. No doubt the meaning is, 'the various banners.'

stuck in his girdle, addresses all before him with his face to the north.

15. Then the son of Heaven, in his martial ornaments, with his bow in one hand, and the arrows under the armpit of the other, proceeds to hunt. (Finally), he gives orders to the superintendent of Sacrifices, to offer some of the captured game to (the spirits of) the four quarters.

16. In this month the plants and trees become yellow and their leaves fall, on which the branches are cut down to make charcoal.

17. Insects in their burrows all try to push deeper, and from within plaster up the entrances. In accordance with (the season), they hurry on the decision and punishment of criminal cases, wishing not to leave them any longer undealt with. They call in emoluments that have been assigned incorrectly, and minister to those whose means are insufficient for their wants.

18. In this month the son of Heaven eats dog's flesh and rice, first presenting some in the apartment at the back of the ancestral temple.

19. If, in this last month of autumn, the proceedings proper to summer were observed, there would be great floods in the states; the winter stores would be injured and damaged; there would be many colds and catarrhs among the people. If those proper to winter were observed, there would be many thieves and robbers in the states; the borders would be unquiet; and portions of territory would be torn from the rest. If those proper to spring were observed, the warm airs would come; the energies of the people would be relaxed and languid; and the troops would be kept moving about.

SECTION IV. PART I.

1. In the first month of winter the sun is in Wei, the constellation culminating at dusk being Wei, and the constellation culminating at dawn *Kh*ih-hsing[1].

2. Its days are the *z*ăn and kwei.

3. Its divine ruler is *K*wan-hsü, and the (attending) spirit is Hsüan-ming[2].

4. Its creatures are the shell-covered.

5. Its musical note is Yü, and its pitch-tube is Ying *K*ung[3].

6. Its number is six. Its taste is salt. Its smell is that of things that are rotten.

7. Its sacrifice is that at (the altar of) the path, and

---

[1] Wei (尾) comprehends ε, μ Scorpio; Wei (危, as on page 272) corresponds to stars in Aquarius and Pegasus. *Kh*ih Hsing (as on p. 262) corresponds to stars in Hydra.

[2] *K*wan-hsü is the dynastic designation of the grandson of Hwang Tî, the commencement of whose reign is assigned in B.C. 2510. He is known also by the personal designation of Kâo-yang, from the name of his second capital. Among the elements his reign is assigned to water, and thence to the north; and hence the designation of his minister as Hsüan-ming, 'the dark and mysterious,' who was called Hsiû (脩) and Hsî (熙), and is said to have been a son of Shâo Hâo.

[3] Yü is the fifth of the notes of the scale; and Ying *K*ung, 'the responsive tube,' the name of the last of the tubes giving the six lower musical accords.

among the parts of the victim the kidneys have the foremost place[1].

8. Water begins to congeal. The earth begins to be penetrated by the cold. Pheasants enter the great water and become large mollusks[2]. Rainbows are hidden and do not appear.

9. The son of Heaven occupies the apartment on the left of the Hsüan Thang (Fane); rides in the dark-coloured carriage, drawn by the iron black horses, and bearing the dark-coloured flag; is dressed in the black robes, and wears the dark-coloured jade. He eats millet and sucking-pig. The vessels which he uses are large and rather deep.

10. In this month there takes place the inauguration of winter. Three days before this ceremony, the Grand recorder informs the son of Heaven, saying, 'On such-and-such a day is the inauguration of winter. The character of the season is fully seen in

---

[1] This altar was outside the gate leading to the ancestral temple, on the west of it. Many say that here was the 'well' supplying the water used for the temple, and would read ȝăng (井) for hsing (行).

[2] The 'great water' here is said in the 'Narratives of the States' (Book XV) to be the Hwâi. The *kh*ăn is said to be a large species of the *k*o, into which small birds are transformed (p. 292). Of course the transmutation of the pheasants into these is absurd. Professor Douglas has found in a Chinese Enclyclopædia a statement that *kh*ăn is sometimes an equivalent of phû lû (蒲 蘆), 'sweet flags and rushes.' The lû, however, is sometimes read lô, and said to have the same sound and meaning as 螺, 'a spiral univalve;' but the great objection to Professor Douglas' view is the meaning he puts on the 爲, as pointed out on p. 292. The text cannot be construed as he proposes.

water.' On this the son of Heaven devotes himself to self-adjustment; and on the day of the inauguration he leads in person the three ducal ministers, the nine high ministers, and his Great officers to meet the winter in the northern suburbs. On his return he rewards (the descendants of) those who died in the service (of the kingdom), and shows his compassion to orphans and widows.

11. In this month orders are given to the Grand recorder to smear with blood the tortoise-shells and divining stalks[1], and by interpreting the indications of the former and examining the figures formed by the latter, to determine the good and evil of their intimations. (In this way) all flattery and partizanship in the interpretation of them (will become clear), and the crime of the operators be brought home. No concealment or deceit will be allowed.

12. In this month the son of Heaven sets the example of wearing furs.

13. Orders are issued to the proper officers in the words:—'The airs of heaven are ascended on high, and those of earth have descended beneath. There is no intercommunion of heaven and earth. All is shut up and winter is completely formed.'

14. Orders are given to all the officers to cover up carefully the stores (of their departments). The minister of Instruction is also ordered to go round (among the people and see) that they have formed their stores, and that nothing is left ungathered.

15. The city and suburban walls are put in good

---

[1] See in Mencius, I, 7, 4, on the consecration of a bell by smearing parts of it with blood.

repair; the gates of towns and villages are looked after; bolts and nuts are put to rights; locks and keys are carefully attended to; the field-boundaries are strengthened; the frontiers are well secured; important defiles are thoroughly defended; passes and bridges are carefully seen after; and narrow ways and cross-paths are shut up.

16. The rules for mourning are revised; the distinctions of the upper and lower garments are defined; the thickness of the inner and outer coffins is decided on; with the size, height and other dimensions of graves. The measures for all these things are assigned, with the degrees and differences in them according to rank.

17. In this month orders are given to the chief Director of works to prepare a memorial on the work of the artificers; setting forth especially the sacrificial vessels with the measures and capacity (of them and all others), and seeing that there be no licentious ingenuity in the workmanship which might introduce an element of dissipation into the minds of superiors; and making the suitability of the article the first consideration. Every article should have its maker's name engraved on it, for the determination of its genuineness. When the production is not what it ought to be, the artificer should be held guilty and an end be thus put to deception.

18. In this month there is the great festivity when they drink together, and each of the stands bears half its animal roasted[1].

[1] Wang Thâo understands this paragraph as meaning that at this season all, both high and low, feast in expression and augmentation of their joy. The characters will bear this inter-

19. The son of Heaven prays for (a blessing on) the coming year to the Honoured ones of heaven; sacrifices with an ox, a ram, and a boar at the public altar to the spirits of the land, and at the gates of towns and villages; offers the sacrifice three days after the winter solstice with the spoils of the chase to all ancestors, and at the five (household) sacrifices;—thus cheering the husbandmen and helping them to rest from their toils[1].

20. The son of Heaven orders his leaders and commanders to give instruction on military opera-

---

pretation. The *k*ăng, of the text however, has also the meaning which appears in the translation; though on that view the statement is not so general. See the 'Narratives of the States,' I, ii. 8.

[1] The most common view seems to be that we have here the various parts of one sacrificial service, three days after the winter solstice, called *k*â (蜡), in the time of *K*âu, and lâ (臘), in that of *Kh*in. While the son of Heaven performed these services, it must have been at different places in the capital I suppose, analogous and modified services were celebrated generally throughout the kingdom.

There is no agreement as to who are intended by 'the Honoured ones of heaven.' Many hold that they are 'the six Honoured ones,' to whom Shun is said to have sacrificed in the second part of the Shû King. But the *Kh*ien-lung editors contend that the want of 'six' is a fatal objection to this view. Kâo Yû, supposing the six Honoured ones to be meant, argued that 'heaven, earth, and the four seasons' were intended by them,—those seasons co-operating with heaven and earth in the production of all things; but the same editors show, from the passages in the Shû, that heaven can in no sense be included among the six Honoured ones. They do not say, however, who or what is intended by the designation in the text. The lâ in the paragraph is taken in a pregnant sense, as if it were lieh (獵, and not 臘), meaning 'to sacrifice with the spoils of the chase.'

tions, and to exercise (the soldiers) in archery and chariot-driving, and in trials of strength.

21. In this month orders are given to the superintendent of waters and the master of fishermen to collect the revenues from rivers, springs, ponds, and meres, taking care not to encroach in any way on any among the myriads of the people, so as to awaken a feeling of dissatisfaction in them against the son of Heaven. If they do this, they shall be punished for their guilt without forgiveness.

22. If, in the first month of winter, the proceedings of government proper to spring were observed, the cold that shuts up all beneath it would not do so tightly; the vapours of the earth would rise up and go abroad; many of the people would wander away and disappear. If those proper to summer were observed, there would be many violent winds in the states; winter itself would not be cold; and insects would come forth again from their burrows. If those proper to autumn were observed, the snow and hoarfrost would come unseasonably; small military affairs would constantly be arising; and incursions and loss of territory would occur.

PART II.

1. In the second month of winter the sun is in Tâu, the constellation culminating at dusk being the eastern Pî, and that culminating at dawn *K*ăn[1].

---

[1] Tâu comprehends ζ, λ, μ, σ, τ, φ of Sagittarius; the eastern Pî, the fourteenth of the Chinese constellations, consists of Algenib or γ Pegasus, and α of Andromeda; *K*ăn is the last of the constellations, and contains β, γ, δ, and ε of Corvus.

2. Its days are *z*ăn and kwei. Its divine ruler is *K*wan-hsü, and the (attending) spirit is Hsüan-ming. Its creatures are the shell-covered. Its musical note is Yü, and its pitch-tube is Hwang *K*ung[1].

3. Its number is six. Its taste is salt. Its smell is that of things that are rotten. Its sacrifice is that at (the altar of) the path, and of the parts of the victim the kidneys have the foremost place.

4. The ice becomes more strong. The earth begins to crack or split. The night bird ceases to sing. Tigers begin to pair[2].

5. The son of Heaven occupies the Grand Fane Hsüan Thang; rides in the dark-coloured carriage, drawn by the iron black horses, and bearing the dark-coloured flag. He is dressed in the black robes, and wears the dark-coloured gems of jade. He eats millet and sucking-pig. The vessels which he uses are large and rather deep.

6. All things relating to the dead are revised and regulated[3].

7. Orders are given to the proper officer to the following effect[4]:—'There should nothing be done in

---

[1] See page 281, paragraph 5.

[2] 'The earth begins to crack;' some say from the increasing intensity of the cold; others from the warmth which has begun to return. The returning warmth is indicated by the undivided line with which Fŭ, the hexagram of the eleventh month, commences—䷗. 'The night bird' sings during the night till the dawn; 'a hill bird, like a fowl.'

[3] See paragraph 16, page 299. The paragraph may be inadvertently introduced here.

[4] 'The proper officer' here is said to be 'the minister of Instruction,' or 'the officer of the People.'

works of earth; care should be taken not to expose anything that is covered, nor to throw open apartments and houses, and rouse the masses to action; —that all may be kept securely shut up. (Otherwise) the genial influences of earth will find vent, which might be called a throwing open of the house of heaven and earth. In this case all insects would die; and the people be sure to fall ill from pestilence, and various losses would ensue.' This charge is said to be giving full development to the (idea of the) month.

8. In this month orders are given to the Director of the eunuchs to issue afresh the orders for the palace, to examine all the doors, inner and outer, and look carefully after all the apartments. They must be kept strictly shut. All woman's-work must be diminished, and none of an extravagant nature permitted. Though noble and nearly related friends should come to visit the inmates, they must all be excluded.

9. Orders are given to the Grand superintendent of the preparation of liquors to see that the rice and other glutinous grains are all complete; that the leaven-cakes are in season; that the soaking and heating are cleanly conducted; that the water be fragrant; that the vessels of pottery be good; and that the regulation of the fire be right. These six things have all to be attended to, and the Grand superintendent has the inspection of them, to secure that there be no error or mistake.

10. The son of Heaven issues orders to the proper officers to pray and sacrifice to (the spirits presiding over) the four seas, the great rivers (with

their) famous sources, the deep tarns, and the meres, (all) wells and springs[1].

11. In this month, if the husbandmen have any productions in the fields, which they have not stored or collected, or if there be any horses, oxen or other animals, which have been left at large, any one may take them without its being inquired into.

12. If there be those who are able to take from the hills and forests, marshes and meres, edible fruits[2], or to capture game by hunting, the wardens and foresters should give them the necessary information and guidance. If there be among them those who encroach on or rob the others, they should be punished without fail.

13. In this month the shortest day arrives. The principle of darkness and decay (in nature) struggles with that of brightness and growth[3]. The elements of life begin to move. Superior men give themselves to self-adjustment and fasting. They keep retired in their houses. They wish to be at rest in their

---

[1] Winter is the season in which the element of water predominates, and it was in virtue of this that the dynasty of Ȝhin professed to rule. The Khwăn-lun mountains (Koulkun), between the desert of Gobi and Thibet, are the source of the Hwang Ho; Yüan-min, the source of the *K*iang; Thung-po, that of the Hwâi; the *K*î grew out of the Yen, rising from the hill of Wang-wû. See Chinese Classics, vol. iii, pp. 127–140.

[2] Hazel-nuts and chestnuts are given as examples of the former; and the water-caltrops and Euryale ferox, or 'cock's head,' of the latter.

[3] This description of the month is well illustrated by the lines of Fû, the hexagram of it referred to above,—䷗; the lowest line representing the principle of light and growth, which just found readmission in the year, and is seeking to develop itself.

persons; put away all indulgence in music and beautiful sights; repress their various desires; give repose to their bodies and all mental excitements. They wish all affairs to be quiet, while they wait for the settlement of those principles of darkness and decay, and brightness and growth.

14. Rice begins to grow. The broom-sedge rises up vigorously[1]. Worms curl[2]. The moose-deer shed their horns[3]. The springs of water are (all) in movement.

15. When the shortest day has arrived, they fell trees, and carry away bamboos, (especially) the small species suitable for arrows.

16. In this month offices in which there is no business may be closed, and vessels for which there is no use may be removed.

17. They plaster (and repair) the pillars and gateways (of the palace), and the courtyard (within), and also doors and other gateways; rebuilding (also all) prisons, to co-operate with the tendency of nature to shut up and secure (the genial influences at this season).

18. If in this second month of winter the proceedings of government proper to summer were observed,

---

[1] This is called by Dr. Williams 'a species of iris.' The roots are made into brooms.

[2] This is a fancy. The commentators say that the worms curl and twist, with their heads turned downwards, as if seeking to return to the warmth beneath the surface.

[3] The shedding of the horns in winter shows that the mî here, (麋), is a species of the elk or moose-deer, and different from the lû (鹿), which sheds its horns in the sixth month. The mî is described as being fond of the water, and as large as a small ox.

there would be droughts in the states; vapours and fogs would shed abroad their gloom, and thunder would utter its voice. If those proper to autumn were observed, the weather would be rainy and slushy; melons and gourds would not attain their full growth; and there would be great wars in the states. If those proper to spring were observed, locusts would work their harm; the springs would all become dry; and many of the people would suffer from leprosy and foul ulcers.

Part III.

1. In the third month of winter the sun is in Wû-nü, the constellation culminating at dusk being Lâu, and that culminating at dawn Tî[1].

2. Its days are *z*ăn and kwei. Its divine ruler is *K*wan-hsü, and the (attendant) spirit is Hsüan-ming. Its creatures are the shell-covered. Its musical note is Yü, and its pitch-tube is Tâ Lü[2].

3. Its number is six. Its taste is salt. Its smell is that of things that are rotten. Its sacrifice is that at (the altar of) the path; and the part of the victim occupying the foremost place is the kidneys.

4. The wild geese go northwards. The magpie begins to build. The (cock) pheasant crows[3]. Hens hatch.

---

[1] Wû-nü, as in paragraph 1, page 268. Lâu corresponds to α, β, γ, ι in the head of Aries; Tî, to α, β, δ, ι, μ, ν Libra.

[2] Tâ Lü is the first of the tubes giving the six lower musical accords.

[3] As is said in the Shih, II, v, 3, 5:—

'Crows the pheasant at the dawn,
And his mate is to him drawn.'

5. The son of Heaven occupies the apartment on the right of the Hsüan Thang (Fane); rides in the dark-coloured carriage, drawn by the iron-black horses, and bearing the dark-coloured flag. He is dressed in the black robes, and wears the dark-coloured gems of jade. He eats millet and sucking-pig. The vessels which he uses are large and rather deep.

6. He issues orders to the proper officers to institute on a great scale all ceremonies against pestilence, to have (animals) torn in pieces on all sides, and (then) to send forth the ox of earth, to escort away the (injurious) airs of the cold[1].

7. Birds of prey fly high and rapidly[2].

8. They now offer sacrifices all round to (the spirits of) the hills and rivers, to the great ministers of the (ancient) deified sovereigns, and to the spirits of heaven (and earth)[3].

9. In this month orders are given to the master of the Fishermen to commence the fishers' work. The son of Heaven goes in person (to look on). He partakes of the fish caught, first presenting some in the apartment at the back of the ancestral temple[4].

---

[1] Compare par. 16, p. 266. The 'ox of earth' is still seen in China.

[2] This evidently is one of the natural phenomena of the season, and should belong to paragraph 4. The translation of the first two characters by 'Birds of prey' is sufficiently close and exact.

[3] The *Kh*ien-lung editors point out the difficulties in explaining the three sacrifices here referred to, and seem to think they were practices of *Kh*in, about which we have little information. 'The great ministers of the Tî' in the second member were probably those mentioned at the commencement of each season. They supplement the concluding member, as I have done, from Lü's *Kh*un *Kh*iû.

[4] Compare paragraphs 7, p. 263; 17, p. 271. In paragraph 7,

10. The ice is now abundant; thick and strong to the bottom of the waters and meres. Orders are given to collect it, which is done, and it is carried into (the ice-houses).

11. Orders are given to make announcement to the people to bring forth their seed of the five grains. The husbandmen are ordered to reckon up the pairs which they can furnish for the ploughing; to repair the handles and shares of their ploughs; and to provide all the other instruments for the fields.

12. Orders are given to the chief director of Music to institute a grand concert of wind instruments; and with this (the music of the year) is closed[1].

13. Orders are given to the four Inspectors[2] to collect and arrange the faggots to supply the wood and torches for the suburban sacrifices, those in the ancestral temple, and all others.

14. In this month the sun has gone through all his mansions; the moon has completed the number of her conjunctions; the stars return to (their places) in the heavens. The exact length (of the year) is nearly completed, and the year will soon begin again. (It is said), 'Attend to the business of your husbandmen. Let them not be employed on anything else.'

15. The son of Heaven, along with his ducal and

---

p. 263, the sovereign gets himself into a boat, a thing now impossible through the ice. Fish are in their prime condition in winter and spring.

[1] Compare paragraph 16, p. 261, et al. Wind instruments were supposed to suit the quiet and meditativeness of autumn and winter, better than the drums and dances of the other seasons.

[2] 'The four Inspectors.' Compare paragraph 8, p. 277. Some read thien (田) for sze (四), 'Inspectors of the fields.'

other high ministers and his Great officers, revises the statutes for the states, and discusses the proceedings of the different seasons; to be prepared with what is suitable for the ensuing year.

16. Orders are given to the Grand recorder to make a list of the princes of the states according to the positions severally assigned to them[1], and of the victims required from them to supply the offerings for the worship of God dwelling in the great heaven, and at the altars of (the spirits of) the land and grain. Orders were also given to the states ruled by princes of the royal surname to supply the fodder and grain for the (victims used in the worship of the) ancestral temple. Orders are given, moreover, to the chief minister to make a list of (the appanages of) the various high ministers and Great officers, with the amount of the land assigned to the common people, and assess them with the victims which they are to contribute to furnish for the sacrifices to (the spirits presiding over) the hills, forests, and famous streams. All the people under the sky, within the nine provinces, must, without exception, do their utmost to contribute to the sacrifices:—to God dwelling in the great heaven; at the altars of the (spirits of the) land and grain; in the ancestral temple and the apartment at the back of it; and of the hills, forests, and famous streams.

17. If, in the last month of winter, the governmental proceedings proper to autumn were observed, the white dews would descend too early; the shelly crea-

[1] As being of the same surname as the royal house, or otherwise; the degree of their rank; the size of their territory.

tures would appear in monstrous forms[1]; throughout the four borders people would have to seek their places of shelter. If those proper to spring were observed, women with child and young children would suffer many disasters; throughout the states there would be many cases of obstinate disease; fate would appear to be adverse. If those proper to summer were observed, floods would work their ruin in the states; the seasonable snow would not fall, the ice would melt, and the cold disappear.

[1] This is the proper force of the characters. Wang Thâo interprets them as meaning that the creatures would bore through dykes and boats, so that the former would let the water through and the latter sink.

BOOK V. THE QUESTIONS OF ȜĂNG-ȜZE[1].

Section I.

1. Ȝăng-ȝze asked, 'If a ruler dies and a son and heir is born (immediately after), what course should be adopted?'

Confucius said, 'The high nobles[2], Great officers and (other) officers, following the chief (minister), who takes charge of the government for the time, (should collect) at the south of the western steps, with their faces towards the north[3]. (Then) the Grand officer of prayer, in his court robes and cap, bearing in his hands a bundle of rolls of silk, will go up to the topmost step, and (there), without ascending the hall, will order the wailing to cease. Mournfully clearing his voice three times[4], he will make announcement (to the spirit of the deceased ruler), saying, "The son of such and such a lady has been born. I venture to announce the fact." He will then go up, and place the silks on a stool on the east of the body in the coffin[5], wail, and descend. All the relatives of the deceased who are there (at the mourning), the high nobles, the Great and other

---

1 See the introduction, pp. 21, 22.

2 These were also ministers; see paragraph 4, page 213.

3 The usual place was at the eastern steps.

4 To call the attention of the spirit of the deceased.

5 The rolls of silk were, I suppose, the introductory present proper on an interview with a superior.

officers, (with the women) in the apartments, all will wail, but without the leaping. When this burst of sorrow is over, they will return to their (proper) places, and proceed forthwith to set forth the mourning offerings to the dead. The minor minister will ascend, and take away the bundle of silks[1].

2. 'On the third day, all the relatives, high nobles, Great and other officers, should take their places as before, with their faces to the north. The Grand minister, the Grand master of the ancestral temple, and the Grand officer of prayer, should all be in their court-robes and caps. The master for the child[2] will carry the child in his arms on a mat of sackcloth. The officer of prayer will precede, followed by the child, and the minister and master of the temple will come after. Thus they will enter the door (of the apartment where the coffin is), when the wailers will cease. The child has been brought up by the western steps[3], and is held in front of the coffin with his face to the north, while the officer of prayer stands at the south-east corner of it. Mournfully clearing his voice three times, he will say, "So and So, the son of such and such a lady, and we, his servants, who follow him, presume to appear before you." The boy is (then made) to do obeisance, with his forehead on the ground, and to wail. The officer of prayer, the minister, the officer of the temple, all the relatives, the high nobles, with the Great and other officers,

[1] And bury it in the court between the two flights of stairs.

[2] Thus early is it made to appear that the child is put under a master; P. Zottoli translates the name by secundus magister.'

[3] The child had been brought by the master from the women's apartments, and carried to the court, that he might thus go up again to the hall by these steps.

will wail and leap[1], leaping three times with each burst of grief. (Those who had gone up to the hall then) descend, and go back to their proper places on the east; where all bare the left arm and shoulder. The son (in the arms of his bearer is made) to leap, and (the women) in the apartments also leap. Thrice they will do so, leaping three times each time. (The bearer for the son) will cover up his sackcloth[2], walk with a staff, (ascend and) set forth the offerings by the dead, and then quit the scene. The Grand minister will charge the officer of prayer and the recorder to announce the name all round, at the five altars of the house, and at those (to the spirits) of the hills and streams[3].'

3. Ȝăng-ȝze asked, 'If the son and heir have been born after the burial (of the) ruler, what course should be followed?'

Confucius said, 'The Grand minister and the Grand master of the ancestral temple will follow the Grand officer of prayer, and announce the fact before the spirit tablet (of the deceased ruler)[4]. Three months after they will give the name in the same place, and announce it all round[5], and also at the altars to (the

[1] A most expressive indication of the sorrow proper to the occasion.

[2] The breast and shoulder of the child had also been bared.

[3] The 'five household altars' are those at which the sacrifices were offered in the palace or house, often mentioned in the last Book.

[4] The characters of the text, 'in the shrine temple of the father,' denote the special shrine or smaller temple assigned to the father in the great ancestral temple; but that was not assigned till after all the rites of mourning were over. The characters here denote the spirit tablet which had been before the burial set up over the coffin, and which was now removed to a rear apartment. P. Zottoli simply has 'coram tabellâ.'

[5] At the courts of the sovereign and of the other princes.

spirits of) the land and grain, in the ancestral temple, and (at the altars of) the hills and streams.'

4. Confucius said, 'When princes of states are about to go to the (court of the) son of Heaven, they must announce (their departure) before (the shrine of) their grandfather, and lay their offerings in that of their father[1]. They then put on the court cap, and go forth to hold their own court. (At this) they charge the officer of prayer and the recorder to announce (their departure) to the (spirits of the) land and grain, in the ancestral temple, and at the (altars of the) hills and rivers. They then give (the business of) the state in charge to the five (subordinate) officers[2], and take their journey, presenting the offerings to the spirits of the road[3] as they set forth. All the announcements should be completed in five days. To go beyond this in making them is contrary to rule. In every one of them they use a victim and silks. On the return (of the princes) there are the same observances.'

5. 'When princes of states are about to visit one another, they must announce (their departure) before

---

[1] The characters here are the same as in the preceding paragraph, but here they have their usual force. Announcement and offerings were made at both shrines.

[2] The most likely opinion is that these five officers were—two belonging to the department of the minister of Instruction, two to that of the minister of Works, and one to that of the minister of War. On them, for reasons which we may not be able to give, devolved on such occasions the superintendence of the state.

[3] There seems to be no doubt of the meaning here, but this significance of 道 is not given in the Khang-hsî dictionary. The more common term is 祖.

the shrine of their father[1]. They will then put on their court robes, and go forth to hold their own court. (At this) they charge the officer of prayer and the recorder to announce (their departure) at the five shrines in the ancestral temple, and at the altars of the hills and rivers which they will pass. They then give (the business of) the state in charge to the five officers, and take their journey, presenting the offerings to the spirits of the road as they set forth. When they return, they will announce (the fact) in person to their grandfather and father[1], and will charge the officer of prayer and the recorder to make announcement of it at the altars where they announced (their departure). (When this has been done), they enter and give audience in the court.'

6. Ȝăng-ȝze asked, 'If the funerals of both parents[2] take place together, what course is adopted? Which is first and which last?'

Confucius said, 'The rule is that the burying of the less important (mother) should have the precedence, and that of the more important (father) follow, while the offerings to them are set down in the opposite order. From the opening of the apartment and conveying out the coffin (of the mother) till its interment no offerings are put down; when the coffin is on the route to the grave, there is no wailing at the regular place for that ceremony. When they return from this interment, they set down the offerings (to the father), and afterwards announce (to his spirit) when the removal of his coffin will take

[1] There would seem to be an omission in the former of these sentences of the announcement to the grandfathers.

[2] Or grandparents.

place, and proceed to arrange for the interment. It is the rule that the sacrifice of repose should first be offered to the more important (father), and afterwards to the less important (mother).'

7. Confucius said[1], 'The eldest son, even though seventy, should never be without a wife to take her part in presiding at the funeral rites. If there be no such eldest son, the rites may be performed without a presiding wife.'

8. Ȝăng-ȝze asked, 'It has been proposed to invest a son with the cap, and the investors have arrived, and after exchanging bows and courtesies (with the master of the house), have entered. If then news should come that the death of some relative has occurred, for whom a year's mourning or that of nine months must be worn, what should be done?'

Confucius said, 'If the death has taken place within (the circle of the same surname), the ceremony should be given up[2]; but if without (that circle), it will go on, but the sweet wine will not be presented to the youth. The viands will be removed and the place swept, after which he will go to his proper position and wail. If the investors have not yet arrived, the capping will be given up (for the time)[3].

9. 'If the arrangements for the capping have been

---

[1] The words of Confucius are here, as in some other paragraphs, not preceded by the formula, 'Ȝăng-ȝze asked.' Some say this is an omission, intentional or unintentional, of the compiler. Some commentators deride the judgment (see especially Ho *K*ung-yü), holding it unworthy of Confucius.

[2] Because then a festal and a mourning service would come together in the ancestral temple.

[3] The investors may have previously heard of the death, and not kept their appointment.

made, but before the day arrives, an occasion for the one year's mourning, or for that of nine months, or five months, have arrived, the youth shall be capped in his mourning dress.'

10. 'When all mourning is over, may a son continue to wear the cap which he has hitherto worn[1]?'

Confucius said, 'When the son of Heaven gives to the (young) prince of a state or a Great officer his robes and the cap proper to each in the grand ancestral temple, the youth on his return home will set forth his offering (in his own ancestral temple), wearing the robes that have been given to him, and here he will drink the cup of capping (as if) offered by his father[2], without the cup of wine at the ceremony.

11. 'When a son is (thus) capped after his father's death, he is considered to be properly capped; he will sweep the ground, and sacrifice at his father's shrine. This being done, he will present himself before his uncles, and then offer the proper courtesies to the investors.'

12. Ȝăng-ȝze asked, 'Under what circumstances is it that at sacrifice they do not carry out the practice of all drinking to one another?'

Confucius said, 'I have heard that at the close of the one year's mourning, the principal concerned in it

---

[1] Till he was capped, a youth wore nothing on his head. But in the case supposed the youth's time for capping had arrived; and he had assumed a cap without the ceremony.

[2] When a father gave orders to his son about his capping or marriage, he gave him a cup of ordinary wine. The sweet wine was given to the youth by a friend or friends who had invested him with the cap. The real answer to Ȝăng-ȝze's question is in paragraph 11.

sacrifices in his inner garment of soft silk, and there is not that drinking all round. The cup is set down beside the guests, but they do not take it up. This is the rule. Formerly duke *K*âo of Lû [1], while in that silken garment, took the cup and sent it all round, but it was against the rule; and duke Hâo [2], at the end of the second year's mourning, put down the cup presented to him, and did not send it all round, but this also was against the rule.'

13. Ȝăng-ȝze asked, 'In a case (of the) mourning for nine months, can (the principal) take part in contributing to the offerings (to the dead of others)?'

Confucius said, 'Why speak only of (the mourning for) nine months? In all cases from (the mourning for) three years downwards, it may be done. This is the rule.'

Ȝăng-ȝze said, 'Would not this be making the mourning of little importance, and attaching (undue) importance to mutual helpfulness?'

Confucius said, 'This is not what I mean. When there is mourning for the son of Heaven or the prince of a state, (all) who wear the sackcloth with the jagged edges (will contribute to) the offerings. At the mourning of a Great officer, (all) who wear the sackcloth with the even edges will do so. At the mourning of an ordinary officer, his associates and friends will do so. If all these be not sufficient, they may receive contributions from all who should mourn for nine months downwards; and if these be still insufficient, they will repeat the process [3].'

---

[1] B.C. 541–510.

[2] B.C. 795–769. This is going a long way back.

[3] On this paragraph P. Zottoli says:—'Ȝăng-ȝze petit an

14. Ȝăng-ȝze asked, 'In a case of the mourning for five months, may (the principal) take part in the other sacrifices (of mourning)[1]?'

Confucius said, 'Why speak only of the mourning for five months? In all cases from the mourning for three years downwards, (the principals) take part in those sacrifices.'

Ȝăng-ȝze said, 'Would not this be making the mourning of little importance, and giving (undue) importance to the sacrifices?'

Confucius said, 'In the mourning sacrifices for the son of Heaven and the prince of a state, none but those who wear the sackcloth with the jagged edges take part in them. In those for a Great officer, they who wear the sackcloth with the even edges do so. In those for another officer, if the participants be insufficient, they add to them from their brethren who should wear mourning for nine months downwards.'

15. Ȝăng-ȝze asked, 'When acquaintances are in mourning, may they participate in one another's sacrifices?'

Confucius said, 'When wearing the three months' mourning, one has no occasion to sacrifice (in his own ancestral temple), and how should he assist another man (out of his own line)?'

---

aliquis in novem mensium luctu constitutus possit adjuvare alterius funestae familiae oblationem. Confucius intelligit de adjuvanda proprii funeris oblatione.' There appears to be a similar misunderstanding between the two in the next paragraph.

[1] Khung Ying-tâ makes this out to be the sacrifices of repose, and at the end of the wailing. I think the reference is more general.

16. Ȝăng-ȝze asked, 'When one has put off his mourning, may he take part in contributing to the offerings (for the dead of another)?'

Confucius said, 'To take part in the offerings (to another's dead), on putting off one's own sackcloth, is contrary to the rule. Possibly, he may perform the part of assisting him in receiving visitors.'

17. Ȝăng-ȝze asked, 'According to the rules for marriages, the presents have been received and a fortunate day has been fixed;—if then the father or mother of the young lady die, what course should be adopted?'

Confucius said, 'The son-in-law will send some one to condole; and if it be his father or mother that has died, the family of the lady will in the same way send some to present their condolences. If the father have died, (the messenger) will name the (other) father (as having sent him); if the mother, he will name the (other) mother. If both parents be dead (on both sides), he will name the oldest uncle and his wife. When the son-in-law has buried (his dead), his oldest uncle will offer a release from the engagement to the lady, saying, "My son, being occupied with the mourning for his father or mother, and not having obtained the right to be reckoned among your brethren, has employed me to offer a release from the engagement." (In this case) it is the rule for the lady to agree to the message and not presume to (insist on) the marriage (taking place immediately). When the son-in-law has concluded his mourning, the parents of the lady will send and request (the fulfilment of the engagement). The son-in-law will not (immediately come to) carry her (to his house), but afterwards she will be married to him; this is the rule. If it be the father or mother of the lady who died, the son-in-law will follow a similar course[1].'

18. Ȝăng-ȝze asked, 'The son-in-law has met the lady in person, and she is on the way with him:—if (then) his father or mother die, what course should be adopted?'

Confucius said, 'The lady will change her dress[2]; and in the long linen robe[3], with the cincture of white silk round her hair, will hasten to be present at the mourning rites. If, while she is on the way, it be her own father or mother who dies, she will return[4].'

19. 'If the son-in-law have met the lady in person, and before she has arrived at his house, there occur a death requiring the year's or the nine months' mourning, what course should be adopted?'

Confucius said, 'Before the gentleman enters, he will change his dress in a place outside. The lady will enter and change her dress in a place inside. They will then go to the proper positions and wail.'

Ȝăng-ȝze asked, 'When the mourning is ended, will they not resume the marriage ceremonies?'

---

[1] Is the final marriage of the lady to the original betrothed 'son-in-law,' or bridegroom as we should say; or to another, that she may not pass the proper time for her marrying? Khung Ying-tâ, and other old commentators, advocate the latter view. Others, and especially the *Kh*ien-lung editors, maintain the former; and I have indicated in the version my agreement with them. There are difficulties with the text; but Confucius would hardly have sanctioned the other course.

[2] At the house of him who was now her husband.

[3] This, called 'the deep garment,' had the body and skirt sown together. See Book XXXIV.

[4] This would be done, it is said, by Hsü Sze-ȝhăng (Ming dynasty), to allow play to her filial piety, but she would live at the house of 'the son-in-law.'

Confucius said, 'It is the rule, that when the time of sacrifice has been allowed to pass by, it is not then offered. Why in this case should they go back to what must have taken place previously?'

20. Confucius said, 'The family that has married a daughter away, does not extinguish its candles for three nights, thinking of the separation that has taken place. The family that has received the (new) wife for three days has no music; thinking her bridegroom is now in the place of his parents[1]. After three months she presents herself in the ancestral temple, and is styled "The new wife that has come." A day is chosen for her to sacrifice at the shrine of her father-in-law; expressing the idea of her being (now) the established wife.'

21. Ȝăng-ȝze asked, 'If the lady die before she has presented herself in the ancestral temple, what course should be adopted?'

Confucius said, '(Her coffin) should not be removed to the ancestral temple, nor should (her tablet) be placed next to that of her mother-in-law. The husband should not carry the staff; nor wear the shoes of straw; nor have a (special) place (for wailing). She should be taken back, and buried among her kindred of her own family;—showing that she had not become the established wife.'

22. Ȝăng-ȝze asked, 'The fortunate day has been fixed for taking the lady (to her new home), and she dies (in the meantime):—what should be done?'

Confucius said, 'The son-in-law will come to condole, wearing the one year's mourning, which he will

[1] This and the statements that follow suppose that the bridegroom's parents are dead.

lay aside when the interment has taken place. If it be the husband who dies, a similar course will be followed on the other side.'

23. Ȝăng-ȝze asked, 'Is it according to rule that at the mourning rites there should be two (performing the part of) the orphan son (and heir, receiving visitors)[1], or that at a temple-shrine there should be two spirit-tablets?'

Confucius said, 'In heaven there are not two suns; in a country there are not two kings[2]; in the seasonal sacrifices, and those to Heaven and Earth[3], there are not two who occupy the highest place of honour. I do not know that what you ask about is according to rule. Formerly duke Hwan of Khî[4], going frequently to war, made fictitious tablets and took them with him on his expeditions, depositing them on his return in the ancestral temple[5]. The practice of having two tablets in a temple-shrine originated from duke Hwan. As to two (playing the part of the) orphan son, it may be thus explained:—Formerly, on occasion of a visit to Lû by duke Ling of Wei, the mourning rites of *K*î Hwan-ȝze were in progress. The ruler of Wei requested leave to offer his condolences. Duke Âi (of Lû)[6] declined (the ceremony), but could not

---

[1] The Chinese characters mean simply 'two orphans.' Neither Khang-hsî nor any English-Chinese dictionary explains the peculiar use of the term here; nor is Confucius' explanation satisfactory, or to the point.

[2] Compare paragraphs 5, 8, III, iii, pages 224–226.

[3] See the 'Doctrine of the Mean,' 19, 6, Chinese Classics, vol. i.

[4] B.C. 685–643.

[5] Literally 'the temple-shrine of his grandfather;' but I think the name must have the general meaning I have given.

[6] It has been shown that the ruler of Wei here could not be

enforce his refusal. He therefore acted as the principal (mourner), and the visitor came in to condole with him. Khang-ȝze stood on the right of the gate with his face to the north. The duke, after the usual bows and courtesies, ascended by the steps on the east with his face towards the west. The visitor ascended by those on the west, and paid his condolences. The duke bowed ceremoniously to him, and then rose up and wailed, while Khang-ȝze bowed with his forehead to the ground, in the position where he was. The superintending officers made no attempt to put the thing to rights. The having two now acting as the orphan son arose from the error of *K*î Khang-ȝze.'

24. Ȝăng-ȝze asked, 'Anciently when an army went on an expedition, was it not first necessary to carry with it the spirit-tablets that had been removed from their shrines[1]?'

Confucius said, 'When the son of Heaven went on his tours of Inspection, he took (one of) those tablets along with him, conveying it in the carriage of Reverence, thus intimating how it was felt necessary to have with him that object of honour[2]. The practice

---

duke Ling. He must have been duke *Kh*û. But this error discredits the view of the statement having come from Confucius.

[1] See note 2 and plan of the royal ancestral temple of *K*âu on pages 223-225.

[2] This, it is said, was the tablet of the royal ancestor which had been last removed from its shrine, and placed in the shrine-house for all such removed tablets. The carriage of Reverence was the 'metal-guilt' carriage of the king, second to that adorned with jade, in which he rode to sacrifice. Zottoli renders :—'Imperator perlustrans custodita, cum translatitii delubri tabella peragrabat, imposita super casti curru, significatum necessariam praesentiam superioris.'

now-a-days of taking the tablets of the seven temple-shrines along with them on an expedition is an error. No shrine in all the seven (of the king), or in the five of the prince of a state, ought to be (left) empty. A shrine can only be so left without its tablet, when the son of Heaven has died, or the prince of a state deceased, or left his state, or when all the tablets are brought together at the united sacrifice, in the shrine-temple of the highest ancestor. I heard the following statement from Lâo Tan[1] :—"On the death of the son of Heaven, or of the prince of a state, it is the rule that the officer of prayer should take the tablets from all the other shrines and deposit them in that of the high ancestor[2]. When the wailing was over, and the business (of placing the tablet of the deceased in its shrine) was completed, then every other tablet was restored to its shrine. When a ruler abandoned his state, it was the rule that the Grand minister should take the tablets from all the shrines and follow him. When there was the united sacrifice in the shrine of the high ancestor, the officer of prayer met (and received) the tablets from the four shrines. When they were taken from their shrines or carried back to them all were required to keep out of the way." So said Lâo Tan.'

---

[1] This was, most probably, Lâo-ȝze, though some of the commentators deny it. *K*ăng says: 'Lâo Tan, the title of old for men of longevity, was a contemporary of Confucius;' and *Kh*ăn Hâo quotes a note on this from Wang of Shih-liang, that 'This was not the author of the "Five thousand words,"' i. e. of the Tâo Teh *K*ing.

[2] While the special sacrifices and other funeral rites were going on, the other sacrifices, which belonged to a different category of rites, were suspended.

25. Ȝăng-ȝze asked, 'Anciently, when they marched on an expedition, and carried no displaced tablets with them, what did they make their chief consideration?'

Confucius said, 'They made the instructions from the tablet their chief consideration[1].'

'What does that mean?' asked the other.

Confucius said, 'When the son of Heaven or the prince of a state was about to go forth, he would, with gifts of silk, skins, and jade-tokens, announce his purpose at the shrines of his grandfather and father. He then took those gifts with him, conveying them on the march in the carriage of Reverence. At every stage (of the march), he would place offerings of food by them, and afterwards occupy the station. On returning, they would make announcement (at the same shrines), and when they had set forth (again) their offerings, they would collect the silk and jade, and bury them between the steps (leading) up to the fane of the high ancestor; after which they left the temple. This was how they made the instructions they received their chief consideration.'

26. Ȝze-yû asked, 'Is it the rule to mourn for a foster-mother[2] as for a mother?'

---

[1] Zottoli gives for this phrase simply 'adhaerebant numini,' subjoining no note on it. The parties spoken of put down their offerings before the shrines, announcing that they were about to undertake such an expedition; and taking it for granted that their progenitors approved of their object, proceeded to carry it out, as if they had received a charge from them to do so, carrying the offerings with them in token of that charge from the spirits in the tablets of the shrines. This view is distinctly set forth by Hwang Khan (end of early Sung dynasty) and others.

[2] This foster-mother was not what we call 'a nurse;' but a lady

Confucius said, 'It is not the rule. Anciently, outside the palace, a boy had his master, and at home his foster-mother; they were those whom the ruler employed to teach his son;—what ground should these be for wearing mourning for them? Formerly duke *K*âo of Lû having lost his mother when he was little, had a foster-mother, who was good; and when she died, he could not bear (not) to mourn for her, and wished to do so. The proper officer on hearing of it, said, "According to the ancient rule, there is no mourning for a foster-mother. If you wear this mourning, you will act contrary to that ancient rule, and introduce confusion into the laws of the state. If you will after all do it, then we will put it on record, and transmit the act to the future;—will not that be undesirable?" The duke said, "Anciently the son of Heaven, when unoccupied and at ease, wore the soft inner garment, assumed after the year's mourning, and the cap." The duke could not bear not to wear mourning, and on this he mourned for his foster-mother in this garb. The mourning for a foster-mother originated with duke *K*âo of Lû[1].'

of the harem to whom the care of an orphan boy was entrusted;—it may have been after he ceased to be suckled. The reasoning of Confucius goes on the assumption that mourning should be worn only in cases of consanguinity or affinity; and it may be inferred from this that concubinage was not the most ancient rule in China.

[1] See the eleventh article in the forty-third chapter of the 'Narratives of the School,' where a similar, probably the same, conversation, with some variations, is found. The duke of Lû in it, however, is not *K*âo, but Hâo; see paragraph 12, page 315.

Section II.

1. Ȝăng-ȝze asked, 'The princes are assembled in a body to appear before the son of Heaven; they have entered the gate, but are not able to go through with the rites (of audience);—how many occurrences will make these be discontinued?'

Confucius said, 'Four.' 'May I ask what they are?' said the other. The reply was:—'The grand ancestral temple taking fire; an eclipse of the sun; funeral rites of the queen; their robes all unsightly through soaking rain. If, when the princes are all there, an eclipse of the sun take place, they follow the son of Heaven to save it[1]; each one dressed in the colour of his quarter, and with the weapon proper to it[2]. If there be a fire in the grand ancestral temple, they follow him to extinguish it without those robes and weapons.'

2. Ȝăng-ȝze said, 'Princes are visiting one another. (The strangers) have entered the gate after the customary bowings and courtesies, but they are not able to go through with the rites (of audience);—how many occurrences will make these be discontinued?'

Confucius said, 'Six;' and, in answer to the ques-

---

[1] The phenomenon of an eclipse suggested the idea of some enemy or adverse influence devouring the sun's disk.

[2] The colour appropriate to the east was green, and the weapon the spear with two hooks; the colour of the south was red, and the weapon the spear with one hook and two points; the colour of the west was white, and the weapon the bow; the colour of the north was black, and the weapon the shield; the colour of the centre was yellow, and the weapon the drum.

tion as to what they were, replied:—'The death of the son of Heaven; the grand ancestral temple taking fire; an eclipse of the sun; the funeral rites of the queen or of the princess of the state; and their robes all unsightly through soaking rain.'

3. Ȝăng-ȝze said, 'At the seasonal sacrifices of the son of Heaven, at those to Heaven and Earth, and at (any of) the five sacrifices of the house, after the vessels, round and square, with their contents have been set forth, if there occur the death of the son of Heaven or mourning rites for the queen, what should be done?'

Confucius said, 'The sacrifice should be stopped.' The other asked, 'If, during the sacrifice, there occur an eclipse of the sun, or the grand ancestral temple take fire, what should be done?' The reply was, 'The steps of the sacrifice should be hurried on. If the victim have arrived, but has not yet been slain, the sacrifice should be discontinued.

4. 'When the son of Heaven has died and is not yet coffined, the sacrifices of the house are not offered. When he is coffined, they are resumed; but at any one of them the representative of the dead takes (only) three mouthfuls (of the food), and is not urged (to take more). He is then presented with a cup, but does not respond by presenting another, and there is an end (of the ceremony). From the removal of the coffin to the return (from the burial) and the subsequent wailing, those sacrifices (again) cease. After the burial they are offered, but when the officer of prayer has finished the cup presented to him, they stop.'

5. Ȝăng-ȝze asked, 'At the sacrifices to the spirits

of the land and grain proper to the feudal princes, if, after the stands and vessels, with their contents, have been arranged, news arrive of the death of the son of Heaven or of the mourning rites for his queen, or if the ruler die or there be mourning rites for his consort, what should be done?'

Confucius said, 'The sacrifice should be discontinued. From the ruler's death to the coffining, and from the removal of the coffin to the return (from the burial) and the (subsequent) wailing, they will follow the example set by the son of Heaven[1].'

6. 3ăng-ȝze asked, 'At the sacrifices of a Great officer[2], when the tripods and stands have been arranged, and the dishes of bamboo and wood, with their contents, have been set forth, but they are not able to go through with the rites, how many occurrences will cause them to be discontinued?'

Confucius said, 'Nine;' and when asked what they were, he added:—'The death of the son of Heaven; funeral rites for his queen; the death of the ruler (of the state); funeral rites for his consort; the ruler's grand ancestral temple taking fire; an eclipse of the sun; (a call to) the three years' mourning; to that of one year; or to that of nine months. In all these cases the sacrifice should be given up. If the mourning be merely for relatives by affinity, from all degrees of it up to the twelve months, the sacrifice will go on. At one where the mourning is worn for twelve months, the representative of the dead, after entering, will take (only) three mouthfuls (of the food), and not be urged to take (any more).

[1] As given in the preceding paragraphs.

[2] In his ancestral temple.

He will be presented with a cup, but will not respond by presenting one in return, and there will be an end (of the ceremony). Where the mourning is for nine months, after he has presented the responsive cup, the thing will end. Where it is for five or for three months, it will not end till all the observances in the apartment are gone through. What distinguishes the proceedings of an ordinary officer is, that he does not sacrifice when wearing the three months' mourning. He sacrifices, however, if the dead to whom he does so had no relationship with him requiring him to wear mourning.'

7. Ȝăng-ȝze asked, 'May one, wearing the three years' mourning for a parent, go to condole with others?'

Confucius said, 'On the completion of the first of the three years, one should not be seen standing with others, or going along in a crowd. With a superior man the use of ceremonies is to give proper and elegant expression to the feelings. Would it not be an empty form [1] to go and condole and wail with others, while wearing the three years' mourning?'

8. Ȝăng-ȝze asked, 'If a Great officer or ordinary officer be in mourning for a parent [2] he may put it off [3]; and if he be in mourning for his ruler, under what conditions will he put that off?'

Confucius said, 'If he have the mourning for his

---

[1] How could he, occupied with his own sorrow, offer anything but an empty form of condolence to others?

[2] Literally 'private mourning,' as below; but evidently the master and disciple both had the mourning for a parent in mind.

[3] On his having to go into mourning for his ruler.

ruler on his person, he will not venture to wear any private mourning;—what putting off can there be? In this case, even if the time be passed (for any observances which the private mourning would require), he will not put it off. When the mourning for the ruler is put off, he will then perform the great sacrifices (of his private mourning)[1]. This is the rule.'

9. Ȝăng-ȝze asked, 'But is it allowable thus to give up all the mourning rites for a parent through this keeping on of the mourning (for a ruler)?'

Confucius said, 'According to the ceremonies as determined by the ancient kings, it is the rule that when the time has passed (for the observance of any ceremony), there should be no attempt to perform it. It is not that one could not keep from not putting off the mourning; but the evil would be in his going beyond the definite statute. Therefore it is that a superior man does not offer a sacrifice, when the proper time for doing so has passed.'

10. Ȝăng-ȝze said, 'If, when the ruler has died, and is now lying in his coffin, the minister be called to the funeral rites for his father or mother, what course will he pursue?'

Confucius said, 'He should go home and remain there; going indeed to the ruler's for the great

[1] That is, the rightful son and heir may then perform the sacrifice marking the close of the first year's mourning for a parent, and that marking the close of the second year's mourning in the month after. But *Kh*ăn Hâo argues that it was only the rightful son who could thus go back and offer the sacrifices proper to the mourning rites for parents, and that the other sons could not do so. This is the case underlying the next paragraph.

services (to the departed), but not for those of every morning and evening[1].'

11. (Ȝăng-ȝze asked), 'If, when they have begun to remove the coffin, the minister be called to the funeral rites for his father or mother, how should he do?'

Confucius said, 'He should go home and wail, and then return and accompany the funeral of the ruler.'

12. 'If,' said (Ȝăng-ȝze), 'before the ruler has been coffined, a minister be called to the funeral rites for his father or mother, what should be his course?'

Confucius said, 'He should go home, and have the deceased put into the coffin, returning (then) to the ruler's. On occasion of the great services, he will go home, but not for those of every morning and evening. In the case of a Great officer, the chief servant of the household will attend to matters; in the case of an ordinary officer, a son or grandson. When there are the great services at the ruler's, the wife of the Great officer will also go there, but not for those of every morning and evening.'

13. One in a low position should not pronounce the eulogy of another in a high, nor a younger man that of one older than himself. In the case of the son of Heaven, they refer to Heaven as giving his

[1] It has been seen that morning and evening offerings to the dead were placed near the coffin. On the first and fifteenth of the month these were on a great scale, and with special observances,—at the new and full moon. They were 'the great services.' The practice still continues.

eulogy. It is not the rule for princes of states to deliver the eulogy of one another[1].

14. Ʒăng-ʒze asked, 'When a ruler goes across the boundary of his own state, he takes with him his inner coffin as a precaution for the preparations against the three years' (mourning rites) for him[2]. If he die (abroad), what are the proceedings on his being brought back?'

Confucius said, 'The clothes to be put on him after the coffining having been provided, the son in the linen cap, with the sackcloth band round it, wearing coarse sackcloth and the shoes of straw, and carrying a staff, will enter by the opening made in the wall of the apartment for the coffin, having ascended by the western steps. If the slighter dressing (preparatory to the coffining) have still (to be made), the son will follow the bier without a cap, enter by the gate, and ascend by the steps on the east. There is one and the same rule for a ruler, a Great officer, and an ordinary officer.'

15. Ʒăng-ʒze asked, 'If one is occupied in drawing (the carriage with the bier on it) at the funeral rites of his ruler, and is then called to the funeral rites of his father or mother, what should he do?'

---

[1] The eulogy has in China for more than a thousand years taken the form of inscriptions on tombs and sacrificial compositions; of which there are many elegant and eloquent specimens. It should be summed up in the honorary title. Truth, however, might require that that should be the reverse of eulogistic; and perhaps this led to its being conferred, as a rule, by one superior in rank and position. The honorary title of a deceased sovereign was first proclaimed at the great sacrifice to Heaven at the winter solstice; and hence it is referred to in the text as coming from Heaven!

[2] That is, I think, simply, 'as a precaution against his dying while abroad.' Zottoli renders:—'Regulus excedens confinia, ut in tres annos praecaveatur, habit sandapilam sequacem.'

Confucius said, 'He should complete what he is engaged in; and when the coffin has been let down into the grave, return home, without waiting for the departure of the (ruler's) son.'

16. Ȝăng-ȝze asked, 'If one, occupied with the funeral rites of a parent, has (assisted in) drawing the bier to the path (to the grave), and there hear of the death of his ruler, what should he do?'

Confucius said, 'He should complete the burial; and, when the coffin has been let down, he should change his dress, and go to (the ruler's).'

17. Ȝăng-ȝze asked, 'If the eldest son by the proper wife be (only) an officer, and a son by a secondary wife be a Great officer, how will the latter proceed in his sacrificing?'

Confucius said, 'He will sacrifice, with the victims belonging to his higher rank, in the house of the eldest son. The officer of prayer will say, "So and So, the filial son, in behalf of So and So, the attendant son, presents his regular offering[1]."'

18. 'If the eldest son, now the head of the family, be residing, in consequence of some charge of guilt, in another state, and a son by a secondary wife be a Great officer, when (the latter) is offering a sacrifice (for the other), the officer of prayer will say, "So

[1] Here two things were in collision. The oldest son by the proper wife was the representative of the father, and only he could preside at the service in the ancestral temple of the family. But here an inferior son has been advanced to a higher rank than his older brother. As a Great officer he is entitled to have three shrine temples; but it would be contrary to the solidarity of the family for him to erect an ancestral temple for himself. The difficulty is met in the way described, the sacrifice being ascribed to the elder brother, as head of the family.

and So, the filial son, employs the attendant son, So and So, to perform for him the regular service." (In this case, however), the principal in this vicarious service will not conduct the sacrifice so as to see that the spirit of the deceased is satisfied to the full; nor send the cup round among all who are present, nor receive the blessing (at the close); nor lay on the ground the portions of the sacrifice as thank-offerings; nor have with him (the wife of the elder brother) who should appear before the spirit-tablet of her mother-in-law, the wife of the deceased. He will put down the cup before the (principal) guests, but they will put it down (in another place), and not send it round. He will not send to them portions of the flesh. In his address to the guests (at the beginning of the service), he will say, "My honoured brother, the honoured son (of our father), being in another state, has employed me, So and So, to make announcement to you[1].""

19. Ȝăng-ȝze asked, 'If the eldest son have gone and is in another state, while a son by a secondary

[1] This paragraph continues the case in the preceding, with the additional circumstances that the head of the family is a fugitive from it, and that the sacrifice referred to in it is performed by the inferior brother remaining in the state, in lieu of him. It is difficult to translate without amplification so as to be intelligible, because of what may be called the technical terms in it. The five points in which the service was deficient, different from what it would have been, if performed by the proper brother, are given in the reverse order of their regular occurrence; whether designedly or not, we cannot tell. For that portion of the paragraph P. Zottoli gives:—'Sed vicarius dominus vacabit satisfactionis sacrificio; vacabit universali propinatione; vacabit benedictione; vacabit consternationis sacrificio; vacabit copulatione;' appending a note to explain the terms.

wife, and without rank, remains at home, may the latter offer the sacrifice?'

Confucius said, 'Yes, certainly.' 'And how will he sacrifice?' 'He will rear an altar in front of the (family-)grave, and there he will sacrifice at the different seasons. If the oldest son die, he will announce the event at the grave, and afterwards sacrifice in the house, calling himself, however, only by his name, and abstaining from the epithet "filial." This abstinence will cease after his death.' The disciples of Ȝze-yû, in the case of sons by inferior wives sacrificing, held that this practice was in accordance with what was right. Those of them who sacrifice now-a-days do not ground their practice on this principle of right;—they have no truthful ground for their sacrifices[1].

20. Ȝăng-ȝze asked, 'Is it necessary that there should be a representative of the dead in sacrifice? or may he be dispensed with as when the satisfying offerings are made to the dead?'

Confucius said, 'In sacrificing to a full-grown man for whom there have been the funeral rites, there must be such a representative, who should be a grandson; and if the grandson be too young, some one must be employed to carry him in his arms. If there be no grandson, some one of the same surname should be selected for the occasion. In sacrificing to one who has died prematurely, there are (only) the satisfying offerings, for he was not

[1] These last two sentences evidently should not be ascribed to Confucius. It was only after his death that Ȝze-yû would have a school of his own. They must have been written moreover after the death of Ȝze-yû.

full-grown. To sacrifice to a full-grown man, for whom there have been the funeral rites without a representative, would be to treat him as if he had died prematurely.'

21. Confucius said, 'There is the offering of satisfaction made in the dark chamber, and that made in the brighter place.'

Ȝăng-ȝze answered with a question, 'But to one who has died prematurely there is not made a complete sacrifice; what do you mean by speaking of two satisfying offerings, the dark and the bright?'

Confucius said, 'When the oldest son, who would take the father's place, dies prematurely, no brother by an inferior wife can be his successor. At the auspicious sacrifice to him[1], there is a single bullock; but the service being to one who died prematurely, there is no presentation (of the lungs), no stand with the heart and tongue, no dark-coloured spirits[2], no announcement of the nourishment being completed. This is what is called the dark satisfying offering. In regard to all others who have died prematurely and have left no offspring, the sacrifice is offered to them in the house of the oldest son, where the apartment is most light, with the vases in the chamber on the east. This is what is called the bright satisfying offering.'

22. Ȝăng-ȝze asked, 'At a burial, when the bier has been drawn to the path (leading to the place), if there happen an eclipse of the sun, is any change made or not?'

---

[1] The first auspicious sacrifice took place when the ceremony of wailing was over.

[2] A name for water.

Confucius said, 'Formerly, along with Lâo Tan[1], I was assisting at a burial in the village of Hsiang, and when we had got to the path, the sun was eclipsed. Lâo Tan said to me, "*Kh*iû, let the bier be stopped on the left of the road[2]; and then let us wail and wait till the eclipse pass away. When it is light again, we will proceed." He said that this was the rule. When we had returned and completed the burial, I said to him, "In the progress of a bier there should be no returning. When there is an eclipse of the sun, we do not know whether it will pass away quickly or not, would it not have been better to go on?" Lâo Tan said, "When the prince of a state is going to the court of the son of Heaven, he travels while he can see the sun. At sun-down he halts, and presents his offerings (to the spirit of the way). When a Great officer is on a mission, he travels while he can see the sun, and at sun-down he halts. Now a bier does not set forth in the early morning, nor does it rest anywhere at night; but those who travel by star-light are only criminals and those who are hastening to the funeral rites of a parent. When there is an eclipse of the sun, how do we know that we shall not see the stars? And moreover, a superior man, in his performance of rites, will not expose his relatives to the risk of distress or evil." This is what I heard from Lâo Tan.'

23. Ȝăng-ȝze asked, 'In the case of one dying where he is stopping, when discharging a mission for

---

[1] This was Lâo-ȝze, 'the old master.' It seems better to keep Lâo as if it had been the surname. See paragraph 24, p. 325.

[2] The east of the road. Graves were north of the towns.

his ruler, the rules say[1] that, (if he die) in a government hotel his spirit shall be recalled; but not, (if he die) in a private one[2]. But to whatever state a commissioner may be sent, the lodging which may be assigned to him by the proper officer becomes a public hotel;—what is the meaning of his spirit not being recalled, (if he die) in a private one?'

Confucius said, 'You have asked well. The houses of a high minister, a Great officer, or an ordinary officer, may be called private hotels. The government hotel, and any other which the government may appoint, may be called a public hotel. In this you have the meaning of that saying that the spirit is recalled at a public hotel.'

24. Ȝăng-ȝze asked, 'Children dying prematurely, between eight and eleven, should be buried in the garden in a brick grave, and carried thither on a contrivance serving the purpose of a carriage, the place being near; but now if the grave is chosen at a distance, what do you say about their being buried there?'

Confucius said, 'I have heard this account from Lâo Tan:—"Formerly," he said, "the recorder Yî had a son who died thus prematurely, and the grave was distant. The duke of Shâo said to him, 'Why not shroud and coffin him in your palace?' The recorder said, 'Dare I do so?' The

---

[1] Where these rules are to be found I do not know.

[2] I use 'hotel' here in the French meaning of the term. We must suppose that 'the private hotel' about which Ȝăng-ȝze asked was one to which the commissioner had gone without the instructions of the state; and, as the *Kh*ien-lung editors say, 'the rites were therefore so far diminished.'

duke of Shâo spoke about it to the duke of *K*âu, who said, 'Why may it not be done?' and the recorder did it. The practice of coffins for boys who have died so prematurely, and shrouding them began with the recorder Yî."'

25. Ȝăng-ȝze asked, 'A minister or a Great officer is about to act the part of a personator of the dead for his ruler. If, when he has received (orders) to pass the night in solemn vigil, there occur in his own family an occasion for him to wear the robe of hemmed sackcloth, what should he do?'

Confucius said, 'The rule is for him to leave (his house) and lodge in a state hotel, and wait till (the ruler's) business is accomplished.'

26. Confucius said, 'When one who has represented the dead comes forth in the (officer's) leathern cap, or the (Great officer's) tasseled cap (which he has worn), ministers, Great officers, and other officers, all will descend from their carriages (when his passes). He will bow forward to them, and he will also have a forerunner (to notify his approach).'

27. Ȝze-hsiâ asked, 'There is such a thing as no longer declining military service, after the wailing in the three years' mourning has come to an end. Is this the rule? or was it at first required by the officers (of the state)?'

Confucius said, 'Under the sovereigns of Hsiâ, as soon as the coffining in the three years' mourning was completed, they resigned all their public duties. Under Yin they did so as soon as the interment was over. Is not this the meaning of what we find in the record, that "the ruler does not take from men their affection to their parents, nor do men take from their parents their filial duty?"'

28. 3ze-hsiâ asked, 'Is then not declining military service (during mourning) to be condemned?'

Confucius said, 'I heard from Lâo Tan that duke Po-*kh*in engaged once in such service, when there was occasion for it; but I do not know if I should allow it in those who seek (by it) their own advantage during the period of the three years' mourning[1].'

---

[1] Po-*kh*in was the son of the duke of *K*âu, and the first marquis of Lû. The time of his entering on the rule of that state was a very critical one in the kingdom; and though it was then, it would appear, the period of his mourning for his mother's death, he discharged his public duty in the time of his own grief.

BOOK VI. WĂN WANG SHIH 3ZE

OR

KING WĂN AS SON AND HEIR[1].

Section I.

1. Thus did king Wăn act when he was eldest son and heir:—Thrice a day he made a visit in due form to king *K*î. When the cock first crowed he dressed himself, and going to the outside of the bedroom, asked one of the servants of the interior who was in attendance how the king was and if he were well. When told that he was well, the prince was glad. At midday he repeated the visit in the same way; and so he did again in the evening[2]. If the king were not so well as usual, the servant would tell the prince, and then his sorrow appeared in his countenance, and his walk was affected and disturbed. When king *K*î took his food again, Wăn recovered his former appearance. When the food went up (to the king), he would examine it and see if it were cold and hot as it ought to be[3]. When it came down, he asked of what dishes the king had eaten. He gave orders to the cook that none of the dishes should go up again, and withdrew on receiving the cook's assurance accordingly[4].

---

[1] See the introduction, pages 22, 23.

[2] It was the duty of a son to wait on his father twice a day,—at morning and night. King Wăn showed his filial duty by paying king *K*î a third visit.

[3] According to the season.

[4] According to the ordinary dates in Chinese chronology, king

2. King Wû acted according to the example (of Wăn), not presuming to go (in anything) beyond it. When king Wăn was ill, Wû nursed him without taking off his cap or girdle. When king Wăn took a meal, he also took a meal; and when king Wăn took a second, he did the same. It was not till after twelve days that he intermitted his attentions.

King Wăn said to Wû, 'What have you been dreaming?' 'I dreamt,' was the reply, 'that God gave me nine ling?' 'And what do you think was the meaning?' King Wû said, 'There are nine states in the west;—may it not mean that you will yet bring them all under your happy sway?' Wăn said, 'That was not the meaning. Anciently they called a year ling. The age is also called ling. I am 100; and you are 90. I give you three years.' King Wăn was 97 when he died, and king Wû was 93[1].

3. King *Kh*ăng, being quite young, could not perform his part at the eastern steps[2]. The duke of *K*âu acted as regent, trod those steps, and adminis-

---

Wăn was born in B.C. 1258, and named *Kh*ang (昌). King *K*î died in 1185, when he was in his seventy-fourth year.

[1] It is difficult to understand and interpret the latter half of this paragraph. The *Kh*ien-lung editors say that, according to the ordinary accounts, king Wû was born when Wăn was fifteen years old, and there was an elder son, Yî-khâo, who died prematurely; whereas king Wû died at 93, leaving his son Sung (king *Kh*ăng) only seven years old. 'Wăn,' they said, 'must have married very early, and Wû very late.' They say also that they cannot understand the text that Wăn gave to his son 'three years,' &c., and suppose that some erroneous tradition has here been introduced.

[2] The king received his nobles at the top of the eastern steps. The phrase = 'in the government of the kingdom.'

tered the government. He illustrated the rules for the behaviour of a young heir in his treatment of Po-*kh*in, that king *Kh*ăng might thereby know the courses to be pursued by father and son, ruler and minister, old and young. When he committed an error, the duke punished Po-*kh*in. This was the way in which he showed king *Kh*ăng his duty as the son and heir.

4. So much on the way in which king Wăn acted as son and heir.

5. In teaching the heir-sons (of the king and feudal princes), and young men (chosen from their aptitude) for learning[1], the subjects were different at different seasons. In spring and summer they were taught the use of the shield and spear; in autumn and winter that of the feather and flute:—all in the eastern school. The inferior directors of Music[2] taught the use of the shield aided by the great assistants. The flute masters taught the use of the spear, aided by the subdirectors, while the assistants regulated by the drum (the chanting of) the Nan[3].

In spring they recited (the pieces), and in summer

---

[1] These 'scholars,' no doubt, were those of whose selection for the higher instruction we have an account in the fourth and other paragraphs of Section IV, Book III.

[2] These are mentioned in the 'Royal Regulations,' though the title does not occur in the *K*âu Lî. They are supposed to be the same as its 'music masters' (Yo Sze, Book XXII).

[3] This clause about the 'drum' is perplexing to a translator. It destroys the symmetry of the paragraph. What we are to understand by the 'Nan' is also much disputed. I suppose the term should embrace the two Nan, or two first Books of the Shih, Part I. Compare the Shih II, vi, 4. 4.

they played on the guitar,—being taught by the grand master in the Hall of the Blind[1]. In autumn they learned ceremonies,—being instructed by the masters of ceremonies. In winter they read the book of History,—being instructed by the guardians of it. Ceremonies were taught in the Hall of the Blind; the book in the upper school.

---

[1] The names of these different schools are also very perplexing; and I here give a note about them by Liû *Kh*ang of our eleventh century. 'Under the *K*âu dynasty they had its own schools and those of the three former dynasties; four buildings, all erected in proximity to one another. Most in the centre was the Pî Yung of *K*âu itself. On the north of it was the school of Shun (the lord Yü); on the east that of Hsiâ; and on the west that of Shang. Those who were learning the use (in dancing) of the shield and spear, and of the plume and flute, went to the eastern school; those who were learning ceremonies went to that of Shang; and those who were learning history, to that of Shun. In the Pî Yung the son of Heaven nourished the old, sent forth his armies, matured his plans, received prisoners, and practised archery. When he came to the Pî Yung, they came from all the other three schools, and stood round the encircling water to look at him. There were also schools on the plan of Shun—the hsiang (庠)—in the large districts (the 鄉, containing 12500 families); others on the plan of Hsiâ—the hsü (序)—in the *K*âu, or smaller districts (the 州, containing 2500 families); and others still on the plan of Shang—the hsiâo (校)—in the Tang (黨), or those still smaller (containing 500 families). These were all schools for young boys. The most promising scholars (in the family schools) were removed to the hsiang; the best in the hsiang, again to the hsü; and the best in the hsü, to the hsiâo. The best in these were removed finally to the great school (or college) in the suburbs (of the capital).' Such is the account of Liû *Kh*ang. Other scholars differ from him in some points; but there is a general agreement as to the existence of a system of graduated training.

6. All the rules about sacrificial offerings[1] and at the nourishing of the old begging them to speak (their wise counsels)[2] and the conversation at general reunions, were taught by the lower directors of Music in the eastern school.

7. The Grand director of Music taught how to brandish the shield and axe. He also delivered the graduated rules relating to conversations and the charges about begging the old to speak. The Grand perfecter (of Instruction)[3] discussed all about (these matters) in the eastern school.

8. Whenever a pupil was sitting with the Grand completer (of Instruction), there was required to be between them the width of three mats. He might put questions to him; and when he had finished, sit back on the mat near to the wall. While the instructor had not finished all he had to say on any one point, he did not ask about another.

9. In all the schools, the officer (in charge), in spring set forth offerings to the master who first taught (the subjects); and in autumn and winter he did the same[4].

10. In every case of the first establishment of a school the offerings must be set forth to the earlier

[1] Probably, not sacrifices in general, but offerings to sages, distinguished old men, &c.

[2] This asking the old men to speak was a part of the festal nourishment of them.

[3] I do not think this officer appears in the lists of the *K*âu Lî. He seems to be named as giving the finishing touch to the training of the young princes.

[4] No mention is made of summer; but, no doubt, there were then the same observances as in the other seasons,—a tribute to the merit of the past, and a stimulus to the students.

sages and the earlier teachers; and in the doing of this, pieces of silk must be used.

11. In all the cases of setting forth the offerings, it was required to have the accompaniments (of dancing and singing). When there were any events of engrossing interest in a state (at the time), these were omitted.

12. When there was the accompaniment of music on a great scale, they proceeded immediately to feast the aged.

13. At all examinations in the suburban schools, the rule was to select the best and mark out the most talented. The pupils might be advanced for their virtue, or commended for something they had accomplished, or distinguished for their eloquence[1]. Those who had studied minor arts were encouraged and told to expect a second examination[2]. If they (then) had one of the three things (above mentioned), they were advanced to a higher grade, according to their several orders, and were styled 'Men of the schools.' They were (still, however,) kept out of the royal college[3], and could not receive the cup from the vase restricted to the superior students.

14. On the first establishment of schools (in any state), when the instruments of music were

---

[1] See paragraphs 2–4, pp. 231–233.

[2] These minor arts, it is understood, were such as medicine and divination.

[3] The name for this college here perhaps indicates that on reaching it, all from the other schools were 'on the same level.' The youths would appear to have passed into it with a festive ceremony. The 'suburban schools' were those in the note on p. 346, with the addition of the 'Eastern *K*iâo' (東膠), which it is not easy to distinguish from 'the eastern school,' already mentioned.

completed[1], offerings of silk were set forth; and afterwards those of vegetables[2]. But there was no dancing and (consequently) no giving out of the spears and other things used in it. They simply retired and received visitors in the eastern school. Only one cup was passed round. The ceremony might pass without (parade of) attendants or conversation.

15. (All these things) belonged to the education of the young princes.

16. In the education of the crown princes adopted by the founders of the three dynasties the subjects were the rules of propriety and music. Music served to give the interior cultivation; the rules to give the external. The two, operating reciprocally within, had their outward manifestation, and the result was a peaceful serenity,—reverence of inward feeling and mild elegance of manners.

17. The Grand tutor and the assistant tutor were appointed for their training, to make them acquainted with the duties of father and son, and of ruler and minister. The former made himself perfectly master of those duties in order to exhibit them; the latter guided the princes to observe the virtuous ways of the other and fully instructed him about them. The Grand tutor went before them, and the assistant came

---

[1] 'Were completed,' should be, according to Khang-*kh*ăng, 'were consecrated.' For the character in the text he would substitute that which we find in Mencius, I, i, 7, 4, applied to the consecration of a bell. Compare vol. iii, p. 323.

[2] The ordinary offerings (see above, paragraph 9); but now a sequel to the offerings of silk. These two offerings, it is understood, were in the school on the west (the hsiang), and thence the parties officiating adjourned to that on the east (the hsü).

after them. In the palace was the guardian, outside it was the master; and thus by this training and instruction the virtue (of the princes) was completed. The master taught them by means of occurring things, and made them understand what was virtuous. The guardian watched over their persons, and was as a stay and wings to them, leading them in the right way. The history says, 'Under the dynasties of Yü, Hsiâ, Shang, and *K*âu, there were the master, the guardian, the Î, and the *Kh*ăng, and there were appointed the four aides and the three ducal ministers. That these offices should all be filled was not so necessary as that there should be the men for them;'—showing how the object was to employ the able[1].

18. When we speak of 'a superior man' we intend chiefly his virtue. The virtue perfect and his instructions honoured; his instructions honoured and the (various) officers correct; the officers correct and order maintained in the state:—these things give the ideal of a ruler[2].

---

[1] The *Kh*ien-lung editors seem to say that 'the Grand tutor' and 'the assistant tutor,' who had the charge of the young prince from his infancy, must have been ladies of the harem; so that, in fact, the government of a ruler's household was regulated after the model of the government of the state in his maturer years. There are no materials to illustrate the duties of the ministers who are called 'the Î and the *Kh*ăng.'

[2] Wû *Kh*ăng thinks that the first three characters here should be translated—'The superior man (*K*ün-ȝze) says;' a sequel to 'The history says' of the preceding paragraph. He then proposes to suppress one of the virtues (德) that follow. But the structure of the whole will not admit this way of dealing with it. There is a play on the characters rendered 'a superior man' and 'a ruler,'—Kün-ȝze (君子) and Kün (君); like our English 'a noble man' and 'a noble,' 'a princely man' and 'a prince.'

19. *K*ung-nî said, 'Formerly, when the duke of *K*âu was administering the government, he did so while he (continued to) go up by the eastern steps. He (also) set forth the rules for a crown prince in (his dealing with) Po-*kh*in, and it was thus that he secured the excellence of king *Kh*ăng. I have heard it said, "A minister will sacrifice himself to benefit his ruler, and how much more will he swerve from the ordinary course to secure his excellence!" This was what the duke of *K*âu did with ease and unconcern.

20. 'Therefore he who knows how to show himself what a son should be can afterwards show himself what a father should be; he who knows how to show himself what a minister should be can afterwards show himself what a ruler should be; he who knows how to serve others can afterwards employ them. King *Kh*ăng, being quite young, could not discharge the duties of the government. He had no means of learning how to show himself what the crown prince should be[1]. On this account the rules for a crown prince were exhibited in (the treatment of) Po-*kh*in, and he was made to live with the young king that the latter might thus understand all that was right between father and son, ruler and minister, elders and youngers[2].'

---

[1] His father being dead.

[2] With reference to this paragraph, which, he thinks, appears here as from Confucius, Wû *Kh*ăng says:—'When king Wû died, *Kh*ăng was quite young. (His uncles of) Kwan and Ȝhâi sent their reports abroad, and the people of Yin planned their rebellion. Then the duke of *K*âu left the capital, and dwelt in the east, and Po-*kh*in went to his jurisdiction, and defeated the people of Hsü and the *Z*ung. Three years afterwards the duke of

21. Take the case of the sovereign and his son and heir. Looked at from the standpoint of affection, the former is father; from that of honour, he is ruler. If the son can give the affection due to the father, and the honour due to the ruler, hereafter he will (be fit to) be the lord of all under the sky. On this account the training of crown princes ought to be most carefully attended to.

22. It is only in the case of the crown prince that by the doing of one thing three excellent things are realised; and it is with reference to his taking his place in the schools according to his age that this is spoken. Thus it is that when he takes his place in them in this way, the people observing it, one will say, 'He is to be our ruler, how is it that he gives place to us in the matter of years?' and it will be replied, 'While his father is alive, it is the rule that

---

*K*âu returned, took the regency and made his expedition to the east,—it was impossible for *Kh*ăng and Po-*kh*in to be always together. Perhaps the duke made them keep so, while king Wû was alive; and the account in the text was an erroneous tradition.' To this the *Kh*ien-lung editors reply:—'Immediately on the death of king Wû, the duke of *K*âu must have adopted the method described in the text. Thâi Kung was Grand master; the duke of Shâo, Grand guardian; and the duke of *K*âu himself Grand tutor. They, no doubt, made Po-*kh*in, *K*ün *Kh*ăn, Lü *K*î, Wang-sun Mâu, and others associate with the young king. In the winter of his first year, the duke removed to the eastern capital, while the other two continued in their places, and Po-*kh*in was daily with *Kh*ăng, and there was no change in the rules for a son and heir. Next year happened the storm which changed the king's views about the duke, who returned to the court. The third year saw the removal of the people of Yen, and Po-*kh*in proceeded to his jurisdiction in Lû. But by this time king *Kh*ăng's virtue and ability were matured. Wû's objections to the ordinary view of the text are without foundation.'

he should do so.' Thus all will understand the right course as between father and son. A second will make the same remark, and put the same question; and it will be replied, 'While the ruler is alive, it is the rule that he should do so;' and thus all will understand the righteousness that should obtain between ruler and minister. To a third putting the same question it will be said, 'He is giving to his elders what is due to their age;' and thus all will understand the observances that should rule between young and old. Therefore, while his father is alive, he is but a son; and, while his ruler is alive, he may be called merely a minister. Occupying aright the position of son and minister is the way in which he shows the honour due to a ruler and the affection due to a father. He is thus taught the duties between father and son, between ruler and minister, between old and young; and when he has become master of all these, the state will be well governed. The saying,

'Music's Director the foundation lays;
The Master this doth to perfection raise.
Let him but once the great and good be taught,
And all the states are to correctness brought,'

finds its application in the case of the heir-son.

23. So much for the duke of *K*âu's going up by the eastern steps.

SECTION II.

1. The Shû-ȝze[1], who had the direction of the (other) members of the royal and princely families,

[1] See Book XLIV, paragraph 1, and note. The Shû-ȝze or *K*û-ȝze belonged to the department of the Sze-mâ. They were two,—Great officers of the third grade; and under them thirty assistants,—officers and employés. The superintendents of the Lists in the

inculcated on them filial piety and fraternal duty, harmony and friendship, and kindly consideration; illustrating the righteousness that should prevail between father and son, and the order to be observed between elders and juniors.

2. When they appeared at court, if it were at a reception in the innermost (courtyard of the palace), they took their places, facing the east, those of the most honourable rank among them, as ministers, being to the north (of the others); but they were arranged according to their age. If it were a reception in the outer (and second courtyard), they were arranged according to their offices;—(as in the former case), by the superintendents of the official lists.

3. When they were in the ancestral temple, they took their places as at the reception in the outer (and second courtyard); and the superintendent of the temple[1] assigned his business to each according to rank and office. In their ascending (to the hall), partaking of what had been left (by the personator of the dead), presenting (the cup to him), and receiving it (from him)[2], the eldest son by the wife took the precedence. The proceedings were regulated by the Shû-ʒze. Although one might have received three of the gifts of distinction, he did not take precedence of an uncle or elder cousin.

4. At the funeral rites for rulers, they were arranged according to the character of their mourning-

paragraph belonged to the same department;—also two of the same rank as the Shû-ʒze, and under them sixty-eight others. The functions of both are described in the *K*âu Lî, Book XXXI.

[1] See the *K*âu Lî, Book XXVII.

[2] These ceremonies do not appear to be mentioned here in the order of their occurrence.

dress in the fineness or coarseness of the material. In case of such rites among themselves, the same order was observed, the principal mourner, however, always taking precedence of all others.

5. If the ruler were feasting with his kindred, then all of a different kindred were received as guests. The cook acted as master of the ceremonies[1]. The ruler took place among his uncles and cousins according to age. Each generation of kindred took a lower place as it was a degree removed from the parent-stem.

6. When with the army, the kindred guarded the spirit-tablets that had been brought from their shrines. If any public duties called the ruler beyond the limits of the state, those officers of the kindred employed the members of it, who had not other duties, to guard the ancestral temple and the apartments of the palace, the eldest sons by the proper wives guarding the temple of the Grand ancestor; the various uncles, the most honoured temple-shrines and apartments; the other sons and grandsons, the inferior shrines and apartments.

7. All descended from any of the five rulers to whom the temple-shrines were dedicated, even those who were now classed among the common people, were required to announce the events of capping and marriage, so long as the temple-shrine of the (Grand ancestor) had not been removed. Their deaths had to be announced; and also their sacrifices during the

[1] We have here an instance of the important part which the cook played in the establishments of the kings and princes of those days; see vol. iii, pp. 356, 422. The ruler was too dignified to drink with the guests.

period of mourning. In the relations of the kindred among themselves, the proper officers punished any neglect of the regulations for condoling and not condoling, leaving off and not leaving off the cap (in mourning). There were the correct rules for the mourning gifts of articles, money, robes, and jade to put into the mouth (of the deceased).

8. When one of the ruler's kindred was found guilty of a capital offence, he was hanged by some one of the foresters' department. If the punishment for his offence were corporal infliction or dismemberment, it was also handed over to the same department. No one of the ruler's kindred was punished with castration.

When the trial was concluded, the proper officer reported the sentence to the ruler. If the penalty were death, he would say, 'The offence of So and So is a capital crime.' If the penalty were less, he would say, 'The offence of So and So has received a lighter sentence.' The ruler would say, 'Let the sentence be remitted for another;' and the officer would say, 'That is the sentence.' This was repeated till the third time, when the officer would make no answer, but hurry off and put the execution into the hands of the appointed forester. Still the ruler would send some one after him, and say, 'Yes, but grant forgiveness,' to which there would be the reply, 'It is too late.' When the execution was reported to the ruler, he put on white clothes, and did not have a full meal or music, thus changing his usual habits. Though the kinsman might be within the degree for which there should be mourning rites, the ruler did not wear mourning, but wailed for him himself (in some family of a different surname).

9. That the ruler's kindred appeared at the reception in the innermost (court) showed how (the ruler) would honour the relatives of his own surname. That they took places according to their age, even those among them of high rank, showed the relation to be maintained between father and son. That they took places at the reception in the outer court according to their offices, showed how (the ruler) would show that they formed one body with (the officers of) other surnames[1].

10. Their taking their places in the ancestral temple according to rank served to exalt the sense of virtue. That the superintendent of the temple assigned to them their several services according to their offices was a tribute of honour to worth. That the eldest son by the proper wife was employed to ascend, take precedence in partaking of what had been left, and in receiving the cup, was to do honour to their ancestor[2].

11. That the distinctions at the funeral rites were arranged according to the fineness or coarseness of their mourning robes was not to take from any one the degree of his relationship[3].

12. The ruler, when feasting with his kindred, took his place among them according to age, and thus development was given to filial piety and fraternal duty. That each generation took a lower place as it was removed a degree from the parent-stem showed the graduation of affection among relatives[4].

---

[1] See paragraph 2, above.
[2] See paragraph 3, above.
[3] See paragraph 4, above.
[4] See paragraph 5, above.

13. The guard maintained during war over the spirit-tablets in the army showed the deep sense of filial piety and love. When the eldest son by the proper wife guarded the temple of the Grand ancestor, honour was done to the temple by the most honoured, and the rule as between ruler and minister was exhibited. When the uncles guarded the most honoured shrines and apartments, and the cousins those that were inferior, the principles of subordination and deference were displayed[1].

14. That the descendants of the five rulers, to whom the temple-shrines were dedicated, were required, so long as the shrine of the Grand ancestor had not been removed, to announce their cappings and marriages, and their death was also required to be announced, showed how kinship was to be kept in mind[2]. While the kinship was yet maintained, that some were classed among the common people showed how mean position followed on want of ability. The reverent observance of condoling, wailing, and of presenting contributions to the funeral rites in articles and money, was the way taken to maintain harmony and friendliness[3].

15. Anciently, when the duties of these officers of the royal or princely kindred were well discharged, there was a constant model for the regions and states; and when this model was maintained, all knew to what to direct their views and aims[4].

---

[1] See paragraph 6, above. [2] See paragraph 12, above.

[3] See paragraph 7, above.

[4] This paragraph is evidently out of place, and should follow the

16. When any of the ruler's kindred were guilty of offences, notwithstanding their kinship, they were not allowed to transgress with impunity, but the proper officers had their methods of dealing with them:—this showed the regard cherished for the people. That the offender was punished in secret[1], and not associated with common people, showed (the ruler's) concern for his brethren. That he offered no condolence, wore no mourning, and wailed for the criminal in the temple of a different surname, showed how he kept aloof from him as having disgraced their ancestors. That he wore white, occupied a chamber outside, and did not listen to music, was a private mourning for him, and showed how the feeling of kinship was not extinguished. That one of the ruler's kindred was not subjected to castration, showed how he shrank from cutting off the perpetuation of their family.

17. When the son of Heaven was about to visit the college, the drum was beaten at early dawn to arouse all (the students). When all were come together, the son of Heaven then arrived and ordered the proper officers to discharge their business, proceeding in the regular order, and sacrificing to the former masters and former sages. When

next. Some of the critics endeavour very ingeniously to account for its having been designedly placed where it stands.

[1] This refers to the statement in paragraph 8, that members of the ruler's kindred, instead of being executed or exposed in the court or market-place, were handed over to be dealt with in the country, by the foresters' department. On that department and the duties and members of it, see the *K*âu Lî, Book I, 11; IV, 64–69.

they reported to him that everything had been done, he then began to go to the nourishing (of the aged).

18. Proceeding to the school on the east, he unfolded and set forth the offerings to the aged of former times, and immediately afterwards arranged the mats and places for the three (classes of the) old, and the five (classes of the) experienced, for all the aged (indeed who were present)[1].

19. He (then) went to look at the food and examine the liquor. When the delicacies for the nourishment of the aged were all ready, he caused the song to be raised (as a signal for the aged to come). After this he retired; and thus it was that he provided for (the aged) his filial nourishment.

20. When (the aged) had returned (to their seats after partaking of the feast), the musicians went up and sang the *Kh*ing Miâo[2], after which there was

[1] There is great difference of opinion about 'the three old' and 'the five experienced.' A common view is that the former name denotes the old men of 80, 90, and 100; which appears to have been first propounded by Tû Yü (A. D. 222–284). The *Kh*ien-lung editors speak contemptuously of it, and ask what analogous division is to be made of the five classes of the experienced. Callery has a note on the paragraph, to the effect that there were two old men, one called 'the san-lâo,' and the other 'the wû-kăng.' The emperor of the *Kh*ien-lung period, he tells us, because of the great age at which he had himself arrived, wished to restore the ancient practices in honour of old age. His proposal, however, was so vigorously opposed in council, especially by a Chinese minister, that he was obliged to abandon it. 'Many volumes,' he says, 'have been written on the origin and meaning of the denominations in the text, but nothing certain is known on the subject.'

[2] '*Kh*ing Miâo' is the name of the first of 'The Sacrificial Odes of *K*âu;' see vol. iii, pp. 313, 314.

conversation to bring out fully its meaning. They spoke of the duties between father and son, ruler and minister, elders and juniors. This union (of the conversation) with the highest description of virtue in the piece constituted the greatest feature of the ceremony.

21. Below (in the court-yard), the flute-players played the tune of the Hsiang[1], while the Tâ-wû was danced, all uniting in the grand concert according to their parts, giving full development to the spirit (of the music), and stimulating the sense of virtue. The positions of ruler and minister, and the gradations of noble and mean were correctly exhibited, and the respective duties of high and low took their proper course.

22. The officers having announced that the music was over, the king then charged the dukes, marquises, earls, counts, and barons, with all the officers, saying, 'Return, and nourish the aged and the young[2] in your eastern schools.' Thus did he end (the ceremony) with (the manifestation of) benevolence.

23. The above statements show how the sage (sovereign) bore in mind the various steps (of this ceremony)[3]. He anxiously thought of it as its greatness deserved; his love for the aged was blended

[1] 'Hsiang' was the name of a piece of music played to the dance Tâ-wû, in memory of the kings Wăn and Wû. It is hardly possible to give any more detailed description either of the piece or of the dance.

[2] 'The young' is supposed to be an interpolation.

[3] This sentence is difficult. Callery translates it:—'En vue de tout cela l'empereur vertueux repasse dans sa mémoire ce que (les anciens) ont fait (pour honorer la vieillesse, afin de les imiter).'

with reverence; he carried the thing through with attention to propriety; he adorned it with his filial nourishing; he connected with it the exhibition of the legitimate distinctions (of rank); and concluded it with (the manifestation of) benevolence. In this way the ancients, in the exhibition of this one ceremony, made all know how complete was their virtue. Among them, when they undertook any great affair, they were sure to carry it through carefully from beginning to end, so that it was impossible for any not to understand them. As it is said in the Yüeh Ming[1], 'The thoughts from first to last should be fixed on (this) learning.'

24. The Record of (king Wăn's) son and heir says, 'Morning and evening he went to the outside of the door of the great chamber, and asked the attendant of the interior whether his father were well, and how he was. If told that he was well, his joy appeared in his countenance. If his father were not so well, the attendant would tell him so, and then his sorrow and anxiety appeared, and his demeanour was disturbed. When the attendant told him that his father was better, he resumed his former appearance. Morning and evening when the food went up, he would examine it and see if it were hot or cold as it ought to be. When it came down, he asked what his father had eaten. He made it a point to know what viands went in, and to give his orders to the cook; and then he retired.

'If the attendant reported that his father was ill, then he himself fasted and waited on him in his dark-coloured dress. He inspected with reverence the

[1] See the 'Charge to Yueh,' in vol. iii, p. 117.

food prepared by the cook, and tasted himself the medicine for the patient. If his father ate well of the food, then he was able to eat. If his father ate but little, then he could not take a full meal. When his father had recovered, then he resumed his former ways[1].'

---

[1] This is evidently an unskilful reproduction of the first paragraph of Section i. We try in vain to discover why the compiler inserted it here.

BOOK VII. THE LÎ YUN

OR

CEREMONIAL USAGES; THEIR ORIGIN, DEVELOPMENT, AND INTENTION[1].

SECTION I.

1. Formerly *K*ung-nî was present as one of the guests at the *K*â sacrifice[2]; and when it was over, he went out and walked backwards and forwards on the terrace over the gate of Proclamations[3], looking sad and sighing. What made him sigh was the state of Lû[4]. Yen Yen was by his side, and said to him, 'Master, what are you sighing about?' Confucius replied, 'I never saw the practice of the Grand course[5], and the eminent men of the three dynasties[6]; but I have my object (in harmony with theirs).

2. 'When the Grand course was pursued, a public and common spirit ruled all under the sky; they

---

[1] See the introduction, pages 23, 24.

[2] Offered in the end of the year, in thanksgiving for all the crops that had been reaped. See in Book IX, ii, paragraphs 9, 10.

[3] The gateway where illustrated copies of the laws and punishments were suspended. It belonged of right only to the royal palace, but it was among the things which Lû had usurped, or was privileged to use.

[4] As usurping royal rites, and in disorder.

[5] This sounds Tâoistic. It is explained of the time of the five Tîs.

[6] The founders of the Hsiâ, Shang, and *K*âu, and their great ministers.

chose[1] men of talents, virtue, and ability; their words were sincere, and what they cultivated was harmony. Thus men did not love their parents only, nor treat as children only their own sons. A competent provision was secured for the aged till their death, employment for the able-bodied, and the means of growing up to the young. They showed kindness and compassion to widows, orphans, childless men, and those who were disabled by disease, so that they were all sufficiently maintained. Males had their proper work, and females had their homes. (They accumulated) articles (of value), disliking that they should be thrown away upon the ground, but not wishing to keep them for their own gratification[2]. (They laboured) with their strength, disliking that it should not be exerted, but not exerting it (only) with a view to their own advantage[2]. In this way (selfish) schemings were repressed and found no development. Robbers, filchers, and

[1] 'They chose;' who are intended by the 'they?' Shall we find them in the 'all under the sky' of the preceding clause? Callery has:—'Sous le grand règne de la vertu, l'empire était la chose publique. On choisissait pour le gouverneur les hommes éminents,' &c. Khung Ying-tâ explains the clause by 'They made no hereditary princes.' Perhaps it would be well to translate passively,—'Men of virtue and ability were chosen (to govern).' The writer has before him the Tâoistic period of the primitive simplicity, when there was no necessity for organised government as in after ages.

[2] It is rather difficult to construe and translate these two sentences. Callery give for them, not very successfully:—'Quant aux objets matériels, ceux qu'on n'aimait pas, on les abandonnait (aux personnes qui en avaient besoin), sans les mettre en réserve pour soi. Les choses dont on était capable, on regardait comme fort mauvais de ne pas les faire, lors même que ce n'était pas pour soi.'

rebellious traitors did not show themselves, and hence the outer doors remained open, and were not shut. This was (the period of) what we call the Grand Union.

3. 'Now that the Grand course has fallen into disuse and obscurity, the kingdom is a family inheritance. Every one loves (above all others) his own parents and cherishes (as) children (only) his own sons. People accumulate articles and exert their strength for their own advantage. Great men imagine it is the rule that their states should descend in their own families. Their object is to make the walls of their cities and suburbs strong and their ditches and moats secure. The rules of propriety and of what is right are regarded as the threads by which they seek to maintain in its correctness the relation between ruler and minister; in its generous regard that between father and son; in its harmony that between elder brother and younger; and in a community of sentiment that between husband and wife; and in accordance with them they frame buildings and measures; lay out the fields and hamlets (for the dwellings of the husbandmen); adjudge the superiority to men of valour and knowledge; and regulate their achievements with a view to their own advantage. Thus it is that (selfish) schemes and enterprises are constantly taking their rise, and recourse is had to arms; and thus it was (also) that Yü, Thang, Wăn and Wû, king *Kh*ăng, and the duke of *K*âu obtained the distinction. Of these six great men every one was very attentive to the rules of propriety, thus to secure the display of righteousness, the realisation of sincerity, the exhibition of errors, the exemplification of benevolence, and

the discussion of courtesy, showing the people all the normal virtues. Any rulers who did not follow this course were driven away by those who possessed power and position, and all regarded them as pests. This is the pe iod of what we call Small Tranquillity[1].'

4. Yen Yen again asked, 'Are the rules of Propriety indeed of such urgent importance?' Confucius said, 'It was by those rules that the ancient kings sought to represent the ways of Heaven, and to regulate the feelings of men. Therefore he who neglects or violates them may be (spoken of) as dead, and he who observes them, as alive. It is said in the Book of Poetry,

"Look at a rat—how small its limbs and fine!
Then mark the course that scorns the proper line.
Propriety's neglect may well provoke
A wish the man would quickly court death's stroke[2]."

Therefore those rules are rooted in heaven, have their correspondencies in earth, and are applicable to spiritual beings. They extend to funeral rites, sacrifices, archery, chariot-driving, capping, marriage, audiences, and friendly missions. Thus the sages made known these rules, and it became possible for the kingdom, with its states and clans, to reach its correct condition.'

5. Yen Yen again asked, 'May I be allowed to hear, Master, the full account that you would give of

---

[1] The Tâoism in this and the preceding paragraph is evident, and we need not be surprised that Wang of Shih-liang should say that they ought not to be ascribed to Confucius. The *Kh*ien-lung editors try to weaken the force of his judgment by a theory of misplaced tablets and spurious additions to the text.

[2] The Shih, I, iv, 8; metrical version, page 99.

these rules?' Confucius said, 'I wished to see the ways of Hsiâ, and for that purpose went to *Kh*î. But it was not able to attest my words, though I found there "The seasons of Hsiâ." I wished to see the ways of Yin, and for that purpose went to Sung. But it was not able to attest my words, though I found there "The Khwăn *Kh*ien." In this way I got to see the meanings in the Khwăn *Kh*ien, and the different steps in the seasons of Hsiâ[1].

6. 'At the first use of ceremonies, they began with meat and drink. They roasted millet and pieces of pork[2]; they excavated the ground in the form of a jar, and scooped the water from it with their two hands; they fashioned a handle of clay, and struck with it an earthen drum. (Simple as these arrangements were), they yet seemed to be able to express by them their reverence for Spiritual Beings.

7. '(By-and-by)[3], when one died, they went upon

---

[1] Compare with this paragraph the ninth in the third Book of the Analects. In that Confucius tells of his visits to *Kh*î and Sung; but says nothing of his finding any book or fragment of a book in either, dwelling instead on the insufficiency of their records. 'The seasons of Hsiâ,' which it is said here 'he got in *Kh*î,' is supposed to be the 'small calendar of Hsiâ,' preserved by the Greater Tâi, and 'the Khwăn *Kh*ien' to have been the 'Kwei Ȝhang Yî,' attributed by many to the Shang dynasty. But all this is very uncertain.

[2] In an unartificial manner, we are told, 'by placing them on heated stones.' It is only the last sentence of the paragraph which makes us think that the previous parts have anything to do with sacrifice or religion.

[3] Khung Ying-tâ thinks that this describes the practices of the period of 'the five Tîs.' The north is the quarter of darkness and decay, the south that of brightness and life. 'The paragraph

the housetop, and called out his name in a prolonged note, saying, "Come back, So and So." After this they filled the mouth (of the dead) with uncooked rice, and (set forth as offerings to him) packets of raw flesh. Thus they looked up to heaven (whither the spirit was gone), and buried (the body) in the earth. The body and the animal soul go downwards; and the intelligent spirit is on high. Thus (also) the dead are placed with their heads to the north, while the living look towards the south. In all these matters the earliest practice is followed.

8. 'Formerly the ancient kings[1] had no houses. In winter they lived in caves which they had excavated, and in summer in nests which they had framed. They knew not yet the transforming power of fire, but ate the fruits of plants and trees, and the flesh of birds and beasts, drinking their blood, and swallowing (also) the hair and feathers. They knew not yet the use of flax and silk, but clothed themselves with feathers and skins.

9. 'The later sages then arose, and men (learned) to take advantage of the benefits of fire. They moulded the metals and fashioned clay, so as to rear towers with structures on them, and houses with windows and doors. They toasted, grilled, boiled, and roasted. They produced must and sauces. They dealt with the flax and silk so as to form linen and silken fabrics. They were thus able to nourish the living, and to make offerings to the dead; to serve

teaches us,' says Hsu Shih-ȝang, 'that the burial and other mourning ceremonies were not inventions of later sages, but grew from the natural feelings and sorrow of the earliest men.'

[1] This was, says *K*ăng, 'the time of the highest antiquity;' 'the time,' says Ying-tâ, 'before the five Tîs.'

the spirits of the departed and God[1]. In all these things we follow the example of that early time.

10. 'Thus it is that the dark-coloured liquor is in the apartment (where the representative of the dead is entertained)[2]; that the vessel of must is near its (entrance) door; that the reddish liquor is in the hall; and the clear, in the (court) below. The victims (also) are displayed, and the tripods and stands are prepared. The lutes and citherns are put in their places, with the flutes, sonorous stones, bells, and drums. The prayers (of the principal in the sacrifice to the spirits) and the benedictions (of the representatives of the departed) are carefully framed. The

[1] According to Ying-tâ, 'this is descriptive of the times of Shan Năng in middle antiquity, of the five Tîs, and of the three kings.' This would extend it over a very long space of time. When it is said that men in their advancing civilisation were able to serve the spirits of the departed and God, the peculiarity of style by which those spirits (literally, the Kwei Shăn) are placed before God (Shang Tî) does not fail to attract the notice of the student. The explanation of it was given ingeniously, and I believe correctly, by Dr. Medhurst (Theology of the Chinese, page 78), who says, 'it was done, probably, in order to distinguish the one from the other, and to prevent the reader from imagining that the Kwei Shăns belonged to the Shang Tî, which mistake might have occurred had the characters been differently arranged.' I translate the last sentence in the present tense, the speaker having, I think, his own times in mind.

[2] The 'dark-coloured' liquor was water, which was employed in the earliest times, before there was any preparation of liquor made from grain, either by fermentation or distillation, and the use of it was continued in the subsequent times of which this paragraph speaks, in honour of the practice of antiquity; and is continued, probably, to the present day. The other liquors are mentioned in the order of their invention, following one another in the historical line of their discovery, the older always having a nearer and more honourable place.

object of all the ceremonies is to bring down the spirits from above, even their ancestors[1]; serving (also) to rectify the relations between ruler and ministers; to maintain the generous feeling between father and son, and the harmony between elder and younger brother; to adjust the relations between high and low; and to give their proper places to husband and wife. The whole may be said to secure the blessing of Heaven.

11. 'They proceed to their invocations, using in each the appropriate terms. The dark-coloured liquor is employed in (every) sacrifice. The blood with the hair and feathers (of the victim) is presented. The flesh, uncooked, is set forth on the stands[2]. The bones with the flesh on them are sodden; and rush mats and coarse cloth are placed underneath and over the vases and cups. The robes of dyed silk are put on. The must and clarified liquor are presented. The flesh, roasted and grilled, is brought forward[3]. The ruler and his wife take alternate parts in presenting these offerings, all being done to please the souls of the departed, and constituting a union (of the living) with the disembodied and unseen.

---

[1] Dr. Medhurst rendered this—'to bring down the Shăns of the upper world, together with the manes of their first ancestors.' In giving to the two phrases one and the same reference I am following Ying-tâ and others.

[2] The last three observances were in imitation of what was done in the earliest antiquity.

[3] In these six things the ways of 'middle antiquity' were observed. The whole paragraph is descriptive of a sacrifice in the ancestral temple under *K*âu, where an effort was made to reproduce all sacrificial customs from the earliest times.

12. 'These services having been completed, they retire, and cook again all that was insufficiently done. The dogs, pigs, bullocks, and sheep are dismembered. The shorter dishes (round and square), the taller ones of bamboo and wood, and the soup vessels are all filled. There are the prayers which express the filial piety (of the worshipper), and the benediction announcing the favour (of his ancestors). This may be called the greatest omen of prosperity; and in this the ceremony obtains its grand completion[1].'

Section II.

1. Confucius said, 'Ah! Alas! I look at the ways of *K*âu. (The kings) Yû[2] and Lî[3] corrupted them indeed, but if I leave Lû, where shall I go (to find them better)? The border sacrifice of Lû, (however,) and (the association with it of) the founder of the line (of *K*âu) is contrary to propriety;—how have (the institutions of) the duke of *K*âu fallen into decay[4]! At the border sacrifice in *Kh*î, Yü was the assessor, and at that in Sung, Hsieh; but these were observ-

[1] This last paragraph appears to me to give a very condensed account of the banquet to a ruler's kindred, with which a service in the ancestral temple concluded. Paragraphs 10, 11, 12 are all descriptive of the parts of such a service. Compare the accounts of it in the Shih II, vi, ode 5, and other pieces.

[2] B.C. 781–771.

[3] B.C. 878–828.

[4] That the sacrificial ceremonies of Lû were in many things corrupted in Lû in the time of Confucius is plain to the reader of the Analects. How the corruption first began is a subject of endless controversy. It seems to be established that special privileges were granted in this respect to the duke of *K*âu and his son, Po-*kh*in. Guarded at first and innocent, encroachments were made by successive princes, as the vigour of the royal authority declined; and by-and-by as those princes became them-

ances of the sons of Heaven, preserved (in those states by their descendants). The rule is that (only) the son of Heaven sacrifices to heaven and earth, and the princes of states sacrifice at the altars to the spirits of the land and grain.'

2. When no change is presumptuously made from the constant practice from the oldest times between the prayer and blessing (at the beginning of the sacrifice)[1] and the benediction (at the end of it)[1], we have what might be called a great and happy service.

3. For the words of prayer and blessing and those of benediction to be kept hidden away by the officers of prayer of the ancestral temple, and the sorcerers and recorders, is a violation of the rules of propriety. This may be called keeping a state in darkness[2].

---

selves more and more weak, their ministers followed in their wake, and usurped the same ceremonies in their own services.

The commentators throw little light on the special corruption selected here for condemnation by Confucius. I have interpreted it by the analogy of the cases of *Kh*î and Sung. The lords of those states were descended from the sovereigns of Hsiâ and Shang respectively, and were invested with them at the rise of the *K*âu dynasty, that they might continue in them the sacrifices of their royal ancestors. They did so not as the lords of *Kh*î and Sung, but as representing the lines of Hsiâ and Shang. But the case was different with the lords of Lû, belonging to the time of *K*âu, but not representing it. Its kings were still reigning. Whether the words of Confucius should be extended over all the paragraph is a doubtful point.

[1] See paragraph 12 of the last section.

[2] In this way new forms of prayer and benediction came into use, and the old forms were forgotten. The sorcerers; see page 172, paragraph 42.

4. (The use of) the *k*an cup (of Hsiâ) and the *k*iâ cup (of Yin), and (the pledging in them) between the representative of the dead and the ruler are contrary to propriety;—these things constitute 'a usurping ruler[1].'

5. (For ministers and Great officers to) keep the cap with pendents and the leathern cap, or military weapons, in their own houses is contrary to propriety. To do so constitutes 'restraint of the ruler[2].'

6. For Great officers to maintain a full staff of employés, to have so many sacrificial vessels that they do not need to borrow any; and have singers and musical instruments all complete, is contrary to propriety. For them to do so leads to 'disorder in a state[3].'

7. Thus, one sustaining office under the ruler is called a minister, and one sustaining office under the head of a clan is called a servant. Either of these, who is in mourning for a parent, or has newly married, is not sent on any mission for a year[4].

---

[1] It would be of little use to give representations of those cups, as they are ordinarily figured. Only in *Kh*î, Sung, and Lû could they be used with any degree of propriety. In the times referred to in these paragraphs they were used by other states; which was an act of usurpation.

[2] Certain styles of these caps were peculiar to the king, and of course could not be used by inferiors. Others might be used by them, but were kept in public offices, and given out when required. Sometimes they were conferred by special gift; but none could make them for themselves.

[3] A Great officer, if he had land, might have a ruler or steward, to whom everything was entrusted; and he might have some sacrificial vessels, but not a complete set. He did not have music at his sacrifices, unless it were by special permission.

[4] Compare Deuteronomy xxiv. 5.

To enter court in decayed robes, or to live promiscuously with his servants, taking place among them according to age:—all these things are contrary to propriety. Where we have them, we have what is called 'ruler and minister sharing the state.'

8. Thus, the son of Heaven has his domain that he may settle there his sons and grandsons; and the feudal princes have their states; and Great officers their appanages that they may do the same for theirs. This constitutes 'the statutory arrangement.'

9. Thus, when the son of Heaven goes to visit a feudal prince, the rule is that he shall lodge in the ancestral temple, and that he do not enter it without having with him all the rules to be observed. If he act otherwise, we have an instance of 'The son of Heaven perverting the laws, and throwing the regulations into confusion.' A prince, unless it be to ask about the sick or to condole with a mourner, does not enter the house of a minister. If he act otherwise, we have the case of 'ruler and minister playing with each other.'

10. Therefore, ceremonies form a great instrument in the hands of a ruler. It is by them that he resolves what is doubtful and brings to light what is abstruse; that he conducts his intercourse with spiritual beings, examines all statutory arrangements, and distinguishes benevolence from righteousness; it is by them, in short, that government is rightly ordered, and his own tranquillity secured.

11. When government is not correct, the ruler's seat is insecure. When the ruler's seat is insecure,

the great ministers revolt, and smaller ones begin pilfering. Punishments (then) are made severe, and manners deteriorate. Thus the laws become irregular, and the rules of ceremony uncertain. When these are uncertain, officers do not perform their duties; and when punishments become severe, and manners deteriorate, the people do not turn (to what is right). We have that condition which may be described as 'an infirm state.'

12. In this way government is the means by which the ruler keeps and protects his person, and therefore it must have a fundamental connection with Heaven. This uses a variety of ways in sending down the intimations of Its will. As learned from the altars of the land, these are (receptivity and docility) imparted to the earth. As learned from the ancestral temple, they are benevolence and righteousness. As learned from the altars of the hills and streams, they are movement and activity. As learned from the five sacrifices of the house, they are the statutes (of their various spirits). It is in this way that the sage rulers made provision for the safe keeping of their persons[1].

---

[1] On this paragraph M. Callery has the following note:—'Très difficile à comprendre dans nos idées, ce passage offre un sens tout simple et naturel aux Chinois, dont la bizarre métaphysique va chercher dans la nature une analogie essentielle entre les accidents divers des êtres, et les phénomènes rationnels ou psychologiques. Ainsi, suivant les philosophes Chinois, tant anciens que modernes, la société présente des inégalités dans ses classes d'individus, comme la terre présente à sa surface des montagnes et des vallées; telle loi provoque l'action et le mouvement, comme les rivières pleines de poissons et les montagnes couvertes de forêts sont des foyers de vie et de développement; telle autre loi

13. Hence the sage forms a ternion with Heaven and Earth, and stands side by side with spiritual beings, in order to the right ordering of government. Taking his place on the ground of the principles inherent in them, he devised ceremonies in their order; calling them to the happy exercise of that in which

---

impose des obligations humanitaires, comme les temples inspirent la piété filiale envers les ancêtres, ou le respect envers les Dieux. Ces analogies sont quelquefois poussées jusqu'au dernier ridicule; mais les Chinois ne les trouvent jamais forcées, et semblent faire très peu de cas de la logique Européenne, qui ne les admire pas.'

The *Kh*ien-lung editors say on it:—'Hsiâo (殽) gives the idea of distribution. All the principles under the sky are simply expressive of the mind of the one Heaven. Heaven is everywhere, and its distributions from which we see its ordinations are also everywhere. *Kh*ien (乾), 'great and originating,' contains all the meaning belonging to the name Heaven. Earth (坤) obediently receives the influences of heaven. Consequently, when we see how earth supports all things, we know how the ordination of Heaven has descended on it. Heaven is the author of all things. It produced men, and men go on to produce one another, in succession. From this we see that every man has his ancestor, and know how the ordination of Heaven has descended on the ancestral temple. Hills and streams are also the productions of Heaven, but every one of them is also able to produce other things; and when we see their productiveness, we know that the ordination of Heaven to that effect has descended on them. The productive power of Heaven is distributed in the five elements, and their results, which are most important to men, are exhibited in the five sacrifices of the house, so that we see those results in these, and know that the ordination of Heaven has descended on them. Now the ancestral temples, the hills and streams, and those five altars of the house, are all distributed on the earth, but in reality have their root in Heaven. And so it is that the sages after the pattern of Heaven made their ordinations; and their filial piety and righteousness, and all the duties enjoined by them, effective, though unseen, secure the issues of government.'

they find pleasure, he secured the success of the government of the people.

14. Heaven produces the seasons. Earth produces all the sources of wealth. Man is begotten by his father, and instructed by his teacher. The ruler correctly uses these four agencies, and therefore he stands in the place where there is no error[1].

15. Hence the ruler is he to whose brightness men look; he does not seek to brighten men. It is he whom men support; he does not seek to support men. It is he whom men serve; he does not seek to serve men. If the ruler were to seek to brighten men, he would fall into errors. If he were to seek to nourish men, he would be unequal to the task. If he were to seek to serve men, he would be giving up his position. Therefore the people imitate the ruler, and we have their self-government; they nourish their ruler, and they find their security in doing so; they serve the ruler, and find their distinction in doing so. Thus it is by the universal application of the rules of propriety, that the lot and duty (of different classes) are fixed; thus it is that men, (acting contrary to those rules,) would all have to account death a boon, and life an evil.

16. Therefore (the ruler), making use of the wisdom of others, will put away the cunning to which that wisdom might lead him; using their courage, he will (in the same way) put away

---

[1] 'If the ruler,' says Khung Ying-tâ, 'were to undertake to do all the work of these agencies himself, he would commit many errors. Employing them according to the natural operation of each, the work is easily performed, and without error.'

passion; and using their benevolence, he will put away covetousness[1].

17. Therefore, when calamity comes on a state, for the ruler to die for its altars is to be regarded as right; but for a Great officer to die for the ancestral temple is to be regarded as a change (of the duty required from him)[2].

18. Therefore when it is said that (the ruler being) a sage can look on all under the sky as one family, and on all in the Middle states as one man, this does not mean that he will do so on premeditation and purpose. He must know men's feelings, lay open to them what they consider right, show clearly to them what is advantageous, and comprehend what are their calamities. Being so furnished, he is then able to effect the thing.

19. What are the feelings of men? They are joy, anger, sadness, fear, love, disliking, and liking. These seven feelings belong to men without their learning them. What are 'the things which men consider right?' Kindness on the part of the father, and filial duty on that of the son; gentleness on the part of the elder brother, and obedience on that of

---

[1] I have here followed the *Kh*ien-lung editors in preference to *K*ăng Khang-*kh*ăng and others. The latter consider that the cunning, passion, and covetousness are those of the men whom the ruler employs,—vices generally found along with the good qualities belonging to them.

[2] It is not easy to see the ground of the reprehension of the devotion of a Great officer which is here implied. 'The care of the state is a trust committed to the ruler by the sovereign,—he should die in maintaining it. An officer has services to discharge, and not trusts to maintain. When the services can no longer be discharged, he may leave them and save himself' (?).

the younger; righteousness on the part of the husband, and submission on that of the wife; kindness on the part of elders, and deference on that of juniors; with benevolence on the part of the ruler, and loyalty on that of the minister;—these ten are the things which men consider to be right. Truthfulness in speech and the cultivation of harmony constitute what are called 'the things advantageous to men.' Quarrels, plundering, and murders are 'the things disastrous to men.' Hence, when a sage (ruler) would regulate the seven feelings of men, cultivate the ten virtues that are right; promote truthfulness of speech, and the maintenance of harmony; show his value for kindly consideration and complaisant courtesy; and put away quarrelling and plundering, if he neglect the rules of propriety, how shall he succeed?

20. The things which men greatly desire are comprehended in meat and drink and sexual pleasure; those which they greatly dislike are comprehended in death, exile, poverty, and suffering. Thus liking and disliking are the great elements in men's minds. But men keep them hidden in their minds, where they cannot be fathomed or measured. The good and the bad of them being in their minds, and no outward manifestation of them being visible, if it be wished to determine these qualities in one uniform way, how can it be done without the use of the rules of propriety (implied in the ceremonial usages)?

Section III.

1. Man is (the product of) the attributes of Heaven and Earth, (by) the interaction of the dual

forces of nature, the union of the animal and intelligent (souls), and the finest subtile matter of the five elements[1].

2. Heaven exercises the control of the strong and light force, and hangs out the sun and stars. Earth exercises the control of the dark and weaker force, and gives vent to it in the hills and streams. The five elements are distributed through the four seasons, and it is by their harmonious action that the moon is produced, which therefore keeps waxing for fifteen days and waning for fifteen[2].

---

[1] Callery's translation of this paragraph is the following:—'L'homme émane, (pour le moral), de la vertu du Ciel et de la Terre; (pour le physique il émane) de la combinaison des (deux principes) Yin et Yang; (pour la partie spirituelle, il émane) de la réunion des esprits et des Dieux; et pour la forme qui lui est propre, il émane de l'essence la plus subtile des cinq éléments.' To this he subjoins the following note:—'Il m'est difficile de croire que les Chinois eux-mêmes aient jamais rien compris à ces théories androgénésiques, dont tout le mérite gît dans le vague de l'énoncé.' The *Kh*ien-lung editors say:—'The characteristic attributes of Heaven and Earth are blended and hid in the two forces of nature; and this is called the truth that is unlimited. If we speak of those forces in their fundamental character, we call them the Yin and Yang. If we speak of them as they develop their power, we call them Kwei and Shăn. If we speak of them as they become substantial, we call them the five elements. And this is what is called the essence of what is meant by the second and fifth lines of the Khien hexagram,' &c. &c.

[2] Callery says here:—'C'est toujours l'application de la théorie des affinités naturelles dont nous avons parlé (see note, p. 281) et dont il importe de bien se pénétrer lorsqu'on veut comprendre quelque chose aux dissertations philosophiques des Chinois.' But after the student has done his best to get hold of the theory, he will often be baffled in trying to follow the applications of it. For example, I cannot get hold of what is said here about the genesis of the moon. Much of the next four paragraphs is very obscure.

3. The five elements in their movements alternately displace and exhaust one another. Each one of them, in the revolving course of the twelve months of the four seasons, comes to be in its turn the fundamental one for the time.

4. The five notes of harmony, with their six upper musical accords, and the twelve pitch-tubes, come each, in their revolutions among themselves, to be the first note of the scale.

5. The five flavours, with the six condiments, and the twelve articles of diet, come each one, in their revolutions (in the course of the year), to give its character to the food.

6. The five colours, with the six elegant figures, which they form on the two robes, come each one, in their revolutions among themselves, to give the character of the dress that is worn.

7. Therefore Man is the heart and mind of Heaven and Earth, and the visible embodiment of the five elements. He lives in the enjoyment of all flavours, the discriminating of all notes (of harmony), and the enrobing of all colours[1].

A little light seems to flash on them from parts of different sections of Book IV, but it is neither bright nor steady.

[1] For this paragraph M. Callery gives:—'L'homme est donc le cœur du Ciel et de la Terre, la fine essence des cinq éléments, et vit en mangeant des choses sapides, en distinguant les sons, et en s'habillant de différentes couleurs (contrairement à la brute, dont les goûts sont grossiers, et les instincts sans raison).' Of course the first predicate about man, and, we might almost say, the second also, are metaphorical. 'La fine essence' is not a correct translation of the text in the second predicate, the Chinese character so rendered is different from the two characters in paragraph 1. On the former predicate Hsiang An-shih (Sung dynasty) says:—

8. Thus it was that when the sages would make rules (for men), they felt it necessary to find the origin (of all things) in heaven and earth; to make the two forces (of nature) the commencement (of all); to use the four seasons as the handle (of their arrangements); to adopt the sun and stars as the recorders (of time), the moon as the measurer (of work to be done), the spirits breathing (in nature) as associates[1], the five elements as giving substance (to things), rules of propriety and righteousness as (their) instruments, the feelings of men as the field (to be cultivated), and the four intelligent creatures as domestic animals (to be reared)[2].

9. The origin of all things being found in heaven and earth, they could be taken in hand, one after the other. The commencement of these being found in the two forces (of nature), their character and tendencies could be observed. The four seasons being used as a handle, (the people) could be stimulated to the business (of each). The sun and stars being constituted the measures of time,

---

'The heart of Heaven and Earth is simply benevolence. The perfect benevolence of Heaven and Earth is lodged in man. Given the human body, and forthwith there is the benevolent heart. Hence it is said (Mencius VII, ii, 16), "Man is benevolence;" "Benevolence is the heart of man." Moreover, the heart of Heaven and Earth is seen in the very idea of life, so that the heart (or kernel) of all fruits is called žăn (仁) or benevolence, which is again a name for man (仁者人也).'

[1] Callery has for this:—'Les Esprits et les Dieux pour compagnons;' Medhurst, 'the Kwei Shins, as the associates.' *K*ăng and Khung say that by Kwei Shăn are to be understood 'the hills and streams of last section,' paragraph 12, for 'those help the respiration of the earth.'

[2] See paragraph 10.

that business could be laid out in order. The moon being taken as the measure (of work to be done), that work could be accomplished successfully. The spirits breathing (in nature) being considered as associates, what is done will be maintained permanently. The five elements being considered as giving substance (to things), what has been done could be repeated. Rules of propriety and righteousness being viewed as the instruments, whatever was done would be completed. The feelings of men being the field to be cultivated, men would look up (to the sages) as to their lords. The four intelligent creatures being made to become domestic animals, there would be constant sources of food and drink.

10. What were the four intelligent creatures[1]? They were the *Kh*î-lin, the phœnix, the tortoise, and the dragon. When the dragon becomes a domestic animal, (all other) fishes and the sturgeon do not lie hidden from men (in the mud). When the phœnix becomes so, the birds do not fly from them in terror. When the *Kh*î-lin does so, the beasts do not scamper away. When the tortoise does so, the feelings of men take no erroneous course.

---

[1] Callery calls these four creatures 'le cerf, l'aigle, la tortue, et le dragon;' and says:—'D'après la mythologie historique des Chinois, ces quatre animaux ne se montrent sur la terre que sous le règne des empereurs d'une vertu extraordinaire. Alors, la plus grande paix règne dans l'univers; tous les hommes sont heureux; personne ne manque de rien:—C'est l'âge d'or, moins les idées poétiques des Grecs et des Latins.' All the four excepting the tortoise are fabulous animals, and even Confucius believed in them (Ana. IX, 8). The lesson drawn from the text by many is that men's goodness is the pledge of, and the way to, all prosperity.

SECTION IV.

1. The ancient kings made use of the stalks and the tortoise-shell; arranged their sacrifices; buried their offerings of silk; recited their words of supplication and benediction; and made their statutes and measures. In this way arose the ceremonial usages of the states, the official departments with their administrators, each separate business with its own duties, and the rules of ceremony in their orderly arrangements.

2. Thus it was that the ancient kings were troubled lest the ceremonial usages should not be generally understood by all below them. They therefore sacrificed to God in the suburb (of the capital), and thus the place of heaven was established. They sacrificed at the altar of the earth inside the capital, and thus they intimated the benefits derived from the earth. Their sacrifices in the ancestral temple gave their fundamental place to the sentiments of humanity. Those at the altars of the hills and streams served to mark their intercourse with the spirits breathing (in nature). Their five sacrifices (of the house) were a recognition of the various business which was to be done.

For the same reason, there are the officers of prayer in the ancestral temple; the three ducal ministers in the court; and the three classes of old men in the college. In front of the king there were the sorcerers, and behind him the recorders; the diviners by the tortoise-shell and by the stalks, the blind musicians and their helpers were all on his left and right. He himself was in the centre. His mind had nothing to do, but to maintain what was entirely correct.

3. By means of the ceremonies performed in the suburb, all the spirits receive their offices. By means of those performed at the altar of the earth, all the things yielded (by the earth) receive their fullest development. By means of those in the ancestral temple, the services of filial duty and of kindly affection come to be discharged. By means of those at the five sacrifices of the house, the laws and rules of life are correctly exhibited. Hence when the ideas in these sacrifices in the suburb, at the altar of the earth, in the ancestral temple, at the altars of the hills and streams, and of the five sacrifices of the house are fully apprehended, the ceremonies used are found to be lodged in them[1].

4. From all this it follows that rules of ceremony must be traced to their origin in the Grand Unity[2].

---

[1] *K*ăng explains 'all the spirits' in the first sentence of this paragraph by 'all the constellations.' Khung agrees with him. *Kh*ăn Hâo (Yüan dynasty) explains it of 'wind, rain, cold, and heat.' The *Kh*ien-lung editors say that the two explanations must be united. But why are these phenomena described as all or 'the hundred spirits?' Is it by personification? or a kind of pantheism?

[2] Medhurst translated this name by 'the Supreme One;' Callery, as I do, by 'la Grande Unité,' adding in parentheses, 'principe de toutes choses.' Does the name denote what we are to consider an Immaterial Being, acting with wisdom, intention, and goodness? Medhurst came to this conclusion. He says:—'Thâi Yî (太一) must mean the Supreme One, or the infinitely great and undivided one. Bearing in mind also that this paragraph follows another in which Tî (帝), the ruling Power, is honoured with the highest adoration, and that this ruling Power is the same

This separated and became heaven and earth. It revolved and became the dual force (in nature).

with the being here called the Supreme One, there can be no doubt that the reference in the whole passage is to the Almighty One who rules over all things' (Dissertation on the Theology of the Chinese, p. 85). He goes on to say that 'the Critical Commentary makes this still more plain by saying that this Supreme One is the source of all others, and that he existed before the powers of nature were divided, and before the myriad things were produced, the one only being. The operations ascribed to him of dividing heaven and earth, of revolving light and darkness, of changing the four seasons, and of appointing the various Kwei Shins to their several offices, are all indicative of that omnipotent power which must be ascribed to him alone.' But the operations referred to in this last sentence are mentioned in the text, not as performed by the Supreme One, but as undergone by the Grand Unity. And, moreover, 'the Critical Commentary' yields a testimony different from what Dr. Medhurst supposed. Khung Ying-tâ says:—'The name Thâi Yî means the original vapoury matter of chaos, before the separation of heaven and earth (太一謂天地未分,混沌之元氣);' and there is nothing in any of the other commentators contrary to this. But the concluding sentence of the paragraph, that 'The law and authority (of all the lessons in the rules of ceremony) is in Heaven,' seems to me to imply 'a recognition (indistinct it may be) of a Power or Being anterior to and independent of the Grand Unity.' Wû *Kh*ăng says:—'The character Thien (Heaven) is used to cover the five things—the Grand Unity, heaven and earth, the (dual force of) Yin and Yang, the four seasons, and the Kwei Shăn.' The attempt, apparent in the whole treatise, to give Tâoistic views a place in the old philosophy of the nation, is prominent here. Medhurst is not correct in saying that the Tî (帝) in paragraph 2 is the same as the Thâi Yî in this paragraph, but It, or rather He, is the same as the Thien (天) with which it concludes. The earliest Chinese adopted Thien or Heaven as the name for the supreme Power, which arose in their minds on the contemplation of the order of nature, and the principles of love and righteousness developed in the constitution of man and the course of providence, and

It changed and became the four seasons. It was distributed and became the breathings (thrilling in the universal frame). Its (lessons) transmitted (to men) are called its orders; the law and authority of them is in Heaven.

5. While the rules of ceremony have their origin in heaven, the movement of them reaches to earth. The distribution of them extends to all the business (of life). They change with the seasons; they agree in reference to the (variations of) lot and condition. In regard to man, they serve to nurture (his nature). They are practised by means of offerings, acts of strength, words and postures of courtesy, in eating and drinking, in the observances of capping, marriage, mourning, sacrificing, archery, chariot-driving, audiences, and friendly missions.

6. Thus propriety and righteousness are the great elements for man's (character); it is by means of them that his speech is the expression of truth and his intercourse (with others) the promotion of harmony; they are (like) the union of the cuticle and cutis, and the binding together of the muscles and bones in strengthening (the body). They constitute the great methods by which we nourish the living,

---

proceeded to devise the personal name of Tî or God, as the appellation of this; and neither Tâoism, nor any other form of materialistic philosophising, has succeeded in eradicating the precious inheritance of those two terms from the mind of peasant or scholar.

Callery has misconstrued the paragraph by making 'Les Rites,' or the 'toutes choses' of his gloss, the subject of all the predicates in it:—'Les rites ont pour origine essentielle la Grande Unité (principe de toutes choses). Ils se divisent ensuite, les uns pour le Ciel, les autres pour la Terre,' &c.

bury the dead, and serve the spirits of the departed. They supply the channels by which we can apprehend the ways of Heaven and act as the feelings of men require. It was on this account that the sages knew that the rules of ceremony could not be dispensed with, while the ruin of states, the destruction of families, and the perishing of individuals are always preceded by their abandonment of the rules of propriety.

7. Therefore the rules of propriety are for man what the yeast is for liquor [1]. The superior man by (his use of them) becomes better and greater. The small man by his neglect of them becomes meaner and worse.

8. Therefore the sage kings cultivated and fashioned the lever of righteousness and the ordering of ceremonial usages, in order to regulate the feelings of men. Those feelings were the field (to be cultivated by) the sage kings. They fashioned the rules of ceremony to plough it. They set forth the principles of righteousness with which to plant it. They instituted the lessons of the school to weed it. They made love the fundamental subject by which to gather all its fruits, and they employed the training in music to give repose (to the minds of learners).

---

[1] On this comparison Callery says:—'Ce que les Chinois appellent du vin (酒) n'étant une autre chose qu'une eau de vie de grains obtenue par la distillation, plus il y a de ferment dans la macération primitive, plus la fermentation vineuse est forte, et plus il y a d'alcool quand on la passe par l'alambic. De là cette comparaison entre le degré d'urbanité chez le sage et le degré de force dans le vin.'

9. Thus, rules of ceremony are the embodied expression of what is right. If an observance stand the test of being judged by the standard of what is right, although it may not have been among the usages of the ancient kings, it may be adopted on the ground of its being right.

10. (The idea of) right makes the distinction between things, and serves to regulate (the manifestation of) humanity. When it is found in anything and its relation to humanity has been discussed, the possessor of it will be strong.

11. Humanity is the root of right, and the embodying of deferential consideration. The possessor of it is honoured.

12. Therefore to govern a state without the rules of propriety would be to plough a field without a share. To make those rules without laying their foundation in right would be to plough the ground and not sow the seed. To think to practise the right without enforcing it in the school would be to sow the seed and not weed the plants. To enforce the lessons in the schools, and insist on their agreement with humanity, would be to weed and not to reap. To insist on the agreement of the lessons with humanity, and not give repose to (the minds of) the learners by music, would be to reap, and not eat (the product). To supply the repose of music and not proceed to the result of deferential consideration would be to eat the product and get no fattening from it.

13. When the four limbs are all well proportioned, and the skin is smooth and full, the individual is in good condition. When there is generous affection between father and son, harmony between brothers,

and happy union between husband and wife, the family is in good condition. When the great ministers are observant of the laws, the smaller ministers pure, officers and their duties kept in their regular relations and the ruler and his ministers are correctly helpful to one another, the state is in good condition. When the son of Heaven moves in his virtue as a chariot, with music as his driver, while all the princes conduct their mutual intercourse according to the rules of propriety, the Great officers maintain the order between them according to the laws, inferior officers complete one another by their good faith, and the common people guard one another with a spirit of harmony, all under the sky is in good condition. All this produces what we call (the state of) great mutual consideration (and harmony).

14. This great mutual consideration and harmony would ensure the constant nourishment of the living, the burial of the dead, and the service of the spirits (of the departed). However greatly things might accumulate, there would be no entanglement among them. They would move on together without error, and the smallest matters would proceed without failure. However deep some might be, they would be comprehended. However thick and close their array, there would be spaces between them. They would follow one another without coming into contact. They would move about without doing any hurt to one another. This would be the perfection of such a state of mutual harmony.

15. Therefore the clear understanding of this state will lead to the securing of safety in the midst of danger. Hence the different usages of ceremony,

and the maintenance of them in their relative proportions as many or few, are means of keeping hold of the feelings of men, and of uniting (high and low, and saving them from) peril.

16. The sage kings showed their sense of this state of harmony in the following way:—They did not make the occupants of the hills (remove and) live by the streams, nor the occupants of the islands (remove and live) in the plains; and thus the (people) complained of no hardship. They used water, fire, metal, wood, and the different articles of food and drink, each in its proper season. They promoted the marriages of men and women, and distributed rank and office, according to the years and virtues of the parties. They employed the people with due regard to their duties and wishes. Thus it was that there were no plagues of flood, drought, or insects, and the people did not suffer from bad grass or famine, from untimely deaths or irregular births. On account of all this heaven did not grudge its methods; earth did not grudge its treasures; men did not grudge (the regulation of) their feelings. Heaven sent down its fattening dews[1]; earth sent forth its springs of sweet wine[1]; hills produced implements and chariots[2]; the Ho sent forth the horse with the map (on his

---

[1] *K*âo Yî in his Filial Miscellanies, Book III, art. 9, contends that these are only different names for the same phenomenon. Few readers will agree with him, though the language means no more than that 'the dews were abundant, and the water of the springs delicious.'

[2] There must have been some legend which would have explained this language, but I have not succeeded in finding any trace of it.

back)[1]. Phœnixes and *Kh*î-lins were among the trees of the suburbs, tortoises and dragons in the ponds of the palaces, while the other birds and beasts could be seen at a glance in their nests and breeding places. All this resulted from no other cause but that the ancient kings were able to fashion their ceremonial usages so as to convey the underlying ideas of right, and embody their truthfulness so as to secure the universal and mutual harmony. This was the realisation of it.

[1] The famous 'River Map' from which, it has been fabled, Fû-hsî fashioned his eight trigrams. See vol. xvi, pp. 14–16.

BOOK VIII. THE LÎ *KH*Î

OR

RITES IN THE FORMATION OF CHARACTER[1].

SECTION I.

1. The rules of propriety serve as instruments to form men's characters, and they are therefore prepared on a great scale. Being so, the value of them is very high. They remove from a man all perversity, and increase what is beautiful in his nature. They make him correct, when employed in the ordering of himself; they ensure for him free course, when employed towards others. They are to him what their outer coating is to bamboos, and what its heart is to a pine or cypress[2]. These two are the best of all the productions of the (vegetable) world. They endure through all the four seasons, without altering a branch or changing a leaf. The superior man observes these rules of propriety, so that all in a wider circle are harmonious with him, and those in his narrower circle have no dissatisfactions with him. Men acknowledge and are affected by his goodness, and spirits enjoy his virtue.

2. The rules as instituted by the ancient kings had their radical element and their outward and

---

[1] See the introductory notice, p. 25.

[2] The author evidently knew the different conditions of their structure on which the growth and vigour of Endogens (the monocotyledonous plants) and Exogens (dicotyledons) respectively depend.

elegant form. A true heart and good faith are their radical element. The characteristics of each according to the idea of what is right in it are its outward and elegant form. Without the radical element, they could not have been established; without the elegant form, they could not have been put in practice[1].

3. (The things used in performing) the rites should be suitable to the season, taken from the resources supplied by the ground, in accordance with (the requirements of) the spirits[2], and agreeable to the minds of men;—according to the characteristics of all things. Thus each season has its productions, each soil its appropriate produce, each sense its peculiar power, and each thing its advantageousness. Therefore what any season does not produce, what any soil does not nourish, will not be used by a superior man in performing his rites, nor be enjoyed by the spirits. If mountaineers were to (seek to) use fish and turtles in their rites, or the dwellers

[1] Callery gives for this short paragraph :—'Les rites établis par les anciens rois ont leur essence intimé et leur dehors; la droiture est l'essence des rites; leur accord patent avec la raison en est le dehors. Sans essence, ils ne peuvent exister; sans dehors ils ne peuvent fonctionner.' He appends a long note on the difficulty of translation occasioned by the character 文 (wăn), which he renders by 'le dehors,' and I by 'the outward, elegant form;' and concludes by saying, 'Traduise mieux qui pourra.' I can only say that I have done the best I could (at the time) with this and every other paragraph.

[2] Khung Ying-tâ says here that 'the spirits were men who, when alive, had done good service, and were therefore sacrificed to when dead. From which it follows that what was agreeable to the minds of men would be in accordance with (the requirements of) the spirits.'

near lakes, deer and pigs, the superior man would say of them that they did not know (the nature of) those usages.

4. Therefore it is necessary to take the established revenues of a state as the great rule for its ceremonial (expenditure). Important for the determination of this is the size of its territory. The amount of the offerings (also) should have regard to the character of the year as good or bad. In this way, though the harvest of a year may be very defective, the masses will not be afraid, and the ceremonies as appointed by the superiors will be economically regulated.

5. In (judging of) rites the time[1] should be the great consideration. (Their relation to) natural duties, their material substance, their appropriateness to circumstances, and their proportioning are all secondary.

Yâo's resignation of the throne to Shun, and Shun's resignation of it to Yü; Thang's dethronement of *K*ieh; and the overthrow of *K*âu by Wăn and Wû:—all these are to be judged of by the time. As the Book of Poetry says,

'It was not that he was in haste to gratify his wishes;
It was to show the filial duty that had come down to him.'

[1] 'The time' comes about by the ordering of heaven. The instances given of it are all great events in the changing of dynasties. But such changes can hardly be regarded as rites. Perhaps the writer thought that the abdication in some cases, and the violent dethroning in others, were precedents, which might be regarded as having that character. For the quotation from the Shih, which is not very happy, see Part III, ode 10, 2.

The sacrifices to heaven and earth; the services of the ancestral temple; the courses for father and son; and the righteousness between ruler and minister:—these are to be judged of as natural duties.

The services at the altars of the land and grain and of the hills and streams; and the sacrifices to spirits:—these are to be judged of by the material substance of the offerings. The use of the funeral rites and sacrifices; and the reciprocities of host and guest:—these are to be judged of by their appropriateness to circumstances.

Sacrificing with a lamb and a sucking pig, by the multitude of officers, when yet there was enough; and sacrificing with an ox, a ram, and a boar, when yet there was nothing to spare:—in these we have an instance of the proportioning.

6. The princes set great store by the tortoise, and consider their jade-tokens as the insignia of their rank, while the (chiefs of) clans have not the tortoises that are so precious, nor the jade-tokens to keep (by themselves), nor the towered gateways:—these (also) are instances of the proportioning.

7. In some ceremonial usages the multitude of things formed the mark of distinction. The son of Heaven had 7 shrines in his ancestral temple; the prince of a state, 5; Great officers, 3; and other officers, 1. The dishes of the son of Heaven on stands were 26; of a duke, 16; of another prince, 12; of a Great officer of the upper class, 8; of one of the lower class, 6. To a prince there were given 7 attendants and 7 oxen; and to a Great officer, 5 of each. The son of Heaven sat on 5 mats placed over one another; a prince, on 3; and a Great officer,

on 2. When the son of Heaven died, he was buried after 7 months, in a fivefold coffin, with 8 plumes; a prince was buried after 5 months, in a threefold coffin, with 6 plumes; a Great officer after 3 months, in a twofold coffin, with 4 plumes. In these cases, the multitude of things was the mark of distinction[1].

8. In other usages, the paucity of things formed the mark of distinction. To the son of Heaven there were given no attendants[2], and he sacrificed to Heaven with a single victim; when he visited the princes (on his tours of inspection), he was feasted with a single bullock. When princes went to the courts of one another, fragrant spirits were used in libations, and there were no dishes on stands, either of wood or bamboo. At friendly missions by Great officers, the ceremonial offerings were slices of dried meat and pickles. The son of Heaven declared himself satisfied after 1 dish; a prince, after 2; a Great officer and other officers, after 3; while no limit was set to the eating of people who lived by their labour. (The horses of) the Great carriage had 1 ornamental tassel at their breast-bands; those of the other carriages had 7 (pieces of) jade for rank-tokens; and libation cups were presented singly; as also the tiger-shaped and yellow cups. In sacrificing to spirits a single mat was used; when princes were giving audience to their ministers, they (bowed to) the Great officers one by one, but to all the other officers

[1] The different views in attempting to verify all the numbers and other points in the specifications here are endless.

[2] The attendants waited on the visitors. But the son of Heaven was lord of all under the sky. He was at home everywhere; and could not be received as a visitor.

together. In these cases the fewness of the things formed the mark of distinction.

9. In others, greatness of size formed the mark. The dimensions of palaces and apartments; the measurements of dishes and (other) articles; the thickness of the inner and outer coffins; the greatness of eminences and mounds[1]:—these were cases in which the greatness of size was the mark.

10. In others, smallness of size formed the mark. At the sacrifices of the ancestral temple, the highest in rank presented a cup (of spirits to the representative of the dead), and the low, a san (containing five times as much): (at some other sacrifices), the honourable took a *kh*ih (containing 3 cups), and the low a horn (containing 4). (At the feasts of viscounts and barons), when the vase went round 5 times, outside the door was the earthenware fâu (of supply), and inside, the hû; while the ruler's vase was an earthenware wû:—these were cases in which the smallness of size was the mark of distinction[2].

11. In others, the height formed the mark of

---

[1] Both these names refer, probably, to mounds raised over the dead. Those over the emperors of the Ming dynasty, about midway between Peking and the Great Wall, and that over Confucius at *Kh*ü-fû in Shan-tung, are the best specimens of these which I have seen.

[2] It is difficult to explain fully and verify all the statements in this paragraph, for want of evidence. The unit in them is the shăng (升), or 'pint,' now = 1·031 litre; the cup, (ȝio, 爵) contained one shăng; the *kh*ih (觶), three; the *k*iŏ (角), four; and the san (散), five. The hû (壺) contained one 'stone' (石), = 10·310 litre; and the wû (甒) = 51·55. The size of the fâu (缶) is unknown.

distinction. The hall of the son of Heaven was ascended by 9 steps[1]; that of a prince, by 7; that of a Great officer, by 5; and that of an ordinary officer, by 3. The son of Heaven and the princes had (also) the towered gateway. In these cases height was the mark.

12. In others, the lowness formed the mark. In sacrificing, the highest reverence was not shown on the raised altar, but on the ground beneath, which had been swept. The vases of the son of Heaven and the princes were set on a tray without feet[2]; those of Great and other officers on one with feet (3 inches high). In these cases the lowness was the mark of distinction.

13. In others, ornament formed the mark. The son of Heaven wore his upper robe with the dragons figured on it; princes, the lower robe with the axes embroidered on it; Great officers, their lower robe with the symbol of distinction; and other officers, the dark-coloured upper robe, and the lower one red. The cap of the son of Heaven had 12 pendents of jade beads set on strings hanging down of red and green silk; that of princes, 9; that of Great officers of the highest grade, 7; and if they were of the lowest grade, 5; and that of other officers, 3. In these cases the ornament was the mark of distinction.

14. In others, plainness formed the mark. Acts of the greatest reverence admit of no ornament.

---

[1] This literally is 'nine cubits;' each step, it is said, was a cubit high.

[2] This tray was four cubits long, two cubits four inches wide, and five inches deep.

The relatives of a father do not put themselves into postures (like other visitors). The Grand jade-token has no engraving on it. The Grand soup has no condiments. The Grand carriage is plain, and the mats in it are of rushes. The goblet with the victim-ox carved on it is covered with a plain white cloth. The ladle is made of white-veined wood. These are cases in which plainness is the mark.

15. Confucius said, 'Ceremonial usages should be most carefully considered.' This is the meaning of the remark that 'while usages are different, the relations between them as many or few should be maintained[1].' His words had reference to the proportioning of rites.

16. That in the (instituting of) rites the multitude of things was considered a mark of distinction, arose from the minds (of the framers) being directed outwards. The energy (of nature) shoots forth and is displayed everywhere in all things, with a great discriminating control over their vast multitude. In such a case, how could they keep from making multitude a mark of distinction in rites? Hence the superior men, (the framers), rejoiced in displaying (their discrimination).

But that in (the instituting of) rites the paucity of things was (also) considered a mark of distinction, arose from the minds (of the framers) being directed inwards. Extreme as is the energy (of nature) in production, it is exquisite and minute. When we look at all the things under the sky, they do not

[1] See page 392, paragraph 15. We may conclude that the Lî Yun was compiled and published before the Lî *Khî*; or it may be that the sentences common to them both had long been in use.

seem to be in proportion to that energy. In such a case, how could they keep from considering paucity a mark of distinction? Hence the superior men, (the framers), watched carefully over the solitude (of their own thoughts)[1].

17. The ancient sages (thus) gave honour to what was internal, and sought pleasure in what was external; found a mark of distinction in paucity, and one of what was admirable in multitude; and therefore in the ceremonial usages instituted by the ancient kings we should look neither for multitude nor for paucity, but for the due relative proportion.

18. Therefore, when a man of rank uses a large victim in sacrifice, we say he acts according to propriety, but when an ordinary officer does so, we say he commits an act of usurpation.

19. Kwan *K*ung had his sacrificial dishes of grain carved, and red bands to his cap; fashioned hills on the capitals of his pillars, and pondweed on the small pillars above the beams[2]:—the superior man considered it wild extravagance.

20. An Phing-*k*ung, in sacrificing to his father, used a sucking-pig which did not fill the dish, and went to court in an (old) washed robe and cap:—the superior man considered it was niggardliness[3].

---

[1] Callery thinks that the theory about rites underlying this paragraph is 'éminemment obscure.' One difficulty with me is to discover any connection between its parts and what is said in paragraphs 7 and 8 about the 'multitude and paucity of rites.'

[2] See the Analects, V, xvii, and the note there. In that passage the extravagance is charged on the 3ang Wăn-*k*ung of paragraph 23.

[3] An Phing-*k*ung was a Great officer of *Kh*î, and ought not to have been so niggardly.

21. Therefore the superior man thinks it necessary to use the utmost care in his practice of ceremonies. They are the bond that holds the multitudes together; and if the bond be removed, those multitudes fall into confusion. Confucius said, 'If I fight, I overcome; when I sacrifice, I receive blessing[1].' He said so, because he had the right way (of doing everything).

22. A superior man will say[2], 'The object in sacrifices is not to pray; the time of them should not be hastened on; a great apparatus is not required at them; ornamental matters are not to be approved; the victims need not be fat and large; a profusion of the other offerings is not to be admired.'

23. Confucius said, 'How can it be said that Ȝang Wăn-*k*ung was acquainted with the rules of propriety? When Hsiâ Fû-*kh*î went right in the teeth of sacrificial order[3], he did not stop him, (nor could he

[1] It is understood that the 'I' is not used by Confucius of himself, but as personating one who knew the true nature of ceremonial usages. See the language again in the next Book, Sect. i, 22; it is found also in the 'Narratives of the School.'

[2] *Kh*ăn Hâo remarks that the compiler of the Book intends himself by 'the superior man.' Thus the compiler delivers his own judgment in an indirect way. Most of what he says will be admitted. It is to the general effect that simple offerings and sincere worship are acceptable, more acceptable than rich offerings and a formal service. But is he right in saying that in sacrificing we should not 'pray?' So long as men feel their own weakness and needs, they will not fail to pray at their religious services. So it has been in China in all the past as much as elsewhere.

[3] Hsiâ Fû-*kh*î was the keeper, or minister in charge, of the ancestral temple of Lû, and contemporary with Ȝang Wăn-*k*ung during the marquisates of *K*wang, Wăn, and Hsî. He introduced at least one great irregularity in the ancestral temple, placing the

prevent) his burning a pile of firewood in sacrificing to the spirit of the furnace. Now that sacrifice is paid to an old wife. The materials for it might be contained in a tub, and the vase is the (common) wine-jar.'

Section II.

1. The rules of propriety may be compared to the human body. When the parts of one's body are not complete, the beholder[1] will call him 'An imperfect man;' and so a rule which has been made unsuitably may be denominated 'incomplete.'

Some ceremonies are great, and some small; some are manifest, and some minute. The great should not be diminished, nor the small increased. The manifest should not be hidden, nor the minute made great. But while the important rules are 300, and the smaller rules 3000, the result to which they all lead is one and the same[2]. No one can enter an apartment but by the door.

2. A superior man in his observance of the rules, where he does his utmost and uses the greatest care, is extreme in his reverence and the manifestation of sincerity. Where they excite admiration and an

---

tablet of Hsî above that of Wăn; and Wăn-*k*ung made no protest. Of the other irregularity mentioned in the text we have not much information; and I need not try to explain it. It seems to me that it must have been greater than the other.

[1] The text has here 'the superior man,' for which Callery has 'au dire du sage.'

[2] See Book XXVIII, ii, paragraph 38. What the 300 and 3000 rules are is very much disputed. The 'one and the same result' is, according to most, 'reverence and sincerity;' according to some, 'suitability.'

elegant attractiveness, there is (still) that manifestation of sincerity.

3. A superior man, in his consideration of the rules, finds those which are carried directly into practice; those in which one has to bend and make some modification; those which are regular and the same for all classes; those which are diminished in a certain order; those in which (a kind of) transplantation takes place, and (the ceremony) is distributed; those in which individuals are pushed forward and take part in the rules of a higher grade; those in which there are ornamental imitations (of natural objects); those in which the ornamental imitations are not carried out so fully; and those where appropriation (of higher observances) is not deemed usurpation[1].

4. The usages of the three dynasties had one and the same object, and the people all observed them. In such matters as colour, whether it should be white or dark, Hsiâ instituted and Yin adopted (its choice, or did not do so)[2].

5. Under the *K*âu dynasty the representatives of

---

[1] Nine peculiarities in ceremonial usages are here indicated. It would be possible to illustrate them fully after the most approved commentators; but there would be little advantage in thus recalling the past which has for the most part passed away,—even in China.

[2] Callery takes a different view of the second sentence in this paragraph, and translates it:—'(Si quelque chose a subi des modifications, ce n'a été que) la couleur blanche ou la couleur verte (caractéristique de telle ou telle autre dynastie; en dehors de ces choses peu importantes, pour tout ce qui est essentiel) la dynastie des Yin s'est scrupuleusement conformée à ce qui a été établi par les Hsiâ.' His view of the whole paragraph, however, comes to much the same as mine.

the dead, sat. Their monitors and cup-suppliers observed no regular rules. The usages were the same (as those of Yin), and the underlying principle was one. Under the Hsiâ dynasty, the personators had stood till the sacrifice was ended, (whereas) under Yin they sat. Under *K*âu, when the cup went round among all, there were six personators[1]. 3ăng-3ze said, 'The usages of *K*âu might be compared to those of a subscription club[2].'

6. A superior man will say, 'The usages of ceremony that come closest to our human feelings are not those of the highest sacrifices; (as may be seen in) the blood of the border sacrifice; the raw flesh in the great offering (to all the royal ancestors) of the ancestral temple; the sodden flesh, where the spirits are presented thrice; and the roast meat, where they are presented once[3].'

7. And so those usages were not devised by

[1] This would be on occasion of the united sacrifice to all the ancestors; the personator of Hâu *K*î being left out of the enumeration, as more honourable than the others.

[2] That is, all stand equally as if each had paid his contribution to the expenses.

[3] The greatest of all sacrifices was that to Heaven in a suburb of the capital; the next was the great triennial or quinquennial sacrifice in the ancestral temple; the third was that at the altars of the land and grain, and of the hills and rivers, which is supposed to be described here as that at which 'the cup' was thrice presented; and the last in order and importance were small sacrifices to individual spirits. The four offerings in the text were presented at the first three; but not in the same order. That to Heaven began with blood; that in the ancestral temple with raw flesh. Those farthest from our human feelings had the place of honour in the greatest services. We must seek for a higher and deeper origin of them than our ordinary feelings.

superior men in order to give expression to their feelings. There was a beginning of them from (the oldest times); as when (two princes) have an interview, there are seven attendants to wait on them and direct them. Without these the interview would be too plain and dull. They reach (the ancestral temple) after the visitor has thrice declined the welcome of the host, and the host has thrice tried to give precedence to the other. Without these courtesies the interview would be too hurried and abrupt.

In the same way, when in Lû they were about to perform the service to God (in the suburb), they felt it necessary first to have a service in the college with its semicircular pool. When they were about in ʒin to sacrifice to the Ho, they would first do so to the pool of Wû. When in *Kh*î they were about to sacrifice to mount Thâi, they would do so first in the forest of Phei.

Moreover, the keeping the victims (for the altar of Heaven) for three months (in the stable); the abstinence (of the worshippers) for seven days; and the vigil of three days:—all showed the extreme degree of (preparatory) care (for the service).

The ritual arrangements, further, of the reception (of guests) and communication between them and the host, and for assisting and guiding the steps of the (blind) musicians, showed the extreme degree of kindly (provision)[1].

---

[1] It is not easy to construe this paragraph, nor to discover and indicate the connexion between its different parts. Generally we may say that it illustrates the previous statement about the rites as not simply the expression of natural feeling, but of that feeling wisely guided and embodied so as to be most beneficial to the

8. In ceremonial usages we should go back to the root of them (in the mind), and maintain the old (arrangements of them), not forgetting what they were at first. Hence there is no (need to be) calling attention to the demonstrations expressive of grief[1]; and those which (more particularly) belong to the court are accompanied by music. There is the use of sweet spirits, and the value set on water; there is the use of the (ordinary) knife, and the honour expressed by that furnished with (small) bells; there is the comfort afforded by the rush and fine bamboo mats, and the (special) employment of those which are made of straw. Therefore the ancient kings in their institution of the rules of propriety had a ruling idea, and thus it is that they were capable of being transmitted, and might be learned, however many they were.

9. The superior man will say, 'If a man do not have in himself the distinctions (embodied in ceremonies), he will contemplate that embodiment without any intelligent discrimination; if he wish to exercise that discrimination, and not follow the guidance of the rules, he will not succeed in his object. Hence if his practice of ceremonies be not according to the rules, men will not respect them;

---

individual and society. The auxiliary services in the first part of it were all preparatory to the great services that followed. That in the great college of Lû was concerned with Hâu *K*î, the ancestor of the House of *K*âu and all its branches, and preliminary to the place he was to occupy at the great sacrifice to Heaven.

The remaining two paragraphs show how the natural feeling was quietly nourished, guided, and modified.

[1] Yet much is said in the Than Kung about those demonstrations of grief in the mourning rites.

and if his words be not according to those rules, men will not believe them. Accordingly it is said, "The rules of ceremony are the highest expression of (the truth of) things."'

10. Hence it was that in old times, when the ancient kings instituted ceremonies, they conveyed their idea by means of the qualities of the articles and observances which they employed. In their great undertakings, they were sure to act in accordance with the seasons; in their doings morning and evening, they imitated the sun and moon; in what required a high situation, they took advantage of mounds and hillocks, and in what required a low situation, of the (banks of the) rivers and lakes. Hence each season has its rains and benefits, and those wise men sought to make use of them with intelligence with all the earnestness they could command[1].

11. The ancient kings valued (men's) possession of virtue, honoured those who pursued the right course, and employed those who displayed ability. They selected men of talents and virtue, and

---

[1] See Callery's translation of this paragraph. He says on it:—'Cette période offre, par son incohérence, des difficultés sérieuses qui me font supposer une grave altération du texte primitif;' and justifies his own version by the remark, 'Je me suis dit qu'après tout il vaut mieux embellir que défigurer.' He takes the whole, like *K*ăng, as referring to the ceremonies of different sacrifices. Ying Yung (Sung dynasty; earlier than *K*û Hsî) understood it more generally of other royal and imperial doings. The *Kh*ien-lung editors say that the two views must be united. They remark on the last sentence that, as 'every season has its appropriate productions and every situation its own suitabilities, we must examine them in order to use things appropriately.'

appointed them. They assembled the whole of them and solemnly addressed them[1].

12. Then in accordance with (the height of) heaven they did service to Heaven, in accordance with (the lower position of) earth they did service to Earth; taking advantage of the famous hills they ascended them, and announced to Heaven the good government (of the princes). When thus at the felicitous spot (chosen for their capitals) they presented their offerings to God in the suburb and announced to Heaven (the general good government from the famous hills), the phœnix descended, and tortoises and dragons made their appearance[2]. When they presented their offerings to God in the suburb the winds and rains were duly regulated, and the cold and heat came each in its proper time, so that the sage (king) had only to stand with his face to the south, and order prevailed all under the sky.

13. The courses of the heavenly (bodies) supply the most perfect lessons, and the sages possessed the highest degree of virtue. Above, in the hall of the ancestral temple, there was the jar, with clouds and hills represented on it on the east, and that with the victim represented on it on the west. Below the hall the larger drums were suspended on the west, and the smaller drums answering to them on the east. The ruler appeared at the (top of the) steps on the east; his wife was in the apartment on the west. The great luminary makes his appearance in

---

[1] The 'selection' here, it is understood, was of the functionaries to take part in the sacrificial ceremonies, and the solemn address was on the duties they had to perform.

[2] See pp. 392, 393, paragraph 16.

the east; the moon makes her appearance in the west. Such are the different ways in which the processes of darkness and light are distributed in nature, and such are the arrangements for the positions (corresponding thereto) of husband and wife. The ruler fills his cup from the jar with an elephant represented on it; his wife fills hers from that with clouds and hills. With such reciprocation do the ceremonies proceed above, while the music responds in the same way below;—there is the perfection of harmony.

14. It is the object of ceremonies to go back to the circumstances from which they sprang, and of music to express pleasure in the results which first gave occasion to it. Thus it was that the ancient kings, in their institution of ceremonies, sought to express their regulation of circumstances, and, in their cultivation of music, to express the aims they had in mind. Hence by an examination of their ceremonies and music, the conditions of order and disorder in which they originated can be known. *K*ü Po-yü[1] said, 'A wise man, by his intelligence, from the sight of any article, knows the skill of the artificer, and from the contemplation of an action knows the wisdom of its performer.' Hence there is the saying, 'The superior man watches over the manner in which he maintains his intercourse with other men.'

15. Within the ancestral temple reverence prevailed. The ruler himself led the victim forward,

[1] A friend, and perhaps a disciple of Confucius, an officer of the state of Wei. He is mentioned in the Confucian Analects and in Mencius.

while the Great officers assisted and followed, bearing the offerings of silk. The ruler himself cut out (the liver) for (the preliminary) offering, while his wife bore the dish in which it should be presented. The ruler himself cut up the victim, while his wife presented the spirits.

The high ministers and Great officers followed the ruler; their wives followed his wife. How grave and still was their reverence! How were they absorbed in their sincerity! How earnest was their wish that their offerings should be accepted! The arrival of the victim was announced (to the spirits) in the courtyard; on the presentation of the blood and the flesh with the hair on it, announcement was made in the chamber; on the presentation of the soup and boiled meat, in the hall. The announcement was made thrice, each time in a different place; indicating how they were seeking for the spirits, and had not yet found them. When the sacrifice was set forth in the hall, it was repeated next day outside (the gate of the temple); and hence arose the saying, 'Are they there? Are they here?'

16. One offering of the cup showed the simplicity of the service; three offerings served to ornament it; five, to mark discriminating care; and seven, to show (the reverence for) the spirits[1].

17. Was not the great quinquennial sacrifice a service belonging to the king? The three animal victims, the fish, and flesh, were the richest tributes for the

[1] The sacrifices where only one cup was presented were, it is said, the smallest; three cups belonged to the altars of the land and grain; five, to those of the hills and rivers; and seven, to those in the ancestral temple. All this is quite uncertain.

palate from all within the four seas and the nine provinces. The fruits and grain presented in the high dishes of wood and bamboo were the product of the harmonious influences of the four seasons. The tribute of metal showed the harmonious submission (of the princes). The rolls of silk with the round pieces of jade placed on them showed the honour they rendered to virtue. The tortoise was placed in front of all the other offerings, because of its knowledge of the future; the tribute of metal succeeded to it, showing the (hold it has on) human feelings. The vermilion, the varnish, the silk, the floss, the large bamboos and the smaller for arrows—the articles which all the states contribute; with the other uncommon articles, which each state contributed according to its resources, even to those from the remote regions:—(these followed the former). When the visitors left they were escorted with the music of the Sze Hsiâ[1]. All these things showed how important was the sacrifice.

18. In the sacrifice to God in the suburb, we have the utmost expression of reverence. In the sacrifices of the ancestral temple, we have the utmost expression of humanity. In the rites of mourning, we have the utmost expression of leal-heartedness. In the preparation of the robes and vessels for the dead, we have the utmost expression of affection. In

[1] We are told in the *K*âu Lî, Book XXIII, art. 32, that the bell master, with bells and drums, performed the nine Hsiâ pieces, on the occasions appropriate to them. The second of them was 'the Sze Hsiâ,' as here, but the occasion for it in the text would be inappropriate. The eighth, or Kâi Hsiâ, would be appropriate here, and hence *K*ăng said that sze was a mistake for kâi (陔).

the use of gifts and offerings between host and guest, we have the utmost expression of what is right. Therefore when the superior man would see the ways of humanity and righteousness, he finds them rooted in these ceremonial usages.

19. A superior man has said, 'What is sweet may be tempered; what is white may be coloured. So the man who is right in heart and sincere can learn the (meaning of the) rites.' The rites should not be perfunctorily performed by the man who is not right in heart and sincere. Hence it is all important (in the performance of them) to get the proper men.

20. Confucius said, 'One may repeat the three hundred odes, and not be fit to offer the sacrifice where there is (but) one offering of the cup. He may offer that sacrifice, and not be fit to join in a great sacrifice. He may join in such a sacrifice, and not be fit to offer a great sacrifice to the hills. He may perform that fully, and yet not be able to join in the sacrifice to God. Let no one lightly discuss the subject of rites [1].'

---

[1] It is not easy to trace satisfactorily the progress of thought here from one sacrificial service to another. 'The great sacrifice' is understood to be the triennial or quinquennial sacrifice to all the ancestors of the ruling House. It is a great step to that from a small sacrifice where only one cup was presented. What 'the great sacrifice to the hills was' is uncertain. It is in the text Tâ Lü (大旅). The meaning of Lü as a sacrifice to the spirit of a hill is well established from the Analects III, 6. Once the phrase Tâ Lü appears as used in the *K*âu Lî, Book V, 91, of the royal sacrifice to God ('Lorsque l'empereur offre un grand sacrifice au Seigñeur Suprême,' Biot); but it cannot have that meaning here, because the text goes on to speak of that sacrifice as superior to this. *K*ăng Hsüan made Tâ Lü to be the sacrifice to the 'five Tîs,' or the five Planetary Gods, which view, as

21. When 3ze-lû was steward to the House of *K*î, its chief had been accustomed to commence his sacrifices before it was light, and when the day was insufficient for them, to continue them by torchlight. All engaged in them, however strong they might appear, and however reverent they might be, were worn out and tired. The officers limped and leaned, wherever they could, in performing their parts, and the want of reverence was great. Afterwards, when 3ze-lû took the direction of them, the sacrifices proceeded differently. For the services in the chamber, he had parties communicating outside and inside the door; and for those in the hall, he had parties communicating at the steps. As soon as it was light, the services began, and by the time of the evening audience all were ready to retire. When Confucius heard of this management, he said, 'Who will say that this Yû does not understand ceremonies[1]?'

---

the *Kh*ien-lung editors point out, cannot be adopted. And how any sacrifice to the hills, however great, could be represented as greater than the quinquennial sacrifice in the ancestral temple, I cannot understand. I must leave the paragraph in the obscurity that belongs to it.

[1] The *Kh*ien-lung editors say:—'3ze-lû was a leal-hearted and sincere man, and the Book ends with this account of him. From the mention of the preparation of the rites on a great scale and of their high value at the beginning of the Book down to this tribute to 3ze-lû as understanding ceremonies, its whole contents show that what is valuable in the rites is the combination of the idea of what is right with the elegant and outward form as sufficient to remove from a man all perversity and increase what is good in his nature, without a multiplicity of forms which would injure the natural goodness and sincerity, and lead their practiser to a crooked perversity. Deep and far-reaching is the idea of it!'

BOOK IX. THE *K*IÂO THEH SĂNG

OR

THE SINGLE VICTIM AT THE BORDER SACRIFICES[1].

SECTION I.

1. At the border sacrifices a single victim was used, and at the altars to (the spirits of) the land and grain there was (the full complement of) three victims[2]. When the son of Heaven went on his

---

[1] See the introductory notice, p. 26.

[2] The object of the statements here and some other paragraphs is to show that the degree of honour was expressed by the 'paucity' of the articles; compare last Book, Sect. i, paragraph 8. Perhaps the name *K*iâo (郊) in the title should be translated in the plural as the name for all the border sacrifices, or those offered in the suburbs of the capital. There were several of them, of which the greatest was that at the winter solstice, on the round hillock in the southern suburb. Besides this, there was in the first month the border sacrifice for 'grain,'—to pray for the blessing of Heaven on the agricultural labours of the year, in which Hâu *K*î, the father of the line of *K*âu, and its 'Father of Husbandry,' was associated by that dynasty. There were also the five seasonal border sacrifices, of which we have mention in the different parts of Book IV, though, so far as what is said in them goes, the idea of Heaven falls into the background, and the five deified ancient sovereigns come forward as so many Tîs. In the first month of summer there was, further, a great border sacrifice for rain, and in the last month of autumn a great border sacrifice of thanksgiving. 'Of all these border sacrifices,' say the *Kh*ien-lung editors, 'there is clear evidence in classical texts.' Into the discussions growing out of them about 'one Heaven,' or 'five Heavens,' and about their origin, it is not necessary that I should enter; it would be foreign, indeed, to my object in this translation to do so. The

inspecting tours to the princes, the viands of the feast to him were composed of a (single) calf; and when they visited him, the rites with which he received them showed the three regular animals. (The feasting of him in such a manner) was to do honour to the idea of sincerity [1]. Therefore if the animal happened to be pregnant, the son of Heaven did not eat of it, nor did he use such a victim in sacrificing to God [2].

2. The horses of the Grand carriage had one ornamental tassel at the breast; those of the carriages that preceded had three; and those of the carriages that followed had five [3]. There were the blood at the border sacrifice; the raw flesh in the great offering of the ancestral temple; the sodden flesh where spirits are presented thrice; and the roast meat where they are presented once [3]:—these were expressive of the greatest reverence, but the taste was not valued; what was held in honour was the scent of the air [4]. When the princes appeared as guests,

border sacrifices were the greatest religious or ceremonial services of the ancient Chinese; and the fact to which our attention is called in this Book, is that at them there was used only a single victim.

[1] Why 'a calf?' 'Because of its guileless simplicity,' says *K*âu Hsü of our eleventh century; earlier than *K*û Hsî, who adopted his explanation. The calf, whether male or female, has not yet felt the appetency of sex, and is unconscious of any 'dissipation.' This is a refinement on the Hebrew idea of the victim lamb, 'without blemish.'

[2] This might be referred to his unwillingness to take life unnecessarily, but for what has just been said about the calf.

[3] See last Book, Sect. i, 8; and Sect. ii, 6.

[4] Little is said on the meaning of this statement, which appears to say that the most subtle and ethereal thing in sacrifices, the

they were presented with herb-flavoured spirits, because of their fragrance; at the great entertainment to them the value was given to (the preliminary) pieces of flesh prepared with cinnamon and nothing more.

3. At a great feast (to the ruler of another state), the ruler (who was the host) received the cup seated on his three mats. (On occasion of a visit through a minister or Great officer) when the cup was thrice presented, the ruler received it on a single mat:—so did he descend from the privilege of his more honourable rank, and assume the lower distinction (of his visitor).

4. In feasting (the orphaned young in spring) and at the vernal sacrifice in the ancestral temple they had music; but in feeding (the aged) and at the autumnal sacrifice they had no music:—these were based in the developing and receding influences (prevalent in nature). All drinking serves to nourish the developing influence; all eating to nourish the receding influence. Hence came the different character of the vernal and autumnal sacrifices; the feasting the orphaned young in spring, and the feeding the aged in autumn:—the idea was the same. But in the feeding and at the autumnal sacrifice there was no music. Drinking serves to nourish the developing influence and therefore is accompanied with music. Eating serves to nourish the receding influ-

'sweet savour' of the offerings, was the most important, and should excite the worshippers to add to their sincerity and reverence all other graces of character. The same lesson was given to the feudal princes when they were entertained as visitors at the royal court.

ence, and therefore is not accompanied with music. All modulation of sound partakes of the character of development.

5. The number of tripods and meat-stands was odd, and that of the tall dishes of wood and bamboo was even [1]; this also was based in the numbers belonging to the developing and receding influences. The stands were filled with the products of the water and the land. They did not dare to use for them things of extraordinary flavours [2] or to attach a value to the multitude and variety of their contents, and it was thus that they maintained their intercourse with spiritual intelligences.

6. When the guests had entered the great door [3], the music struck up the Sze Hsiâ [4], showing the blended ease and respect (of the king). (While feasting), at the end of (every) cup the music stopped (for a moment), a practice of which Confucius often indicated his admiration. When the last cup had been put down, the performers ascended the hall, and sang; —exhibiting the virtues (of host and guests). The singers were (in the hall) above, and the organists were (in the court) below;—the honour being thus

[1] Every Chinese scholar knows that odd numbers all belong to the category of Yang (———), and even numbers to that of Yin (— —).

[2] The meaning of this clause is uncertain, and I have not found it anywhere sufficiently explained, considering what the characters are (褻味).

[3] This paragraph and the next describe ceremonies on occasion of the king's reception of the great nobles, when they appeared in great force at court. With this the expurgated Lî *K*î begins.

[4] See note 1, page 413.

given to the human voice. Music comes from the expanding influence (that operates in nature); ceremonies from the contracting. When the two are in harmony, all things obtain (their full development).

7. There were no fixed rules for the various articles of tribute. They were the different products of the different territories according to their several suitabilities, and were regulated by their distances (from the royal domain). The tortoises were placed in front of all the other offerings;—because (the shell) gave the knowledge of the future. The bells succeeded to them;—because of their harmony, they were a symbol of the union of feeling that should prevail[1]. Then there were the skins of tigers and leopards;—emblems of the fierce energy with which insubordination would be repressed; and there were the bundles of silks with disks of jade on them,—showing how (the princes) came to (admire and experience) the virtue (of the king).

8. (The use of) a hundred torches in his courtyard began with duke Hwan of *Kh*î. The playing of the Sze Hsiâ (at receptions) of Great officers began with *K*âo Wăn-ʒze[2].

9. When appearing at another court, for a Great officer to have a private audience was contrary to propriety. If he were there as a commissioner, bearing

[1] As we have no account anywhere of bells, made, being sent as tribute, many understand the name as merely = 'metal.'

[2] This and the five paragraphs that follow seem the work of another hand, and are not in the expurgated *K*î. Duke Hwan was the first and greatest of 'the five presiding princes' of the *Kh*un *Kh*iû period. He died B.C. 643. *K*âo Wăn-ʒze was a Great officer and chief minister of Ʒin about a century after. The king alone might have a hundred torches in his courtyard.

his own prince's token of rank, this served as his credentials. That he did not dare to seek a private audience showed the reverence of his loyalty. What had he to do with the tribute-offerings in the court of the other prince that he should seek a private audience? The minister of a prince had no intercourse outside his own state; thereby showing how he did not dare to serve two rulers.

10. For a Great officer to receive his ruler to an entertainment was contrary to propriety. For a ruler to put to death a Great officer who had violently exercised his power was (held) an act of righteousness; and it was first seen in the case of the three Hwan[1].

The son of Heaven did not observe any of the rules for a visitor or guest;—no one could presume to be his host. When a ruler visited one of his ministers, he went up to the hall by the steps proper to the master;—the minister did not presume in such a case to consider the house to be his own. According to the rules for audiences, the son of Heaven did not go down from the hall and meet the princes. To descend from the hall and meet the princes, was an error on the part of the son of Heaven, which began with king Î[2], and was afterwards observed.

---

[1] The 'three Hwan' intended here were three sons of duke Hwan' of Lû, known as *Kh*ing-fû, Yâ, and *K*î-yû; see the Ȝo *K*wan, and Kung-yang, on the last year of duke *K*wang. Instances of the execution of strong and insubordinate officers in different states, more to the point, had occurred before; but the writer had in mind only the history of Lû.

[2] Î was the ninth of the sovereigns of *K*âu (B.C. 894–879); with him appeared the first symptoms of decline in the dynasty.

11. For the princes to suspend (their drums and bells) in four rows like the walls of an apartment (after the fashion of the king), and to use a white bull in sacrificing[1]; to strike the sonorous jade; to use the red shields with their metal fronts and the cap with descending tassels in dancing the Tâ-wû; and to ride in the grand chariot:—these were usages which they usurped. The towered gateway with the screen across the path, and the stand to receive the emptied cups; the axes embroidered on the inner garment with its vermilion colour:—these were usurpations of the Great officers. Thus, when the son of Heaven was small and weak, the princes pushed their usurpations; and when the Great officers were strong, the princes were oppressed by them. In this state (those officers) gave honour to one another as if they had been of (high) degree; had interviews with one another and made offerings; and bribed one another for their individual benefit: and thus all usages of ceremony were thrown into disorder. It was not lawful for the princes to sacrifice to the king to whom they traced their ancestry, nor for the Great officers to do so to the rulers from whom they sprang. The practice of having a temple to such rulers in their private families, was contrary to propriety. It originated with the three Hwan[2].

12. The son of Heaven[3] preserved the descend-

[1] That a white bull was used in Lû in sacrificing to the duke of *K*âu, appears from the fourth of the Praise Odes of Lû. See vol. iii, p. 343.

[2] These must be the three families of Lû, so powerful in the time of Confucius, all descended from duke Hwan. The expression 'in this (state)' shows that the writer was a man of Lû.

[3] We must think of this 'son of Heaven' as the founder of a

ants of (the sovereigns of) the two (previous) dynasties, still honouring the worth (of their founders). But this honouring the (ancient) worthies did not extend beyond the two dynasties.

13. Princes did not employ as ministers refugee rulers[1]. Hence anciently refugee rulers left no son who continued their title.

14. A ruler stood with his face towards the south, to show that he would be (in his sphere) what the influence of light and heat was (in nature). His ministers stood with their faces to the north, in response to him. The minister of a Great officer did not bow his face to the ground before him, not from any honour paid to the minister, but that the officer might avoid receiving the homage which he had paid himself to the ruler.

15. When a Great officer was presenting (anything to his ruler), he did not do so in his own person; when the ruler was making him a gift, he did not go to bow in acknowledgment to him:—that the ruler might not (have the trouble of) responding to him.

16. When the villagers were driving away pestilential influences, Confucius would stand at the top of his eastern steps, in his court robes, to keep the spirits (of his departed) undisturbed in their shrines[2].

---

new dynasty. Thus it was that king Wû of *K*âu enfeoffed the duke of Sung as representing the kings of Shang, and the rulers of Kü as representing those of Hsiâ.

[1] Rulers expelled from their own state. But the princes might employ their sons as ministers, who ceased to be named from their former dignity.

[2] See the Confucian Analects X, 10, 2, and note. Dr. Williams (on 禓) says that the ceremony is now performed by the Board of Rites ten days before the new year.

17. Confucius said, 'The practice of archery to the notes of music (is difficult). How shall the archer listen, and how shall he shoot, (that the two things shall be in harmony)?'

Confucius said, 'When an officer is required to shoot, if he be not able, he declines on the ground of being ill, with reference to the bow suspended at the left of the door (at his birth)[1].'

18. Confucius said, 'There are three days' fasting on hand. If one fast for the first day, he should still be afraid of not being (sufficiently) reverent. What are we to think of it, if on the second day he beat his drums[2]?'

19. Confucius said, 'The repetition of the sacrifice next day inside the Khû gate; the searching for the spirits in the eastern quarter; and the holding the market in the morning in the western quarter:—these all are errors.'

20. At the Shê, they sacrificed to (the spirits of) the land, and on the tablet rested the power of the darker and retiring influence of nature. The ruler stands (in sacrificing) with his face to the south at the foot of the wall on the north, responding to the idea of that influence as coming from the north. A *k*iâ day is used (for the sacrifice),—to employ a commencing day (in the Cycle)[3].

---

[1] Every gentleman was supposed to learn archery as one of the 'six liberal arts;' and a bow was suspended near the door on the birth of a boy in recognition of this. The excuse in the paragraph is a lame one. See the 'Narratives of the School,' article 28; and Book XLIII, 19.

[2] 'Narratives of the School,' XLIV, 9.

[3] There are of course six decades of days in the Cycle, each beginning with a *k*iâ day.

The great Shê altar of the son of Heaven was open to receive the hoarfrost, dew, wind, and rain, and allow the influences of heaven and earth to have full development upon it. For this reason the Shê altar of a state that had perished was roofed in, so that it was not touched by the brightness and warmth of Heaven. The altar (of Yin) at Po[1] had an opening in the wall on the north, so that the dim and cold (moon) might shine into it.

21. In the sacrifice at the Shê altars they dealt with the earth as if it were a spirit. The earth supported all things, while heaven hung out its brilliant signs. They derived their material resources from the earth; they derived rules (for their courses of labour) from the heavens. Thus they were led to give honour to heaven and their affection to the earth, and therefore they taught the people to render a good return (to the earth). (The Heads of) families provided (for the sacrifice to it) at the altar in the open court (of their houses); in the kingdom and the states they did so at the Shê altars; showing how it was the source (of their prosperity).

When there was a sacrifice at the Shê altar of a village[2], some one went out to it from every house. When there was such a sacrifice in preparation for a hunt, the men of the state all engaged in it. When there was such a sacrifice, from the towns, small and large, they contributed their vessels of rice, thereby

[1] Po had been the capital of the Shang dynasty. The site was in the present Ho-nan; changed more than once, but always retaining the name. We have the Northern, the Southern, and the Western Po.

[2] See page 259, paragraph 7.

expressing their gratitude to the source (of their prosperity) and going back in their thoughts to the beginning (of all being).

22. In the last month of spring[1], the fire star having appeared, they set fire to (the grass and brushwood). When this was done, they reviewed the chariots and men, numbering the companies of a hundred and of five. Then the ruler in person addressed them in front of the Shê altar, and proceeded to exercise their squadrons, now wheeling to the left, now wheeling to the right, now making them lie down, now making them rise up; and observing how they practised these evolutions. When the game came in sight and the desire of capturing it was exerted, (he watched) to see that (the hunters) did not break any of the rules (for their proceedings). It was thus sought to bring their wills into subjection, and make them not pursue the animals (in an irregular way). In this way such men conquered in fight, and such sacrificing obtained blessing.

Section II.

1. The son of Heaven, in his tours (of Inspection) to the four quarters (of the kingdom), as the first thing (on his arrival at each) reared the pile of wood (and set fire to it)[2].

---

[1] Perhaps 'the last month' should be 'the second month.' There is much contention on the point.

[2] This paragraph is not in the expurgated Lî. It does seem out of place, for the book goes on to speak of the border or suburban sacrifices presented in the vicinity of the capital, and having nothing to do with the tours of Inspection, of which we

2. At the (Great) border sacrifice, he welcomed the arrival of the longest day. It was a great act of thanksgiving to Heaven, and the sun was the chief object considered in it[1]. The space marked off for it was in the southern suburb;—the place most open to the brightness and warmth (of the heavenly

---

first read in the Canon of Shun, in the Shû. Those tours, however, were understood to be under the direction of Heaven, and the lighting of the pile of wood, on reaching the mountain of each quarter, is taken as having been an announcement to Heaven of the king's arrival.

[1] P. Callery has here the following note:—'Il résulte de ce passage et de plusieurs autres des chapitres suivants, que dès les temps les plus anciens, les Chinois rendaient au soleil un véritable culte, sans même y supposer un esprit ou génie dont il fût la demeure, ainsi qu'ils le faisaient pour les montagnes, les rivières et tous les autres lieux auxquels ils offraient des sacrifices. De nos jours encore on sacrifie au soleil et à la lune; mais c'est plutôt un acte officiel de la part des autorités, qu'une pratique de conviction, car le peuple Chinois n'a pas, comme les Japonais, une grande dévotion pour l'astre du jour. Voyez la fin du chapitre XVIII.'

The text conveys no idea to me of such an ancient worship, but I call the attention of the reader to Callery's view. The other passages to which he refers will be noticed as they occur. For my, 'and the sun was the principal object regarded in it,' he says, 'C'est le soleil qui est le principal objet (des adorations).' The original text is simply 而主日. I let my translation stand as I first made it; but on a prolonged consideration, I think, it would be more accurate to say, 'and the sun was considered (for the occasion) as the residence of (the spirit of) Heaven.' Such an acceptation of 主 is quite legitimate. The sun became for the time the 'spirit-tablet (神主)' of Heaven. Fang *K*üeh says:—'(The Son of Heaven) was welcoming the arrival of the longest day, and therefore he regarded the sun as the residence (for the time) of the spirit of Heaven. That spirit could not be seen; what could be looked up to and beheld were only the sun, moon, and stars.'

influence). The sacrifice was offered on the ground which had been swept for the purpose;—to mark the simplicity (of the ceremony). The vessels used were of earthenware and of gourds;—to emblem the natural (productive power of) heaven and earth. The place was the suburb, and therefore the sacrifice was called the suburban or border. The victim was red, that being the colour preferred by the (*K*âu) dynasty; and it was a calf;—to show the estimation of simple sincerity.

3. For (all) sacrifices in the border they used a hsin day[1]; because when *K*âu first offered the border sacrifice, it was the longest day, and its name began with hsin.

4. When divining about the border sacrifice, (the king) received the reply in the fane of his (great) ancestor, and the tortoise-shell was operated on in that of his father;—honour being thus done to his ancestor, and affection shown to his father. On the day of divination, he stood by the lake[2], and listened himself to the declarations and orders which were

[1] The mention of the 'hsin day' requires that we should understand *k*iâo (郊) here of other sacrifices so called, and not merely of the great one at the winter solstice. The *Kh*ien-lung editors say:—'The border sacrifices for which they used the hsin days were those at which they prayed for a good year. They used such a day, because when king Wû offered his great sacrifice after the battle of Mû-yêh, and announced the completion of his enterprise, the day was hsin-hâi, and from it dated *K*âu's possession of the kingdom, and the hsin days became sacred days for the dynasty.' There were of course three hsin days in every month.

[2] The 'lake' here must be a name for the royal college with the water round it. So Lû Tien and others explain it (澤蓋學

delivered[1],—showing an example of receiving lessons and reproof. (The officers) having communicated to him the orders (to be issued), he gives warning notice of them to all the officers (of a different surname from himself), inside the Khû gate (of the palace), and to those of the same surname, in the Grand temple.

5. On the day of the sacrifice, the king in his skin cap waits for the news that all is ready,—showing the people how they ought to venerate their superiors. Those who were engaged in mourning rites did not wail nor venture to put on their mourning dress. (The people) watered and swept the road, and turned it up afresh with the spade; at (the top of) the fields in the neighbourhood they kept torches burning,—thus without special orders complying with (the wish of) the king[2].

6. On that day, the king assumed the robe with the ascending dragons on it as an emblem of the heavens[3]. He wore the cap with the pendants of jade-pearls, to the number of twelve[4], which is the

---

宫辟雍), and Yüan Yüan's dictionary with reference to this paragraph, defines it as 'the place where they practised ceremonies.'

[1] By the officers as the result of the divination.

[2] It was an established custom that they should do so.

[3] 'The robe with the dragons on it,'—Kwăn (衮),—is thus described in the dictionary. But there must have been also some emblazonry of the heavenly figures on it also; otherwise it would not have emblemed the heavens. But I have not been able to find this in any dictionary.

[4] Having now changed the skin cap mentioned in the preceding paragraph.

number of heaven[1]. He rode in the plain carriage, because of its simplicity. From the flag hung twelve pendants, and on it was the emblazonry of dragons, and the figures of the sun and moon, in imitation of the heavens. Heaven hangs out its brilliant figures, and the sages imitated them. This border sacrifice is the illustration of the way of Heaven.

7. If there appeared anything infelicitous about the victim intended for God, it was used for that intended for *K*î[2]. That intended for God required to be kept in its clean stall for three months. That intended for *K*î simply required to be perfect in its parts. This was the way in which they made a distinction between the spirits of Heaven and the manes of a man[3].

8. All things originate from Heaven; man originates from his (great) ancestor. This is the reason

---

[1] 'The heavenly number;'—with reference, I suppose, to the twelve months of the year.

[2] *K*î, better known as Hâu *K*î, 'the prince, the minister of agriculture,' appears in the Shû as Shun's minister of agriculture (*Kh*î 棄, vol. iii, pp. 42, 43), and one of the principal assistants of Yü, in his more than Herculean achievement (vol. iii, pp. 56–58); and in the Shih as the father of agriculture (vol. iii, pp. 396–399). To him the kings of *K*âu traced their lineage, and they associated him with God at the Great border sacrifice. See the ode to him, so associated, vol. iii, p. 320. In that service there was thus the expression of reverence for God and of filial piety, the second virtue coming in as the complement of the other. It would seem to be implied that they used the ox for *K*î for the blemished one.

[3] By 'spirit' and 'manes' I have endeavoured to come as near as I could to the different significance of the characters shăn (神) and kwei (鬼).

why *K*î was associated with God (at this sacrifice). In the sacrifices at the border there was an expression of gratitude to the source (of their prosperity and a going back in their thoughts to the beginning of (all being).

9. The great *k*â sacrifice of the son of Heaven consisted of eight (sacrifices). This sacrifice was first instituted by Yin *Kh*î[1]. (The word) *k*â expresses the idea of searching out. In the twelfth month of a year, they brought together (some of) all the productions (of the harvest), and sought out (the authors of them) to present them to them as offerings.

10. In the *k*â sacrifice, the principal object contemplated was the Father of Husbandry. They also presented offerings to (ancient) superintendents of husbandry, and to the (discoverers of the) various grains, to express thanks for the crops which had been reaped.

They presented offerings (also) to the (representatives of the ancient inventors of the overseers of the) husbandmen, and of the buildings marking out the boundaries of the fields, and of the birds and beasts. The service showed the highest sentiments of benevolence and of righteousness.

The ancient wise men had appointed all these agencies, and it was felt necessary to make this

---

[1] Who this Yin *Kh*î was is unknown. *K*ăng thought he was an ancient sovereign. The *Kh*ien-lung editors seem to prove in opposition to him and others that he was the minister of some ancient sovereign. His descendants were subordinate ministers under *K*âu, having to do with sacrifice. They are mentioned at the end of the 37th Book of the *K*âu Lî.

return to them. They met the (representatives of the) cats, because they devoured the rats and mice (which injured the fruits) of the fields, and (those of) the tigers, because they devoured the (wild) boars (which destroyed them). They met them and made offerings to them. They offered also to (the ancient Inventors of) the dykes and water-channels;—(all these were) provisions for the husbandry[1].

11. They said,—

'May the ground no sliding show,
Water in its channels flow,
Insects to keep quiet know;
Only in the fens weeds grow!'

They presented their offerings in skin caps and white robes;—in white robes to escort the closing year (to its grave). They wore sashes of dolychos cloth, and carried staffs of hazel,—as being reduced forms of mourning. In the *k*â were expressed the highest sentiments of benevolence and righteousness.

---

[1] This and the other paragraphs down to 13 about the *k*â sacrifice are not in the expurgated copies. It is difficult to understand what it really was. What is said of it leads us to think of it as a Chinese Saturnalia at the end of the year, when all the crops had been gathered in, and the people abandoned themselves to license and revel under the form of sacrificial services. 'The Father of Husbandry' was probably Shăn Năng, the successor of Fû-hsî; see vol. iii, pp. 371, 372. 'The Superintendents of Husbandry' would be Hâu *K*î and others, though Hâu *K*î appears in the Shih as really the father of agriculture. 'The overseer' occurs in the Shih (vol. iii, p. 371 et al.) as 'the surveyor of the fields.' The commentators, so far as I have read, are very chary of giving us any information about the offerings to 'the cats and tigers.' *K*iang *K*âo-hsî says, 'They met the cats and tigers, that is, their spirits (迎貓虎,卽其神也).'

(After this)[1] they proceeded to sacrifice in yellow robes and yellow caps,—releasing the field-labourers from the toils (of the year). Countrymen wore yellow hats, which were made of straw.

12. The Great Netter[2] was the officer who had the management for the son of Heaven of his birds and (captured) beasts, and to his department belonged (all such creatures) sent by the princes as tribute. (Those who brought them)[3] wore hats of straw or bamboo splints, appearing, by way of honour to it, in that country dress. The Netter declined the deer and women (which they brought)[4], and announced to the visitors the message (of the king) to this effect, that they might warn the princes with it:—

> 'He who loves hunting and women,
> Brings his state to ruin.'

The son of Heaven planted gourds and flowering plants; not such things as might be reaped and stored[5].

---

[1] This seems to introduce another service, following that of the *k*â. It is understood to be the lâ sacrifice of *Kh*in, described on page 300, paragraph 19.

[2] We find 'the Netter' called Lo (羅氏), as if Lo had become the surname of the family in which the office was hereditary, as the last but one of the departments described in the 30th Book of the *K*âu Lî.

[3] Those would be 'Great officers' from the various states, personating for the occasion hunters or labouring men.

[4] The 'deer' would be taken in the chase; the 'women,' attractive captives, taken in war. But they would not have such to present from year to year. We can say nothing more about this article of tribute.

[5] Many take this concluding sentence as part of the king's message. The *Kh*ien-lung editors decide against that view; its meaning is that the king never farmed for his own gain.

13. The *k*â with its eight sacrifices served to record (the condition of the people) throughout all the quarters (of the country). If in any quarter the year had not been good, it did not contribute to those services,—out of a careful regard to the resources of the people. Where the labours of a good year had been successfully completed, they took part in them,—to give them pleasure and satisfaction. All the harvest having by this time been gathered, the people had nothing to do but to rest, and therefore after the *k*â wise (rulers) commenced no new work[1].

14. The pickled contents of the ordinary dishes were water-plants produced by the harmonious powers (of nature); the brine used with them was from productions of the land. The additional dishes contained productions of the land with the brine from productions of the water.

The things in the dishes on stands were from both the water and land. They did not venture to use in them the flavours of ordinary domestic use, but variety was considered admirable. It was in this way that they sought to have communion with the spirits; it was not intended to imitate the flavours of food[2].

15. The things set before the ancient kings served as food, but did not minister to the pleasures of the palate. The dragon-robe, the tasseled cap, and

[1] This paragraph treats of the *k*â as celebrated in the states.

[2] The conclusion of this paragraph leads us to take all the dishes spoken of in it as containing sacrificial offerings. It would take too long to discuss all that is said about the 'regular' and the 'additional' dishes in the first part.

the great carriage served for display, but did not awaken a fondness for their use.

The various dances displayed the gravity of the performers, but did not awaken the emotion of delight. The ancestral temple produced the impression of majesty, but did not dispose one to rest in it. Its vessels might be employed (for their purposes in it), but could not be conveniently used for any other. The idea which leads to intercourse with spiritual Beings is not interchangeable with that which finds its realisation in rest and pleasure.

16. Admirable as are the spirits and sweet spirits, a higher value is attached to the dark spirit and the bright water[1],—in order to honour that which is the source of the five flavours. Beautiful as is the elegant embroidery of robes, a higher value is set on plain, coarse cloth,—going back to the commencement of woman's work. Inviting as is the rest afforded by the mats of fine rushes and bamboos, the preference is given to the coarse ones of reeds and straw,—distinguishing the (character of the service in which they were employed). The Grand soup is unseasoned,—in honour of its simplicity. The Grand symbols of jade have no engraving on them,—in admiration of their simple plainness. There is the beauty of the red varnish and carved border

[1] We have seen, before, that 'the dark spirit' is water. Was there a difference between this and 'the bright water?' The *Khien-lung* editors think so, and refer to the functions of the Sze Hsüan officer (司烜氏, *Kâu Lî*, Book XXXVII, 41-44), who by means of a mirror drew the bright water from the moon. How he did so, I do not understand. The object of the writer in this part of the section is to exhibit the value of simple sincerity in all religious services.

(of a carriage), but (the king) rides in a plain one,—doing honour to its plainness. In all these things it is simply the idea of the simplicity that is the occasion of the preference and honour. In maintaining intercourse with spiritual and intelligent Beings, there should be nothing like an extreme desire for rest and ease in our personal gratification. It is this which makes the above usages suitable for their purpose.

17. The number of the tripods and meat-stands was odd, but that of the tall dishes of wood and bamboo was even,—having regard to the numbers belonging to the developing and receding influences of nature[1]. The vase with the yellow eyes[2] was the most valued of all, and contained the spirit with the fragrant herbs. Yellow is the colour (of earth) which occupies the central place[3]. In the eye the energy (of nature) appears most purely and brilliantly. Thus the spirit to be poured out is in that cup, the (emblem of the) centre, and (the symbol of) what is most pure and bright appears outside[4].

---

[1] See the fifth paragraph of Section i, and the note. It may be added here, after Khung Ying-tâ, that 'the tripod and stand contained the body of the victim, which, as belonging to an animal that moved, was of the category of Yang, but the dishes contained the products of trees and vegetables, which were of the category of Yin.'

[2] In pictures, this vase was figured with two eyes. They were carved on the substance of the vessel and then gilt, so as to appear yellow.

[3] On the central place assigned to the element of earth and its yellow colour, see the supplementary section appended to Book IV, Section ii, Part iii.

[4] P. Callery characterises the reasoning of this paragraph as 'puéril et grotesque;' and concludes a long note on it with the

18. When sacrificing to Heaven, the earth is swept, and the sacrifice presented on the ground,—from a regard to the simplicity of such an unartificial altar. Admirable as are the vinegar and pickles, suet boiled and produced through evaporation is preferred,—to do honour to the natural product of heaven. An ordinary knife might be employed (to kill the victim), but that fitted with bells is preferred,—giving honour to the idea thereby indicated; there is the harmony of sound, and then the cutting work is done.

SECTION III.

1. (As to) the meaning of (the ceremony of) capping[1]:—The cap used for the first act of the service was of black cloth,—the cap of the highest antiquity. It was originally of (white) cloth, but the colour when it was used in fasting was dyed black. As to its strings, Confucius said, 'I have not heard anything about them.' This cap, after it had been once put upon (the young man), might be disused.

2. The son by the wife proper was capped by the eastern stairs (appropriate to the use of the master), to show how he was in their line of succes-

---

sentence:—'Je laisse à ceux qui peuvent suivre ce logogriphe dans le texte Chinois, le soin d'en saisir toutes les finesses; car, à mon sens, ce n'est qu'une ineptie.'

[1] These paragraphs about capping are not in the expurgated copy of the Lî, and many commentators, especially Wang of Shih-liang, would relegate them to Book XI. And they are not all easy to be understood. The capping was thrice repeated, and each time with a different cap. So much is clear. The names and forms of the caps in paragraph 3 have given rise to much speculation, from which I purposely abstain; nor do I clearly comprehend its relation to the threefold capping in the ceremony.

sion to him. The father handed him a cup in the guests' place (without receiving one in return). The capping showed that he had reached maturity. The using of three caps was to give greater importance (to the ceremony), and show its object more clearly. The giving the name of maturity in connexion with the ceremony was to show the reverence due to that name.

3. The wei-mâo was the fashion of *K*âu; the *k*ang-fû, that of Yin; and the mâu-tui, that of the sovereigns of Hsiâ. *K*âu used the pien; Yin, the hsü; and Hsiâ, the shâu. The three dynasties all used the skin cap, with the skirt-of-white gathered up at the waist.

4. There were no observances peculiar to the capping (in the families) of Great officers, though there were (peculiar) marriage ceremonies. Anciently a man was fifty when he took the rank of a Great officer; how should there have been peculiar ceremonies at his cappings? The peculiar ceremonies at the cappings as used by the princes arose in the end of the Hsiâ dynasty.

5. The eldest son of the son of Heaven by his proper queen (was capped only as) an ordinary officer. There was nowhere such a thing as being born noble. Princes received their appointments on the hereditary principle, (to teach them) to imitate the virtue of their predecessors. Men received office and rank according to the degree of their virtue. There was the conferring of an honourable designation after death; but that is a modern institution. Anciently, there was no rank on birth, and no honorary title after death.

6. That which is most important in ceremonies is to understand the idea intended in them. While the idea is missed, the number of things and observances in them may be correctly exhibited, as that is the business of the officers of prayer and the recorders. Hence that may all be exhibited, but it is difficult to know the idea. The knowledge of that idea, and the reverent maintenance of it was the way by which the sons of Heaven secured the good government of the kingdom.

7. By the united action of heaven and earth all things spring up. Thus the ceremony of marriage is the beginning of a (line that shall last for a) myriad ages. The parties are of different surnames; thus those who are distant are brought together, and the separation (to be maintained between those who are of the same surname) is emphasised[1]. There must be sincerity in the marriage presents; and all communications (to the woman) must be good. She should be admonished to be upright and sincere. Faithfulness is requisite in all service of others, and faithfulness is (specially) the virtue of a wife. Once mated with her husband, all her life she will not change (her feeling of duty to him), and hence, when the husband dies she will not marry (again)[2].

---

[1] I do not see how Callery translates here:—'On rapproche ce qui était éloigné, et on unit ce qui était distinct.' He says, however, in a note:—'Ceci se rapporte à l'antique loi, encore en vigueur, qui interdit le mariage entre personnes d'un même nom, parce que lors même qu'il n'existe entre elles aucune trace de parenté, il est possible qu'elles proviennent de la même souche, et se trouvent ainsi sur la ligne directe, où les Chinois admettent une parenté sans fin.'

[2] This brief sentence about a woman not marrying again is not

8. The gentleman went in person to meet the bride, the man taking the initiative and not the woman,—according to the idea that regulates the relation between the strong and the weak (in all nature). It is according to this same idea that heaven takes precedence of earth, and the ruler of the subject.

9. Presents are interchanged before (the parties) see each other[1];—this reverence serving to illustrate the distinction (that should be observed between man and woman). When this distinction (between husband and wife) is exhibited, affection comes to prevail between father and son. When there is this affection, the idea of righteousness arises in the mind, and to this idea of righteousness succeeds (the observance of) ceremonies. Through those ceremonies there ensues universal repose. The absence of such distinction and righteousness is characteristic of the way of beasts.

10. The bridegroom himself stands by (the carriage of the bride), and hands to her the strap (to assist her in mounting[2]),—showing his affection. Having

in the expurgated copies. Callery, however, says upon it:—'Dans certains textes du Lî Kî, on trouve à la suite de ce passage une phrase qui restreint à la femme cette immutabilité perpétuelle dans le mariage. En effet, les lois Chinoises ont de tout temps permis à l'homme de se remarier après la mort de sa première femme, tandis que pour les veuves, les secondes noces ont toujours été plus ou moins flétries, ou par la loi, ou par l'usage.'

[1] Callery has for this:—'Les présents que porte l'époux dans ses visites.' But the young people did not see each other till the day of the marriage.

[2] On the 'strap' to help in mounting the carriage, see p. 45, et al. Callery has here 'les rênes.' The text would seem to say that the bridegroom was himself driving, and handed the strap to help the other up; but that would have been contrary to all etiquette;

that affection, he seeks to bring her near to him. It was by such reverence and affection for their wives that the ancient kings obtained the kingdom. In passing out from the great gate (of her father's house), he precedes, and she follows, and with this the right relation between husband and wife commences. The woman follows (and obeys) the man:—in her youth, she follows her father and elder brother; when married, she follows her husband; when her husband is dead, she follows her son. 'Man' denotes supporter. A man by his wisdom should (be able to) lead others.

11. The dark-coloured cap, and the (preceding) fasting and vigil, (with which the bridegroom meets the bride, makes the ceremony like the service of) spiritual beings, and (the meeting of) the bright and developing and receding influences (in nature). The result of it will be to give the lord for the altars to the spirits of the land and grain, and the successors of the forefathers of the past;—is not the utmost reverence appropriate in it? Husband and wife ate together of the same victim,—thus declaring that they were of the same rank. Hence while the wife had (herself) no rank, she was held to be of the rank of her husband, and she took her seat according to the position belonging to him[1].

---

and they appear immediately, not sitting together, but following each other.

[1] It is exceedingly difficult to construe this sentence, nor do the commentators give a translator much help. Rendering ad verbum, all that we have is this:—'The dark-coloured cap, self-purification (and) abstinence; spiritual beings, Yin (and) Yang.' *K*ăng's explanation is very brief:—'The dark-coloured cap (was) the dress in sacrificing. Yin (and) Yang mean husband and wife.' I have

12. The old rule at sacrifices was to have the vessels (only) of earthenware and gourds; and when the kings of the three dynasties instituted the (partaking of the) victim, those were the vessels employed. On the day after the marriage, the wife, having washed her hands, prepared and presented (a sucking-pig) to her husband's parents; and when they had done eating, she ate what was left,—as a mark of their special regard. They descended from the hall by the steps on the west, while she did so by those on the east;—so was she established in the wife's (or mistress's) place.

13. At the marriage ceremony, they did not employ music,—having reference to the feeling of solitariness and darkness (natural to the separation from parents). Music expresses the energy of the bright and expanding influence. There was no congratulation on marriage;—it indicates how (one generation of) men succeeds to another[1].

---

tried to catch and indicate the ideas in the mind of the writer. Taken as I have done, the passage is a most emphatic declaration of the religious meaning which was attached to marriage. Dr. Medhurst (Theology of the Chinese, pp. 88, 89) has translated the greater part of the paragraph, but not very successfully, thus:—'A black crown, with fasting and watching, is the way to serve the Kwei Shins, as well as the male and female principle of nature. The same is the case also (with regard to marriages which are contracted) with the view of obtaining some one to perpetuate the lares domestici (社稷); and principally respect obtaining successors for our ancestors:—can they therefore be conducted without reverence?'

[1] See p. 322, paragraph 20; where Confucius says that in a certain case the bridegroom's family has no music for three days, on the ground that the bridegroom had lost his parents, and sorrow was more suitable than mirth as he thought of their

14. At the sacrifices in the time of the lord of Yü the smell was thought most important. There were the offerings of blood, of raw flesh, and of sodden flesh;—all these were employed for the sake of the smell.

15. Under the Yin, sound was thought most important. Before there was any smell or flavour, the music was made to resound clearly. It was not till there had been three performances of it that they went out to meet (and bring in) the victim. The noise of the music was a summons addressed to all between heaven and earth.

16. Under the *K*âu, a pungent odour was thought most important. In libations they employed the smell of millet-spirits in which fragrant herbs had been infused. The fragrance, partaking of the nature of the receding influence, penetrates to the deep springs below. The libations were poured from cups with long handles of jade, (as if) to employ (also) the smell of the mineral. After the liquor was poured, they met (and brought in) the victim, having first diffused the smell into the unseen realm. Artemisia along with millet and rice having then been burned (with the fat of the victim), the fragrance penetrates through all the building. It was for this reason that, after the cup had been put down, they burnt the fat with the southernwood and millet and rice.

17. So careful were they on all occasions of sacri-

---

being gone. This statement was generalised by the writer; but in the Shih, as in ordinary life, music is an accompaniment of marriage. See the paraphrase of the 'Amplification of the fourth of the Khang-hsî precepts.'

fice. The intelligent spirit returns to heaven; the body and the animal soul return to the earth; and hence arose the idea of seeking (for the deceased) in sacrifice in the unseen darkness and in the bright region above. Under the Yin, they first sought for them in the bright region; under *K*âu, they first sought for them in the dark.

18. They informed the officer of prayer in the apartment; they seated the representative of the departed in the hall; they killed the victim in the courtyard. The head of the victim was taken up to the apartment. This was at the regular sacrifice, when the officer of prayer addressed himself to the spirit-tablet of the departed. If it were (merely) the offering of search, the minister of prayer takes his place at the inside of the gate of the temple. They knew not whether the spirit were here, or whether it were there, or far off, away from all men. Might not that offering inside the gate be said to be a searching for the spirit in its distant place?

19. That service at the gate was expressive of the energy of the search. The stand with the heart and tongue of the victim (set forth before the personator) was expressive of reverence. (The wish of the principal) for wealth (to those assisting him) included all happiness. The (presentation of the) head was (intended as) a direct (communication with the departed). The presence (of the representative) was that the spirit might enjoy (the offerings). The blessing (pronounced by him) was for long continuance, and comprehensive. The personator (seemed) to display (the departed).

20. The (examination of the) hair and the (taking

of the) blood was an announcement that the victim was complete within and without. This announcement showed the value set on its being perfect[1]. The offering of the blood was because of the breath which is contained in it. They offered (specially) the lungs, the liver, and the heart, doing honour to those parts as the home of the breath.

21. In offering the millet and the glutinous millet, they presented the lungs along with it. In offering the various prepared liquors, they presented the bright water;—in both cases acknowledging their obligations to the dark and receding influence (in nature). In taking the fat of the inwards and burning it, and in taking the head up (to the hall), they made their acknowledgments to the bright and active influence.

22. In the bright water and the clear liquor the thing valued was their newness. All clarifying is a sort of making new. The water was called 'bright' because the principal in the service had purified it.

23. When the ruler bowed twice with his head to the ground, and, with breast bared, himself applied

[1] From the middle of paragraph 10 to 18 inclusive is not in the expurgated edition, which closes with the nineteenth paragraph and the half of the twenty-first. I need not quote Callery's translation of this portion, but he says on it:—'Ce passage est un de ceux qui se refusent le plus à la traduction, et qui renferment, au fond, le moins d'idées claires et raisonnables. L'auteur a voulu, ce me semble, donner une explication mystique à des mots et à des coutumes qui n'en étaient point susceptibles, et il lui est arrivé, comme à certains commentateurs bibliques du moyen âge, de faire un galimatias, auquel lui même, sans doute, ne comprenait rien.'—On what the author says about the hair and blood, compare vol. iii, page 370.

the knife, this expressed his extreme reverence. Yes, his extreme reverence, for there was submission in it. The bowing showed his submission; the laying the head on the ground did that emphatically; and the baring his breast was the greatest (outward) exhibition of the feeling.

24. When the sacrificer styled himself 'the filial son,' or 'the filial grandson,' he did so (in all cases) according to the meaning of the name. When he styled himself 'So and So, the distant descendant,' that style was used of (the ruler of) a state or (the Head of) a clan. (Though) there were the assistants at the service, the principal himself gave every demonstration of reverence and performed all his admirable service without yielding anything to any one.

25. The flesh of the victim might be presented raw and as a whole, or cut up in pieces, or sodden, or thoroughly cooked; but how could they know whether the spirit enjoyed it? The sacrificer simply showed his reverence to the utmost of his power.

26. (When the representative of the departed) had made the libation with the *k*iâ cup, or the horn, (the sacrificer) was told (to bow to him) and put him at ease. Anciently, the representative stood when nothing was being done; when anything was being done, he sat. He personated the spirit; the officer of prayer was the medium of communication between him and the sacrificer.

27. In straining (the new liquor) for the cup, they used the white (mâo) grass and obtained a clear cup. The liquor beginning to clear itself was further clarified by means of pure liquor. The juice

obtained by boiling aromatics (with the extract of millet) was clarified by mingling with it the liquor which had begun to clear itself:—in the same way as old and strong spirits are qualified by the brilliantly pure liquor or that which has begun to clear itself[1].

---

[1] He would be a bold man who would say that he had given a translation of this paragraph, which he was sure represented exactly the mind of the author. The interpretation given of it even by *K*ăng Hsüan is now called in question in a variety of points by most scholars; and the *Kh*ien-lung editors refrain from concluding the many pages of various commentators, which they adduce on it, with a summary and exposition of their own judgment. Until some sinologist has made himself acquainted with all the processes in the preparation of their drinks at the present day by the Chinese, and has thereby, and from his own knowledge of the general subject, attained to a knowledge of the similar preparations of antiquity, a translator can only do the best in his power with such a passage, without being sure that it is the best that might be done.

In the *K*âu Lî, Book V, 23–36, we have an account of the duties of the Director of Wines (酒正; Biot, 'Intendant des Vins'). Mention is made of 'the three wines (三酒),' which were employed as common beverages, and called shih *k*iû (事酒), hsî *k*iû (昔酒), and *kh*ing *k*iû (清酒); in Biot, 'vin d'affaire, vin âgé, and vin clair.' Consul Gingell, in his useful translation of 'The Institutes of the *K*âu Dynasty Strung as Pearls' (London: Smith, Elder, and Co., 1852), calls them—'wine made specially for any particular occasion; wine which has become ripe; and old, clear, and fine wine.'

In addition to these three *k*iû, the Director had to do with the five *k*î (五齊; Biot, 'les cinque sorts de vins sacrés'), and called fan *k*î (泛齊), lî *k*î (醴齊), ang *k*î (盎齊), thî *k*î (緹齊), and *kh*ăn *k*î (沈齊); in Biot, after *K*ăng Hsüan, 'vin surnageant, vin doux, vin qui se clarifie, vin substantiel, vin reposé;' in Gingell, 'rice-water which has undergone

28. Sacrifices were for the purpose of prayer, or of thanksgiving, or of deprecation.

29. The dark-coloured robes worn during vigil and purification had reference to the occupation of the thoughts with the dark and unseen. Hence after the three days of purification, the superior man was sure (to seem) to see those to whom his sacrifice was to be offered[1].

---

fermentation, wine in which dregs have formed, wine in which the dregs have risen to the surface, wine in which the dregs have congealed, and of which the colour has become reddish, and pure clear wine in which the dregs are subsiding.' Whether Biot be correct or not in translating *k*î (perhaps should be read *k*âi, = 齋) 'vin sacré,' the five preparations so called were for use at sacrifices. 'They were,' say the *Kh*ien-lung editors, 'for use at sacrifices, and not as ordinary drinks.' 'They were all thin, and unpalatable; for the cup, and not for the mouth.'

[1] The *Kh*ien-lung editors say that from paragraph 14 to this. the compiler mentions promiscuously a great many particulars about the ancient sacrifices, the different places in which the services at them were performed, the things used in them, &c., showing how sincere and earnest those engaged in them must be to attain to the result mentioned in this last paragraph; and that this is the fundamental object of the whole treatise.

I have called attention to this promiscuous nature of the contents of many of the Books towards the end of them, in the introduction, page 34, as a characteristic of the collection.

BOOK X. THE NÊI ȜEH

OR

THE PATTERN OF THE FAMILY[1].

SECTION I.

1. The sovereign and king orders the chief minister to send down his (lessons of) virtue to the millions of the people.

2. Sons[2], in serving their parents, on the first crowing of the cock, should all wash their hands and rinse their mouths, comb their hair, draw over it the covering of silk, fix this with the hair-pin, bind the hair at the roots with the fillet, brush the dust from that which is left free, and then put on their caps, leaving the ends of the strings hanging down. They should then put on their squarely made black jackets, knee-covers, and girdles, fixing in the last their tablets. From the left and right of the girdle they should hang their articles for use:—on the left side, the duster and handkerchief, the knife and whetstone, the small spike, and the metal speculum for getting fire from the sun ; on the right, the archer's thimble for the thumb and the armlet, the tube for writing instruments, the knife-case, the larger spike, and the borer for getting fire from wood. They should put on their leggings, and adjust their shoe-strings.

---

[1] See the introductory notice, pp. 26, 27.

[2] The 'sons' here are young gentlemen of good families, shih (士), who might be employed as ordinary officers.

3. (Sons') wives should serve their parents-in-law as they served their own. At the first crowing of the cock, they should wash their hands, and rinse their mouths; comb their hair, draw over it the covering of silk, fix this with the hair-pin, and tie the hair at the roots with the fillet. They should then put on the jacket, and over it the sash. On the left side they should hang the duster and handkerchief, the knife and whetstone, the small spike, and the metal speculum to get fire with; and on the right, the needle-case, thread, and floss, all bestowed in the satchel, the great spike, and the borer to get fire with from wood. They will also fasten on their necklaces[1], and adjust their shoe-strings.

4. Thus dressed, they should go to their parents and parents-in-law. On getting to where they are, with bated breath and gentle voice, they should ask if their clothes are (too) warm or (too) cold, whether they are ill or pained, or uncomfortable in any part; and if they be so, they should proceed reverently to stroke and scratch the place. They should in the same way, going before or following after, help and support their parents in quitting or entering (the apartment). In bringing in the basin for them to wash, the younger will carry the stand and the elder the water; they will beg to be allowed to pour out

[1] 'Necklaces' is only a guess at the meaning. *Kh*ăn Hâo and others make the character to mean 'scent bags.' But this also is only a guess. There is nothing in its form to suggest such a meaning; and as many other critics point out, it is inconsistent with the usage in paragraph 5. These acknowledge that they do not understand the phrase 衿纓. See I, i, 3. 34, but the use of ying there is considered inappropriate here.

the water, and when the washing is concluded, they will hand the towel. They will ask whether they want anything, and then respectfully bring it. All this they will do with an appearance of pleasure to make their parents feel at ease. (They should bring) gruel, thick or thin, spirits or must, soup with vegetables, beans, wheat, spinach, rice, millet, maize, and glutinous millet,—whatever they wish, in fact; with dates, chestnuts, sugar and honey, to sweeten their dishes; with the ordinary or the large-leaved violets, leaves of elm-trees, fresh or dry, and the most soothing rice-water to lubricate them; and with fat and oil to enrich them. The parents will be sure to taste them, and when they have done so, the young people should withdraw[1].

5. Youths who have not yet been capped, and maidens who have not yet assumed the hair-pin, at the first crowing of the cock, should wash their hands, rinse their mouths, comb their hair, draw over it the covering of silk, brush the dust from that which is left free, bind it up in the shape of a horn, and put on their necklaces. They should all hang at their girdles[2] the ornamental (bags of) perfume; and as soon as it is daybreak, they should (go to) pay their respects (to their parents) and ask what they will eat

[1] The structure of this and the preceding sentences is easy enough, but it is not easy for a translator to assure himself that he is rendering every Chinese character by its correct equivalent in his own language.

[2] They hang on these instead of the useful appendages mentioned in paragraphs 2 and 3, as being too young to employ these. This determines the meaning of 長者 in the last clause as I have given it. Zottoli's rendering is:—'Si nondum comederint, tunc adjuturi majores inspectabunt praeparata.

and drink. If they have eaten already, they should retire; if they have not eaten, they will (remain to) assist their elder (brothers and sisters) and see what has been prepared.

6. All charged with the care of the inner and outer parts (of the house), at the first crowing of the cock, should wash their hands and mouths, gather up their pillows and fine mats, sprinkle and sweep out the apartments, hall, and courtyard, and spread the mats, each doing his proper work. The children go earlier to bed, and get up later, according to their pleasure. There is no fixed time for their meals.

7. From the time that sons receive an official appointment, they and their father occupy different parts of their residence. But at the dawn, the son will pay his respects, and express his affection by (the offer of) pleasant delicacies. At sunrise he will retire, and he and his father will attend to their different duties. At sundown, the son will pay his evening visit in the same way.

8. When the parents wish to sit (anywhere), the sons and their wives should carry their mats, and ask in what direction they shall lay them. When they wish to lie down, the eldest among them should carry the mats, and ask where they wish to place their feet, while the youngest will carry a (small) bench for them to lean on while they stretch out their legs. (At the same time) an attendant will place a stool by them. They should take up the mat on which they had been lying and the fine mat over it, hang up the coverlet, put the pillow in its case, and roll up the fine mat and put it in its cover.

9. (Sons and their wives) should not move the clothes, coverlets, fine mats, or undermats, pillows, and stools of their parents[1]; they should reverently regard their staffs and shoes, but not presume to approach them; they should not presume to use their vessels for grain, liquor, and water, unless some of the contents be left in them; nor to eat or drink any of their ordinary food or drink, unless in the same case.

10. While the parents are both alive, at their regular meals, morning and evening, the (eldest) son and his wife will encourage them to eat everything, and what is left after all, they will themselves eat[2]. When the father is dead, and the mother still alive, the eldest son should wait upon her at her meals; and the wives of the other sons will do with what is left as in the former case. The children should have the sweet, soft, and unctuous things that are left.

11. When with their parents, (sons and their wives), when ordered to do anything, should immediately respond and reverently proceed to do it. In going forwards or backwards, or turning round, they should be careful and grave; while going out or coming in, while bowing or walking, they should not presume to eructate, sneeze, or cough, to yawn or stretch themselves, to stand on one foot, or to lean against anything, or to look askance. They should not dare to spit or snivel, nor, if it be cold, to put on more clothes, nor, if they itch anywhere, to scratch

[1] That is, the parents of the husband, and parents-in-law of the wife.

[2] 'That nothing,' says Khung Ying-tâ, 'may be served up again.'

themselves. Unless for reverent attention to something[1], they should not presume to unbare their shoulders or chest. Unless it be in wading, they should not hold up their clothes. Of their private dress and coverlet, they should not display the inside. They should not allow the spittle or snivel of their parents to be seen[2]. They should ask leave to rinse away any dirt on their caps or girdles, and to wash their clothes that are dirty with lye that has been prepared for the purpose; and to stitch together, with needle and thread, any rent.

Every five days they should prepare tepid water, and ask them to take a bath, and every three days prepare water for them to wash their heads. If in the meantime their faces appear dirty, they should heat the water in which the rice has been cleaned, and ask them to wash with it; if their feet be dirty, they should prepare hot water, and ask them to wash them with it. Elders in serving their youngers, and the low in serving the noble, should all observe these rules.

12. The men should not speak of what belongs to the inside (of the house), nor the women of what belongs to the outside. Except at sacrifices and funeral rites, they should not hand vessels to one another. In all other cases when they have occasion to give and receive anything, the woman should receive it in a basket. If she have no basket, they should both sit down, and the other put the thing on

---

[1] As for archery. The meaning is, I suppose, that none of the things mentioned should be seen or known, while they are waiting on their parents.

[2] But instantly wipe it off, according to *Kh*ăn Hâo.

the ground, and she then take it up. Outside or inside[1], they should not go to the same well, nor to the same bathing-house. They should not share the same mat in lying down; they should not ask or borrow anything from one another; they should not wear similar upper or lower garments. Things spoken inside should not go out, words spoken outside should not come in. When a man goes into the interior of the house, he should not whistle nor point. If he have occasion to move in the night, he should use a light; and if he have no light, he should not stir. When a woman goes out at the door, she must keep her face covered. She should walk at night (only) with a light; and if she have no light, she should not stir. On the road, a man should take the right side, and a woman the left.

13. Sons and sons' wives, who are filial and reverential, when they receive an order from their parents should not refuse, nor be dilatory, to execute it[2]. When (their parents) give them anything to eat or drink, which they do not like, they will notwithstanding taste it and wait (for their further orders); when they give them clothes, which are not to their mind, they will put them on, and wait (in the same way)[3]. If (their parents) give them anything to do, and then employ another to take their place,

[1] Zottoli has for this—'viri mulieresque.' The writer is speaking of men and women, indeed; but the characters have reference to place, and = 'out of the house or in it.'

[2] That is, they will not presume on any indulgence which they might expect from the impression made by their general character and behaviour.

[3] 'Orders,' consequent on their parents' seeing that the food or garment is not to their mind.

although they do not like the arrangement, they will in the meantime give it into his hands and let him do it, doing it again, if it be not done well.

14. When the sons and their wives are engaged with laborious tasks, although (their parents) very much love them, yet they should let them go on with them for the time;—it is better that they take other occasions frequently to give them ease.

When sons and their wives have not been filial and reverential, (the parents) should not be angry and resentful with them, but endeavour to instruct them. If they will not receive instruction, they should then be angry with them. If that anger do no good, they can then drive out the son, and send the wife away, yet not publicly showing why they have so treated them[1].

15. If a parent have a fault, (the son) should with bated breath, and bland aspect, and gentle voice, admonish him. If the admonition do not take effect, he will be the more reverential and the more filial; and when the father seems pleased, he will repeat the admonition. If he should be displeased with this, rather than allow him to commit an offence against any one in the neighbourhood or countryside, (the son) should strongly remonstrate. If the parent be angry and (more) displeased, and beat him till the blood

[1] This last sentence is enigmatical in the original text. Zottoli says:—'Si non possint coerceri, filium ejice nurum exclude, quin tamen patefacius agendi morem;' adding as an explanation of that 'agendi morem,' 'siquidem eos haud certe in finem sic ejectos voles.' Different views of the Chinese have been given by different critics; and it would not be difficult to add to their number.

flows, he should not presume to be angry and resentful, but be (still) more reverential and more filial.

16. If parents have a boy born (to the father) by a handmaid, or the son or grandson of one of his concubines, of whom they are very fond, their sons should after their death, not allow their regard for him to decay so long as they live.

If a son have two concubines, one of whom is loved by his parents, while he himself loves the other, yet he should not dare to make this one equal to the former whom his parents love, in dress, or food, or the duties which she discharges, nor should he lessen his attentions to her after their death. If he very much approves of his wife, and his parents do not like her, he should divorce her[1]. If he do not approve of his wife, and his parents say, 'she serves us well,' he should behave to her in all respects as his wife,—without fail even to the end of her life.

17. Although his parents be dead, when a son is inclined to do what is good, he should think that he will thereby transmit the good name of his parents, and carry his wish into effect. When he is inclined to do what is not good, he should think that he will thereby bring disgrace on the name of his parents, and in no wise carry his wish into effect.

18. When her father-in-law is dead, her mother-in-law takes the place of the old lady[2]; but the wife of the eldest son, on all occasions of sacrificing and receiving guests, must ask her directions in every-

[1] *Kh*ăn Hâo quotes here from the Lî of the elder Tâi (Book XIII, chapter 26) the 'seven grounds of divorce,' the first of them being the wife's 'want of accordance with her husband's parents.'

[2] Who now retires from the open headship of the family.

thing, while the other sons' wives must ask directions from her. When her parents-in-law employ the eldest son's wife, she should not be dilatory, unfriendly, or unpolite to the wives of his brothers (for their not helping her). When the parents-in-law employ any of them, they should not presume to consider themselves on an equality with the other; walking side by side with her, or giving their orders in the same way, or sitting in the same position as she.

19. No daughter-in-law, without being told to go to her own apartment, should venture to withdraw from that (of her parents-in-law). Whatever she is about to do, she should ask leave from them. A son and his wife should have no private goods, nor animals, nor vessels; they should not presume to borrow from, or give anything to, another person. If any one give the wife an article of food or dress, a piece of cloth or silk, a handkerchief for her girdle, an iris or orchid, she should receive and offer it to her parents-in-law. If they accept it, she will be glad as if she were receiving it afresh. If they return it to her, she should decline it, and if they do not allow her to do so, she will take it as if it were a second gift, and lay it by to wait till they may want it. If she want to give it to some of her own cousins, she must ask leave to do so, and that being granted, she will give it.

20. Eldest cousins in the legitimate line of descent and their brothers should do reverent service to the son, who is the representative chief of the family and his wife[1]. Though they may be richer and

[1] These are all legitimate members of the same surname or clan, but the honoured cousin is the chief of it in the direct line. He is

higher in official rank than he, they should not presume to enter his house with (the demonstrations of) their wealth and dignity. Although they may have in attendance many chariots and footmen, these should stop outside, and they enter it in more simple style with a few followers.

If to any of the younger cousins there have been given vessels, robes, furs, coverlets, carriages and horses, he must offer the best of them (to his chief), and then use those that are inferior to this himself. If what he should thus offer be not proper for the chief, he will not presume to enter with it at his gate, not daring to appear with his wealth and dignity, to be above him who is the head of all the clan with its uncles and elder cousins.

A wealthy cousin should prepare two victims, and present the better of them to his chief. He and his wife should together, after self-purification, reverently assist at his sacrifice in the ancestral temple. When the business of that is over, they may venture to offer their own private sacrifice.

21. Of grain food, there were millet, the glutinous rice, rice, maize, the white millet, and the yellow maize, cut when ripe, or when green.

Of prepared meats, there were beef soup, mutton soup, pork soup, and roast beef; pickle, slices of beef, pickle and minced beef; roast mutton, slices

---

the chieftain of the clan. They are heads of subordinate branches of it. They may have become more wealthy and attained to higher rank in the service of their common ruler, but within the limits of the clan, he is their superior, and has duties of sacrifice to the ancestors of it, with which they cannot of themselves intermeddle.

of mutton, pickle, and roast pork; pickle, slices of pork, mustard sauce, and minced fish; pheasant, hare, quail, and partridge[1].

22. Of drinks, there was must in two vessels, one strained, the other unstrained, made of rice, of millet, or of maize. In some cases, thin preparations were used as beverages, as millet gruel, pickle, with water syrup of prunes, and of steeped rice; clear wine and white[2].

Of confections, there were dried cakes, and rice-flour scones.

23. For relishes, snail-juice and a condiment of the broad-leaved water-squash were used with pheasant soup; a condiment of wheat with soups of dried slices and of fowl; broken glutinous rice with dog soup and hare soup; the rice-balls mixed with these soups had no smart-weed in them.

A sucking-pig was stewed, wrapped up in sonchus leaves and stuffed with smart-weed; a fowl, with the same stuffing, and along with pickle sauce; a fish, with the same stuffing and egg sauce; a tortoise, with the same stuffing and pickle sauce.

For meat spiced and dried they placed the brine of ants; for soup made of sliced meat, that of hare; for a ragout of elk, that of fish; for minced fish, mustard sauce; for raw elk flesh, pickle sauce; for preserved peaches and plums, egg-like suet.

24. All condiments for grain food were of a

---

[1] In all, four rows of prepared meats, consisting of four dishes each.

[2] Both the old wine and occasional wine, mentioned in the note on page 447, were 'white.' The *kiû* here, probably, were the three *kiû* there.

character corresponding to the spring; for soup, to the summer; for sauces, to the autumn; and for beverages, to the winter.

In all attempering ingredients, sour predominated in the spring; bitter, in the summer; acrid, in the autumn; and salt, in the winter:—with the due proportioning of the unctuous and sweet.

The glutinous rice (was thought) to suit beef; millet, to suit mutton; glutinous millet, to suit pork; maize, to suit dog; wheat, to suit goose; and the broad-leaved squash, to suit fish.

25. Lamb and sucking-pig were (thought to be) good in spring, fried with odorous (beef) suet; dried pheasant and fish, in summer, fried with the strong-smelling suet (of dog); veal and fawn, in autumn, fried with strong suet (of fowl); fresh fish and goose, in winter, fried with the frouzy suet (of goat).

26. There were dried beef, and dried stalks of deer's flesh, of wild pig's, of elk's, and of the muntjac's. Elk's flesh, deer's, wild pig's, and muntjac's, was (also eaten uncooked; and) cut in large leaf-like slices. Pheasants and hares were (made into soup) with the duckweed. There were sparrows and finches, partridges, cicadas, bees, lichens, small chestnuts, the water-caltrops, the hovenia dulcis, the zizyphus, chestnuts, hazel-nuts, persimmons, cucumbers, peaches, plums, ballaces, almonds, haws, pears, ginger, and cinnamon [1].

---

[1] In this there are the names of more than thirty condiments or relishes, which, according to most commentators, were, or might be, served up at the meals of the rulers of states. But from paragraph 21 we have a list of viands, drinks, and their accom-

27. If a Great officer, at his ordinary meals, had mince, he did not have, at the same time, dried slices of meat; and if he had the latter, he did not have the former. An ordinary officer did not have two kinds of soup, or sliced flesh. (But) old men of the common people, did not eat their meat alone without accompaniments.

28. Mince was made in spring, with onions; in autumn, with the mustard plant. Sucking-pig was used in spring, with scallions; in autumn, with smart-weed. With lard they used onions; with fat, chives. With the three victim-animals they used pepper, and employed pickle as an accompaniment. For wild animals' flesh they used plums. In quail soup, fowl soup, and with the curlew, the condiment was smart-weed. Bream and tench were steamed; pullets, roasted; and pheasants, (boiled), with fragrant herbs and no smart-weed.

29. Things not eaten were the turtle, when hatching; the intestines of the wolf, which were removed, as also the kidneys of the dog; the straight spine of the wild cat; the rump of the hare; the head of the fox; the brains of the sucking-pig; the yî-like bowels of fish[1]; and the perforated openings of the turtle[1].

30. (Bones and sinews) were taken from the flesh; the scales were scraped from fish; dates were made to appear as new; chestnuts were

---

paniments with no information as to when and by whom they were used. To descend to further particulars about them would be troublesome.

[1] 乙. It is uncertain what some of these forbidden articles really were.

selected; peaches were made smooth; *k*â and pears had the insects drilled out of them[1].

31. When an ox lowed at night, its flesh was (considered) to be rank; that of a sheep, whose long hair showed a tendency to get matted, to be frouzy; that of a dog which was uneasy and with (the inside of) its thighs red, to be coarse; that of birds when moulting and with their voices hoarse, to be fetid; that of pigs, when they looked upwards and closed their eyes, to be measly; that of a horse, black along the spine and with piebald fore-legs, to smell unpleasantly.

A pullet, whose tail could not be grasped by the hand, was not eaten, nor the rump of a tame goose, nor the ribs of a swan or owl, nor the rump of a tame duck, nor the liver of a fowl, nor the kidneys of a wild goose, nor the gizzard of the wild goose without the hind-toe, nor the stomach of the deer.

32. Flesh cut small was made into mince; cut into slices it was made into hash. Some say that the flesh of elks, deer, and fish was pickled; that of muntjacs also, being cut in small pieces; that of fowls and wild pigs, in larger pieces; of hares, the stomach was pickled. Onions and scallions were mixed with the brine to soften the meat[2].

---

[1] The explanation of these brief notes is also perplexing. Zottoli makes the *k*â to have been a kind of medlar (azarolus). Medhurst calls it, after the Khang-hsî dictionary, 'a kind of pear.' Williams, explaining it under a synonym (of the same sound), 'a sour red fruit of the size of a cherry, a kind of hawthorn.'

[2] The manner of these preparations has not been definitely explained. The meaning is uncertain. So also is what is said of the cupboards in the next paragraph.

33. Soup and boiled grain were used by all, from the princes down to the common people, without distinction of degree. Great officers did not regularly have savoury meat, but when seventy they had their cupboards. The cupboards of the son of Heaven were five on the right (of the dining hall), and five on the left; those of dukes, marquises, and earls were five, all in one room; those of Great officers three (in a side chamber), and other officers had one on their buffet.

SECTION II.

1. In nourishing the aged[1], (Shun), the lord of Yü, used the ceremonies of a drinking entertainment; the sovereigns of Hsiâ, those (at entertainments after) a reverent sacrifice or offering; the men of Yin, those of a (substantial) feast; and the men of *K*âu cultivated and used all the three[2].

Those of fifty years were entertained in the schools of the districts; those of sixty, in the school of the capital; and those of seventy, in the college. This rule extended to the feudal states. An old man of eighty made his acknowledgment for the ruler's invitation by kneeling once and bringing his head to the ground twice. The blind did the same. An

---

[1] *Kh*ăn Hâo says:—The nourishment of the aged took place in four cases: 1st, in the case of the three classes of ancients; 2nd, in that of the father and grandfather of one who had died in the service of the country; 3rd, in that of officers who had retired from age; and 4th, in that of the aged of the common people. On seven occasions of the year it was done formally.

[2] On the different designations of the dynasties, see on Confucian Analects, III, 21.

old man of ninety employed another to receive (the message and gift for him).

For those of fifty, the grain was (fine and) different (from that used by younger men). For those of sixty, there was meat kept in store (from the day before). For those of seventy, there was a second service of savoury meat. Those of eighty were supplied regularly with delicacies. For those of ninety, food and drink were never out of their chambers; wherever they wandered, it was deemed right that savoury meat and drink should follow them.

After sixty (the coffin and other things for the funeral) were seen to be in readiness (once) a year; after seventy, once a season; after eighty, once a month; and after ninety, they were every day kept in good repair. The bandages, however, the sheet, the larger coverlets, and the cases were prepared after death[1].

At fifty, one was supposed to begin to decay; at sixty, not to feel satisfied unless he had flesh to eat. At seventy, he was thought to require silk in order to make him feel warm; at eighty, to need some one (to sleep) with him, to keep him warm; and at ninety, not to feel warm even with that.

At fifty, one kept his staff in his hand in the family; at sixty, in his district; at seventy, in the city; at eighty, (an officer) did so in the court. If the son of Heaven wished to put questions to (an officer of) ninety, he went to his house, and had rich food carried after him.

---

[1] The sheet was for the slighter dressing of the corpse immediately after death; the coverlets for the fuller dressing at the coffining; the cases were for the upper part of the corpse and for the legs.

At seventy, (an officer) did not wait till the court was over (before he retired). At eighty, he reported every month (to the ruler's messenger) that he was still alive; at ninety, he had (delicate food) sent to him regularly every day.

At fifty, one was not employed in services requiring strength; at sixty, he was discharged from bearing arms along with others; at seventy, he was exempted from the business of receiving guests and visitors; at eighty, he was free from the abstinences and other rites of mourning.

When one received at fifty the rank (of a Great officer), at sixty he did not go in person to the school[1]. At seventy he resigned office; and then and afterwards, in mourning he used only the unhemmed dress of sackcloth (without adopting the privations of the mourning rites)[1].

The kings of the three dynasties, in nourishing the old, always caused the members of families who were advanced in years to be brought to their notice[2] Where an officer was eighty, one of his friends was free from all service of government; where he was ninety, all the members of his family were exempted from them. So also it was in the case of the blind.

(Shun), the lord of Yü, entertained the aged (who had retired from the service) of the state in (the school called) the higher hsiang, and the aged of the common people in (the school called) the lower

[1] Does this intimate, that if he had learned better at school, when young, he might have become a Great officer earlier? He was now too old to learn.

[2] The government could not attend to all the aged; but it wished to hear of all cases of remarkable age, and would then do what it could for them.

hsiang. The sovereigns of the line of Hsiâ entertained the former in (the school called) the hsü on the east, and the latter in (that called) the hsü on the west. The men of Yin entertained the former in the School of the Right, and the latter in that of the Left. The men of *K*âu entertained the former in the *k*iâo on the east, and the latter in the Yü hsiang. This was in the suburb of the capital on the west.

The lord of Yü wore the hwang cap in sacrificing (in the ancestral temple), and the white robes in entertaining the aged. The sovereigns of Hsiâ sacrificed in the shân cap, and entertained the aged in the dark garments of undress. Those of Yin sacrificed in the hsü cap, and entertained in the garments of white thin silk. Those of *K*âu sacrificed in the mien cap, and entertained the aged in the dark upper garment (and the lower white one)[1].

2. Ȝăng-ȝze said, 'A filial son, in nourishing his aged, (seeks to) make their hearts glad, and not to go against their wishes; to promote their comfort in their bed-chambers and the whole house; and with leal heart to supply them with their food and drink:—such is the filial son to the end of life. By "the end of life," I mean not the end of parents' lives, but the end of his own life. Thus what his parents loved he will love, and what they reverenced he will reverence. He will do so even in regard to all their

[1] The above long paragraph constitutes, with very little difference, the first twelve paragraphs of Section v of Book III. *K*û Hsî says that in this Book we have 'old text,' whereas Book III is a compilation of the Han dynasty; and that the authors of it incorporated this passage. I am willing to allow that they did so; but it may be doubted if this Book in its present form be older than the time of Han.

dogs and horses, and how much more in regard to the men (whom they valued)!'

3. In all their nourishment of the aged, (the object of) the five Tîs was to imitate (their virtue), while the kings of the three dynasties also begged them to speak (their lessons). The five Tîs taking them as models, sought to nourish their bodily vigour, and did not beg them to speak; but what good lessons they did speak were taken down by the faithful recorders. The three (lines of) kings also took them as models, and after nourishing their age begged them to speak. If they (seemed to) diminish the ceremonies (of entertainment), they all had their faithful recorders as well (to narrate their virtue).

4. For the Rich Fry, they put the pickled meat fried over rice that had been grown on a dry soil, and then enriched it with melted fat. This was called the Rich Fry.

5. For the Similar Fry, they put the pickled meat fried over the millet grains, and enriched it with melted fat. This was called the Similar Fry.

6. For the Bake, they took a sucking-pig or a (young) ram, and having cut it open and removed the entrails, filled the belly with dates. They then wrapped it round with straw and reeds, which they plastered with clay, and baked it. When the clay was all dry, they broke it off. Having washed their hands for the manipulation, they removed the crackling and macerated it along with rice-flour, so as to form a kind of gruel which they added to the pig. They then fried the whole in such a quantity of melted fat as to cover it. Having prepared a large pan of hot water, they placed in it a small tripod,

which was filled with fragrant herbs, and the slices of the creature which was being prepared. They took care that the hot water did not cover this tripod, but kept up the fire without intermission for three days and nights. After this, the whole was served up with the addition of pickled meat and vinegar.

7. For the Pounded Delicacy, they took the flesh of ox, sheep, elk, deer and muntjac, a part of that which lay along the spine, the same in quantity of each, and beat it now as it lay flat, and then turning it on its side; after that they extracted all the nerves. (Next), when it was sufficiently cooked, they brought it (from the pan), took away the outside crust, and softened the meat (by the addition of pickle and vinegar).

8. For the Steeped Delicacy, they took the beef, which was required to be that of a newly killed animal, and cut it into small pieces, taking care to obliterate all the lines in it. It was then steeped from one morning to the next in good wine, when it was eaten with pickle, vinegar, or the juice of prunes.

9. To make the Grill, they beat the beef and removed the skinny parts. They then laid it on a frame of reeds, sprinkled on it pieces of cinnamon and ginger, and added salt. It could be eaten thus when dried. Mutton was treated in the same way as beef, and also the flesh of elk, deer, and muntjac. If they wished the flesh wet, they added water and fried it with pickled meat. If they wished it dry, they ate it as eaten (at first).

10. For the (Soup) Balls, they took equal quantities of beef, mutton and pork, and cut them small. Then they took grains of rice, which they mixed

with the finely cut meat, two parts of rice to one of meat, and formed cakes or balls, which they fried.

11. For the Liver and Fat, they took a dog's liver, and wrapped it round with its own fat. They then wet it and roasted it, and took it in this condition and scorched it. No smartweed was mixed with the fat.

12. They took the grains of rice and steeped them in prepared rice-water. They then cut small the fat from a wolf's breast, and with it and the grains of rice made a fry[1].

13. The observances of propriety commence with a careful attention to the relations between husband and wife. They built the mansion and its apartments, distinguishing between the exterior and interior parts. The men occupied the exterior; the women the interior. The mansion was deep, and the doors were strong, guarded by porter and eunuch. The men did not enter the interior; the women did not come out into the exterior.

14. Males and females did not use the same stand or rack for their clothes. The wife did not presume to hang up anything on the pegs or stand of her husband; nor to put anything in his boxes or satchels; nor to share his bathing-house. When her husband had gone out (from their apartment), she put his pillow in its case, rolled up his upper and under mats, put them in their covers, and laid them away in their proper receptacles. The young served the old; the low served the noble;—also in this way.

---

[1] This and the other paragraphs from 4 are understood to describe the 'eight delicacies (八珍),' which were specially prepared for the old. See the *K*âu Lî, Book IV, par. 18.

15. As between husband and wife, it was not until they were seventy, that they deposited these things in the same place without separation. Hence though a concubine were old, until she had completed her fiftieth year, it was the rule that she should be with the husband (once) in five days. When she was to do so, she purified herself, rinsed her mouth and washed, carefully adjusted her dress, combed her hair, drew over it the covering of silk, fixed her hair-pins, tied up the hair in the shape of a horn, brushed the dust from the rest of her hair, put on her necklace, and adjusted her shoe-strings. Even a favourite concubine was required in dress and diet to come after her superior. If the wife were not with the husband, a concubine waiting on him, would not venture to remain the whole night[1].

16. When a wife was about to have a child, and the month of her confinement had arrived, she occupied one of the side apartments, where her husband sent twice a day to ask for her. If he were moved and came himself to ask about her[2], she did not presume to see him, but made her governess dress herself and reply to him.

When the child was born, the husband again sent twice a day to inquire for her. He fasted now, and did not enter the door of the side apartment. If the child were a boy, a bow was placed on the left of the door; and if a girl, a handkerchief on the

[1] This paragraph has given rise to a great deal of discussion and writing among the commentators, into which it is not desirable to enter.

[2] The first character in this clause occasions difficulty to a translator. Zottoli has:—'Negotiisque ipsemet interrogabit illam.' Wang Tâo understands it as I have done.

right of it. After three days the child began to be carried, and some archery was practised for a boy, but not for a girl.

17. When a son and heir to the ruler of a state was born, and information of the fact was carried to him, he made arrangements to receive him at a feast where the three animals should all be provided; and the cook took in hand the (necessary) preparations. On the third day the tortoise-shell was consulted for a good man to carry the child; and he who was the lucky choice, kept a vigil over night, and then in his court robes, received him in his arms outside the chamber. The master of the archers then took a bow of mulberry wood, and six arrows of the wild rubus, and shot towards heaven, earth, and the four cardinal points. After this the nurse received the child and carried it in her arms. The cook (at the same time) gave (a cup of) sweet wine to the man who had carried the child, and presented him with a bundle of silks, and the tortoise-shell was again employed to determine the wife of an officer, or the concubine of a Great officer, who should be nurse.

18. In all cases of receiving a son, a day was chosen; and if it were the eldest son of the king, the three animals were killed (for the occasion). For the son of a common man, a sucking-pig was killed; for the son of an officer, a single pig; for the son of a Great officer, the two smaller animals; and for the son of the ruler of a state, all the three. If it were not the eldest son, the provision was diminished in every case one degree.

19. A special apartment was prepared in the

palace for the child, and from all the concubines and other likely individuals there was sought one distinguished for her generosity of mind, her gentle kindness, her mild integrity, her respectful bearing, her carefulness and freedom from talkativeness, who should be appointed the boy's teacher; one was next chosen who should be his indulgent mother, and a third who should be his guardian mother. These all lived in his apartment, which others did not enter unless on some (special) business.

20. At the end of the third month a day was chosen for shaving off the hair of the child, excepting certain portions,—the horn-like tufts of a boy, and the circlet on the crown of a girl. If another fashion were adopted, a portion was left on the left of the boy's head, and on the right of the girl's. On that day the wife with the son appeared before the father. If they were of noble families, they were both in full dress. From the commissioned officer downwards, all rinsed their mouths and washed their heads. Husband and wife rose early, bathed and dressed as for the feast of the first day of the month. The husband entered the door, going up by the steps on the east, and stood at the top of them with his face to the west. The wife with the boy in her arms came forth from her room and stood beneath the lintel with her face to the east.

21. The governess then went forward and said for the lady, 'The mother, So and So, ventures to-day reverently to present to you the child!' The husband replied, 'Reverently (teach him to) follow the right way.' He then took hold of the right hand of his son, and named him with the smile and voice of a child. The wife responded, 'We will remember.

May your words be fulfilled!' She then turned to the left, and delivered the child to his teacher, who on her part told the name all round to the wives of the relatives of all ranks who were present. The wife forthwith proceeded to the (festal) chamber.

22. The husband informed his principal officer of the name, and he in turn informed all the (young) males (of the same surname) of it. A record was made to the effect—'In such a year, in such a month, on such a day, So and So was born,' and deposited. The officer also informed the secretaries of the hamlets, who made out two copies of it. One of these was deposited in the office of the village, and the other was presented to the secretary of the larger circuit, who showed it to the chief of the circuit; he again ordered it to be deposited in the office of the circuit. The husband meanwhile had gone into (the festal chamber), and a feast was celebrated with the ceremonies of that with which a wife first entertains her parents-in-law.

23. When an heir-son has been born, the ruler washed his head and whole body, and put on his court robes. His wife did the same, and then they both took their station at the top of the stairs on the east with their faces towards the west. One of the ladies of quality, with the child in her arms, ascended by the steps on the west. The ruler then named the child; and (the lady) went down with it.

24. A (second) son or any other son by the wife proper was presented in the outer chamber[1], when

---

[1] It seems plain that the sons in this paragraph were all by the proper wife or chief lady of the harem, for it is not till paragraph 26 that sons by inferior members of it are spoken of. The *Kh*ien-

(the ruler) laid his hand on its head, and with gentle voice named it. The other observances were as before, but without any words.

25. In naming a son, the name should not be that of a day or a month or of any state, or of any hidden ailment[1]. Sons of Great and other officers must not be called by the same name as the heir-son of the ruler.

26. When a concubine was about to have a child, and the month of her confinement had arrived, the husband sent once a day to ask for her. When the son was born, at the end of three months, she washed her mouth and feet, adjusted herself early in the morning and appeared in the inner chamber (belonging to the wife proper). There she was received with the ceremonies of her first entrance into the harem. When the husband had eaten, a special portion of what was left was given to her by herself; and forthwith she entered on her duties of attendance.

27. When the child of an inferior member of the ruler's harem was about to be born, the mother went to one of the side apartments, and at the end of three months, having washed her head and person, and

lung editors clearly establish this point. *K*ăng Hsüan took a different view, saying that '"the (second) son" was a brother of the heir-son (in paragraph 23), and "any other son" a son by a concubine,' and P. Zottoli adopts this view:—'Reguli haeres (世子), ejus germanus frater (適子), a subnuba filius (庶子);' adding, 'Regulus excipiebat primum in praecipua diaeta (路寢); secundum in postica diaeta (燕寢), quae hic exterior dicitur relate ad adjacentes aedes, quibus nobilis puerpera morari solebat; tertium excipiebat in adjacentibus aedibus (側室).' But these 'side apartments' are not mentioned till paragraph 27.

[1] See page 78, paragraph 42.

put on her court robes, she appeared before the ruler. (One of) her waiting women (also) appeared with the child in her arms. If (the mother) was one to whom the ruler had given special favours, he himself named the son. In the case of such children generally, an officer was employed to name them.

28. Among the common people who had no side chambers, when the month of confinement was come, the husband left his bed-chamber, and occupied a common apartment. In his inquiries for his wife, however, and on his son's being presented to him, there was no difference (from the observances that have been detailed).

29. In all cases though the father is alive, the grandson is presented to the grandfather, who also names him. The ceremonies are the same as when the son is presented to the father; but there is no (interchange of) words (between the mother and him).

30. The nurse of the ruler's boy[1] quitted the palace after three years, and, when she appeared before the ruler, was rewarded for her toilsome work. The son of a Great officer had a nurse. The wife of an ordinary officer nourished her child herself.

31. The son of a commissioned officer and others above him on to the Great officer was presented (to the father once) in ten days. The eldest son of a ruler was presented to him before he had eaten, when he took him by the right hand; his second or any other son by the wife proper[2] was presented after he had eaten, when he laid his hand on his head.

32. When the child was able to take its own food,

---

[1] See above, par. 17.

[2] See above, par. 24.

it was taught to use the right hand. When it was able to speak, a boy (was taught to) respond boldly and clearly; a girl, submissively and low. The former was fitted with a girdle of leather; the latter, with one of silk[1].

[1] The account which follows this of the teaching and training of the brothers and sisters is interesting; and we may compare it with what is said in volume iii, p. 350, of the different reception given to sons and daughters in the royal family, though the distinction between them is not accentuated here so strongly. The passage treats of the children in a family of the higher classes, but those of the common people would be dealt with in a corresponding manner according to their circumstances. And even in the early feudal times the way was open for talent and character to rise from the lower ranks in the social scale, and be admitted to official employment. The system of competitive examinations was even then casting a shadow before. To number the days was, and is, a more complicated affair in China than with us, requiring an acquaintance with all the terms of the cycle of sixty, as well as the more compendious method by decades for each month. The education of a boy, it will be seen, comprehended much more than what we call the three Rs. The conclusion of paragraph 33 gives the translator some difficulty. Zottoli has—'et petet exerceri lectionibus sermonisque veritate,' and my own first draft was—'he would ask to be exercised in (reading) the tablets, and in truthful speaking.' But it is making too much of the boys of ancient China to represent them as anxious to be taught to speak the truth. The meaning of the concluding characters, as given in the text, is that assigned to them by *K*ăng Hsüan.

There is nothing in what is said of the daughters to indicate that they received any literary training. They were taught simply the household duties that would devolve on them in their state of society; though among them, be it observed, were the forms and provision for sacrifice and worship. It will be observed, also, at how early an age all close intercourse between them and their brothers came to an end, and that at ten they ceased to go out from the women's apartments. On what is said about the young men marrying at the age of thirty I have spoken in a note on page 65.

33. At six years, they were taught the numbers and the names of the cardinal points; at the age of seven, boys and girls did not occupy the same mat nor eat together; at eight, when going out or coming in at a gate or door, and going to their mats to eat and drink, they were required to follow their elders:—the teaching of yielding to others was now begun; at nine, they were taught how to number the days.

At ten, (the boy) went to a master outside, and stayed with him (even) over the night. He learned the (different classes of) characters and calculation; he did not wear his jacket or trousers of silk; in his manners he followed his early lessons; morning and evening he learned the behaviour of a youth; he would ask to be exercised in (reading) the tablets, and in the forms of polite conversation.

34. At thirteen, he learned music, and to repeat the odes, and to dance the *k*o (of the duke of *K*âu)[1]. When a full-grown lad, he danced the hsiang (of king Wû)[1]. He learned archery and chariot-driving. At twenty, he was capped, and first learned the (different classes of) ceremonies, and might wear furs and silk. He danced the tâ hsiâ (of Yü)[1], and attended sedulously to filial and fraternal duties. He might become very learned, but did not teach others;—(his object being still) to receive and not to give out.

35. At thirty, he had a wife, and began to attend

[1] It is difficult to describe exactly, amid the conflict of different views, these several dances. Dances were of two kinds, the civil and military. The *k*o was, perhaps, the first of the civil dances, ascribed to the duke of *K*âu (vol. iii, p. 334); and the hsiang, the first of the martial. The two are said to have been combined in the tâ hsiâ.

to the business proper to a man. He extended his learning without confining it to particular subjects. He was deferential to his friends, having regard to the aims (which they displayed). At forty, he was first appointed to office; and according to the business of it brought out his plans and communicated his thoughts. If the ways (which he proposed) were suitable, he followed them out; if they were not, he abandoned them. At fifty, he was appointed a Great officer, and laboured in the administration of his department. At seventy, he retired from his duties. In all salutations of males, the upper place was given to the left hand.

36. A girl at the age of ten ceased to go out (from the women's apartments). Her governess taught her (the arts of) pleasing speech and manners, to be docile and obedient, to handle the hempen fibres, to deal with the cocoons, to weave silks and form fillets, to learn (all) woman's work, how to furnish garments, to watch the sacrifices, to supply the liquors and sauces, to fill the various stands and dishes with pickles and brine, and to assist in setting forth the appurtenances for the ceremonies.

37. At fifteen, she assumed the hair-pin; at twenty, she was married, or, if there were occasion (for the delay), at twenty-three. If there were the betrothal rites, she became a wife; and if she went without these, a concubine. In all salutations of females, the upper place was given to the right hand.

TRANSLITERATION OF ORIENTAL ALPHABETS ADOPTED FOR THE TRANSLATIONS OF THE SACRED BOOKS OF THE EAST.

CONSONANTS.	MISSIONARY ALPHABET.			Sanskrit.	Zend.	Pehlevi.	Persian.	Arabic.	Hebrew.	Chinese.
	I Class.	II Class.	III Class.							
Gutturales.										
1 Tenuis	k	...	...	क	𐬐	𐭪	ک	ك	כּ	k
2 ,, aspirata	kh	...	...	ख	𐬑	𐭧	...	...	כ	kh
3 Media	g	...	...	ग	𐬔	𐭢	گ	...	גּ	...
4 ,, aspirata	gh	...	...	घ	𐬖	𐭢	...	...	ג	...
5 Gutturo-labialis	q	...	...	...	...	...	ق	ق	ק	...
6 Nasalis	ṅ (ng)	...	...	ङ	{ 𐬢 (ng) / 𐬣 (N) }	...	...	...	...	...
7 Spiritus asper	h	...	...	ह	𐬵 (𐬓 *hv*)	𐭤	ه	ه	ה	h, hs
8 ,, lenis	’	...	...	...	...	...	ا	ا	א	...
9 ,, asper faucalis	‘h	...	...	...	...	...	ح	ح	ח	...
10 ,, lenis faucalis	’h	...	...	...	...	...	ع	ع	ע	...
11 ,, asper fricatus	...	‘*h*	...	...	...	...	خ	خ	ח	...
12 ,, lenis fricatus	...	’*h*	...	...	...	...	...	...	...	...
Gutturales modificatae (palatales, &c.)										
13 Tenuis	...	*k*	...	च	𐬗	𐭰	چ	...	...	*k*
14 ,, aspirata	...	*kh*	...	छ	...	...	...	...	...	*kh*
15 Media	...	*g*	...	ज	𐬘	𐭰, 𐭩	ج	ج	...	...
16 ,, aspirata	...	*gh*	...	झ	...	...	غ	غ	...	...
17 ,, Nasalis	ñ	...	...	ञ	...	...	...	...	...	...

CONSONANTS (*continued*).	MISSIONARY ALPHABET. I Class.	II Class.	III Class.	Sanskrit.	Zend.	Pehlevi.	Persian.	Arabic.	Hebrew.	Chinese.
18 Semivocalis	y	...	...	य	𐬌𐬌, 𐬫 [illegible] init.	𐭉	ي	ي	י	y
19 Spiritus asper	...	(ẙ)	...	...	...	...	...	...	...	...
20 „ lenis	...	(y̓)	...	...	...	...	...	...	...	...
21 „ asper assibilatus	...	*s*	...	श	𐬱	𐭔	ش	ش	...	...
22 „ lenis assibilatus	...	*z*	...	...	𐬲	[illegible]	ژ	...	...	*z*
Dentales.										
23 Tenuis	t	...	...	त	𐬙	𐭕	ت	ت	תּ	t
24 „ aspirata	th	...	...	थ	𐬚	...	...	...	ת	th
25 „ assibilata	...	...	TH	...	...	...	ث	ث	...	...
26 Media	d	...	...	द	𐬛	𐭃	د	د	דּ	...
27 „ aspirata	dh	...	...	ध	𐬜	...	...	...	ד	...
28 „ assibilata	...	...	DH	...	...	...	ذ	ذ	...	...
29 Nasalis	n	...	...	न	𐬥	[illegible]	ن	ن	נ	n
30 Semivocalis	l	...	...	ल	...	𐭋	ل	ل	ל	l
31 „ mollis 1	...	*l*	...	ळ	...	...	...	...	...	...
32 „ mollis 2	...	...	L	...	...	...	...	...	...	...
33 Spiritus asper 1	s	...	...	स	𐬯	𐭎	س (ث)	س	שׂ	s
34 „ asper 2	...	...	s (ʃ)	...	...	...	...	...	ס	...
35 „ lenis	z	...	...	...	𐬰	𐭆	ز (ذ)	ز	ז	z
36 „ asperrimus 1	...	...	z (ʒ)	...	...	...	ص	ص	צ	ʒ, ʒh
37 „ asperrimus 2	...	...	ẓ (ʒ̣)	...	...	...	ض	...	...	...

Dentales modificatae (linguales, &c.)										
38 Tenuis	...	*t*	....	ट	....	...	ط	ط	ט	...
39 ,, aspirata	...	*th*	....	ठ	....	...	ظ	ظ	...	...
40 Media	...	*d*	....	ड	[illegible]	[illegible]	...	...	...	...
41 ,, aspirata	...	*dh*	....	ढ	....	...	...	ض	...	...
42 Nasalis	...	*n*	....	ण	[illegible]	...	...	...	...	...
43 Semivocalis	r	...	....	र	[illegible]	[illegible]	ر	ر	ר	...
44 ,, fricata	...	*r*	....	...	....	...	...	...	...	*r*
45 ,, diacritica	...	...	R	...	....	...	...	...	...	...
46 Spiritus asper	sh	...	....	ष	[illegible]	[illegible]	...	...	...	sh
47 ,, lenis	zh	...	....	...	....	...	...	...	...	...
Labiales.										
48 Tenuis	p	...	....	प	𐬞	[illegible]	پ	...	פּ	p
49 ,, aspirata	ph	...	....	फ	....	...	...	...	פ	ph
50 Media	b	...	....	ब	𐬠	[illegible]	ب	ب	בּ	...
51 ,, aspirata	bh	...	....	भ	....	...	...	...	ב	...
52 Tenuissima	...	*p*	....	...	....	...	...	...	...	...
53 Nasalis	m	...	....	म	𐬨	[illegible]	م	م	מ	m
54 Semivocalis	w	...	....	...	[illegible]	...	...	...	...	w
55 ,, aspirata	hw	...	....	...	....	...	...	...	...	...
56 Spiritus asper	f	...	....	...	𐬟	[illegible]	ف	ف	...	f
57 ,, lenis	v	...	....	व	»	[illegible]	و	و	ו	...
58 Anusvâra	...	*m*	....	अं	[illegible] ã	...	...	...	...	...
59 Visarga	...	*h*	....	अः	....	...	...	...	...	...

VOWELS.	MISSIONARY ALPHABET. I Class.	II Class.	III Class.	Sanskrit.	Zend.	Pehlevi.	Persian.	Arabic.	Hebrew.	Chinese.
1 Neutralis	0	...	...	...	...	...	...	...	ְ	ă
2 Laryngo-palatalis	ĕ	...	...	...	...	...	...	...	...	...
3 „ labialis	ŏ	...	...	...	...	𐭠 fin.	...	...	...	...
4 Gutturalis brevis	a	...	...	अ	𐬀	𐭠 init.	َ	َ	ַ	a
5 „ longa	â	(*a*)	...	आ	𐬁	𐭠	َا	َا	ָ	â
6 Palatalis brevis	i	...	...	इ	𐬌	...	ِ	ِ	ִ	i
7 „ longa	î	(*i*)	...	ई	𐬍	𐭩	ِي	ِي	ִי	î
8 Dentalis brevis	*li*	...	...	ऌ	...	...	...	...	...	...
9 „ longa	*lî*	...	...	ॡ	...	...	...	...	...	...
10 Lingualis brevis	*ri*	...	...	ऋ	...	...	...	...	...	...
11 „ longa	*rî*	...	...	ॠ	...	...	...	...	...	...
12 Labialis brevis	u	...	...	उ	𐬎	...	ُ	ُ	ֻ	u
13 „ longa	û	(*u*)	...	ऊ	𐬏	𐭥	ُو	ُو	וּ	û
14 Gutturo-palatalis brevis	e	...	...	...	𐬆(e) 𐬇(*e*)	...	...	...	ֶ	e
15 „ longa	ê (ai)	(*e*)	...	ए	𐬉, 𐬈	𐭩	...	...	ֵ	ê
16 Diphthongus gutturo-palatalis	âi	(*ai*)	...	ऐ	...	...	َيْ	َيْ	...	âi
17 „ „	ei (ĕi)	...	...	...	...	...	...	...	...	ei, êi
18 „ „	oi (ŏu)	...	...	...	...	...	...	...	...	...
19 Gutturo-labialis brevis	o	...	...	...	𐬊	...	...	...	ָ	o
20 „ longa	ô (au)	(*o*)	...	ओ	𐬋	𐭥	...	...	וֹ	...
21 Diphthongus gutturo-labialis	âu	(*au*)	...	औ	𐬁𐬎 (*au*)	...	َوْ	َوْ	...	âu
22 „ „	eu (ĕu)	...	...	...	...	...	...	...	...	...
23 „ „	ou (ŏu)	...	...	...	...	...	...	...	...	...
24 Gutturalis fracta	ä	...	...	...	...	...	...	...	...	...
25 Palatalis fracta	ï	...	...	...	...	...	...	...	...	...
26 Labialis fracta	ü	...	...	...	...	...	...	...	...	ü
27 Gutturo-labialis fracta	ö	...	...	...	...	...	...	...	...	...